T0318190

# Organizational Space and Beyond

Through the focus on organizational space, using the reception and significance of the seminal work on the subject by sociologist Henri Lefebvre, this book demonstrates why and how Lefebvre's work can be used to inform and elaborate organizational studies, especially in view of the current interest in the "socio-material" dimension of organizations.

As the "spatial turn" in organizational research exposed the importance of spatial design in inducing power and cultural relations, Lefebvre's perspective has become an inspiring, theoretical framework. However, Organizational Space and Beyond explores how Lefebvre's work could be of a much wider relevance, especially given his profound theoretical engagement with diverse schools of philosophical and sociological thought, including Nietzsche, Marx, Sartre and Foucault.

This book brings together a range of authors that collectively develop a broader understanding of Lefebvre's relevance to organizational studies, including areas of management concern such as strategy and diversity studies, and ultimately draw on Lefebvre's work to rethink, reimagine and reshape scholarship in organizational studies. It will be of relevance to researchers, academics, students and organizational professionals in the fields of organization studies, management studies, cultural studies, architecture and sociology.

**Sytze F. Kingma** is a senior lecturer in the Department of Organization Sciences at Vrije Universiteit Amsterdam, Netherlands.

**Karen Dale** is reader and director of teaching in the Department of Organisation, Work and Technology at Lancaster University, UK.

**Varda Wasserman** is a senior lecturer in the Department of Management and Economics at the Open University of Israel, Israel.

# Routledge Studies in Management, Organizations and Society

This series presents innovative work grounded in new realities, addressing issues crucial to an understanding of the contemporary world. This is the world of organised societies, where boundaries between formal and informal, public and private, local and global organizations have been displaced or have vanished, along with other nineteenth-century dichotomies and oppositions. Management, apart from becoming a specialised profession for a growing number of people, is an everyday activity for most members of modern societies.

Similarly, at the level of enquiry, culture and technology, and literature and economics, can no longer be conceived as isolated intellectual fields; conventional canons and established mainstreams are contested. **Management, Organizations and Society** addresses these contemporary dynamics of transformation in a manner that transcends disciplinary boundaries, with books that will appeal to researchers, student and practitioners alike.

Recent titles in this series include:

For a full list of titles in this series, please visit www.routledge.com

# Organizational Space and Beyond

The Significance of Henri Lefebvre
for Organization Studies

Edited by Sytze F. Kingma, Karen Dale,
and Varda Wasserman

 Routledge
Taylor & Francis Group

NEW YORK AND LONDON

First published 2018
by Routledge
605 Third Avenue, New York, NY 10017

and by Routledge
2 Park Square, Milton Park, Abingdon, Oxon, OX14 4RN

First issued in paperback 2020

*Routledge is an imprint of the Taylor & Francis Group, an informa business*

*Library of Congress Cataloging-in-Publication Data*
A catalog record for this book has been requested

ISBN 13: 978-0-367-73426-8 (pbk)
ISBN 13: 978-1-138-23640-0 (hbk)

Typeset in Sabon
by Apex CoVantage, LLC

# Contents

# Contributors

Timon Beyes is professor of sociology of organization and culture at Leuphana University Lüneburg, Germany, and Copenhagen Business School, Denmark. His research focuses on the processes, spaces and aesthetics of organization in the fields of media culture, art, cities as well as higher education. Recent publications include "Colour and Organization Studies" (*Journal of Organization Studies*, 2017), *The Routledge Companion to Reinventing Management Education* (with M. Parker and C. Steyaert, 2016), *Social Media—New Masses* (with I. Baxmann and C. Pias, Chicago 2016) and *Performing the Digital* (with M. Leeker and I. Schipper, Bielefeld, 2017).

Karen Dale works at Lancaster University in the Department of Organization, Work and Technology. She has written on embodiment, materiality, space and architecture in relation to organizations and organizing, including *The Spaces of Organization and the Organization of Space* (Palgrave) with Gibson Burrell.

Gili S. Drori is associate professor of sociology at the Hebrew University of Jerusalem, Israel. Her publications speak to her research interests in institutional theory of organizations and world society theory; globalization and glocalization; science, innovation and higher education; and, culture, knowledge and policy regimes. Gili earned her academic education at Tel Aviv University (BA 1986; and MA 1989) and Stanford University (PhD, 1997, sociology). She served as Director of IR Honors Program and taught at Stanford University for a decade. She also taught at the University of California Berkeley (USA), the Technion (Israel), and University of Bergamo (Italy) and was a guest scholar at Uppsala University (Sweden).

Sytze F. Kingma is senior lecturer in the sociology of organization at the Department of Organization Sciences of the VU University Amsterdam, the Netherlands. His research interests involve the material and virtual dimensions of organizational networks, and the way risk and responsibility are implicated in organizational contexts. He published extensively in the field of gambling and is the editor of *Global Gambling: Cultural Perspectives on Organized Gambling* (Routledge, 2010). His publications deal with risk, responsibility, organizational space and technology; most recent articles are about 'third workspaces' and 'new ways of working'.

**Daniel S. Lacerda** is lecturer of management at Federal University of Rio Grande do Sul (UFRGS), Brazil. He received his PhD in Organization Studies from Lancaster University and has published articles in journals such as *Discourse and Society* and *Third World Quarterly*. His recent work examines the management practices of civil society organizations with an emphasis on the political economy of space

**Jeanne Mengis** is associate professor of organizational communication in the Faculty of Communication Sciences at the University of Lugano (Switzerland), where she is director of the Institute of Marketing and Communication Management. She is a senior research fellow at the research unit for Innovation, Knowledge and Organizational Networks (IKON) at Warwick Business School (WBS). Her work has appeared in *Organization Science* and *Organization Studies,* and she has recently published research on space in *Organization* and *Organizational Research Methods*. Her current research explores the role of spatiotemporality in identity translation work, in the context of film industry festivals.

**Louise Nash** is a lecturer in management at Essex Business School. Prior to this she worked in a variety of marketing-related management roles in financial services and more recently in university administration. Her research interests are in interpretative, qualitative studies of the lived experience of work, particularly in the spatial and temporal rhythms of everyday working life, and in exploring and developing sensory and embodied methods of research.

**Inbal Ofer** is a professor of Modern European history at the department of History, Philosophy and Judaic Studies at the Open University of Israel. She specializes in 20th century Spanish history with an emphasis on gender, urban history and social movements. She is the author of *Señoritas in Blue: The Making of a Female Political Elite in Franco's Spain. The National Leadership of the Sección Femenina de la Falange (1936–1977),* Sussex Academic Press, 2009; and of *Claiming the City and Contesting the State: Squatting, Community Formation and Democratization in Spain (1955–1986),* Routledge, 2017.

**Tuomo Peltonen** is professor of organization and management Åbo Akademi University, Finland. He also holds a docent (adjunct professor) appointment at Aalto University and University of Turku. His current research interests include organization theory and philosophy, wisdom, spirituality and religion; and history of management thought. Tuomo's books include: *Organization Theory: Critical and Philosophical Engagements*

(Emerald); *Spirituality and Religion in Organizing* (Palgrave), *Origins of Organizing* (edited with Hugo Gaggiotti and Peter Case; Edward Elgar) and *Towards Wise Management* (Palgrave; forthcoming).

**Fabio James Petani** is assistant professor in the department of Management and HR at INSEEC Business School and researcher in the chair on Digital Innovation & Artificial Intelligence at INSEEC Business School in Lyon (France). He holds a PhD from the University of Lugano (Switzerland). His research on organizational space has appeared in *Organization*. He is interested in discursive and sociomaterial practices of justification and critique in organizations. His latest research studies how digital technology and urbanization are jointly transforming business organizations, work and social relations more broadly.

**Briana Preminger** is a teaching fellow at the Department of Management at Bar Ilan University and teaching assistant at the Department of Sociology at the Hebrew University of Jerusalem, in Israel. Briana earned her academic education at Bar Ilan University (MBA 2001) and at The Hebrew University (BA 1995; MA 1998; PhD 2017). Her PhD is conferred jointly with SKEMA Business School, in France. Briana's research interests are in institutional theory of organization; value and cocreation; and organization of social space.

**Arja Ropo** is professor of management and organization at the Faculty of Management, University of Tampere, Finland. Her continuing interest is leadership from an embodied and material perspective. Recently, she has studied leadership and physical workplaces. She advances leadership theory as a sociomaterial phenomenon, as an embodied relationship between the human and material. Her work has appeared in the *Leadership Quarterly*, *Leadership*, *Scandinavian Journal of Management*, *Journal of Management & Organization* and *Journal of Corporate Real Estate*, among others.

**Perttu Salovaara** is an adjunct assistant professor at Stern School of Business, New York University, USA, and a leadership researcher at the School of Management, University of Tampere, Finland. Having a background in philosophy, his research focuses on leadership's epistemological and ontological questions. He has recently studied and published on embodiment in leadership, leadership in spaces and places, Lefebvre's triadic space concept, and coworking movement. He has also produced three academic documentary films on leadership and is at the moment studying coworking spaces, craft breweries, and plural and leaderless forms of leadership. Perttu draws inspiration for his research from alpine skiing, guitar playing and home brewing.

**Harriet Shortt** is an associate professor in organization studies at Bristol Business School at the University of the West of England, Bristol, UK.

Her research focuses on organizational space, artefacts and identity and she has an expertise in qualitative research methods including innovative visual methodologies, specifically, participant-led photography. Harriet has led several research projects in both public and private sector organizations that examine spatial change and the impact of work space on employees' everyday working practices. Her research has been published in journals including *Human Relations, Organizational Research Methods, Management Learning, Visual Studies* and the *International Journal of Work, Organization and Emotion.* She is a member of 'inVisio' (The International Network for Visual Studies in Organization) and part of the ESRC RDI funded team that developed 'inVisio *inspire*', an online resource for visual researchers in business and management.

**Sarah Warnes** is a Senior Teaching Fellow at the UCL School of Management and holds a Doctorate from Essex Business School, University of Essex. Her PhD explored the lived dimension of organizational space in an English Cathedral. Sarah joined the School of Management in 2013 and leads on three courses: Understanding Management, Business Research Methods and Dissertation. Sarah has tutored and lectured across both undergraduate and post-graduate programmes in the subjects of management, leadership, strategy, organizational change, research methodology and dissertation completion. Prior to joining the public sector, Sarah worked for a private training company committed to workplace training; here Sarah spent two years setting up operations in the UAE.

**Varda Wasserman** is senior lecturer at the Open University of Israel in the Department of Management & Economics. She is an organizational sociologist, and her research interests are: organizational aesthetics, organizational control and resistance, (un)doing gender, masculinity in organizations, embodiment, religion and organizations, excluded social groups and the army as an organization. She has published in *Organization Science, Organization Studies, Culture and Organization, Organization* and other journals.

**Zhongyuan Zhang** currently works as an associate professor at the School of Management, Zhejiang University. He obtained his PhD in organizational studies from Warwick Business School. He has previously worked and published on the social space of organizations in journals such as *Human Relations* and *Culture & Organization*. Currently, he is studying the social construction of creativity in the cartoon and animation industry.

# 1 Introduction

## Henri Lefebvre and Organization Studies

*Sytze F. Kingma, Karen Dale,*
*and Varda Wasserman*

### Introducing Lefebvre

One of the most important points to make right at the start of this book is the need to not stereotype Henri Lefebvre solely as a theorist of space, as Shields (2001) puts it. Thus we begin with a very brief overview of Lefebvre's life and work, in an attempt to avoid the "mis-recognition" that has tended to characterize Lefebvre's categorization by Anglo-American readers, as Aronowitz (2015: 73) argues, where he is 'placed' only in relation to a very partial view of his work and life.

Henri Lefebvre was born in 1901 and died in 1991, his life thus covering most of the twentieth century with its profound changes and disruptions. He was born and died in the south-west of France, near the Pyrenees, in the intervening decades seeing the transformation of the rural peasantry and the growth of urbanization processes, becoming a key observer and theorist of both. Lefebvre's life and work span not just time, but also academic space. He originally graduated in philosophy from the Sorbonne, but later took up a post in sociology at the University of Strasbourg. In other words, his work defies easy definition and categorization; he speaks and has had influence across multiple academic disciplinary boundaries. As Shields notes, in the 1950s and 1960s, Lefebvre was one of the most translated of French theorists, known predominantly at the time for his work on dialectical materialism. His later work on the production of social space has had a different reception (not originally well received in France and in the context of Marxism, but taken up from the 1980s as a central theory in relation to studies of urbanism) and 'translation' (not being translated into English until 1991, and taken up in relation to critical geography and through this route tending to wend its way into other disciplines in the English speaking world). And his work is much broader than these two examples. He wrote over 60 books and 300 articles. Stanley Aronowitz (2015) comments that the relevance of his work to ecology and to art and aesthetics has still not been recognized. Many of his works were dictated and he did not tend to return to edit them. This makes them challenging to read and interpret. But Lefebvre's life was not confined to academic debates. His whole life was one of activism and is

2 Sytze F. Kingma, Karen Dale, and Varda Wasserman

criss-crossed with the influences of this. He joined the French Communist Party in 1928, and provoked his expulsion from it in 1958 after finally acknowledging the influence of the work of Sartre. He then became one of the critics of the continued Stalinism and structuralism of the Communist Party, and was associated with other activist groups including the Situationists and Maoist groups. He was an active opponent of the Vichy regime during the Second World War, and he was centrally involved with the student occupations of 1968, and the political events during the 1960s which led up to this. Among his students can be counted Jean Baudrillard and Manuel Castells. Both his activism and his diverse working life—at various times he was a factory worker, a taxi driver, the artistic director of a radio station, and did military service—feed in to his approach to his writings. His development of acutely perceptive theory is underpinned throughout with political consciousness and a deep concern for everyday life.

Many details about his life and work can be found in already available excellent introductions to Lefebvre. We will focus on how the significance of Lefebvre and his approach have been portrayed and could be made relevant for organization studies. The most systematic and comprehensive of the introductory texts include Rob Shields his *Lefebvre, Love & Struggle* (1999), Stuart Elden his *Understanding Henri Lefebvre: Theory and the Possible* (2004), and Andy Merrifield his *Henri Lefebvre: A Critical Introduction* (2006). In addition, we refer to an edited volume by Kanishka Goonewardena et al., *Space, Difference, Everyday Life: Reading Henri Lefebvre* (2008), which offers 15 chapters by a range of authors discussing various aspects of Lefebvre's work. These publications (re)present different versions of Lefebvre's ideas, and together, we believe, offer a thorough introduction to Lefebvre's work. In some respects, the works are complementary, although there is, of course, great overlap in the themes covered. As a crude indication, one could perhaps say that Merrifield offers a more emphatic entry to Lefebvre, Shields focusses on the internal coherence of his work, Elden is very comprehensive in interpretations and contexts, and, if you specifically are after particular aspects and backgrounds, Goonewardena et al. would be a good start. The introductions all offer overviews and insights into Lefebvre's ideas and intellectual life, his broad philosophical interests, his dialectical materialist methodology, his lifelong engagement with a broad range of topics, including everyday life, time, space, the urban, politics, the state and globalization. Introductions necessarily offer fragmented impressions of the original works, summarize, prioritize, reorganize and schematize arguments, and frame the work in a different context of scientific debates. This in itself is a valuable and necessary contribution, and a precondition to make original works accessible and understandable, especially in the case of Lefebvre.

The works mentioned are all meant to be introductory texts and, for that reason alone, organization scholars who seek to contribute to Lefebvrian organization studies are well advised to consult the original Lefebvre texts they refer to. This is not only because 'second hand' accounts may raise crude, partial or even false impressions of the original, but also because of the nature of Lefebvre's work: his methodology, use of concepts and particularly his style of writing. His complex philosophical style makes his works difficult to read. The major arguments and concepts are also often difficult to grasp because Lefebvre almost never presents these in a straightforward way. Concepts and insights are gradually developed throughout the texts in which they are empirically and philosophically grounded and contextualized, and repeatedly nuanced, redefined and elaborated upon. In this respect, Lefebvre's writing style is demanding to readers who want to grasp and deduce the basics of his ideas from the text as a whole. This means that the introductory volumes not only come in handy but, paradoxically, may even be considered necessary for readers to grasp the meaning and significance of the original texts. Indeed, for readers who are not yet familiar with Lefebvre's work, it is recommended to start with a good introduction, especially Elden's (2004), not only because this introduction is the most comprehensive but also because it offers a good entry to Lefebvre's work because of its enriching and insightful endnotes. Zhang (2006), one of the contributors to the current volume, explicitly advocated Elden's introduction as an 'indispensable commentary as well as general guide' for organization scholars.

This introductory chapter proceeds as follows. We start with a brief sketch of the influence of Lefebvre's work and how this can be made relevant for organization studies. Secondly, we discuss how Lefebvre was adopted and gained a new relevance in organization studies. Finally, we offer an overview of the studies presented in this volume, and indicate how they might be pertinent for spatial organization studies as an emerging field of interest. In this introduction we do not offer suggestions for future research. Instead, we decided to end the volume with a separate chapter on possible future directions for research into spatial organization.

## Lefebvre's Influence

*The Production of Space* (Lefebvre, 1991 [1974]) is by far Lefebvre's most influential work and will also be frequently referred to in this volume. Lefebvre almost never writes in a programmatic way, that is, a way in which the major contributions, ideas, concepts, arguments and methods are outlined in advance, and subsequently explained and substantiated in a linear fashion. In this respect, his style is essayistic and very French. A notable and important exception concerns the first chapter of *The Production of Space*—explicitly titled 'plan of the present work'—in which Lefebvre provides the reader with a formal account and definitions of the three epistemologically different but always complementary spatial perspectives his work is renowned for—often briefly addressed as Lefebvre's 'spatial triad'.

For Lefebvre, there are always two opposed understandings of space, the *mental space* referring to the images of space as conceived by experts, such as a map, and the *concrete space* referring to the real material properties of space we may all perceive. However, and this is the key of his approach, Lefebvre argues that, in addition, there always is a third understanding of space, which combines the two and mediates between the two. This is our understanding of the simultaneously *real-and-imagined* space we deal with in everyday situations. The logic behind this third perspective, the 'lived space', is that Lefebvre recognizes that all social actors combine the two poles and entertain ideas about the concrete spaces which constitute their life—this logic is akin to that of the living brain, a thinking substance. Lefebvre's triad thus consists of three distinct but related spatial perspectives, the 'conceived', the 'perceived' and the 'lived space'. Zhang (2006) usefully highlights Elden's reading of this, that the lived space addresses our purely subjective informal knowledge of space—which always relates to the conceived and perceived—and that the three perspectives should be understood as particular points of view on the whole space and in this respect overlap, not juxtapose, one another.

However, and the authors of the introductory texts agree, this does not mean that the background and meaning of this deceptively clear classification of perspectives, and the way the perspectives relate or can be put to use, is immediately evident from the first account. This one can find out only by following Lefebvre's uses of the concepts, discussions of the philosophical backgrounds, his comments and applications in the subsequent chapters of the book. For instance, Schmid (2008) argues that Lefebvre's triad can best be understood with reference to 'the trinity of Hegel, Marx, and Nietzsche'. What is more, *The Production of Space* can be understood as a culmination of a large part of Lefebvre's previous work, which constitutes a voluminous but in many respects closely connected oeuvre. In his previous works, especially his works on 'everyday life' (Lefebvre, 1991 [1947]), 'the rural' and 'the urban' (Lefebvre, 2003 [1970]), he gradually developed and grounded various aspects of his arguments and already offered basic rationales and provisional formulations of his spatial perspectives. This implies that one should ideally read a significant part of Lefebvre's work in order to reach a proper understanding of his spatial theory. Furthermore, this argument applies not only to the works previous to *The Production of Space*, but also to the subsequent works; his masterpiece on 'the state' (not translated into English and out of print in French), and especially *Rhythmanalysis* (Lefebvre, 2004 [1992]), which he himself addressed as 'an idea that may be expected to put the finishing touches to the exposition of the production of space' (Lefebvre, 1991 [1974]: 405). For this reason, one can hardly do without good guides such as the introductions mentioned. Although in these ways necessary, the introductions are, of course, not sufficient for developing Lefebvrian organization studies; they need to be supplemented with a close reading of relevant parts of the original work and with contemporary applications in organization studies, such as the ones discussed further on and the ones written for this volume. Finally, in order to actually bring Lefebvre's approach to life, this will have to be tested, applied and specified in actual organizational research practices. The proof of the pudding ultimately lies in the eating.

Another important observation about Lefebvre's work is that his work was taken up on a significant scale by international social science only after his death in 1991, also the year the English translation of *La Production de l'espace*—already published in French in 1974—was released. In the 1990s, this work had a significant impact in the field of social geography and was assigned a prominent role by, in particular, Mark Gottdiener (1985), who discussed *The Production of Space* seriously; David Harvey, who wrote an afterword to *The Production of Space*; and Edward Soja, whose book *Third Space* (1996) in title and content was directly inspired by Lefebvre's approach. Soja was also instrumental in connecting Lefebvre's work with the broader expansion of the interest in space in the wider social sciences, particularly in the cultural studies field. This 'reassertion of space in social theory' (Soja, 1989) was part of a general post-modernist critique of modern social science because of its prioritizing of time and history over space and geography (cf. Jameson, 1991). Kipfer et al. (2008: 3) regard the political-economic geography reading as a 'first' and the post-modern cultural reading as a 'second' reading of Lefebvre. They argue for a 'third' more comprehensive reading which overcomes and combines the two and fuses and balances Lefebvre's political-economic considerations with those of subjectivity and identity. We suggest that the appropriation of Lefebvre in organization studies can by and large be inserted in this third stream of readings of Lefebvre. The first tranch of organization studies papers to make reference to Lefebvre's triad, which we will further discuss below, appeared only in 2004 and 2005 (Ford and Harding, 2004; Dobers and Strannegård, 2004; Dale, 2005; Watkins, 2005).

The late, post-mortem, recognition complicates the application of Lefebvre's work in organization studies. First, by the time that the significance of Lefebvre's work had been recognised in organisation studies, the field had developed sophisticated contemporary approaches in a different direction, of which, for example, neo-institutional theory is a strong example (see Drori and Preminger's discussion in the current volume). Consequently, the more organization studies evolved into alternative directions and developed a framework of reference of its own, the bigger the gap—in time and empirical topics—between organization studies and Lefebvre's approach became, and subsequently the more difficult to overcome. Second, this effect was aggravated because also outside the field of organization studies, and even in the French context, the work of Lefebvre was not systematically built upon, applied and developed further conceptually and empirically. His work seems somewhat frozen in time.

This does not mean that Lefebvre's work was not influential. On the contrary, Lefebvre's work should be regarded as highly influential both upon contemporaries and successors, but this influence was largely indirect and hardly recognizable. On the one hand, Lefebvre did not follow a standard academic career. Although he wrote for a large part of his adult life, his interests and work often were not directly connected to academic positions. Lefebvre was a controversial figure, as Merrifield (2006) points out in some detail, and as much a neo-Marxist thinker and intellectual outside of academia as inside. He can also be considered a left-wing activist, although with his writing and commentaries he was an activist in words rather than deeds. He was an active member of the French communist party (PCF) for 30 years (from 1928 to 1958). He is also known for his support and analysis of the May 1968 student movement (Lefebvre, 1969 [1968]). In French sociology courses, so we have been told, Lefebvre is mainly mentioned with reference to *The Sociology of Marx* (1982 [1966]), a rather straightforward introduction to Marxism but not a significant part of his own contributions. The enormous range of Lefebvre's writings also makes his work difficult to classify. Lefebvre's work went in many directions. He advocated and practiced multidisciplinary approaches, and incorporated economics, politics, philosophy, psychology and the arts. His work was as much grounded in phenomenology as in semiology. His major contributions concerned not only spatial analyses but, equally important, the history of ideas, particularly the ideas about space (remember, there are always two spaces, the 'mental' and the 'concrete'). In his thinking and writing, he extensively engaged with Hegel, Marx, Nietzsche, Heidegger, Sartre and many more. All these factors make his work difficult to classify and to access.

On the other hand, there are also reasons external to Lefebvre's person and work which may account for the poor integration of Lefebvre's work in mainstream social science. This has to do with a particular feature of French sociology, or for post-World War II continental European sociology as contrasted with Anglo-Saxon sociology—this feature may even be typical for a specific phase of development of social science. Leading sociologists developed almost egocentric conceptual frameworks with attached series of studies, which resulted in largely self-referential and closed theoretical systems. This scientific practice characterized Lefebvre's oeuvre but equally that of, for instance, Baudrillard, Foucault or Bourdieu. This practice may lead to a strong internal coherence, diachronic grounding and depth in concepts and studies. However, at the same time, this leads to weak external coherence, synchronic grounding and superficial connections between the various schools of thought. The various sociological schools developed their insights in relative isolation and virtually ignored each other, with some exceptions. A notable exception would be Lefebvre's comments on Foucault's work, which he regarded as particularly 'powerful' but criticized for its neglect of the wider spatial context of the state (Elden, 2004: 240). At the same time there are all kinds of hidden connections in contacts and themes.

As opposed to Baudrillard, Foucault or Bourdieu, Lefebvre's approach remained academically isolated and was hardly translated, applied, elaborated or debated by others. Although not in an explicit manner, large parts of the work of Manuel Castells—in the late 1960s an assistant of Lefebvre—and David Harvey can easily be portrayed as a continuation of Lefebvre's interests and work on the urban. Ironically, both Castells and Harvey initially thought that Lefebvre had developed a flawed Marxist approach to the city, and sought to correct this with a more structuralist focus on the economic forces of production (Elden, 2004: 142). However, in their later work they revised their Marxist position and their work evolved in a direction which was arguably more in line with Lefebvre's approach. In the 1990s, as mentioned above, Harvey was also instrumental for integrating Lefebvre's sociology of space in Anglo-Saxon social geography. By that time, Castells had shifted his interests from the city to a new material phenomenon, that of information technology and the network society, and wrote an ambitious and voluminous sociology of *The Information Age* (Castells, 1996); this development and topic definitely would have fascinated Lefebvre—and he undoubtedly would have commented upon the book. And although without reference to Lefebvre, Castells's work on the information age very much resembles Lefebvre's approach, in style, method and neo-Marxist reasoning. Another intriguing, but different, kind of parallel between Lefebvre's work and contemporary social theory concerns his ideas about the 'colonization of everyday life' by the market and by the state. This is a prominent theme in Lefebvre's three volumes of *Critique of Everyday Life* (2014 [1947, 1961, 1981]) but also a key concern, albeit much more abstractly developed, in German sociologist Jürgen Habermas's *Theory of Communicative Action* (1984 [1981]), a resemblance explicitly pointed out by social geographer Miller (2000: 42–43). Lefebvre surely would have criticized Habermas's approach for not being rooted in materiality; at least this is what he criticized Hegel, Nietzsche and Heidegger for.

Comparing various sociological approaches and schools of thought, and how they do or do not relate, we can better leave to historians of science. Suffice it to note here that the distanciation of Lefebvre's work from organization studies, both because of the time gaps and the intellectual space gaps noted above, raises hindrances which make it comparatively difficult to pick up and integrate Lefebvre's work and develop Lefebvrian organization studies. In any case, in order to apply Lefebvre to contemporary contexts, as suggested by Brenner and Elden (2009), who sought to apply Lefebvre to the field of international political economy, 'Lefebvre's key concepts and analyses must be pushed, challenged, updated, and rearticulated in order to be made relevant' (Brenner and Elden, 2009: 374). The difficulties, perhaps, make it understandable (but not justifiable) that the most abstract parts of Lefebvre's work, such as the triad, appeal to contemporary scholars of organization.

## The Influence of Lefebvre's Work in Organization Studies

In this section we discuss how Lefebvre's work has been appropriated in organization studies. The objective here is not to describe in detail the research which has utilized Lefebvre nor is it able to cover all of such studies (and we apologize now to readers for our omissions and for foregrounding our own work), but to delineate some of the main themes and also, importantly, to consider what strands have not been paid as much attention to thus far.

The interest in Lefebvre's ideas and their application to organizational studies does not constitute a linear history. There are some references to Lefebvre's work in organization studies from the 1990s, such as in Mary Jo Hatch's (1997) *Organization Theory*, which was novel in including a chapter on 'the physical organization' which refers to Lefebvre along with David Harvey and Edward Soja. However, possibly the first paper to draw significantly upon Lefebvre's spatial triad in order to derive a new approach to organizations, is Yeung's (1998) paper in *Organization* on 'The social-spatial constitution of business organizations: a geographical perspective'. Yeung argues that organizations are not only socially but spatially embedded, and that their geographic relations need to be understood because the networks of relations that businesses engage with in order to exist are linked to specific territories. This paper goes further than solely considering the physical location of organizations, in applying Lefebvre's spatial triad to understanding how the practices of organizations are embedded within and transform spatial relations beyond the entity of the organization itself. In this way it connects with Lefebvre's broader concern with the capitalist relations of production, and how these are spatially produced and reproduced.

Lefebvre's triad has certainly found a central place in the literature on organization space, although much of the literature which has taken this up has tended to apply it at the level of the organization itself, with less concern for the perspective across different spatial scales that characterizes Lefebvre's writings. Yeung's (1998) paper therefore marks a less common approach within organization studies (as opposed to economic geography), in arguing for a move from the 'spaces of firms' to understanding how companies are embedded in geographically specific ways within 'spaces of network relations'. In a related though different vein, the second part of Dale and Burrell's (2008) book follows Lefebvre in arguing for a 'political economy of space' that moves beyond 'the spaces of organization' to consider the bigger picture of 'the organization of space'. To date, this has not really been taken up within organization studies. In this way, we can see that there have been restrictions not only in the narrowness of the range of Lefebvre's work which has been taken up within organization studies, but also in the tendency to decontextualize the spatial triad from the broader framework of the abstract spaces of capitalism within which Lefebvre clearly places it.

A further related but different kind of restriction in the early appropriations of Lefebvre's work concerns the often subsidiary role attached to Lefebvre's approach. There is a tendency for Lefebvre's approach to be 'merely' used as a tool. Instead specific organizational processes, such as processes of meaning making, control and resistance are considered to be the main objectives of the analysis. This is understandable, but there is a risk here of imposing a separation between method and theory. This may paradoxically lead to a discussion of organization processes without taking space sufficiently into account. In other words, space can come to be seen merely as 'influencing' organizational processes, simply 'adding in' space rather than developing an integrated account about for instance 'spatial control' and 'spatial meanings'.

However, it is perhaps not surprising that certain elements of Lefebvre's work become foregrounded and others are relatively neglected within organization studies. The papers which have drawn upon Lefebvre's work have tended to articulate it within those issues and debates which have currency within the discipline of organization studies, and perhaps particularly around areas of lived experience, embodiment, sociomateriality, aesthetics and identity. It is also consistent with the dominant approach within the discipline that most studies which use elements of Lefebvre's work focus at the level of the spaces of the organization. It is apparent in many of these papers that a key impetus is to try to get to grips with organizational life as lived experience and to move away from more abstract notions about organizations. Thus, even though Lefebvre's writings on the critique of everyday life are not often explicitly cited, his concern with the quotidian communicates and resonates with many of the concerns of contemporary organization theory. This is also why, as discussed earlier, we would classify much of the appropriation of Lefebvre in organization studies as being part of a third reading of Lefebvre, combining the 'geographical' and 'cultural' reading.

Whilst it is Lefebvre's spatial triad that has generated the greatest interest in organization studies, the ways in which this central analytical device has been taken up are extremely diverse. Watkins' (2005) analysis of theatrical performance has the explicit purpose of introducing Lefebvre's work into organizational analysis, arguing that all three elements of Lefebvre's spatial triad need to be integrated for a deeper understanding of organizational space. He connects the constrictive nature of the dominance of a conceived or of a perceived space with the concerns raised in critical organization literature against the dominance of mental constructions which are detached from their physical and social context (Knights, 1992). According to Lefebvre, such an approach may lead to 'descriptions of' or even 'discourses on' space but it cannot contribute to a true 'knowledge of' space (Lefebvre, 1991 [1974]: 7). Thus Watkins uses Lefebvre's triad both as a critique of organization studies and as an alternative tool for a comprehensive understanding of the actual organization and use of space.

The dialectical relationship between the different aspects of the spatial triad articulated by Lefebvre has been used by a number of writers to cast light upon organizational-spatial dynamics. For example, Kingma's (2008) analysis of Dutch casino spaces shows how a logic of pleasure was historically and spatially produced through the perceived space (in dynamic interaction with the conceived and lived) by a dual process of the 'dissociation' of gambling from the urban environment by the casino building, combined with the 'association' of the casino building with an urban entertainment district. In the conceived space, this logic was spatially achieved through 'scripting' gambling as entertainment combined with the physical 'constraining' of gambling behaviour through access strategies and game area divisions. Lastly, in the lived space this logic was reinforced by constructing professional gamblers and addicts as 'exceptions' and by reducing the gambling experience to 'illusions' of profit and luxury which are confined to the premises of the casino. This work further argues that the controversial entertainment view of casinos can only be fully understood with reference to the wider scale levels of the nation state, of urban space, and of capital accumulation in consumer society (Kingma, 2004, 2011).

Some more recent studies have developed reflections of Lefebvre's work beyond the spatial triad. For example, Wapshott and Mallett's (2011) discussion of home-working is unusual in that it adapts Lefebvre's ideas about dominated and appropriated spaces to discuss multi-dimensional aspects of home/working spaces, and how these co-exist in a state of dialectical tension. This argument also recognizes the Marxian history of the concepts in Lefebvre's work, and addresses how the boundaries between 'home' and 'work' are constructed and dismantled in ways which typically relate to the broader relations of production.

A number of studies use Lefebvre's concepts to explore aspects of control and resistance within organizations. This can be seen in Dale's (2005) study of a new building for a privatized electricity company, which attempted to integrate a new set of organizational values into the design of the space and thus to influence the ways in which employees might 'live through' these spaces. Changes within the company influenced changing experiences of the building, illustrating how conceived, perceived and lived aspects of space are not fixed but in a dynamic interaction with each other. Wasserman and Frenkel (2011) also utilize the spatial triad to analyse attempts to build certain sorts of organizational, cultural and national identities through organizational aesthetics, the lived experiences of this, and the resistances it produces. Aesthetics expressing a desire to connect with modern Western-European culture and distinguish itself from traditional Israeli culture were incorporated into a new Ministry of Foreign Affairs building. The attempt to impose these aesthetic and cultural values generated various acts of resistance, especially through acts of 'culture jamming'—for instance by 'ridiculing symbols' and 'disturbing order'. These can be interpreted as reflecting inherent contradictions between the conceived and lived spaces of the Ministry's building. Zhang, Spicer, and Hancock (2008) examine the relations between control and resistance in social space through the use of J. G.Ballard's novels. The interactions of the dialectical relations of social space are shown when they discuss how hyper-organized—strictly designed and regulated spaces—forms of planned space may in themselves produce novel forms of lived space. Their paper also provides a useful corrective for a sometimes almost romantic assumption of the superiority of 'lived space' over conceived and perceived space, as through the novels of Ballard what we see are 'the seemingly antithetical rationality of debauched lived space' (p. 900) taking over whole communities. 'People's ability to re-interpret and creatively misuse planned spaces' (p. 904) is not necessarily positive.

A number of papers have explored how power relations are reproduced not only through the conceived spaces of organizations, but through spatial practices and lived spaces. Zhang and Spicer (2014) argue that spatial practices are not solely about expressing resistance to dominated spaces. They analyse how minute practices such as walking and daily rituals, as well as apparently ironic stories and mocking jokes, contribute to *reproducing* rather than challenging hierarchical and bureaucratic power relations. This continues the thread of a number of writers who have pointed to the significance of the micro-relations of social space, such as Beyes and Steyaert's (2012) discussion of the importance of bodily movements, successions of actions and affects, and configurations, in seeing 'spacing' as a process and performative rather than as an object to be fixed and reified.

These perspectives relate also to one of the particular resonances which Lefebvre's work has had within organization studies: the emphasis that Lefebvre puts on human embodiment. As he powerfully expresses it: 'the whole of (social) space proceeds from the body' (Lefebvre, 1991 [1974]: 405). Ian Lennie uses this to look at management from an embodied and lived perspective in his book *Beyond Management* (1999). Dale (2005) and Dale and Latham (2015) combine Lefebvre with studies of material culture and particularly Merleau Ponty's (1965 [1945]) theorization of 'embodiment' in which the 'body' and the 'mind' are not dichotomized but entwined. Wasserman and Frenkel (2015) use Lefebvre's triad to explore the relations between organizational spatiality, gender and class exposing the role of space and its embodied enactment by women of various classes in constructing and reconstructing inequality regimes within organizations. Tyler and Cohen (2010) also explore the interrelationship of embodiment of gender performativity and organizational spaces. In doing this, they bring together Lefebvre's conceptualization of representational space with Butler's work on gender performativity. Further, importantly, 'Lefebvre (1991: 17, 35) argues that the social production of space "implies a process of signification" in which subjects "must either recognize themselves or lose themselves"' (Tyler and Cohen, 2010: 181).

One key observation of the way in which literature on organizational space has developed: that is the tendency to combine Lefebvre's approach with other, more contemporary, literatures. This tendency is both understandable and necessary. It is understandable because other literatures are perhaps more familiar and accessible, having a more long-standing contribution to understanding organizational dynamics. It can also be regarded necessary to actualize Lefebvre's approach and connect his work with contemporary organizational contexts, developments and discussions. There is a risk in this of watering down or distorting Lefebvre's approach, but

there are also rich possibilities for different ideas intersecting and informing each other. Ford and Harding directly confront the potential dangers of
bringing together different approaches by describing their reading of Lefebvre through a postmodern lens as 'an insouciant perpetration of violence
upon his Marxist perspective' (2004: 817). However, despite this rider, their
detailed use of the spatial triad in an analysis of how different staff understand their relationship with the merger of two health service trust organizations brings together both the Lefebvrian sense of embodiment in the
production of social space along with a recognition of the political nature
of how the abstract spaces of capital are produced, and the violence inherent in this. They contrast how non-management staff have an embodied
and embedded sense of place with how senior management perceive the
organization, which is conveyed through numerical codes such as budget
figures, numbers of staff, numbers of beds, all held together by management
structures. As in Tyler and Cohen's work they dovetail their case study with
insights from Butler and the power relations of performative spaces which
come to constitute the subject.

In another example, Dobers and Strannegard's (2004) paper on the spatial 'adventures' of a Danish experimental design object, a chair called the
'Cocoon'—designed for possible use in public space to take moments of
relief and shelter from our hectic everyday lives—fuses Lefebvre's approach
with Bruno Latour's actor-network-theory (ANT). This connection makes
sense because in ANT attention is paid to the translation and transformation of objects as they travel through social space. Furthering this, Peltonen's
(2011) analysis of the architecture of a Finnish university brings Lefebvre
together with the work of Callon, and Callon and Law, to discuss the idea
of buildings as scripts, as producing obligatory passage points and evolving assemblages. These appropriations reveal that Lefebvre's approach in
several respects pre-figures and parallels other relevant approaches in organization studies to which it may be fruitfully connected. This approach of
weaving together conceptual insights from Lefebvre with other literatures
is continued in some chapters within this current text, with some novel
combinations.

The range of areas where Lefebvre's writings have been appropriated into
organization studies is diverse and it is impossible to do justice to them
all. Contributions of comparable significance to the ones discussed in this
introduction include for instance Hirst's (2011) analysis of the differential
appropriation of flexible offices spaces; Verduyn's (2015) use of Lefebvre
in developing a process view on entrepreneurship; and Petani and Mengis'
(2016) analysis of the role of 'lost spaces' and 'remembering' in processes
of space planning. These works should all be regarded as indicative of the
rich potential of a Lefebvrian approach for organization studies. We have
discussed a few articles in more detail to draw attention to the disparate
ways in which Lefebvre's concepts have been and can be put to use. In
their influential review of studies of organizational space, Taylor and Spicer

(2007) also recognize and discuss different approaches to space across the literature, categorizing these as studies of space as distance; studies of space as the materialization of power relations; and studies of space as experience. They link these to Lefebvre's triad, which they characterize as practising, planning and imagining. However, they go further than this through an analysis of spatial scale, influenced by Lefebvre's perspective on spatial scale as socially produced (Spicer, 2006). As well as using this to enable the different elements of the triad, or different approaches to space in organization studies, to be articulated in a dialectical way with each other, this also allowed them to explore how the literature in organization studies tends not to range across multiple scales and the interplay between them. This is a state of play which has largely continued through the intervening decade since Taylor and Spicer's analysis, though we hope that some of the chapters in this present book might indicate how engaging with spatial scales might open up productive possibilities (see especially the chapters by Lacerda, Nash, and Zhang).

Another, more general, observation is that Lefebvre's work has been appropriated in a restricted way, with an overwhelming concentration on his model of the spatial triad (particularly Chapter 1 of *The Production of Space*). Although restricted, this 'model' has proved very powerful for first turning space into an object of social analysis and second for analysing the production of the spatial organization as the outcome of dialectical interactions between experience, power and meaning in relation to space. Regarding the use of this model, we would point to the risk of taking this model too literally as a prescriptive objective of static spatial analyses instead of a dynamic heuristic tool. Beyes and Steyaert (2012: 49) explicitly remarked that in the use of the triad, in their view, there is a 'tendency to reify space, to turn spatial becoming into representations of the beings of organizational spaces, to prioritize the spatial products over the processes of their productions'. For a further critique, see also Beyes's chapter in the current volume. In this respect, it is relevant to point out that Lefebvre himself at the end of *The Production of Space* explicitly warned against such an interpretation of his approach, which would 'obscure' his true objective—which is not an analysis of space, but a critique of the established knowledges associated with space—and that he definitely is not aiming to produce 'models, typologies or prototypes of space' (Lefebvre, 1991 [1974]: 404–405). Instead, Lefebvre is concerned to see an 'exposition of the *production of space*', meaning that he seeks to focus on the dynamics behind the processes of production. According to a number of commentators (including Shields (1999), Elden (2004), Merrifield (2006) and Goonewardena et al. (2008)), Lefebvre does not always live up to this ideal in his work, perhaps especially in his extensive overview of the 'history of space' in Chapter 4 of *The Production of Space*, in which he alternates between a process view and rather essentialist accounts of the historical succession of spatial situations and systems. However, Lefebvre clearly formulates his analytical ideal in terms of an *orientation* or a perspective which overcomes the distinction between the process and the product, 'in an organ that perceives, a direction that may be conceived, and a directly lived movement progressing towards the horizon' (Lefebvre, 1991 [1974]: 423). One way to counter the risk of reification, in our view, is to read and use the triad more explicitly in relation to Lefebvre's work as a whole, and relate it to his philosophical discussions and notions of time, the body, everyday life, technology, the urban, the global and abstract space. On the other hand, Lefebvre's radically open approach, and his reluctance against, a distinction between the process and its product, can perhaps also be considered as a shortcoming, as argued by Neil Smith in his introduction to *The Urban Revolution* (Lefebvre, 2003 [1970]: xiv). Smith argues that this prevents Lefebvre from seriously considering 'how certain social meanings become fixed, however temporarily, in and as space and place'. In any case, an analysis of which differences in spaces are made and remade maybe against his ideal but is not entirely at odds with Lefebvre's own substantive analyses. And, as suggested by Smith, this ambivalence might perhaps be overcome by defining spatial products against the backdrop of time.

## Outline of the Present Work

This volume offers a range of Lefebvrian inspired discussions and spatial analysis of organization processes. With this, the volume seeks to explore, and draw attention to, a new approach in the field of organization studies, a field that is currently dominated by a focus on discursive approaches (Carlile et al., 2013). The Lefebvrian (spatial) perspectives can be regarded both as alternatives and as complements to mainstream organization studies. They are alternatives because they place organizations in a new and different light, and offer new insights and interpretations for the social construction of organizations and for the controversies over the products, services and (unintended) consequences these organizations contribute to the wider society. They are complements because they show that organizations are more diverse and complex than specialist spatial analyses or the disembodied and dematerialized accounts of many organization studies seem to suggest.

In some respects, the chapters bring to the surface submerged traditions in organization studies, as is the case with detailed workplace studies, organizational history, geography and design. In other respects organizational analyses are extended in new and relevant directions, as is the case with rhythm-analysis, the urban and the role of the state. The varied contributions all draw upon Lefebvre's work in various ways and connect them to various extents with contemporary illustrations and case studies. They express in all cases a spatial orientation. Serious attention is drawn towards rituals, symbols, meanings, values, legitimations, power relations, (informal) work-relations, and the artifacts involved in the (re)production of spatial organizations. The case studies provide rich and detailed descriptions, they cover a range of organizational sectors, and they stem from a range of countries, including Brazil, Israel, China, Sweden, Spain, Finland, Switzerland and the UK. Although the global and national connectedness of the organizations will be evident, at the same time the case studies stress the unique local embeddedness of organization processes. We do not suggest that the chapters represent a common understanding of Lefebvre or that the editors and the various authors would necessarily agree on each other's uses and interpretations of Lefebvre. We do suggest that there is agreement on the great potential of Lefebvre's work for developing organization studies, and that all contributions share Lefebvre's work as a point of departure for linking his approach to contemporary organizational contexts.

The volume follows a logic of scope, and is organized into parts on theoretical considerations, spaces of organizations, and the organization of spaces, although inevitably there is overlap between the parts. The first part which focuses on theoretical contribution offers discussions on how to broaden the appropriation of Lefebvre's approach, the idea of 'absent spaces' in architectural design, the idea of 'spacing leadership', and a comparison between institutional and Lefebvrian analysis in organization studies. The spaces of organizations part addresses the private and everyday life aspects of organizations, regarding for instance the embodiment of work practices, rhythmanalysis, and the significance of informal spaces and practices at work. The organization of spaces part considers intermediate relations and makes clear that processes of organizing affect and penetrate societies at large, often in many and profound ways. This part includes analyses and considerations of the historical and abstract space relations involved in the spatial construction of the urban and the (nation) state.

Part I (**Theoretical considerations—process, absence, power, institutions**) starts with a chapter by Timon Beyes about politics, embodiment and everyday life as possible themes for extending the significance of Lefebvre's work for organization studies. From the perspective of this volume, Beyes's chapter offers a good start because it shares a key concern of this introduction and this volume, namely that Lefebvre's work can be regarded as of greater relevance for organization studies than the spatial triad alone. Beyes extends our understanding of Lefebvre by situating *The Production of Space* in the broader context of Lefebvre's oeuvre and shifting attention from the triad to three themes on which Lefebvre's insights are considered equally valuable and which have great potential for, and connect with, current interests in organization studies: 'dialectic materialism', 'everyday life', and the 'human body'. These themes reflect 'problems of spatial organization' and are important for further developing, as Beyes stresses, the study of *spaces of organizing*. The themes are in Beyes' terms helpful for formulating and addressing the 'how', 'where' and 'what' questions. Dialectical materialism (the 'how' question) concerns the way Lefebvre conceptualizes the production of space. Lefebvre—different from and against Hegel and Marx—always considers three dimensions which are continuously affecting each other and which, therefore, produce a dialectic and a change process which is open ended by definition. It follows, argues Beyes, that spatio-organizational analyses should focus on the process of production, the emancipatory moments of change, and the significance of self-organization—*autogestion*, in Lefebvre's terms. With the concept of everyday life (the 'where' question) Lefebvre extended his analyses beyond the economic sites of production such as the workplace to include questions of social reproduction, cultural life and the urban. Lefebvre regards everyday life as a key domain for sensing alienation and developing resistance against the forces of organized capitalism and the state. Beyes considers it important to prioritize the study of the mundane aspects of organizing, and participant-observation, over the structural analysis and spatial set-ups of formal organizations. For this purpose he also considers the body (regarding the 'what' question) and Lefebvre's *rhythm-analysis* as important in organizational research. Beyes particularly argues for a critical and politicized engagement with processes of organization.

In Chapter 3, Fabio Petani and Jeanne Mengis consider the use of Lefebvre's spatial triad for analysing the role of 'absent spaces' in a space planning process. Planning always involves the exclusion of alternative possibilities and the production of a range of plans and variations of which only a part (and often nothing) will be materialized. However, argue Petani and Mengis, we need to better understand how, in the practice of conceiving space, discarded spaces may remain relevant and how presences and absences interact over time. This also involves a consideration of how absence and disposal in the pre-production phase of conceiving is 'lived' and experienced by those involved. Petani and Mengis actually understand absent space as 'an expression of how a once conceived, but then disposed space becomes lived'. Theoretically they project this absent space as a mirror image of the perceived space, and as a dialectical moment, in Lefebvre's triad and the production of space. Petani and Mengis illustrate the dynamic of how absent spaces become significant in the narratives of practitioners through two complementary examples from their research on the building of a public culture centre in a small city in Switzerland. These examples concern the inclusion of a museum which was initially excluded from the plans, and the exclusion of a park which was not considered a significant loss. The strategic disposal of the plan for the museum for reasons of cost-cutting was successfully resisted by planners and other stakeholders who emotionally invested meaning in the museum. However, in the complementary case of the park such emotional investment was virtually lacking and the disposal was consequently not regretted. Following Petani and Mengis, a consideration of absence and disposal may reveal hidden meanings and interests in the planning process.

In Chapter 4, Perttu Salovaara and Arja Ropo introduce the notion of 'spacing leadership' in a discussion of changes in organizational power relations from 'power-over' to 'power-with' orientations in the design of a new work space. Salovaara and Ropo compare and combine Lefebvre's understanding of power relations with critical leadership studies in which increasing attention is drawn to the role of materiality and space in leadership. In these novel approaches leadership is considered as a collective rather than an individual activity and not only as a relation between people but also between people and the material environment. The human-material leadership relations Salovaara and Ropo consider in terms of 'spacing leadership'. For this they specifically draw on Lefebvre's analysis of the natural rhythms and constraints of rural life in peasant communities, in which leadership is in their view conceived in terms of collective actions across informal networks. This notion of leadership compares to Mary Parker Follet's notion of 'power with' (as distinguished from 'power over'), a democratic horizontal approach to leadership. Salovaara and Ropo illustrate their dynamic Lefebvrian understanding of spacing leadership with an analysis of a spatial renovation project in a Finnish university building. This case study was characterized by the unique feature of a close involvement of the university staff in the design process. Salovaara and Ropo posit, among other things, that the immediate involvement and influence in the change process by personnel led to a greater sense of ownership and belonging in the new work spaces.

In Chapter 5, Drori and Preminger compare and combine Lefebvre's spatial theory with neo-institutional theory, a dominant theoretical framework in contemporary organization studies. They illustrate their approach with an analysis of Jerusalem's Western Wall. What is called 'neo institutional theory' represents a popular and dominant stream in organization studies which, similar to Lefebvre, is characterized by a multi-dimensional approach. But different from Lefebvre, these theories hardly take materiality into account. Institutional theory largely relies on discursive analysis. Drori and Preminger argue for a need to include spatiality in institutional analysis and build on recent initiatives to do so with their reading of Lefebvre's spatial theory. Lefebvre offers in their view 'new paths for conceptual and empirical advances'. They first show that recently space has been incorporated in institutional theory as a 'relational sphere', a 'professional domain' or as a 'legitimation tool'. Difficulties in comparing the two approaches arise because of the differences in ontological backgrounds—Weberian with a bias on legitimation in the case of institutional theory and Marxist with a bias on power in the case of Lefebvre. Neo-institutional theory might in Drori and Preminger's view benefit from Lefebvre's approach by broadening the scope of spatial analysis, by adding a new dimension or 'sphere' to theoretical considerations, by a stronger focus on power and hierarchy, and by furthering the study of global organization. In their empirical illustration of the holy monument of Jerusalem's Western Wall, Drori and Preminger distinguish between three spatial dimensions of the Western Wall, those of logics—of religion, archeology and nationality—and the subsequent sensemaking and enactment of these logics. Drori and Preminger's exercise reveals some of the difficulties but also the possibilities for integrating Lefebvre's approach with mainstream organization studies.

In part II (Spaces of organization—everyday work life, embodiment, rhythms, boundaries) the focus shifts from theoretical considerations to Lefebvrian analyses of small-scale organizational practices. This second part starts with Chapter 6 by Sarah Warnes, who takes the reader to an English Cathedral where she studied the everyday life aspects of the work of employees and volunteers from an embodied spatial perspective. Warnes shows how organizational members deal with the tensions generated by the dual objectives of this Cathedral, which serves as a religious site for contemplation but also depends on tourism. The analysis is built up from Lefebvre's notions of rhythms and the 'spatial body', which consists of thoughts, movement and gestures that are able to 'fuse a prescribed space with a different space, a lived space'. Warnes seeks to analyse an 'experiential understanding' of how value clashes are mediated by the body. Concepts of 'dwelling' and 'dressage' are of particular relevance here. As a participant-observer in the Cathedral, Warnes focused on the mundane routines of workers, and how they dealt with the differences, combinations and tensions between sacred and secular activities and spaces. She particularly shows how the body is effective in managing the competing value clashes which characterize the organization's problematic. She explains, for instance, how the experience of church workers is one of dwelling at work: feeling comfortable and inhabiting the space through a personalized workplace territory with meaningful pictures, paintings or a screen-saver, which may trigger feelings of being 'at home' or of a momentarily relief from the pressures of work. Other examples relate to organizational dressage in which workers were 'playing out' conflicting values, such as challenging the prescribed walking routes they take through the Cathedral, or the way some challenged prescribed work routines in the Cathedral's shop, which played a key role in terms of revenue generation. In this analysis Warnes uses Lefebvre's approach as an alternative way to explore issues of organizational belonging, identity and resistance, and to further an understanding of spatial production through bodily movement.

In Chapter 7, Louise Nash explores the relevance of Lefebvre's *Rhythmanalysis* (2004 [1992]) for organization studies in her study of the public space of the financial district of London City. Here Nash seeks to research the broader spatial context of a work setting through the experiences of those employed there, thus bringing meaning, space, and organizational-geographic sector together. Nash refers to Thrift's notion of 'patina' to address the City's distinctive aura, appearance and cultural meaning. Rhythms in Nash's research are not only important objects of research but also a methodological key to unlock the experience of this setting, which requires both an immersion in the rhythms and a detached observation of those rhythms. To understand rhythms, the focus falls on the conjunction of time and space, in particular the 'sense of urgency' Nash felt in the City as well as the loss of confidence from the financial crisis which started in 2007. Nash analyses the City's distinctive patina in three themes: the hectic performance of business life; the masculine privatized corporate space—both inside and outside; and the rhythms of order and disorder including the (legitimate) release of pressure in excessive behaviour and cycles of financial crises. Nash sees the City thus as linked with the linear rhythms of the workday and the dynamic of a global financial centre, as a localized part of Greater London and as a public space which often operates as a private space.

Chapter 8 by Tuomo Peltonen and Perttu Salovaara focuses on the tension between the conceived space and the everyday enactment of the perceived and the lived space to better understand the political aspects of the social space. Focusing on a case study of the Lunch Beat disco—Scandinavian workers dancing during lunch breaks—Peltonen and Salovaara exemplify a collective, artistic carnival that attempts to transcend the existing capitalist order. As an embodied practice, dancing during the working day demonstrates not only how body and mind are intertwined in organizational everyday life, but also posits a liminal space where workers could escape to during the day. However, as they claim, a 'reading of the Lunch Beat through Lefebvre's politically expanded triadic model, the movement [the Lunch Beat] had potential for a larger emancipatory effect, but this remained unfulfilled', because it remained oriented towards an increase in productivity and was experienced as a means to enhance well-being at work and produce a motivated, happy employee. Escape practices were reframed as work-oriented tools and consequently, instead of challenging capitalist power relations, the movement has reproduced them.

Chapter 9 by Harriet Shortt focuses on Lefebvre's triad as well and analyses food and eating in workplaces as a mundane and routine activity that takes place in specific spaces. Shortt urges us to take into consideration that space has an important role in constructing social interrelations, and she thus uses the term 'foodscape' to highlight that in order to understand eating as a socio-cultural phenomenon, it is crucial to critically examine how spaces of food are consumed, planned, controlled, resisted, embodied and lived. Based on a study conducted in a governmental organization that was relocated into a new building, Shortt demonstrates how different locations for eating were experienced and interpreted differently by the workers. The tensions between the conceived space and the perceived and lived spaces are exposed through four main themes: conversations during food breaks which took place in various locations, usually not in those which were designated for this purpose, thus creating alternative collaborative working environments; workers seeking 'unmanaged' experiences by escaping to private dining areas within and outside the organization, thus avoiding the organizational expectation 'to socialize' with others; smell as an embodied spatio-cultural experience that disrupts the formal, planned spaces of organizations; and lastly healthy foodscapes imposed by the organization subverted by employees through sharing sweets and cakes in liminal spaces. The chapter is divided into dishes—appetizer, starter, amuse bouche, main dish and dessert—which gives the reader a highly embodied experience. In this respect, the chapter provides a rich Lefebrian analysis which integrates many of Lefebvre's ideas in regard to everyday life, power, domination, resistance, appropriation, politics, embodiment, and socio-cultural production of space.

Part III (**Organization of spaces—Capitalism, urban- and state relations**) is devoted to macro analyses of the production of space and it starts with Chapter 10 by Zhongyuan Zhang on the spatial dynamics of the Chinese city, Hangzhou. Zhang encourages organizational scholars to draw much heavier on Lefebvre's early writings on urban space, looking at the underlying processual dimensions of the city and the dynamic interrelations between the conceived, perceived and lived spaces. Based on Lefebvre's *The Right to the City* and the Marxist concepts of exchange-value and use-value, Zhang analyses the reality of the city both as a product that can be traded and consumed and as an *oeuvre* that people can use in non-economic ways. In this sense, Zhang continues the previous chapter's emphasis on the tension between power and resistance, domination and appropriation. In the chapter, three urban processes/practices are examined: redesigning roads by narrowing bike lanes and abolishing sidewalks thus revoking pedestrians' territorial rights; appropriation of the sidewalk by citizens who (mis)use it for various domestic purposes (such as drying laundry, cooking and eating) and thereby reclaiming their right to space; and square-dancing that often evokes conflicts between residents and dancers that are mediated by local governmental attempts to regulate these activities. In his conclusion, he offers some insights about the implications of his study on the city for organizational studies: putting more emphasis on unintentional subversions of controlled spaces and avoiding an overly romantic view of the resisting power of the lived space, paying more attention to changes in organizational spatial layouts to reveal hidden power rationales and revealing new liminal, in-between spaces within and outside organizations.

Chapter 11 by Inbal Ofer is also based on the concept of the right to the city, but it adds an historical angle to Lefebvre's writing focusing on urbanization processes in Madrid from Franco's dictatorship to the democratic regime. Ofer draws our attention to the state level and their planning regimes by analysing the formation of the city and the changes that occurred in Madrid from a highly segregated and dominated urban space (imposed by the state officials) to the vernacular, informal, resistant spatial practices (carried out by the city inhabitants, the citizens). Ofer shows that even in dictatorial regimes, power is not complete and planned spaces are always disrupted and recreated, but, on the other hand, citizens' participation in democratic regimes is also not exhausted. The chapter is divided into three historical periods: the first refers to Madrid under Franco's regime in the 1950s and 1960s, in which market-driven, hierarchical, and rational planning brought about functional zoning and to highly spatial segregation that reinforced the state's domination; the second relates to the emergence of sporadic, illegal and informal counter-spaces in the late 1960s which offered the citizens much more independence and flexibility and a way to cope with the alienation of the segregation; and third considers the democratization of Spain which brought about new forms of urban knowledge through the participation of citizens in the planning processes. Even though Ofer outlines a process of urban democratization in which new forms of knowledge could emerge from the participation of citizens in planning processes, she doubts the ability of democratic authorities to allow citizens to gain their full rights to the city and to take an active part in designing and regulating their own living environment.

Chapter 12 by Daniel Lacerda also deals with the state's role in urbanization and in its attempts to regulate citizens' appropriation of space, but theoretically it is much more focused on power and even violence. Focusing on the case of Brazilian favelas in Rio de Janeiro, Lacerda examines the various ways the violence of abstraction is perpetrated by the state's attempts to take control over the social space in the favelas. Based on observation, interviews and visual methodologies, the chapter offers an analysis of the coercive practices of the state and of the police, whose aim was to fight against the drug cartels that dominated the favelas but also provided basic public services that the residents did not get from the official state authorities. By applying the Lefebvrian triad and putting a special emphasis on the abstract space, Lacerda describes the struggle between these two entities as contesting political and economical ideologies and violent spatial practices. By analysing this extreme case study, the chapter raises important questions regarding the 'totality of space' and 'the abstract space of capital accumulation' and suggests some insights on how to implement these ideas in the field of organizational studies.

In this introduction, we have not aimed to provide a complete overview of the significance of Lefebvre for organization studies. Likewise, this is not the aim or pretension of the volume. Our objective was to make clear that Lefebvre's work is only beginning to be appropriated in organization studies and that this volume illustrates different possible ways of using Lefebvre. The chapters of this volume only represent part of the possible routes that have been or could be taken towards developing Lefebvrian organization studies; i.e. to studying 'spatial organization'. We will return to and specify this approach in more detail in the final chapter of this volume on 'future directions'. The authors and studies are brought together in the hope that this selection will inspire and challenge organization scholars and practitioners across the world to further explore and develop the rich potential of Lefebvre's work for organization studies.

## References

Aronowitz, S. (2015). Henri Lefebvre: The ignored philosopher and social theorist. In *Against Orthodoxy: Social Theory and Its Discontents* (pp. 73–91). New York: Palgrave Macmillan.

## 22   Sytze F. Kingma, Karen Dale, and Varda Wasserman

Beyes, T. and Steyaert, C. (2012). Spacing organization: Non-representational theory and performing organizational space. *Organization*, 19, 45–61.

Brenner, N. and Elden, S. (2009). Henri Lefebvre on state, space, territory. *International Political Sociology*, 353–377.

Carlile, P. R., Nicolini, D., Langley, A., et al. (2013). *How Matter Matters: Objects, Artifacts, and Materiality in Organization Studies.* Oxford: Oxford University Press.

Castells, M. (1996). *The Information Age: Economy, Society and Culture.* Oxford: Blackwell Publishers Ltd.

Dale, K. (2005). Building a social materiality: Spatial and embodied politics in organizational control. *Organization*, 12, 649–678.

Dale, K. and Burrell, G. (2008). *The Spaces of Organisation & the Organisation of Space. Power, Identity & Materiality at Work.* New York: Palgrave Macmillan.

Dale, K. and Latham, Y. (2015). Ethics and entangled embodiment: Bodies—materialities—organization. *Organization*, 22, 166–182.

Dobers, P. and Strannegård, L. (2004). The cocoon—a traveling space. *Organization*, 11, 825–848.

Elden, S. (2004). *Understanding Henri Lefebvre—Theory and the Possible.* London and New York: Continuum.

Ford, J. and Harding, N. (2004). We went looking for an organization but could find only the metaphysics of its presence. *Sociology*, 38, 815–830.

Goonewardena, K., Kipfer, S., Milgrom, R., et al. (2008). *Space, Difference, Everyday Life: Reading Henri Lefebvre.* New York: Routledge.

Gottdiener, M. (1985). *The Social Production of Urban Space.* Austin: University of Texas Press.

Habermas, J. (1984 [1981]). *The Theory of Communicative Action.* Boston: Boston Beacon Press.

Hatch, M. J. (1997). *Organization Theory.* Oxford: Oxford University Press.

Hirst, A. (2011). Settlers, vagrants and mutual indifference: Unintended consequences of hot-desking. *Journal of Organizational Change Management*, 24, 767–788.

Jameson, F. (1991). *Postmodernism, or, The Cultural Logic of Late Capitalism.* New York: Verso.

Kingma, S. (2004). Gambling and the risk society: The liberalisation and legitimation crisis of gambling in the Netherlands. *International Gambling Studies*, 4, 47–67.

Kingma, S. F. (2008). Dutch casino space or the spatial organization of entertainment. *Culture and Organization*, 14, 31–48.

Kingma, S. F. (2011). Waterfront rise. Urban casino space and boundary construction in the Netherlands. In P. Raento and D. G. Schwartz (Eds.), *Gambling, Space, and Time. Shifting Boundaries and Cultures* (pp. 83–107). Reno & Las Vegas: University of Nevada Press.

Kipfer, S., Goonewardena, K., Schmid, C., et al. (2008). On the production of Henri Lefebvre. In K. Goonewardena, S. Kipfer, R. Milgrom, et al. (Eds.), *Space, Difference, Everyday Life. Reading Henri Lefebvre.* London and New York: Routledge.

Knights, D. (1992). Changing spaces: The disruptive impact of a new epistemological location for the study of management. *Academy of Management Review*, 17, 514–536.

Lefebvre, H. (1969 [1968]). *The Explosion: Marxism and the French Upheaval* (translated by Alfred Ehrenfeld). New York: Modern Reader.

Lefebvre, H. (1982 [1966]). *The Sociology of Marx* (translated from the French by Norbert Guterman). Columbia: Columbia University Press.

Lefebvre, H. (1991 [1947]). *Critique of Everyday Life Introduction* (translated by John Moore, With a Preface by Michel Trebitsch). New York: Verso.

Lefebvre, H. (1991 [1974]). *The Production of Space*. Oxford: Blackwell.

Lefebvre, H. (2003 [1970]). *The Urban Revolution* (translated by Robert Bononno. Foreword by Neil Smith). Minneapolis: University of Minnesota Press.

Lefebvre, H. (2004 [1992]). *Rhythmanalysis. Space, Time and Everyday Life* (translated by Stuart Elden and Gerald Moore, with an introduction by Stuart Elden). New York: Bloomsbury Academic.

Lefebvre, H. (2014 [1947, 1961, 1981]). *Critique of Everyday Life. One Volume Edition. Vol I, II, III* (translated by John Moore and by Gregory Elliott; prefaces by Michel Trebitsch), London: Verso.

Lennie, I. (1999). *Beyond Management*. London: Sage.

Merleau-Ponty, M. P. (1965 [1945]). *Phenomenology of Perception*. London: Routledge.

Merrifield, A. (2006). *Henri Lefebvre. A Critical Introduction*. New York: Routledge.

Miller, B. (2000). *Geography and Social Movements: Comparing Antinuclear Activism in the Boston Area*. Minneapolis: University of Minnesota Press.

Peltonen, T. (2011). Multiple architectures and the production of organizational space in a Finnish university. *Journal of Organizational Change Management, 24*, 806–821.

Petani, F. J. and Mengis, J. (2016). In search of lost space: The process of space planning through remembering and history. *Organization, 23*, 71–89.

Schmid, C. (2008). Henri Lefebvre's theory of the production of space: Towards a three-dimensional dialectic. In K. Goonewardena, S. Kipfer, R. Milgrom, et al. (Eds.), *Space, Difference, Everyday Life*. London and New York: Routledge, 27–45.

Shields, R. (1999). *Lefebvre, Love & Struggle. Spatial Dialectics*. London and New York: Routledge.

Shields, R. (2001). Henri Lefebvre: Philosopher of everyday life. In A. Elliott and B. Turner (Eds.), *Profiles in Contemporary Social Theory*. London: Sage, 226–237.

Soja, E. (1996). *Third Space. Journeys to Los Angeles and Other Real-and-Imagined Places*. Oxford: Basil Blackwell.

Soja, E. W. (1989). *Postmodern Geographies: The Reassertion of Space in Critical Social Theory*. London and New York: Verso.

Spicer, A. (2006). Beyond the convergence–divergence debate: The role of spatial scales in transforming organizational logic. *Organization Studies, 27*(10), 1467–1483.

Taylor, S. and Spicer, A. (2007). Time for space: A narrative review of research on organizational spaces. *International Journal of Management Reviews, 9*, 325–346.

Tyler, M., & Cohen, L. (2010). Spaces that matter: Gender performativity and organizational space. *Organization Studies, 31*(2), 175–198.

Verduyn, K. (2015). Entrepreneuring and process: A Lefebvrian perspective. *International Small Business Journal, 33*, 638–648.

Wapshott, R. and Mallett, O. (2011). The spatial implications of homeworking: A Lefebvrian approach to the rewards and challenges of home-based work. *Organization, 19*, 63–79.

Wasserman, V. and Frenkel, M. (2011). Organizational aesthetics: Caught between identity regulation and culture jamming. *Organization Science, 22*, 503–521.

Wasserman, V. and Frenkel, M. (2015). Spatial work in-between glass ceilings and glass work: Gender-class intersectionality and organizational aesthetics. *Organization Studies, 36,* 1485–1505.

Watkins, C. (2005). Representations of space, spatial practices and spaces of representation: An application of Lefebvre's spatial triad. *Culture and Organization, 11,* 209–220.

Yeung, H. W.-C. (1998). The social-spatial constitution of business organizations: A geographical perspective. *Organization, 5,* 101–128.

Zhang, Z. (2006). What is lived space. *Ephemera. Theory & Politics in Organization, 6,* 219–223.

Zhang, Z., Hancock, P. and Spicer, A. (2008). Hyper-organizational space in the work of J. G. Ballard. *Organization, 13,* 549–567.

Zhang, Z. and Spicer, A. (2014). 'Leader, you first': The everyday production of hierarchical space in a Chinese bureaucracy. *Human Relations, 47,* 739–762.

Part I

# Theoretical Considerations— Process, Absence, Power, Institutions

# 2 Politics, Embodiment, Everyday Life

## Lefebvre and Spatial Organization

*Timon Beyes*

## Introduction

In 1986, Henri Lefebvre and the French architects Serge Renaudie and Pierre Guilbaud submitted a proposal for the International Competition for the New Belgrade Urban Structure Improvement, held by the City of Belgrade in the former Yugoslavia. The call had asked for designs to improve 'the unfinished plan of the central zone and the enlargement of the modern city' (Blagojević, 2009: 120). The proposal, however, began by rejecting the assumptions of definitive design and detailed planning. 'We can only rejoice', Lefebvre and the architects stated, 'that Novi Beograd is unfinished' (Renaudie et al., 2009: 6). To continue the 'neo-rationalist' types of organizing the city and its zoning would fail; 'the resistance of the population . . . expresses an important loss of the "organizational message"' (p. 8). To adopt an eclectic 'post-modern historicism' would not work either, provoking merely endless disagreement on the epoch and styles best adaptable to the present. 'As with every dynamic organization', the authors wrote, 'cities are fluid and mobile and any attempt to stop them in order to analyse and represent them risks killing them' (p. 11).

Eschewing propositions of fixed urban forms in favour of open and radical 'modes of organization' (p. 31), which were predicated on the ideas of the 'right to the city' and self-organization (*autogestion*), the proposal was eliminated in the first round of the jury procedure. Found in the civic archives of Belgrade by the architectural historian Ljiljana Blagojević and published alongside contextual essays by Sabine Bitter and Helmut Weber (2009), the text presents an intriguing point of departure for rethinking "Lefebvre and Organization Studies" in at least three ways. For one, 'Lefebvre's theoretical sensibility pervades the text' (Smith, 2009: 81). The document therefore points to conceptual, programmatic and political implications of enlisting this thinker's writings. These implications echo yet go beyond *The Production of Space*, Lefebvre's great book of spatial theory that seems to dominate (not only) his organization-theoretical reception. Second, what is striking about the proposal is not only the engagement with nitty-gritty aspects of urban design, as Smith notes, but also its adoption of a language and understanding of organization as a processual and contested spatial phenomenon. I know of no other text by Lefebvre that departs from the notion of *autogestion* in order to explicitly thematize the question of spatial organization, with the city as form, medium and outcome of processes of social organization. Third, the proposal's focus on the complexity and the potentiality of the urban everyday presents the organization of the social as a messy and embodied realm of encounters, struggle and possibility, which entails the bodies of architects and scholars. Research here is 'a creative, sensual practice' (Kipfer et al., 2008b: 300) that helps produce space, too.

Guided by these observations, the chapter argues for a more wide-ranging and deeper engagement with Lefebvre's oeuvre in the study of organization, one that is informed by his wider concerns and his politics. Such an engagement should not be limited to his work on space in general and *The Production of Space* in particular. Yet I seek to dwell here on the important thematic of the spatial constitution of organization or, in Lefebvre's words, 'the problems of spatial organization' (2009b: 186). I believe this is important because a reading of Lefebvre's body of work that is both closer and broader can help to further develop the study of organizational space, or rather, the study of *spaces of organizing*. Another way of putting this is to state that there is a need to be aware of, and withstand, a two-fold risk of closure in the organization-theoretical reception of Lefebvre's writings: first, to focus only on *The Production of Space* and, second, to be content with this book's often-quoted and seemingly accessible triad model of conceived, perceived and lived space as laid out in its introductory section (1991: 33).

Withstanding this kind of closure does not mean aiming for a definite account or a finalization of Lefebvre's ideas. Given this thinker's far ranging and evolving engagements with different themes and contexts as well as the sprawling and sometimes contradictory style of his writing, any interpretation of his work, it could be suggested, is necessarily partial.[1] As Merrifield (1995: 295) argued, it seems sensible to interpret Lefebvre's 'tantalizing vague . . . loose, episodic and frequently prolix' style of writing as an indication of the writer's intention to keep his systems of thoughts open. And of course, my own approach to Lefebvre's body of work is not disinterested and impartial. It is coloured by prior attempts at working with what could be called a process-theoretical reading of mainly *The Production of Space* (Beyes and Michels, 2011, 2014), *Rhythmanalysis* (Beyes and Steyaert, 2012) and Lefebvre's writings on the urban (Beyes, 2006, 2012).

To begin with, I discuss the problematic of enlisting Lefebvre within organization studies in the form of relying on (the introductory section of) *The Production of Space*. Reading into Lefebvre's oeuvre, I then suggest dialectical materialism and its politics as the overall logic of *how* to conceptualize the production of space; everyday life as the loci *where* the production of space plays out; and the human body as a crucial component of *what* researchers seek out in order to trace processes of spatial production. As the terms of how, where and what indicate, this text moves towards what can be called a "hermeneutics of spacing": an epistemological approach to the politics of spatial organization. In conclusion, I discuss the notion of the right to the city, which frames the proposal for the architectural competition (Renaudie et al., 2009: 1–2), as an exemplary opening for future inquiries into spaces of organizing.

## Enlisting Lefebvre

When browsing through the social-scientific, Anglo-American academic literature on 'space', one soon encounters references to the French philosopher/sociologist Henri Lefebvre. More often than not, enlisting Lefebvre means elaborating upon, quoting from or gesturing at the 1991 English translation of his 1974 treatise on *The Production of Space*. The book has been praised as 'arguably the most important book ever written about the social and historical significance of human spatiality and the particular powers of the spatial imagination' (Soja, 1996: 8). Its translation into English has been hailed as '*the* event within critical human geography during the 1990s' (Merrifield, 2006: 103, orig. emphasis). Its conceptualization of space 'encompasses a great deal of what, 25 years later, has become stock-in-trade in the social sciences' (Löw, 2008: 29).

For organizational researchers who embark on establishing space as a *sui generis* realm of critical enquiries, Lefebvre's treatise has been a major source of inspiration, with the consequence that a Lefebvre-inspired "spatial turn" has broached its convincing appearance in organizational studies (Beyes and Steyaert, 2012; Taylor and Spicer, 2007). What makes Lefebvre particularly interesting for this context, in a nutshell, is his social ontology of space: 'social relations . . . have no real existence save in and through space. *Their underpinning is spatial*' (Lefebvre, 1991: 404, orig. emphasis). Lefebvre refused to see space as a universal category that would precede praxis, be it a container having its own material reality independent of human beings or a Kantian transcendental structure for subjective perceptions. Going beyond the abstract duality of subject and object, Lefebvre insisted that space is 'something more than the theatre, the disinterested stage or setting, of action' (1991: 410); rather, 'itself the outcome of past actions . . . space is what permits fresh actions to occur, while suggesting others and prohibiting yet others' (1991: 73). This ontological stance establishes organizational space as a new 'lens' (Hernes, 2004) through which organizational life and its very material struggles around power and identity can be understood and analysed (e.g. Beyes and Michels, 2011; Dale and Burrell, 2008; Dale, 2005; Wasserman and Frenkel, 2011, 2015; Zhang, Spicer, and Hancock, 2008; Zhang and Spicer, 2014).

At once produced and producing, both consequence and generative force of social relations, space needs to be thought and explored in its processual becoming and production. In the often-quoted *Plan of the Present Work*, the introduction to *The Production of Space*, Lefebvre developed a threefold heuristic model to grasp the making of space (1991: 33). First, 'perceived space' denotes the routine, embodied and non-reflexive structuring of everyday reality through space-related practices. Second, such spatial practice is permeated with and informed by 'conceived space', which refers to society's dominant conceptual and cognitive, thus ideological 'representations of space' enacted by scientists, planners and technocrats. Third, 'lived space' designates space users' non-specialist and expressive spatial experiences: the symbolic that 'loads' objects with images, emotions, affects and connotations (Schmid, 2005: 236). In organizational spatial studies this triad model has been heavily cited and received, sometimes as if it would epitomize Lefebvre's spatial thought. Here, empirical efforts tend to depart from given organizational spaces (usually in formal and thus spatially demarcated organizations) and to trace episodes of the spatial realities of such organizations as either perceived, conceived or lived spaces, as they appear in, for instance, state bureaucracies (Wasserman and Frenkel, 2011, 2015), universities (Beyes and Michels, 2011; Dobers and Strannegård, 2004; Tyler and Cohen, 2010) and theatre companies (Watkins, 2005).

In these studies, the focus tends to fall either on the "cold calculation" of the conceived, managerial space in colonizing and determining the organizational everyday or on a more romantic focus on the appearance of subversive 'lived' spaces. In fact, Lefebvre's own definitions of 'conceived space' as the 'dominant' space of designers and 'lived space' as 'space of "inhabitants" and "users"' (1991: 38–39) seem to imply stable, dichotomized camps. Correspondingly, studies on organizational space tend to resort to 'conceived' and 'lived' spaces as representing, to a greater or lesser degree, separate realms of power and resistance (Dale and Burrell, 2008; Ford and Harding, 2004; Zhang, Spicer, and Hancock, 2008; Wasserman and Frenkel, 2011). A reading of Lefebvre that is more attuned to social space's processual, non *a priori* nature would caution against such classifications of organizational spaces. Indeed, 'the knowledge sought here [does] not construct models, typologies or prototypes of spaces; rather it offers an exposition of the *production of space*', Lefebvre claimed in the final pages of his book, which ends thus: 'we are concerned with nothing that even remotely resembles a system' (1991: 404, 423; orig. emphasis).

Yet employing *The Production of Space* should only be the beginning. Lefebvre's prolific writing career spans the major part of the 20th century (Merrifield, 2000), and he had published an impressive array of texts on a variety of topics before he came to write *The Production of Space*, his 57th book, discounting edited volumes and re-issues. It is necessary to understand Lefebvre's spatial theories within the context of his lifelong trajectory of thinking (Brenner, 2001), not only because the book is sometimes regarded as a kind of synthesis of Lefebvre's broader intellectual engagements (Soja, 1996), but also because it contains ambiguities and even contradictions that, when such contextualization is absent, gives forth to what some scholars have criticized as 'a classic case of mis-recognition' (Aronowitz, 2001: 133; Kipfer et al., 2008a). As Elden (2001: 820) pointed out, the early, spatially minded Anglo-American discussion of Lefebvre's writings 'has come at the cost of neglect of the political and philosophical aspects of his work'.[2] In this sense, scholars face two critical issues when enlisting Lefebvre (Brenner, 2001: 755): Is their reception accompanied by a reflection on the breadth and details of his work as well as a sensitivity to the political and historical context and aims of his writing? And are intellectual and political impulses as well as contextually embedded ideas turned into a productive reappropriation?

I believe that in order to enable a both more in-depth and wide-ranging engagement with Lefebvre's work, the study of organization needs to face up to these questions, embrace the political and philosophical aspects and contexts of his wider oeuvre and experiment with productive reappropriations of its ideas and impulses for, and in, the study of organization. In this sense, Dale and Burrell's (2008) book-length engagement with *The Production of Space* is an exemplary case, both by reframing the 'spatial triad' as the interplay of emplacement, enchantment and enactment—so as to understand the materialization of power in organizational space and its effects—and with regard to the book's concern with the wider political economy of space.[3] In the following pages, I engage with important works written by the philosopher and sociologist before and after *The Production of Space*. On this basis, I outline three major and in themselves interrelated themes that preoccupied him, namely dialectical materialism, everyday life and the body—concepts that in a dialectical fashion can never be abstracted from their concrete shapes and sites of struggle.

## Thinking the Production of Space: Dialectical Materialism and its Politics

> [T]here is a politics of space because space is political.
>
> (Lefebvre, 2009a: 174)

The proposal by Renaudie, Guilbaud and Lefebvre clearly pursued a Lefebvrian politics, most notably in its radical suggestions for enabling self-organization and the right to the city. In Gottdiener's somewhat hyperbolic terms, Lefebvre 'was perhaps the greatest Marxian thinker since Marx' (1993: 129). An unwavering Marxist, Lefebvre was committed to an idiosyncratic Hegelian version of historical materialism. Already in *Dialectical Materialism*, published in 1940, he stressed the need to both take dialectical materialism seriously and preserve its truth by transcending it (Lefebvre, 1968). He credited Hegel with insisting 'on the fact that all thought and all philosophy, even when it opts for one of the opposed terms by striving to reduce the other, moves amongst contradictions'. Thus, 'Hegel discovered the Third Term . . . it is produced rigorously whenever two terms are in contradiction' (p. 31).

However, Hegel had integrated his 'discovery' into an absolute system of thought. It was Marx, then, who denied the Hegelian road towards the perfect philosophical-political system and who paved the way for 'true materialism': the latter 'determines the *practical* relations inherent in every organized human existence and studies them inasmuch as they are concrete conditions of existence for cultures or ways of life' (Lefebvre, 1968: 85; emphasis added). Instead of sticking to *a priori* constructs, instead of glorifying the concept, the real (or, in a spatial vocabulary, 'concrete space') is determining dialectical thought (p. 86 ff.). To wit, this was a reading of Marx wrestled from and turned back against the economistic thought of 'orthodox' Marxism: 'economic relations are not the only relations but the simplest ones. . . . Dialectical materialism is not an economicism' (p. 85). In writings preceding and foreshadowing *The Production of Space*, for instance, Lefebvre (1996, 2003c) discussed the city and urban struggles as the key sites (and the key stakes) of the organization and unfolding of the dialectics of practical relations of production—a sentiment that informs the architectural proposal for the New Belgrade Urban Structure Improvement.

Apparently, it was Nietzsche's influence that made Lefebvre recall the linear version of historical progress as outlined by dialectical materialism. In *Hegel, Marx, Nietzsche* (Lefebvre, 2003a: 42 ff.), he claimed that the modern world would be not only Hegelian and Marxist, but also Nietzschean: Nietzsche asserted life and the lived against political and economic processes, resistance through poetry, music and theatre as well as hope for 'the extraordinary: the surreal, the supernatural, the superhuman' (see also Lefebvre, 1991: 135 ff.; Elden, 2004b: 73 ff.). In a typical move, Lefebvre insisted on a dialectical third term: 'There are always Three. There is always the Other' (Lefebvre, 2003b: 50). As this quote indicates, he conceptualized the three terms of dialectics as simultaneously affecting each other, instead of seeing the third term as the result or the solution of the first two. Dialectics thus becomes a processual, fluid dynamic, 'the inability of the whole . . . to suppress diversity and difference' (Allen and Pryke, 1994: 454, fn 3). There is no synthesis in the Hegelian sense. This move resembled an opening towards a *non-teleological* dialectic that seems to have 'fuelled' Lefebvre's thinking over the course of a century—as Schmid (2005: 307) remarked, this dialectic is the epistemological key to Lefebvre's whole oeuvre.

With regard to the question of spatial organization, three things follow. First, one can discern an overall pattern for conceptualizing the spatial triad, a dialectical—or trialectical—lesson of *how* to approach the analysis of space: each term of the spatial triad is to be seen as simultaneously affecting and be affected by the others; none of them can be thought of without recourse to the other two. In a dynamic process, all three terms of Lefebvre's spatial dialectics constantly mingle (Merrifield, 2000). It follows that spatio-organizational analysis should focus on the *process* of the production of space through the coming-together of the perceived, the conceived and the lived. To emphasize the processual character of such spatial dialectics is by default closer to an open notion of "spaces of organizing" (that can appear anywhere) than to the comparably bounded point of departure that "organizational spaces" seem to allude to. Such an approach can therefore be aligned with the more radical branch of the process theory of organization that prefers to study organization, or rather organizing, as continuous movement between order and disorder (Cooper, 1986; Holt et al., 2014).

Second, this epistemological key implies an outspoken political stance. It is an emancipatory endeavour which hinges on the critique of power-in-space, as Dale and Burrell (2008) stress. Yet beyond such critique, the point of Lefebvre's idiosyncratic notion of dialectics is precisely that contradictory spatial constellations already contain and constitute emancipatory traces and moments—as his life-long work on the problematic of everyday life, which I turn to below, succinctly demonstrated. A depoliticized reception of *The Production of Space* as "merely" a supplier of a spatial heuristics through which to analyse and categorize organizational spaces thus constitutes a rather partial, if not crippling reading of Lefebvre. At the very least, the implications of subtracting critique, politics and emancipation from his work would need to be acknowledged and reflected upon.

Third, and perhaps most importantly, there is an irony in translating a Lefebvrian spatial sensibility into the study of formal, bounded organizations: Such organizations are of course already "conceived abstractions" (their concrete spaces produced through the constant mingling of the conceived, perceived and the lived). In what Lefebvre in his time called 'the bureaucratic society of controlled consumption' (Lefebvre, 1994: 68), corporations and state administrations are co-constitutive of the abstract space of capitalism. It was especially the 'urban organization' through a kind of bureaucratic capitalist governmentality 'against which Lefebvre endlessly railed', and 'which is a far cry from the organization of an anti-capitalist politics' (Harvey, 2013: 140). With Lefebvre, in other words, the presupposition of formal organizations as given objects of inquiry is far from self-evident. As echoed in the proposal for the urban design competition, the question of organization, on the one hand, takes the form of *autogestion*—literally, self-management or self-governance.[4] It denotes the radical redistribution of power towards processes of self-organization, towards social groups creating and governing the conditions of their practice. It is again not a fixed condition, form or model, but an emancipatory process of struggle over the democratic control of firms, enterprises, universities and political associations, but also areas, neighbourhoods or regions (Lefebvre, 2009d). On the other hand, and relatedly, the city is the form and medium of organization. Lefebvre argued that the issue of *autogestion* would be increasingly enacted through the organization and appropriation of urban space. In this sense, a Lefebvre-inspired study of organization would approach urban constellations as sites of organizing and struggle, allowing for both new and temporary forms and practices of organization and their politics, especially in relation to practices of self-organization and everyday appropriations of urban spaces (Beyes, 2010, 2012, 2015).

## Situating the Production of Space: Everyday Life

Lefebvre's concept of everyday life lies in its introduction of a third term into the most important philosophical opposition of the twentieth century: the opposition between the phenomenological and the structural. Everyday life is neither the realm of the intentional, monadic subject dear to phenomenology; nor does it dwell in the objective structures—the language, institutions, kinship structures—that are perceptible only by bracketing the experience of the individual subject. Neither the subjective (the biographical) nor the objective (the discursive), but both: literally and *dans tous les sens*.

(Ross, 2008: 9, orig. emphasis)

According to Renaudie, Guilbaud and Lefebvre's architectural proposal (2009: 1), the organizational site and medium of the city needed to become a 'space of reappropriation (of daily life, of the social)'. Even in 'strict urban organizations', transgressions invariably take place, 'an overflowing of established frames, proving that everywhere there is an "undefined" that refuses to give itself to instituted paths' (p. 11). This 'undefined' and its potential echoes the romantic notion of the irreducible remainder: There is something that does not add up, that is left over 'after all distinct, superior, specialized, structured activities have been singled out by analysis' (Lefebvre, 2008a: 97), as Lefebvre put it in his most renowned definition of everyday life in the first of his *Critiques of Everyday Life*.

If dialectical materialism and its politics are the key to understanding Lefebvre's overall approach, then the critique of everyday life constitutes the heart of his career-spanning critical project 'to decode the modern world, the bloody riddle, according to the everyday' (Lefebvre and Levich, 1987: 9). This project encompassed the three volumes of *Critique of Everyday Life* (2008a, 2008b, 2008c), first published in 1947, 1961 and 1981, respectively, the 1968 monograph on *Everyday Life in the Modern World* (1994), and the posthumously published sketch on *Rhythmanalysis* (2004), which presented itself as an approach to explore the various rhythms of daily life. Yet also the notion of space as developed in *The Production of Space* and in the books on the urban that preceded it (Lefebvre, 1996, 2003c) 'can be understood as a kind of recoding of his initial concept of everyday life' (Ross, 2008: 9). According to Stanek (2011), rather than merely derived from long-held philosophical positions, Lefebvre's theory of space grew out of his concrete engagement with, and on-the-ground research on, urban and rural development and planning in postwar France.

The question of everyday life was of utmost importance to Lefebvre, surpassing the workplace as the primary site of domination and struggle, enlarging questions of social transformation to more socio-cultural and urban (and more than "simply" economistic) processes—for example to 'sustenance, clothing, furnishing, homes, neighbourhoods, environment' (Lefebvre, 1994: 21). As Roberts (1999: 19) pointed out, Lefebvre pioneered a new kind of Marxist sociology, a critical hermeneutics of the everyday that would focus on the contradictory relations of living subjects and concrete objects instead of merely constituting a philosophical claim of concreteness. The idea that the complexities of the everyday are in and by themselves utterly remarkable had of course already been vividly demonstrated by the Weimar critics Benjamin and Krakauer, as well as by the Surrealists, and was later picked up by the Situationists as well as Debord, Barthes and de Certeau, to name just some of the obvious artists and thinkers (Highmore, 2002)—Lefebvre himself was personally involved with both the Surrealists and the Situationist International (Merrifield, 2006).

However, 'Lefebvre is the first writer actually to codify the "everyday" as phenomenologically co-present with, but conceptually distinct from, mere "everydayness"', the latter signifying 'the modality of capital's administration of atomization and repetition' (Roberts, 1999: 23). In a counter-move to the Heideggerian notion of everydayness as a realm of alienation, then, Lefebvre's version of everyday life is a contradictory, potentially conflict-ridden constellation (Elden, 2004a). Everyday life continually produces irreducible remainders that bear traces of dissent, resistance and subversion, of transformation and critique. In his later life Lefebvre seemed to have become progressively embittered about the colonization of the quotidian and the dwindling possibilities of resistance, but he never gave up on his main intuition.[5] As he wrote in his late third volume of the *Critique of Everyday Life* (2008c: 10): 'with daily life, lived experience is taken up and raised up to critical thinking. It is no longer disdained, regarded as an insignificant residue'.

For Lefebvre, then, 'everyday life is profoundly related to *all* activities, and encompasses them with all their differences and their conflicts' (Lefebvre, 2008a: 97; orig. emphasis): 'the everyday is therefore the most universal and the most unique condition, the most social and the most individuated, the most obvious and the best hidden' (Lefebvre and Levich, 1987: 9). These ideas informed, and resurfaced in, his work on space. Thus, in *The Production of Space*, social space was described as 'at once homogeneous and divided, at once unified and fragmented' (Lefebvre, 1991: 306). In the second volume of the *Critique of Everyday Life*, Lefebvre would, in move that foreshadows the later spatial triad, define everyday life as encompassing the three levels of necessity, appropriation and social control (Lefebvre, 2008b).[6]

Reading *The Production of Space* and the spatial triad in the context of Lefebvre's life-long concern with the problematic of everyday life has important implications for the study of organizational space. The production of space is invariably situated in the mundane contradictions of quotidian encounters. If dialectical materialism supplies the overall pattern of *how* to conceptualize and interpret space, then this *where* of everyday life harbours the fundamental methodological principle for empirical spatial inquiries. Merrifield (2006: 4) described Lefebvre's approach as 'a sort of participant observation' of the everyday: It is here that the conceived manifests itself, the perceived is routinely reproduced, and the lived makes expressive and symbolic use of organizational objects—and it is here that spaces of organizing are produced through the coming-together of these processes. Treating everyday organizational space 'as a repository of larger processes' (Kipfer et al., 2008a: 8) risks silencing the inventiveness of the everyday and thus the dialectical complexities of, and the spatial contradictions inherent in, space production. To put it simply: 'If everyday life is going to challenge us into new ways of thinking and new ways of perceiving, then it will need to practise a kind of heuristic approach to social life that does not start out with predesignated outcomes' (Highmore, 2002: 3). In this sense, one is to study the processes of the production of space that shape the urban everyday more than the products of spatial production; to research quotidian spaces of organizing more than the spatial set-ups of formal organizations. As discussed in the following section, such mundane making of space is invariably tied to human corporeality.

### Exploring the Production of Space: The Body

> The understanding of space cannot reduce the lived to the conceived, nor the body to a geometric or optical abstraction. On the contrary: this understanding must begin with the lived and the body, that is, from a space occupied by an organic, living, and thinking being.
>
> (Lefebvre, 2009c: 229)

If 'Lefebvre's most urgent goal is to recapture genuine experience and free the concrete from its subsumption under the abstract' (Aronowitz, 2001: 154), then it should not come as a surprise that he was keenly attuned to conceptions of the body, and that the latter became a(nother) critical and recurrent figure of his thought (Elden, 2004c). 'As such, the living body has (in general) always been present: a constant reference', Lefebvre remarked in the conclusion to *Rhythmanalysis* (2004: 67), the last book he wrote and the text that most forcefully made the case for '[t]he body. Our body. So neglected in philosophy that it ends up speaking its mind and kicking up a fuss' (p. 20). Never shy of provocative assertions, in *The Production of Space* he claimed that '[w]estern philosophy has *betrayed* the body; it has actively participated in the great process of metaphorization that has *abandoned* the body; and it has *denied* the body' (1991: 407; orig. emphasis).

Importantly, Lefebvre went on to say that 'the living body' would be 'at once subject and object' (1991: 407). Given his notion of dialectical materialism, it is not surprising that he sought to go beyond the rather clear-cut division between the active and generative body, on the one hand, and the body as acted upon, as constructed by outside forces, on the other: 'there is neither separation nor an abyss between so-called material bodies, living bodies, social bodies and representations, ideologies, traditions, projects and utopias' (Lefebvre, 2004: 43). Lefebvre's reflections on the role of the body were therefore deeply related to his life-long concern with the subordination *and* the promises of everyday life. Drawing upon other thinkers, most prominently Heidegger (like him, Lefebvre referred to Hölderlin's notion of 'poetic dwelling', see Lefebvre, 1991: 314) and Nietzsche, he related the emphasis on the body to the desired surpassing of the more orthodox Marxian analysis of social practice. In spatial terms,

> [s]patial practice is neither determined by an existing system, be it urban or ecological, nor adapted to a system, be it economic or political. On the contrary, thanks to potential energies of a variety of groups capable of diverting homogenized space to their own purposes, a theatricalized or dramatized space is liable to arise. Space is liable to be eroticized and restored to ambiguity, to the common birthplace of needs and desires. . . . An unequal struggle, sometimes furious, sometimes more low-key, takes place between the Logos and the Anti-Logos.
>
> (Lefebvre, 1991: 391)

Besides being inspired by Nietzsche's Dionysian celebration of existence, as these words indicate, but far from a post-structuralist mode of thought, as it is sometimes argued (e.g. Taylor and Spicer, 2007: 341), Lefebvre saw himself on clear ontological and phenomenological grounds, departing from the notion of 'a practical and fleshy body conceived of as a totality complete with spatial qualities . . . and energetic properties' (1991: 61)—an image that relates back to the Marxist assumption of the 'total man' (Lefebvre, 1968: 136 ff.). Moreover, the body's everyday life, so to speak, 'the cryptic opacity that is the great secret of the body' (Lefebvre, 1991: 203) was again positioned as the third, this time resorting to a vocabulary of time: 'For the body indeed unites the cyclical and the linear, combining the cycles of time, need and desire with the linearities of gesture, perambulation, prehension and the manipulation of things—the handling of both material and abstract tools. The body subsists precisely at the level of the reciprocal movement between these two realms; their difference—which is lived, not thought—is its habitat' (p. 203). In *Rhythmanalysis*, Lefebvre would further develop this notion by conceptualizing the body as polyrhythmic, as composed of diverse rhythms (Lefebvre, 2004); and making space of multiple rhythms would resurface as one of the propositions in the proposal for the Belgrade architectural competition (Renaudie et al., 2009).

For Lefebvre, then, space invariably was a product of the human body: 'The whole of (social) space proceeds from the body, even though it so metamorphoses the body that it may forget it altogether' (Lefebvre, 1991: 405). His interrogation of the complex relationship between human body and space circled around the history of the shift from the space of the body to the body-in-space: how a living organism is produced in space and simultaneously helps produce that space (p. 195 ff.). In other words, the production of space is an embodied process; the body is always already involved in the making of space. In terms of the spatial triad, the body can be understood 'as a mediator of the relationship between the different [spatial] dimensions' (Simonsen, 2005: 7) that never occur in isolation. As conceived "dressage," the body is worked upon and constructed in specific manners through representations of space (Lefebvre, 2004: 38 ff.). At the same time, it is a precondition for perceived space and the carrying-out of spatial practices that require the use of, for example, hands and sensory organs; and it is a source of excessive energies, a producer of difference that allows for other expressions and imaginations, other spatial representations (lived space).

With regard to spatio-organizational analysis, this amounts to the call for a focus on the *corporeal production of space* (Simonsen, 2005). If the making of spaces of organizing is to be explored through the simultaneity of perceived, conceived and lived spaces, then the body as "polyrhythmic" mediator of these processes becomes an erstwhile "research object." At no moment, to paraphrase Lefebvre (2004: 67), should the analysis of organizational space lose sight of the body. Studying the sheer embodiment of spatial organization (Dale, 2005; Tyler and Cohen, 2010; Wasserman and Frenkel, 2015) therefore helps redress the diagnosis of a 'disembodied organizational analysis', which would treat the body as 'an absent presence' (Hassard, Holliday, and Willmott, 2000: 4–5). Moreover, and to all appearances rather challenging to the disembodied gaze of the organizational scholar, all of this pertains to the researcher's body, too (Beyes and Steyaert, 2012). For Lefebvre, after all, theorizing had a strong sensual dimension; it was entangled with everyday life and fuelled by political passion. Therefore, '[t]he ear, the eyes and the gaze and the hands are in no way passive instruments that merely register and record' (Lefebvre, 2004: 83); he/she 'changes that which he[/she] observes: he[/she] sets it in motion, he[/she] recognises its power' (p. 25). As concerns the conditions and the state of scholarship, these claims would warrant a more expansive discussion. In Merrifield's words (2006: 120), 'a universal capitulation to the conceived over the lived hasn't just taken place in the world: it has taken place in those who should know better, in those who read Lefebvre's work, in those who edit and contribute to radical journals'.

## A Hermeneutics of Spacing and the Right to the City

> When institutional (academic) knowledge sets itself up above lived experience, just as the state sets itself up above everyday life, catastrophe is in the offing. Catastrophe is indeed already upon us.
>
> (Lefebvre, 1991: 415)

My attempt to enrich the study of organizational space through a more wide-ranging reading into Lefebvre's oeuvre has led to the discussion of three central tenets informing his work and, ultimately, his work on space: the reformulation of dialectical materialism, his life-long research into the enigma of everyday life, and the critique of the neglect of the body in western philosophy. While this chapter has stuck to the spatialities of organizing, the reception of Lefebvre should by no means be limited to (the production of) space. Yet these tenets do have significant reverberations for organizational spatial enquiries. Going beyond yet encompassing the triad of conceived, perceived and lived space, they point to a 'hermeneutics of spacing':

First, *accounting for the processes of spatial dialectics*. Lefebvre's non-teleological version of dialectic materialism emphasizes the contradictory dynamics of its three terms, which harbours the ever openness of political possibilities. This kind of politics is thus predicated on the processual, heterogeneous and contested nature of space production. The analytical distinction between conceived, perceived and lived space originated from Lefebvre's dialectical thinking; the three elements of the triad thus need to be understood as interrelated and in tension. It follows that none of the elements in the spatial triad can be taken on its own as representing an empirical organizational space. Rather than being held as distinct spatial categories (perceived, conceived and lived spaces as different organizational spaces within clearly demarcated organizations), the three terms of Lefebvre's spatial dialectics afford a processual view on the production of spatial organization. In this sense, it is appropriate to see the triad as consisting of conceived, perceived and lived *spacings* (Beyes and Steyaert, 2012).

Second, *attending to everyday life*. Lefebvre dialecticized the quotidian the same way he dialecticized the production of space. Rhythms and ruptures, repetitions and novelties, the mundane and its 'irreducible remainders', they reside side by side in everyday life. In tracing the simultaneous and contradictory togetherness of conceived, perceived and lived spacing(s), one is inevitably enmeshed within everyday life. The question of organization therefore becomes one of the myriad and prosaic forms and processes of organizing and reorganizing the social, most notably as they take place in the urban everyday.

Third, *appreciating the body*. As Tyler and Cohen (2010: 181) pointed out with regard to the performance of gendered organizational spaces, 'social space . . . comes into being by being inhabitated'. For Lefebvre the understanding of space began with the body. Space was treated 'as a *product* of the human body, . . . not simply as the physical imposition of a concept, or a space, *upon* the body' (Stewart, 1995: 610; orig. emphasis). It is through the pre-linguistic knowledge of our bodies that the world comes to be registered in our perceptions; it is through spatial forces that bodies or a conception of bodies are constructed in a certain manner (Martin, 2002); and it is through corporeal enactments that organizational space can be transformed. The relation between the production of organizational spaces and bodies is thus a mutually constitutive one—and not a causal or representational one (Grosz, 1998). For organizational scholarship, this would mean to include but also go beyond the question of how architecture 'distributes bodies in a certain space and organizes the flow of communication' (Kornberger and Clegg, 2004: 1100). Conversely, relating embodiment to the category of lived space (Dale, 2005; Tyler and Cohen, 2010) risks falling short of the embodied dialectical interplay of spacings. If the Lefebvrian body is a mediator of spacings—'polyrhythmic', as Lefebvre called it—then the embodiment of space implies the presence of the conceived and the perceived, too.

What I end up with, then, is a perspective that is able to take into account more than 'just' organizational space and power struggles in formal organizations—or, more precisely, that offers a thinking of space which cannot be disentangled from the everyday organizing of the social, its embodied complexities and rhythms. All of this does not exclude the mundane spaces within formal organizations. However, the formal organizations of late capitalism and state bureaucracies are already part of the "conceived" abstraction that Lefebvre never tired of arguing against. *Autogestion* emerges in contradiction to the state (Lefebvre, 2009d). In this sense, a Lefebvrian study of organizing and of spatial organization would be attuned to alternative and temporary spaces of organization and their politics.

In this spirit, I conclude by returning to the proposal for the urban design competition with which this chapter began. The proposal relates the notion of the right to the city—originally formulated in 1967—to the question of organization. Similar to the question of work, which Lefebvre translated from its narrow understanding of (in his time) industrial labour to the manifold and embodied activities of producing and reproducing the urban everyday, the problematic of organization shifts to the city as organizational unit and its processes of organizing. How can a city be organized? Yet as David Harvey points out, 'the right to the city does not arise primarily out of various intellectual fascination and fads. . . . It primarily rises up from the streets, from the neighborhoods, as a cry for help and sustenance by oppressed peoples in desperate times' (Harvey, 2013: xiii). It is again connected to the promise of, and continuous struggle around, *autogestion*—emancipatory 'management associations', in Lefebvre's words, that 'appear in the *weak points* of existing society' (Lefebvre, 2009d: 144; orig. emphasis). In other words, the right to the city poses the question of organization neither in terms of bureaucratic governmentality nor according to the more recent and proliferating discourse on competitive urban entrepreneurialism (Beyes, 2012). Rather, it reactualizes issues of *autogestion* and self-organization. As '*a right to urban life*' (Lefebvre, 1996: 138; orig. emphasis), and thus to fully participate in urban society through everyday practices, it is not granted but to be defined and redefined through quotidian social relations and political actions; it as a right only inasmuch as it is appropriated. As such, it has recently become one of the key watchwords for urban protest and social struggle, picked up and appropriated by a heterogeneous set of initiatives at least in the Western world 'that invoke the concept and try to use it to form alliances across towns and across issues, between housing activists and artists, leftist groups and cultural workers, small business owners and the new precarious groups' (Mayer, 2010: 34).

Such appropriations of Lefebvre's work point to openings for critical and politicized engagements with processes of organization. These processes affect, and are affected by, the colonization and irreducible remainders of everyday life, struggles around embodiment and sexuality, urban and anti-globalization movements as well as questions of citizenship and the right to the city. Whereas Lefebvre's hopes for a different organization of the social was formed in Fordist and Eurocentric times of postwar urbanism and dwelling as well as workers' movements and self-organization, his work offers ample inspiration to explore contemporary, emancipatory forms and processes of organizing.

## Notes

1 'Lefebvre's books are compendia of thoughts that, in a negative light, threaten to disperse into incoherence or, more favourably, are charming, conversational explorations of themes' (Poster 2002: 744). With regard to *The Production of Space*, Lefebvre is therefore best viewed as a theoretical guide who offers 'various alternative routes . . . but no clear path' (Entrikin and Berdoulay 2005: 132).

2 Elden even suggested that Lefebvre's work had 'suffered as a *result* of being read in English and appropriated for a certain type of academic work by certain types of scholars' (Elden 2001: 820; orig. emphasis). However, there seems to be a contradiction between retracing Lefebvre's idiosyncratic use of other thinkers' work while simultaneously criticizing how contemporary scholars eclectically mine Lefebvre's oeuvre (Elden 2004b).

3 There is a tension within the pages of *The Production of Space* (Lefebvre 1991: 229 et seqq.): In the historical discussion of how the capitalist 'way' of producing space emerges, Lefebvre offers a rather teleological narrative of spatial epochs. As I will try to show, however, all of this is based on the methodological prioritisation of everyday life and the everyday production of space (Merrifield 2006).

4 That the proposal reactivated the notion of *autogestion* for the Belgrade competition was no coincidence. After all, Yugoslavia had a much-noticed history of experimenting with forms of workers' self-management (which is also a history of these forms' demise), constituting a Yugoslav version of state socialism that was sometimes discussed as a 'third way'—a history that Lefebvre paid close attention and repeatedly returned to (Erić 2009).

5 Consider the difference between Lefebvre's concept of everyday life and Bourdieu's (later) notion of *habitus*. In a thinly veiled aside to Bourdieu's work, Lefebvre criticized the notion of distinction as 'an abstract principle of classification and nomenclature on the one hand, and a principle of evaluation on the other. . . . The phenomenon theorized by it passes too readily from what is distinct to what is distinguished. In this way, it effects separations by accentuating social distances in the hierarchy' (Lefebvre 2008c: 114).

6 First, 'the *immaterial and natural forms of necessity* (needs, cyclic time scales, affective and vital spontaneity) as well as the seeds of the activity by which those forms are controlled (abstraction, reason, linear time)'; second, 'it encompasses the region where objects and goods are continually *appropriated*, where desires

are elaborated from needs, and where "goods" and desires correspond'—it thus designates 'the realm of the dialectic between "alienation" and "disalienation"', a realm of confrontation between the possible and the impossible; third, the level of social control, denoting 'a set of practices, representations, norms and techniques, established by society itself to regulate consciousness, to give it some "order"— an ambiguous realm, for this social control is sometimes played with, subverted, disobeyed' (Lefebvre 2008b: 62; orig. emphasis).

# References

Allen, J. and Pryke, M. (1994). The production of service space. *Environment and Planning D: Society and Space*, 12(4), 453–475.

Aronowitz, S. (2001). The ignored philosopher and social theorist: The work of Henri Lefebvre. *Situations*, 2(1), 133–155.

Beyes, T. (2006). City of enterprise, city as prey? On urban entrepreneurial spaces. In C. Steyaert and D. Hjorth (Eds.), *Entrepreneurship as Social Change* (pp. 251–270). Cheltenham: Edward Elgar.

Beyes, T. (2010). Uncontained: The art and politics of reconfiguring urban space. *Culture and Organization*, 16(3), 229–245.

Beyes, T. (2012). Organising the entrepreneurial city. In D. Hjorth (Ed.), *Handbook of Organisational Entrepreneurship* (pp. 320–337). Cheltenham: Edward Elgar.

Beyes, T. (2015). Summoning art to save the city. *Ephemera: Theory & Politics in Organization*, 15(1), 207–220.

Beyes, T. and Michels, C. (2011). The production of educational space: Heterotopia and the business university. *Management Learning*, 42(5), 521–536.

Beyes, T. and Michels, C. (2014). Performing university space: Multiplicity, relationality, affect. In P. Temple (Ed.), *The Physical University: Contours of Space and Place in Higher Education* (pp. 15–33). London: Routledge.

Beyes, T. and Steyaert, C. (2012). Spacing organization: Non-representational theory and performing organizational space. *Organization*, 19(1), 45–61.

Bittner, S. and Weber, H. (Eds.) (2009). *Autogestion, or Henri Lefebvre in New Belgrade*. Berlin: Sternberg Press.

Blagojević, L. (2009). The problematic of a "new urban": The right to New Belgrade. In S. Bittner and H. Weber (Eds.), *Autogestion, or Henri Lefebvre in New Belgrade* (pp. 119–133). Berlin: Sternberg Press.

Brenner, N. (2001). Henri Lefebvre in contexts: An introduction. *Antipode*, 33(5), 763–768.

Cooper, R. (1986). Organization/disorganization. *Social Science Information*, 25(2), 299–233.

Dale, K. (2005). Building a social materiality: Spatial and embodied politics in organizational control. *Organization*, 12(5), 649–678.

Dale, K. and Burrell, G. (2008) *The Spaces of Organisation and the Organisation of Space: Power, Identity and Materiality at Work*. Basingstoke: Palgrave Macmillan.

Dobers, P. and Strannegård, L. (2004). The cocoon—a traveling space. *Organization*, 11(6), 825–848.

Elden, S. (2001). Politics, philosophy, geography: Henri Lefebvre in recent Anglo-American scholarship. *Antipode*, 33(5), 809–825.

Elden, S. (2004a). Between Marx and Heidegger: Politics, philosophy and Lefebvre's *The Production of Space*. *Antipode*, 36(1), 86–105.

Elden, S. (2004b). *Understanding Henri Lefebvre: Theory and the Possible*. London: Continuum.

Elden, S. (2004c). Rhythmanalysis: An Introduction. In H. Lefebvre (Ed.), *Rhythm-analysis* (translated by S. Elden and G. Moore) (pp. vii–xv). London: Continuum.

Entrikin, J. N. and Berdoulay, V. (2005). The Pyrenees as place: Lefebvre as guide. *Progress in Human Geography*, 29(2), 129–147.

Erić, Z. (2009). The third way: The experiment of workers' self-management in socialist Yugoslavia. In S. Bittner and H. Weber (Eds.), *Autogestion, or Henri Lefebvre in New Belgrade* (pp. 135–149). Berlin: Sternberg Press.

Ford, J. and Harding, N. (2004). We went looking for an organization but could find only the metaphysics of its presence. *Sociology*, 38(4), 815–830.

Gottdiener, M. (1993). A Marx for our time: Henri Lefebvre and *The Production of Space*. *Sociological Theory*, 11(1), 129–134.

Grosz, E. (1998). Bodies-cities. In H. J. Nast and S. Pile (Eds.), *Places Through the Body* (pp. 42–51). London: Routledge.

Harvey, D. (2013). *Rebel Cities: From the Right to the City to the Urban Revolution*. London: Verso.

Hassard, J., Holliday, R. and Willmott, H. (2000). The body and organization. In J. Hassard, R. Holliday and H. Willmott (Eds.), *Body and Organization* (pp. 1–14). London: Sage.

Hernes, T. (2004). *The Spatial Construction of Organization*. Amsterdam: John Benjamins.

Highmore, B. (2002). Introduction: Questioning everyday life. In B. Highmore (Ed.), *The Everyday Life Reader* (pp. 1–34). London: Routledge.

Holt, R., Hernes, T., Helin, J. and Hjorth, D. (2014). Process is how process does'. In J. Helin et al. (Eds.), *The Oxford Handbook of Process Philosophy and Organization Studies* (pp. 1–16). Oxford: Oxford University Press.

Kipfer, S., Goonewardena, K., Schmid, C. and Milgrom, R. (2008a). On the production of Henri Lefebvre. In K. Goonewardena, S. Kipfer, R. Milgrom and C. Schmid (Eds.), *Space, Difference, Everyday Life: Reading Henri Lefebvre* (pp. 1–23). London: Routledge.

Kipfer, S., Schmid, C., Goonewardena, K. and Milgrom, R. (2008b). Globalizing Lefebvre? In K. Goonewardena, S. Kipfer, R. Milgrom and C. Schmid (Eds.), *Space, Difference, Everyday Life: Reading Henri Lefebvre* (pp. 285–305). London: Routledge.

Kornberger, M. and Clegg, S. (2004). Bringing space back in: Organizing the generative Building. *Organization Studies*, 25(7), 1095–1114.

Lefebvre, H. (1968). *Dialectical Materialism* (translated by John Sturrock). First published 1940. London: Jonathan Cape.

Lefebvre, H. (1991). *The Production of Space* (translated by D. Nicholson-Smith). First published 1974. Oxford: Blackwell.

Lefebvre, H. (1994). *Everyday Life in the Modern World* (translated by S. Rabino-vitch). First published 1968. London: Transaction.

Lefebvre, H. (1996). Right to the city. In E. Kofmann and E. Lebas (Ed. and trans.), *Henri Lefebvre: Writings on Cities* (pp. 63–181). First published 1967. Oxford: Blackwell.

Lefebvre, H. (2003a). Hegel, Marx, Nietzsche (from *Hegel, Marx, Nietzsche ou le royaume des ombres*, first published 1975). In S. Elden, E. Lebas and E. Kofman (Eds.), *Heni Lefebvre: Key Writings* (pp. 42–49). London: Continuum.

Lefebvre, H. (2003b). Triads and Dyads (from *La Présence et l'absence*, first published 1980). In S. Elden, E. Lebas and E. Kofman (Eds.), *Heni Lefebvre: Key Writings* (pp. 50–56). London: Continuum.

Lefebvre, H. (2003c). *The Urban Revolution* (translated by R. Bononno). First published 1970. Minneapolis: University of Minnesota Press.

Lefebvre, H. (2004). *Rhythmanalysis* (translated by S. Elden and G. Moore). First published 1992. London: Continuum.

Lefebvre, H. (2008a). *Critique of Everyday Life, Vol. I* (translated by J. Moore). First published 1947. London: Verso.

Lefebvre, H. (2008b). *Critique of Everyday Life, Vol. II: Foundations for a Sociology of the Everyday* (translated by J. Moore). First published 1961. London: Verso.

Lefebvre, H. (2008c). *Critique of Everyday Life, Vol. III: From Modernity to Modernism* (translated by J. Moore). First published 1981. London: Verso.

Lefebvre, H. (2009a). Reflections on the politics of space (first published in *Espaces et sociétés*, 1970). In N. Brenner and S. Elden (Eds.), trans. G. Moore, N. Brenner and S. Elden, *Henri Lefebvre: State, Space World: Selected Essays* (pp. 167–184). Minneapolis: University of Minnesota Press.

Lefebvre, H. (2009b). Space: Social product and use value (first published in *Critical Sociology: European Perspectives*, ed. J. W. Freiberg, 1979). In N. Brenner and S. Elden (Eds.), translated by G. Moore, N. Brenner and S. Elden, *Henri Lefebvre: State, Space World: Selected Essays* (pp. 185–195). Minneapolis: University of Minnesota Press.

Lefebvre, H. (2009c). Space and the state (from *De l'État*, first published 1978). In N. Brenner and S. Elden (Eds.) translated by G. Moore, N. Brenner and S. Elden, *Henri Lefebvre: State, Space World: Selected Essays* (pp. 223–253). Minneapolis: University of Minnesota Press.

Lefebvre, H. (2009d). Theoretical problems of *Autogestion* (first published in 1966). In N. Brenner and S. Elden (Eds.) translated by G. Moore, N. Brenner and S. Elden, *Henri Lefebvre: State, Space World: Selected Essays* (pp. 138–152). Minneapolis: University of Minnesota Press.

Lefebvre, H. and Levich, C. (1987). The everyday and everydayness. *Yale French Studies*, 73, 7–11.

Löw, M. (2008). The constitution of space: The structuration of spaces through the simultaneity of effect and perception. *European Journal of Social Theory*, 11(1), 24–49.

Martin, P. Y. (2002). Sensations, bodies and the 'Spirit of a Place': Aesthetics in residential organizations for the elderly. *Human Relations*, 55(7), 861–885.

Mayer, M. (2010). *Social Movements in the (Post-)Neoliberal City*. London: Bedford Press.

Merrifield, A. (1995). Lefebvre, anti-logos and Nietzsche: An alternative reading of *The Production of Space*. *Antipode*, 27(3), 294–303.

Merrifield, A. (2000). Henri Lefebvre: A socialist in space. In M. Crang and N. Thrift (Eds.), *Thinking Space* (pp. 167–182). London: Routledge.

Merrifield, A. (2006). *Henri Lefebvre: A Critical Introduction*. London: Routledge.

Poster, M. (2002). Everyday (virtual) life. *New Literary History*, 33(4), 743–760.

Renaudie, S., Guilbaud, P. and Lefebvre, H. (2009). International competition for the new Belgrade urban structure improvement (originally submitted in 1986). In

S. Bittner and H. Weber (Eds.), *Autogestion, or Henri Lefebvre in New Belgrade* (pp. 1–32). Berlin: Sternberg Press.

Roberts, J. (1999). Philosophizing the everyday: The philosophy of praxis and the fate of cultural studies. *Radical Philosophy*, 98(November/December), 16–29.

Ross, K. (2008). *The Emergence of Social Space: Rimbaud and the Paris Commune*. First published 1988. London: Verso.

Schmid, C. (2005). *Stadt, Raum und Gesellschaft: Henri Lefebvre und die Theorie der Produktion des Raumes*. München: Franz Steiner.

Simonsen, K. (2005). Bodies, sensations, space and time: The contribution from Henri Lefebvre. *Geografiska Annaler*, 87B(1), 1–14.

Smith, N. (2009). Preface. In S. Bittner and H. Weber (Eds.), *Autogestion, or Henri Lefebvre in New Belgrade* (pp. 81–86). Berlin: Sternberg Press.

Soja, E. W. (1996). *Thirdspace: Journeys to Los Angeles and Other Real-and-Imagined Places*. Oxford: Blackwell.

Stanek, L. (2011). *Henri Lefebvre on Space. Architecture, Urban Research, and the Production of Theory*. Minneapolis: University of Minnesota Press.

Stewart, L. (1995). Bodies, visions, and spatial politics: A review essay on Henri Lefebvre's *The Production of Space*. *Environment and Planning D: Society and Space*, 13(5), 609–618.

Taylor, S. and Spicer, A. (2007). Time for space: An interpretive review of research on organizational spaces. *International Journal of Management Reviews*, 9(4), 325–346.

Tyler, M. and Cohen, L. (2010). Spaces that matter: Gender performativity and organizational space. *Organization Studies*, 31(2), 175–198.

Wasserman, V. and Frenkel, M. (2011). Organizational aesthetics: Caught between identity regulation and culture jamming. *Organization Science*, 22(2), 503–521.

Wasserman, V. and Frenkel, M. (2015). Spatial work in between glass ceilings and glass walls: Gender-class intersectionality and organizational aesthetics. *Organization Studies*, 36(11), 1485–1505.

Watkins, C. (2005). Representations of space, spatial practices and spaces of representations: An application of Lefebvre's spatial triad. *Culture and Organization*, 11(3), 209–220.

Zhang, Z. and Spicer, A. (2014). 'Leader, you first': The everyday production of hierarchical space in a Chinese bureaucracy. *Human Relations*, 67(6), 739–762.

Zhang, Z., Spicer, A. and Hancock, P. (2008). Hyper-organizational space in the work of J.G. Ballard. *Organization*, 15(6), 889–910.

# 3 Rhythms of Historical Disposal

## The Role of Absent Spaces in the Organizational Process of Space Planning

*Fabio James Petani and Jeanne Mengis*

## Introduction

> *[T]he darkness does not lift but becomes yet heavier as I think how little we can hold in mind, how everything is constantly lapsing into oblivion with every extinguished life, how the world is, as it were, draining itself, in that the history of countless places and objects which themselves have no power of memory is never heard, never described or passed on.*
>
> From *Austerlitz* by W. G. Sebald, 2001: 30–31

> *We can see our forests vanishing, our water-powers going to waste, our soil being carried by floods into the sea; and the end of our coal and our iron is in sight. But our larger wastes of human effort, which go on every day through such of our acts as are blundering, ill-directed, or inefficient . . . are less visible, less tangible, and are but vaguely appreciated.*
>
> From *The Principles of Scientific Management* by F. W. Taylor, 1911: 5

In our attempts to organize and plan the present and the future, much energy goes into conceiving—through meetings, documents and other forms of representation—places and objects that later are discarded. Amongst these absences, we often recall particular possibilities that did not materialize and which, regardless of the alternatives that for better or worse replaced them, we still consider as unachieved potential, a shame, a missed chance, a waste of our time and effort. In this chapter, we focus on this "waste" in the context of spatial planning, aiming to develop a processual understanding of how the planning of space is organizationally lived, in a rhythm punctuated by its most burning defeats and by struggles attempting to make up for or regain some material possibilities.

The history of *absent materiality* is largely undertheorized in organization studies. The analysis of unbuilt or transformed spaces, planned in connection with the construction of a public cultural centre in a small city, aims at better understanding how space is conceived (i.e. planned). To this end, we integrate Lefebvre's original insights on space (1991/1974) with his work on history (1970, 1975, 2014b), rhythm (2004/1992), and temporality (2014a), and develop the production of space through a processual focus on the disposal of planned space. Planning always implies the exclusion of alternative possibilities. In the practice of space planning, such possibilities shed light on the project's organizational history of how absent materiality was lived and interpreted (Giovannoni and Quattrone, 2017; Meyer, 2012). Absent spaces capture the outcomes of hidden power relationships, account for sacrifices lived as unfair, and by contrast shed light on the disposal of planned spaces that do not become significant for their absence, but remain irrelevantly disposed of and materially excluded.

Much frustration of spatial planners lies in realizing how much of their individual and collective work is consumed in a seemingly inconsequential manner, as a lot of spaces fail to be implemented as planned and much design efforts appear to vanish without leaving material traces of their existence beyond paperwork. We argue that this sense of waste clings to particular organizational possibilities that symbolically represent a sort of alternate organizational history, a list of discarded but emotionally charged resources that over time help us to analyse the organizational practice of spatial planning. Some *material absences* become organizationally inhabited by actors, who use them to justify and explain why and how certain objectives were not pursued as expected. This chapter aims at grasping part of *"our larger wastes of human effort . . . [that] are less visible, less tangible, and are but vaguely appreciated"* (Taylor, 1911: 5). We do not attempt to understand how to increase efficiency by *eliminating* these wastes (which appear inescapable in any design process), but to study, in a performative account, how *"the history of countless places and objects which themselves have no power of memory"* and risk *"lapsing into oblivion"* (Sebald, 2001: 31), counts (or fails to count) in space planning. Planned and unbuilt spaces become charged with immaterial qualities of absence in view of the considerable time, energy, emotional attachment and values that practitioners invest in their production.

Important literature on the geographies and practices of disposal has shown that "[o]bjects die but do not disappear: things are dismantled, cast aside, destroyed and disposed of but remain in countless material and immaterial ways" (Crewe, 2011: 27). Clearly, disposing of the material form of something does not erase its semiotic presence. On the contrary, by physically throwing away objects, their semiotic presence might even be heightened (Edensor, 2005), which suggests that the practice of disposing can actually make an absence more present (Hetherington, 2004: 159). For space, such a relational focus on present absences or absent presences (Callon and Law, 2004; Meyer, 2012) suggests that "presence and absence cannot be thought of as two sides, recto and verso of one mental (or social or natural) phenomenon" (Lefebvre, 1980: 225). Rather, space "is defined as the play of absences and presences" (Lefebvre, 1980: 230). This 'play' does not always unfold as a straightforward process, just as production, consumption and disposal do not replace one another over time in a linear, discrete sequence (Hetherington, 2004). A focus on the alternation (and simultaneity) of absences and presences in patterns of repetition and difference allows us to analyse the rhythms (Lefebvre, 2004/1992) of everyday organized life. Absence is immanent in all "acts of human production" (Cooper, 2007: 1567) as a major force, since missing presence haunts and incites production and organization (Cooper, 2006) in latent ways we are not aware of.

In particular, we need to better understand how, in the practice of conceiving space, discarded spaces remain present and how presences and absences perform and interact over time, in view of the power relations at play in the production of space (Lefebvre, 1991). In contrast with a conceived or planned space[1] considered like a cold technical representation dominating society (Lefebvre, 1991: 38–39), detached from spaces lived through concrete and emotional imagination, absent spaces indicate a residual by-product that goes beyond mere technocratic representations. We argue that some of these rejections matter in many planning processes, and particularly in the production of space, since they reverberate rhythms of past energies, inciting critique and motivating actors to win back some of this loss in future plans (Petani and Mengis, 2016). The stories of places that materialized only on paper remain often untold (for a notable exception, see a suggestive 'paperwork alternate history' of New York City in Shanor, 1988). Our analysis of a single construction project reveals that some planned spaces were not easily erased because they remained telling non-occurrences, and absences were mobilized discursively as promising possibilities. We paraphrase Taylor (1911) to explain the rationale of our focus: being attentive to the "draining of the world's untold sacrifice of conceived space" allows us to appreciate how absent materiality (cp. Giovannoni and Quattrone, 2017; Meyer, 2012) performs in the process of organizing.

To this aim, we introduce the concept of absent space and suggest a larger appreciation of Henri Lefebvre's work for organization studies. A spatio-temporal and sociomaterial view of Lefebvre's spatial theory (1991) has shown how spatial planning can narratively and strategically manipulate the past, when—in the attempt to regain a convenient identity—lost spaces are searched for to re-enact a glorious History, or 'remember the future' (Petani and Mengis, 2016). Yet, space planning has also an organizational history with a small h, an everyday life made of paperwork representations, which "end nowhere," or, to be more accurate, that neither *end*, nor actually *become somewhere*. This chapter selects two illustrative vignettes of this representational wasteland of plans suspended in a pendulum between absence and presence.

We provide a longitudinal analysis of the planning and construction of a great public cultural centre, observing the organizational process of space planning with a selective focus on some planned spaces that over time risked (or actually ended up) not being built as originally designed. Existing organizational studies drawing on Lefebvre dwell predominantly on how space is transformed by organizations and practitioners that appropriate 'already constructed' facilities with their practices and imaginations (de Vaujany and Vaast, 2014; Decker, 2014; Ford and Harding, 2004; Wasserman and Frenkel, 2011). Organizational research has shown how space production is a political form of control, against which practitioners are more or less subdued or resistant, producing or reproducing, through their work practices, the spaces conceived to contain and constrain particular uses, attribution of meanings and identities (Dale and Burrell, 2008; Wasserman and Frenkel, 2011). We know less, instead, about how organizational pre-production is lived, that is how the conceiving of space is experienced before or during the physical construction of buildings (although see Giovannoni and Quattrone, 2017). Organization studies attentive to the historical legacies of places have shown that the production of space neither starts with the material re-building or restructuring of facilities (de Vaujany and Mitev, 2013; Gastelaars, 2010), nor does it end with their demolition (Petani and Mengis, 2016). By analysing the lived organizational practices of space planning proper, we answer the recent call to account specifically for the *history of conceived space* (Mitev and De Vaujany, 2013: 327). We complement extant research on organizational space drawing on Lefebvre by shedding light on the interplay between conceived, practiced and lived space (Lefebvre, 1991) when planning a new building, a moment of the production of space in which conflicting spatial possibilities are excluded and are experienced as a waste, or outcomes of undue disposal. In synthesis, we ask two questions. First, how does the 'waste' of planned spaces help us to understand how planning and more specifically space planning is lived and practiced before it gets inhabited by end-users? And second, how does the concept of absent space, by clarifying a lived dimension of conceiving, help us to theorize the untold rhythms of disposal in space planning?

The focus on absent spaces allows us to assess the possibilities that 'leave a trace', a necessary condition that Lefebvre posed for moments to qualify as 'historical' (Lefebvre, 1970). The organizational becoming of space can therefore be understood through its planning process, which is historically marked also by traces of non-occurrences, or significant absences. In the following sections, we introduce our theoretical background, present our empirical case and methods, and present findings under the form of illustrative vignettes, delineating our contribution in a concluding discussion.

## Theory Background

### *Lefebvre's Threefold Production of Space: From Conceived Space to a History-Laden Process of Conceiving*

Henri Lefebvre (1991) critically argued that the concept of space was either used to indicate an abstract, reductive representation of the world, or to indicate its concrete, inert manifestation in the material environment. Because these two appreciations shape concretely the everyday life of users, Lefebvre called for a refined understanding of the lived dimension of space and the history of social practices, shifting from the study of things in space to the social production of space.

Lefebvre's notion of *lived space* intended precisely to grasp the concrete experience of space appropriated by the everyday imagination and experience of dominated users, who saw their needs disconnected from the technical representations that perpetuated the agendas of social control of space planners. Lefebvre thus bridged the political and representational gap between "conceived space," critically defined as the dominating, technocratic *representation of space* (Lefebvre, 1991: 39), identifiable in the abstract space planned by architects, engineers and managers (Dale, 2005: 657), and "perceived space," the concrete space of our material routines of *spatial practice* (Lefebvre, 1991: 38). As an organizational view clarifies, lived space "is balanced carefully between the two poles of conceived space (purely idealism) and perceived space (pure materialism)" (Zhang, 2006: 221).[2] Lefebvre conveys therefore a plural understanding of space as a compromise between opposed sociomaterial forces, in whose dialectic tension lies great historical explanatory power about how space is produced by (and produces) social relations.

Lefebvre's triad has allowed organizational research to study how practitioners use many kinds of organizational space. The contradictions between how space is designed and how it is actually lived and imagined have shown how organizations attempt to control, or otherwise shape their employees' sense of self (Ford and Harding, 2004; Ford and Harding, 2008), and their collective identities (Dale and Burrell, 2008). This social and material work (Dale, 2005) of space may ignite aesthetic fascination (Hancock and Spicer, 2011), resistance against strict codes of behaviour (Wasserman and Frenkel, 2011), or daunting feelings of loathing (Ford and Harding, 2008). Organization scholars have analysed the spatial dynamics of homeworking (Wapshott and Mallett, 2012), gender performativity (Tyler and Cohen, 2010), theatrical performance (Watkins, 2005), high commitment organizations (Fleming and Spicer, 2004), extreme bureaucracies (Zhang and Spicer, 2014), and even the extreme hyper-organizational spaces of modern fiction (Zhang, Spicer, and Hancock, 2008).

The triad however "loses all force if it is treated as an abstract 'model'" (Lefebvre, 1991: 40). The three spaces risk being mistaken for the simple modelling of three temporal sequences of space production, whereby space is first conceived and represented, then perceived and practiced, and only later experienced and lived, charging it with emotions or symbolic meanings. On the contrary, organizational research suggested that the three spaces flow into a single time of space since "spatial practice, spatial planning and spatial imagination come together into a single *moment* of social space" and therefore "must be treated holistically" (Taylor and Spicer, 2007: 335, emphasis added). Similarly, we also view production, consumption and disposal as not clear-cut processes within a simple temporal linear sequence, but as coexisting in multiple temporalities that co-constitute their reciprocal becoming (Hetherington, 2004).

The treatment of time and history is central in the theory of the production of space (Lefebvre, 1991), and in Lefebvre's work more generally (Elden, 2004b: 170). Lefebvre proposed "'a retro' study of social space in its *history and genesis* [. . .] which allows us to glimpse into if not foresee the future and *what is possible*" (1986; 2003: 211, emphasis added). Lefebvre advocated, in the study of space, a historical awareness about the gap between reality and possibility, "because any realization cuts off certain possibilities . . . What is lacking is a *history of space.*"(Lefebvre, 2014b: 89, emphasis in the original).

The suggestion, rarely picked up in organizational research, is to trace the long-term dynamics in the production of space (de Vaujany and Vaast, 2014; Decker, 2014; Gastelaars, 2010; Kingma, 2008), to reconstruct also the history of conceived space (Mitev and De Vaujany, 2013: 327). In a recent account, we have shown how the strategic narratives of certain spaces of the distant past enter the process of conceiving future spaces, involving not only interesting temporal dynamics of repetition (e.g. "remembering the future"), but a tight sociomaterial interplay between perceived, conceived and lived space (Petani and Mengis, 2016). Organizational research seldom employs Lefebvre in a time-sensitive way to analyse the practice of conceiving space (Giovannoni and Quattrone, 2017), most often analysing the end-users' practices and lived experiences of organizational spaces, conceived by anonymous others through unknown or obscure design practices. Organizational literature knows little about the conceiving of space as an everyday organizational history with a small h, made of untold, invisible defeats experienced by the space planners and managers of space production.

A processual account on the conceiving of space benefits from the wider insights Henri Lefebvre offers on temporality, rhythm and history (1970, 1975, 2004/1992, 2014/1947) complementing his theory of spatial production (Lefebvre, 1991) with nuanced sociological appreciations of disposal and absence (Hetherington, 2004; Lefebvre, 1980) as part of our everyday practices of production and consumption.

## Temporality and History in Lefebvre

Lefebvre did not substitute the study of time for that of space, but rather addressed "the relation between space and time, and in the process rethought both concepts" (Elden, 2004b: 170). This relationship interested him very broadly, ranging from historical events (Lefebvre, 1970, 1975) to the mundane practices of everyday life (Lefebvre, 2014a). His broad spatiotemporal concern emerges from the unit of analysis proposed in his latest work: "Everywhere there is interaction between a place, a time and an expenditure of energy, there is **rhythm**" (Lefebvre, 2004/1992: 15, in bold in the original). A rhythm, however, does not unfold in an indistinct, homogeneous and automatic flow, but everyday routines can be disrupted in productive and revelatory "moments" (Elden, 2004b: 170). For Lefebvre, perceived, conceived and lived space are moments (Lefebvre, 1991: 40), and the important concept of moment is defined as "*the attempt to achieve the total realization of a possibility*" (Lefebvre, 2014a: 642, emphasis in original). For Lefebvre, *possibility* was key to understand history: "The introduction of Possibility . . . permits us to conceive the objectivity—while yielding its due to relativity, novelty and inexhaustibility—of history" (Lefebvre, 1975: 35, capital letter in the original). Events do not all unfold as equal to one another in our grasp, but they have their differential rhythms and historical relevance. Something is historical, if it leaves traces (Lefebvre, 2003: 178). We suggest that also unrealized possibilities leave traces and count as historical. When conceived (spatial) events do not occur and are experienced as unresolved, the past remains "both connected to us *and* separated from us" (Dale and Burrell, 2008: 78, emphasis in original; Lefebvre, 1970, 2003): We cannot repeat and repair past moments, which remain detached, inaccessible, although very present to us in their absence, in the negation of their planned and imagined (i.e. conceived and lived) possibilities.

Everyday organizational history of spatial planning leaves interesting traces of absences, which help us to understand the becoming of space, as lived by its producers. Urban planning draws justification from strategically remembering the lost places of a golden history it seeks to regain (Petani and Mengis, 2016). In a related way, planners feel the urge also to make up for or re-present a problematically unachieved potential, whose absence reverberates from the past under certain conditions. A sensitivity towards the production of space through Lefebvre's insights on temporality helps to grasp the 'historical rhythm of organizational planning' as an interesting sociomaterial interplay between successful and failed attempts to achieve possibilities, where even absences count.

### The Role of Disposal and Absence in the Process of Conceiving Space

Lefebvre's aim of capturing the genesis of space out of its historical possibilities, invites tracing the *management of absence*. In a review of the theoretical and practical understandings of representation, Lefebvre overcomes the view of presence-absence as a binary phenomenon, reducible to a linguistic, logic and atemporal representation of opposition (Lefebvre, 1980); instead, he will later analyse such a relationship as a dialectical movement with lived practices and rhythms (Lefebvre, 1980: 227; 2004/1992).

The dialectical, rhythmic movement of absences and presences builds on an understanding of reality as a complementary, processual interaction of visibility and invisibility (Kallinikos, 1995) whereby "forms and objects are constituted [also] by what they are *not*, by their deferral in time and space" (Cooper, 2014: 589, emphasis in the original). Because "presence can be absence; and the absent present[,] . . . we should be putting the oppositions implied in such pairs behind us (. . .) we should be looking at *processes*" (Callon and Law, 2004: 3, emphasis added). Actor network theory friendly organizational research, whose sociomaterial awareness our approach embraces, has discussed spacing and timing as an issue of accounting for alterity, apparent absences or hidden presences in effortful orderings and organizings (Jones, McLean, and Quattrone, 2004).

One way to grasp the role of absence in the representation and production of space is to relate absence to a process inherent in all practices of production and consumption: disposal. Disposal *"is about placing absences and this has consequences for how we think about 'social relations',"* since "[g]etting rid of something is never simply an act of waste disposal. Issues of agency and representation (and nonrepresentation) get drawn in too." (Hetherington, 2004: 159, emphasis in the original). The suggestion is not only that the temporality of discarded plans and ideas provides insights into how planning practices enable or hinder particular spatial and social configurations (Hetherington, 2004). More importantly, during the organizational planning phase, the disposal of conceived spaces or spatial possibilities, involves also the "placing of absences" (Hetherington, 2004: 159) as some of these discarded plans acquire agencies as they are charged with a more-than-representational dimension (Lorimer, 2005).[3]

The notion of absent space can grasp the dialectic process whereby a conceived space, in the form of the organizational representation of a space still to be built, does not translate into a materially perceived space and its disposal gets lived with a sense of non-completion and absence. In other words, in relation to Lefebvre's spatial triad (see Figure 3.1), absent space is an expression of how a once conceived, but then disposed space becomes lived (Lefebvre, 1991). Indeed, planned, albeit temporarily not perceived spaces (except being perceived as paperwork organizational representations) can be lived by planners as 'absent spaces'.

As visualized in Figure 3.1, absent space is in diametrical opposition to perceived space, since it cannot be experienced as a materially practiced space. This does not prevent absent space being lived as an important, historical moment of unrealized possibilities. Indeed, each production of space—with its three moments of conceived, perceived and lived space—casts a shadow of disposal as an inherent part of producing space (see black shadow in Figure 3.1). When the disposal of a conceived space creates a sense of attachment to the lived, yet not materially realized (perceived) space, then this space becomes an absent space. Not all disposed spaces have over time the ability to re-enter the production process, by becoming 'present' as significant absences. The moment of **absent space** is *the attempt to realize materially a conceived spatial possibility, which temporally survives the moment of its disposal by further influencing future planning.*

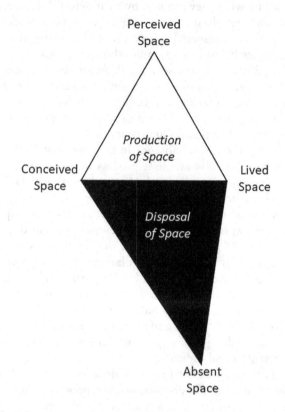

*Figure 3.1* The inherent part of space production involving disposal of space and its emergence as absent space.

Figure by the authors.

It is indeed this performative capacity of the absent space, which makes it relevant to consider in the process of conceiving. Because absent space is lived as a significant organizational waste of conceiving, it remains relevant to the production process as a sour lesson learnt or as an unrealized possibility one wishes to recover.

## Case Study

This study draws on a longitudinal, ethnographic study investigating the coordination of multiple actors involved in the planning and construction of a public cultural centre. With total costs of over 230 million CHF, the centre was a historically important project for a small Swiss city of 60,000 people and included multiple facilities: a museum, a theatre-concert hall, a rehearsal room, a bookshop, a café, administrative offices, a restaurant, a multipurpose conference area, and an underground parking. The centre was built on a plot of land where a former ruinous grand hotel from the nineteenth century was placed. Attached and related to the new centre are an invaluable sixteenth-century Romanesque style church owned by the Canton (region), its former convent, which underwent refurbishment at the same time, a major public square and a hillside area destined to become a public park. The council acted as the project owner and main investor with over 200 million CHF, collaborating with the region as the Canton contributed 5.5 million CHF. Local, private real estate developers in November 2004 acquired from the city the former hotel and built luxury lakefront apartments.

The public project met fierce political resistance by the opposition party on the base of two premises. First, over a period of time the financial crisis dramatically reduced the city's main source of revenues in annual taxes and the public financing of the grand project became a significant burden. During the approval of the funds for building the cultural centre, the opposition party imposed a cutback in costs through a reduction of the museum's exhibition area from two floors to one, arguing on its own Sunday free press that the scarcely profitable elite activity of the museum did not justify the planned space. Second, the contractual formula of the general contract proved an uncomfortable innovation that cut off local builders and assigned the work to a consortium headed by a multinational foreign firm, immediately depicted in the opposition party newspaper as a "lawless invader."

The felt controversy of the project led to much public scrutiny and the over 150 change requests to the original plan and contract were in part also a result of the contested nature of the project.

## Data Collection

Both authors were actively involved in the difficult access to the field, conducting interviews and carrying out observations between November 2011 and July 2014. We collected archival data of 132 public and private documents, collecting both the official documents of the council (e.g. council funding resolutions) and confidential organizational documents (i.e. administrative files on contract management). We interviewed all the major actors involved in planning and construction management activities, conducting 60 semi-structured interviews (all audio-recorded and transcribed verbatim) and 70 ethnographic interviews during observations.

We had repeated interviews with nine key informants: the project manager, the contract manager, the councillor responsible for the project, the director and deputy-director (from the council town planning division); the lead project coordinator, the construction manager, the general manager (from the general contractor), and of course the lead architect. After reconstructing the project and the history of the actors' involvement in the project, our interviews asked very open questions like: "How is the project coming along? What are the major challenges you faced and are currently facing? How did these challenges come about, how were they solved?" Answers often pointed to never-built spaces, as tokens of remorse for unachieved possibilities of space planning practices, but also spaces that risked not happening and were rescued.

Our process-sensitivity focused on: a) the "dramatic" shifts in the project (Pettigrew, 1990); b) the sequence of events describing how particular spaces changed over time (Pettigrew, 1997; Van de Ven, 1992: 169), and c) through which sociomaterial practices (Orlikowski and Scott, 2008) coordination evolved.

We carried out 43 days of observations, during which we attended also of building site meetings (10) and of political steering committee meetings (2) in the presence of the highest political and corporate authorities involved in the project. We also did participant observations at the council general archive (5 days over a 6-month period), helping the project manager to file all the official documentation of the project.

Documents played a crucial role in our ethnographic work, revealing both macro-historical planning narratives on lost spaces in official documents (Petani and Mengis, 2016), and detailed micro-stories of the everyday life of construction project management.

*Data Analysis*

Our research questions narrowed focus on the process of conceiving in planning and construction (so before end-users occupied the centre). We used rhythm, following Lefebvre "as a mode of analysis—a *tool* of analysis rather than just an *object* of it" (Elden, 2004b: xii), addressing the inductively emerging themes of disposal and absence in spatial planning practices. The temporal interest in the socio-material gap between conceived space and perceived space, was inspired by the methodological insight that to understand organizations as they happen (Schatzki, 2006) we need to grasp also what is not happening and what could have happened (Nicolini, 2013: 168). This helped us to uncover power relations and to tell the untold stories of excluded planned possibilities, so absent spaces had the methodological implication of orienting data collection and analysis over time on the conceived and unbuilt, and also on the conceived space temporarily perceived as absent.

Using NVivo software, we coded a closer selection of documents and interviews relating to conceived parts of the project that actors called '*wasted spaces*'. These included: 1) a ground floor restaurant on the square that was never built as planned; 2) the park, once conceived to be entirely walkable, and later transformed and reduced; 3) a planned laboratory for young artists in a donated basement, which instead became an exhibition space for a private art collection; 4) a planned hostel for resident artists at the former convent, later substituted by administrative offices for cultural managers; 5) the initially planned second floor of the cultural centre, temporarily made absent by not financing it, and later approved. We analysed how these wasted spaces over time became related to conceived, perceived and lived spaces and to the rhythmical Lefebvrian issues of "change and repetition, identity and difference, contrast and continuity" (Elden, 2004a: xii). We then coded a subset of these wasted spaces as "absent spaces," indicating discarded spaces that seemed to play a productive role in the practices of conceiving and in the reflexive narratives of practitioners.

The stratified rejected plans began to resemble the telling film negatives of the printed photographs (i.e. the emerged, perceived built space), revealing a submerged organizational history of the planning process. Elaborating on the interviewed practitioners' reflections, rejected spaces could move from a sort of organizational "waste," or merely "consumed and disposed" possibilities (which could also remain so), to a *historical moment* in the planning of space: failing to produce what was planned created frustration or a resisting attachment towards vainly attempted possibilities. We thus followed various moments of rejection to compare and contrast over time different types of the organizational transformation of conceived space.

An abductive dialogue between our data-induced insights and Hetherington's (2004) illuminating review on the sociology of consumption, led us to interpret these spaces, initially inductively coded as 'wasted', as part of the process of disposal, or absence management, a way of ordering that works well on condition that actors do not encounter "absence as unexpected presence, in effect an *unresolved question of value*" (Hetherington, 2004: 170, emphasis added).

## Absent Spaces

In this section, we contrast two conceived spaces of the cultural centre, the museum and the park, which both became radically transformed, being more or less temporarily rejected during the process of conceiving. Together, the two narrative vignettes illustrate the lived practice of conceiving space through instances of disposal, which assume a productive sense of absence in one case, or fail to do so in the other.

### A Temporary Disposal. When Rejection is Historically Resisted and Absence Multiplies Presences: The Museum

At one of the most critical moments in the project's planning history, political representatives of the town entered into a harsh conflict over the planned spaces of the cultural centre and its costs. The planners managing the project were faced with a drastic disposal of a space, and intentionally suspended a conceived space between absence and presence, strategically waiting for a more convenient *moment* to realize particularly valued possibilities (remember how Lefebvre, 2014/1947: 642 defines moment as an attempt to realize a possibility). The temporary absence of this planned space, disposed of in a display of power by the political opposition during the approval of the project's funds, was lived in ways that made a traceable difference on both the conceived and the perceived (i.e. built) spaces of the project, as these presences were organized to fight absence/disposal.

The decision to fund the cultural centre in 2004 imposed a controversial cost-cutting logic of reducing the museum from two floors to one. Many actors experienced it as a major drawback. With only one floor, the museum could no longer both display its permanent collection and hold temporary exhibitions as initially planned. The interviewed museum art director mentioned that "by sacrificing the second floor, the project was one-legged, a tiny museum with only 1200 m² of exhibition space, smaller than the present cantonal museum." Even a council member from an opposition party recalled: "the future use of the new building was absurd . . . we fought against this reduction, which a few years later was effectively reconceived."

The sense of sacrifice and missed opportunity of the absent second floor was so present, at the time of its disposal and thereafter, that actors geared their planning practice towards resisting the decision. Actors bet on the possibility of re-introducing the planned space with support from the regional authority (i.e. the Canton) to fund the second floor's cost, the only argument used for its disposal. This meant fighting absence back in the representational planning practice of preparing, during the 2004–2007 interval, a call for tenders for general contractors (the single most important organizational representation of space of the project's history), that accounted also for the possible future presence of the museum's second floor. The councillor responsible for both town planning and cultural activities explained:

> In the call for tenders, we included a separate section for the extra floor, even if its funding had not been approved. This avoided having to ask at a later stage this estimate to a general contractor, who, having made an initial competitive offer to win the bid, could go in for the kill on the extra floor, had we advanced the request after assigning the contract.

The absence of the museum's second floor led to the flexible strategy in the call for tenders (2007): despite the funding decision's disposal of this space years before (2004), this *absent space was managed as a possible presence in the future*, on condition of meeting certain budgetary requirements. A possible future re-inclusion of the absent space became easier because the costs for its re-inclusion could count on a competitive representation of this possibility, avoiding a later "emergent" request to an already established general contractor in a stronger negotiating position to impose a higher price. This non-linear process of planning uncertain spaces shows how conceived space is not always an abstract and dominating representation of space (Lefebvre, 1991), but can be lived as a conflictual managing of absence against powerful rhythms of disposal. Our data suggest that the lived risk of future spatial absences, incited by the disposal of valued spatial plans, influenced the practice of conceiving: spatial planned possibilities were lived as endangered (i.e. absent spaces), making them more resistant to disposal.

The museum's second floor remained formally absent (i.e. not approved for construction) for several years of the planning practice (2004–2010); in this status it exercised a historically traceable (Lefebvre, 2003: 178) post-disposal agency. During this time it urged the councillor to negotiate with the Canton a swift merger between the town and the state-regional modern art museums. This took place in 2010, when the Canton agreed to contribute 5.5 million CHF towards a 'more than just spatial' event of the project's and the city's organizational history: Not only was the museum's floor recovered, but the merger sealed a long-term city-region institutional cooperation.

The museum thus won back the reintegration of the original two-floor plan not only because it raised extra funds, but also thanks to a completely different set up of institutional relations and circumstances. The second floor's absence signalled an *"unresolved question of value"* (Hetherington, 2004: 170, emphasis added). The absent second floor catalysed the broader process of merging the two museums. The prospective two-floor museum represented a material, necessary condition for enacting the long-term cost reduction plan of not substituting the retiring art director of one of the two merged institutions. A slimmer, integrated public art offer was accelerated through the spatio-historical planning objective of winning the missing floor back.

The absent space proved to be a relevant 'information', understood as a difference that made a difference (Bateson, 1972). The councillor was not alone in resisting the disposal of the museum's second floor. Its absence threatened far higher costs than the construction expenses saved by not building the facility. Powerful private art collectors started reconsidering the prospect of donating to the city their precious art collections in the absence not only of the missing floor, but also of a unique institution where their collection would become part of an extra-urban, state-regional project. These contingent social relations acted as powerful levers in charging the absent floor's resilience. Resistance did not however wait for the merger of museums to materialize in built outcomes (i.e. perceived spaces). In the 2004–2010 interval the museum expanded downward, conquering an extra makeshift space in the basement. During a guided visit at the building site in 2013, the architect explained this historical evolution in the project's conceived and perceived spaces, which we verified on the evolving plans and on site. The museum art-director of the time had taken immediate "mole steps" to transform the underground technical spaces into added exhibition space, a complex operation to realize with zero budget. The temperature and humidity conditions of technical spaces did not comply with strict requirements to host and insure works of art worth millions, which required a retrofit adaptation of the space. The spatial 'plan B' adding the basement floor succeeded in compensating for the unexpected disposal of the museum's second floor. So when the second 'official floor' became present again, its temporary absence had informally but practically multiplied spaces: the museum ended up having three floors.

The processual accountancy of production (Lefebvre, 1991) and disposal (Hetherington, 2004) of conceived and perceived spaces evolving over time clearly shows the effects of absent space. Had the second floor been funded from the start, the extra floor downstairs would not have been planned and realized, as it gained justification only to substitute the absent floor. The example suggests that in the practices of conceiving space, an important absence produced multiple presences, and not only quantitative, in terms of floors, but also qualitative, reflected in the different set up of social relations and merged institutions.

### A Successful Disposal. When Rejected Space Fails to Become Absent: The Park

Not all the spaces that did not get built as planned were lived as a painful disposal, despite embodying substantial changes to the project. The disposal of some spaces was regarded as simply inevitable. When the prospect of a lack of perceived space was organizationally lived as problematic (e.g. the museum's floor), it signalled the gap between planned and constructed space, and absent space became a significant moment of the production of space. Yet, the organizational consumption of some of these conceived possibilities remained in a shadowy disposal of space (see Figure 3.1).

We found that a necessary, though not sufficient condition for rejected planned spaces to become absent and consequential in space planning practices was the strong emotional investment of planners and other stakeholders. Space 'gained in absence' when discarded planned spaces became inhabited, before their end-use, by a multitude of powerful sociomaterial relations that fought disposal, creating a political steadfast attachment to their presence. This is the stronger motivation for participatory planning, an idea pioneered by Lefebvre's notion of a right to the city (Lefebvre, 1968), with citizens joining the lived process of planning by appropriating the space before construction. Interestingly, our case however shows that some planned spaces failed to get 'charged as lived' and were easily disposed of, *despite* strong public communication on them.

A good example of a space that was effectively disposed of is the park. Plans could evolve dramatically without any significant protest, regardless of a demonstrable transformation from what was previously promised during public presentations, and reinforced in *ad hoc* book publications.

The originally conceived park was a major asset of the winning architectural design for the centre, which had a strong urbanist vision strengthening park area. The inspiring representation of green possibilities remained abstract and temporally detached both from both the project's cultural functions developed only later, and from the power relations that shaped the city.

In the initial public documents (e.g. council request of funds, 2004), the park was represented as the "second green reference" (building on the perceived strength of a lakefront park already present) that "embraced" the historical built agglomeration and gave it the necessary "green lungs": many stakeholders valorized this aspect of the urban intervention in the early planning stages, but also during construction. When in 2012 we interviewed the councillor responsible for the project, she explained: "We told ourselves that in a hundred years there will still be a park of 6000 square meters, so something the city needs will remain for future generations."

The park oriented key, early choices of the planning process, so its increasing disappearance struck us the most. The winning project, from its first shortlisting in 2000 out of 104 anonymous competing designs, to the advanced competition between four identified plans in 2002, underwent a historically traceable (Lefebvre, 2003: 178) green shift that helps to explain its final selection. The initial design placed private villas on the hillside to the rear of the cultural centre (where the park is now located), with the former hotel still belonging to the city and filled with public contents (i.e. the theatre in 2000); the later revised plan relocated the private residential space, managed by powerful real estate tycoons, within the more spacious former hotel at the lakefront. Interpreting the will of the town to sell the hotel to support financially the onerous public investment, the changed plan appeared to balance (cover, hide?) with a strengthened green area the loss of a once publicly owned historic hotel. The park was rhetorically depicted as a flagship oasis for the entire urban landscape. It is difficult to exaggerate the emphasis the council and the architect placed on the added value of the park.

A reputed landscape architect was employed in the task of reconstructing the botanical 500-year history of the hill, to restore it in keeping with the practices of the Franciscan monks of the convent, who had cultivated the hills between 1490 and 1848 (see painting on Figure 3.2). A public conference held in May 2012 presented the planned park to the citizens, also

*Figure 3.2* Photos from the monography on the park published for the conference held in May 2012, pp. 17–19.

Courtesy of Studio Pandakovic e Associati.

through an illustrated monograph. The park helped the overall marketing of the project history: first for the architect selling the design to the contest jury and the council; second, for politicians selling it to citizens/voters. Up until 2012 (midway into construction), we can trace the life of the conceived park in the architect's contribution to the bilingual, luxurious monograph published for the conference: "the park is conceived as a LIVING SPACE, an external space expressing the same values we find in the interior" (Anonymized Architect, 2012, monograph: 13, upper case in the original English translation).

The regained park echoed a philosophy of minimal architectural intervention, valorizing the natural landscape through a link with the existing green, lakefront urban areas, and also by recuperating green places of the past. Such spatiotemporal narrative was thus summed up by the conference intervention of the landscape architect: "Every intervention on public spaces is culture, because every place must refer dialogically with what this place has been in its past history." The symbolical value of the park was communicated most explicitly. Figure 3.2, taken from the monograph, shows, on the left, an image of the planned park, criss-crossed by white footpaths enabling the public to climb the hill; on the right, the historical frescoed lunette on the theme of the Calvary (sixteenth century, in the contiguous church) which inspired "a hill scenery reflecting the peaceful Franciscan image of nature and recalling an old farm landscape" as the landscape architect puts it in the monograph (p. 19). Finally, politicians had made also attempts to engage the population in the appropriation of this part of the project by giving citizens the possibility of "adopting and dedicating" a bench or tree at the park.

In these ways, politicians took all possible credit for the planned space ahead of the 2013 local elections—long before the park's material construction—strategically narrating and betting on the space's future (Boje, 2011): in May 2012 in an interview to the local press the councillor responsible for the project envisioned the as yet non existing park as "a slow island of peace in the hustle and bustle of the city."

So far we have offered a glimpse of the representations and the more-than-representational (Lorimer, 2005) affective practices relating to the park before construction. The promised park was however destined to change greatly in perceived size and content.

The cultural centre materially ate up parts of the park, as a close study of the evolution of plans over time indicates. Figure 3.3 shows how, by 2014, the building of the culture centre occupied a significant volume of space conceived in 2002 for the park. In addition, while the design presented in May 2012 still included an entirely pedestrian-friendly link between the hill side of the city and its lake-front and historical centre, a year and a half later, the planned park area, was sacrificed mercilessly, becoming a walled-in sloping back garden, less usable by pedestrians, without the previously designed gently rising paths. The interviewed landscape architect critically resumed this evolution in November 2013: "The garden, because to call it

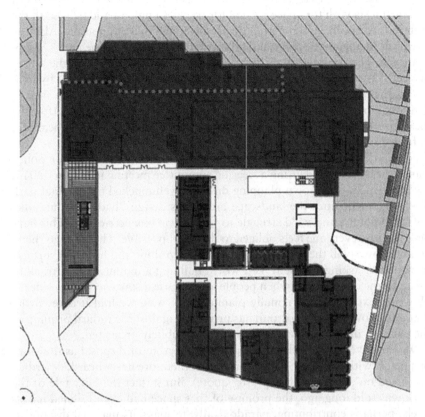

*Figure 3.3* The cultural centre eating up the park: The dotted line shows the original design's boundaries of the cultural centre (2002) respect to its expansion by 2014.

Courtesy of Architects Claudia Scholz and Louise Brandberg Realini.

park now is a bit. . . . Before it was all walkable . . . the paths . . . Now the paths we have left are almost service routes . . . the hillside will now be . . . only to look at from below . . . You won't be able to walk to that part." The council Town Planning director, interviewed during a steering committee meeting in 2014, acknowledged the reduction of the park more coldly, referring to practical reasons that made it necessary: "Yes, it's true, perhaps the urban concept of the green area helped the architect to win the design contest, but it was not compatible with the storage and logistic functions of the museum and theatre, which we later revolutionized. . . . Once we had fixed this aspect, the urban concept of the park died and was buried there, it remained on paper."

The sudden death of an important park for the city out of logistical reasons contrasted strikingly with the inspirational narrative that had accompanied its planning for so long. Since the design contest, the park faced a series of practical tests with the space needed for trucks to unload and deliver all the materials for both museum and theatre being the most important. Also the power of financial resources and political interests explain the park's disappearance. The park was built last and paid the consequences of the whole project's cost overrun, which led to a reduction of the park's budget by half. Lastly, the use of the conceived park to obtain a political return was already consumed by the end of 2013, making the park more disposable. After the local elections, the park remained present, but its gradual disappearance unfolded in a silent disinterest.

The park's partial disposal was not lived as a sacrifice by major politicians, nor by citizens. During a steering committee meeting in January 2014, the abovementioned town planning director even mocked the original park as exaggerated, since the landscape architect's design "had something like 400–500 plants, and we'd struggle to fit in some blueberries. . . . This happens because everyone feels obliged to do the impossible. Then you go there, you see how small the space really is, it's a steep slope and not a flat surface, so you start asking yourself: 'Is it worth building a mountain-type track to go up to the city hillside, when people already use a stairway on the side?' " However extreme the originally planned park was, we find it noteworthy that until now, no citizen group has protested against the radical pruning of the park, so different now from how it was publicly presented.

We ourselves lived such untold planning rhythm of disposal as the story of a place 'with no power of memory that is therefore never heard, described or passed on' (see Sebald's opening quote). But in fact the fairy tale of the park was told long ago, the promise of that space had been fulfilled narratively, perhaps contributing, paradoxically, to make its material disappearance less conspicuous. No powerful stakeholder fought for the park.

The case illustrates how not all discarded spaces become absent and play a productive role in the planning process, yet constitute the shadow that disposal casts over the production of space (see Figure 3.1). It shows how conceived spaces are politically practiced within particular temporal rhythms (i.e. election cycles) that consume their semiotic presence/absence before they can materialize to benefit the majority of stakeholders (i.e. taxpayers, citizens). Disposal did not turn the park into an absent space, but followed almost an opposite trajectory compared to the absent museum floor: While the floor started temporally with a dramatically lived absence and won back a multiple perceived presence, the park, initially represented as an inspirational presence, ended as a decreasingly present conceived and perceived space. The case of the park also suggests that a conceived space, however representationally charged on paper with deep symbolic meanings (i.e. as a lived and almost already perceivable space), and however legitimized by winning a design contest, can organizationally be disposed of, when later developed conceptions collectively impose themselves rendering impracticable the plan selected during the design contest. Representations of space (i.e. conceived spaces) (Lefebvre, 1991) unavoidably change over time, as projects get closer to their material implementations (perceived space). And as the production of space is not concluded with its physical construction, we maintain a small hope that our alternative account of the killing of a planned park may enliven its "absence" for future planning to win back some of the green disposed of.

## Conclusion

Absence is related to disposal and incites a processual thinking towards the complementary reality it (be)comes from: just as absence suggests presence, disposal evokes production and consumption (Hetherington, 2004), and these dialectic tensions capture the sociomaterial relations of a political power struggle (Dale and Burrell, 2008). The spaces of Lefebvre's triad must not only be treated holistically (Taylor and Spicer, 2007: 335, emphasis added), but qualitative studies should get behind or beyond what happens (Schatzki, 2006) to capture also the unachieved organizational possibilities of practices (Nicolini, 2013: 168). Absent space contributes a theorizing on the particular production which, through disposal, transforms over time some conceived and materially absent spaces, into lived and still influential spaces (Meyer, 2012). Practices of conceiving space interplay organizationally with Lefebvre's perceived/practiced and lived/imagined. We have shown specifically how immaterial spaces count (Crewe, 2011: 27) in valorizing (or silencing) the possibilities of historical moments (Lefebvre, 2014/1947: 642) that leave interesting traces (Lefebvre, 1970): both those loudly told by absent spaces and those left untold by disposed ones.

We illustrated how the lived dimension of conceiving makes an important material difference. The second floor of the museum's abrupt and unexpected absence hurt like an amputated limb, creating the historically influential possibility of regaining it as materially present. Instead, the repeated rhetorical celebration of the park made it so vividly present in all its imagined, material, symbolical and historical relations, that it could be perceived as lived even prior to its realization, making its material production less important, as not attuned to the political rhythms of elections and still not lived by the citizens as an absence.

Not all missed historical possibilities of urban planning are lived as such. This suggests that the way planned spaces are affectively experienced matters for whether a disposal is felt and perceived as an absence or not. What provides a quality of absence to conceived spaces is the threat towards future possibilities for powerful actors, who expect an accomplished historical realization from certain perceived spaces. To add specificity to our argument, the living of conceiving cannot be left to scattered participatory planning masking political promotion, with random participation by the general public. Desirable conceived spaces may better resist disposal (i.e. become absent, in the sense of being critically recognized as a lack) in a long-term rhythm and history of everyday organizational struggle, if coupled with powerful institutional and historical organizational support (e.g. agreements between city and cantonal museum; city and private art collectors; city and real estate investors).

We have shown that discarded plans do not all behave in the same way. The difference rests in the lived dimension that over time charges some planned spaces but not others. The everyday lived dimension of conceiving space is made up of a stratification of possibilities, some of which inevitably become impossibilities. Only a selection of rejected planned spaces—through their lived absence—become significant 'moments' in the production of space. By focusing on the presences and absences of disposal, absent spaces contribute to make the organizational history of conceiving more intelligible in its non-linear twists and turns.

The production of space is organizationally lived by the historical ongoing disposal of conceived spaces. Accounting for the material and lived absence of the planned spaces, we traced processually how actors move from plans to the perception of their performative effects. Emotional responses and related imaginations of what is possible feed back into the planning process, to defend practitioners' efforts from becoming historically inconsequential, failing to achieve the possibilities they aimed for.

A longitudinal view on space planning should consider variously charged and lived rhythms of disposal as a management of absences (Hetherington, 2004). To this end, we showed how absences may continue to influence the production of space (Lefebvre, 1991). We added a further moment to Lefebvre's spatial triad (Lefebvre, 1991) that provides a historical, time-sensitive and processual account of conceived space (Mitev and De Vaujany, 2013). Absent space addresses social materiality in the long term, since affectively charged plans continue to reverberate their values, and embody recrimination for the wasted human efforts and the untold stories of possibilities lapsing into oblivion (see opening quotes).

Disposal and absence can be materially traced and shown to be productive (Meyer, 2012). But we want to be clear that there is nothing deterministic in the absence of spaces, conceived or otherwise. As an additional *moment*, absent space shares the features of other moments as "attempts to realize total possibilities" (Lefebvre, 2014/1947: 642). These moments are important turning points, which can fail, succeed, or even accomplish their intended organizational possibilities only partially or temporarily, depending on 'from when' (or by whom) history is told.

This chapter has integrated some of Lefebvre's thoughts on temporality, rhythm and history (Lefebvre, 1970, 1975, 2004/1992, 2014/1947) to advance a processual appreciation of his spatial triad (Lefebvre, 1991), and further adds spatial specificity to his general reflections on representation, absence and presence (Lefebvre, 1980). By looking at what is historically and in everyday practice represented as possible, but then proves not to be, absent space contributes to the ambition of the production of space of being

" 'a retro' study of social space *in its history and genesis* [. . .] which allows us to glimpse into if not foresee the future and *what is possible*" (Lefebvre, 1986; 2003: 211, emphasis added). Absent spaces show qualitatively the performative effects of a recurring and related disposal/production dialectical process within the practice of conceiving space.

Absence is not a planning anomaly. Disposal is in fact an unavoidable political controversy on the value of possibilities, and the absences it produces (and consumes) motivate presences that would not otherwise emerge. This finds support in Lefebvre's reflection: "Absence, as a moment, has nothing pathogenic about it. On the contrary: it provokes, it incites" (Lefebvre, 1980: 231). Absence and disposal thus help a processual view of the production of space in that they provide an emotional counterpart to what physical spaces mean to us, even before (or beside) their materialization. Much as the spaces we use and practice are imbued with a life that often contradicts their abstract design, so the spaces we could never realize, despite having conceived them with great inconsequential effort, reverberate energies hard to dismiss as simply ineffective.

This chapter inevitably has some limitations. First of all, we only addressed partially the question of how the notion of disposal can be applied holistically to Lefebvre's spatial triad (Taylor and Spicer, 2007). This constitutes an interesting agenda for a wider Lefebvre-inspired, process organizational research on space. Here we limited our exploratory analysis to the role that conceived and absent space have in the production of space. A full engagement with the notion of disposal would no doubt include the disposal of perceived spaces, in examining the long term organizational agency of ruins (Edensor, 2005) and of demolitions in the production of space. This seems a rich path for process organization studies, beyond a focus on space. How do we organize by disorganizing, how do we undo what we (or others) did before? How is the creative, innovative force of destruction performed materially and symbolically?

Secondly, within the interesting dynamics of disposal and absence in space production and the way they shape possibilities in planning practices, further reflection on the representation and materiality of conceived spaces and their absences is necessary. Lefebvre himself posed the problem of representing absence: "*Absence?* How to represent it, since the representation fills the voids of absence?" (Lefebvre, 1980: 230). Our study provides only first indications that the representation and 'materialization of absences' matter broadly in the lived practices of conceiving. Future research may address the relationship between representational, more-than-representational (Lorimer, 2005) and material spaces more systematically.

How can these material and immaterial absences and presences be politically managed in space planning? How can researchers, citizens, and planners themselves identify the significantly undesired disappearances from spatial plans? The second floor of the museum was made particularly conspicuous from an early disruptive absenting of its plan, whereby disposal actually transformed an absence and made it more present (Hetherington, 2004: 159). A specular inverted argument can apply to the park, whose early, promotional presentation to the citizens did nothing to prevent the disposal of that plan, almost as if putting the spotlight on that space allowed it somehow to hide its disappearance in plain sight, to silence its absence less visibly, because in many ways already seen. When politicians promise green areas in connection with urban renovation projects, they should be made preventively accountable for respecting those plans, for instance allocating separate untouchable budgets allocated to green areas. This would at least warrant the independent means for certain promises to be kept, avoiding that green areas got easily sacrificed as the temporally last thing to be constructed in big projects. Cost overruns should not be contained at the expense of green areas.

This chapter has foregrounded waste, absence and disposal as organizationally relevant elements in the context of spatial planning, and in planning more generally. A compelling argument sees all architecture as marked by melancholy (Benjamin, 2000) "for each building is what it is, but simultaneously is 'that which is not'. The latter *absence* creates a feeling in all those at the site of 'a loss', *a negation of what might have been*" (Dale and Burrell, 2008: 291, emphasis added). Materially built facilities obscure the realm of possibilities from which they were planned, calling for a specific organizational search into the history of conceiving (Mitev and De Vaujany, 2013: 327). Material spaces do not always reveal, but often conceal their planners' intentions, covering the trails of ruined dreams and merely attempted alternative conceptions of space. In Gyerin's words: "*[o]nce completed, buildings hide the many possibilities that did not get built*, as they bury the interests, politics, and power that shaped the one design that did" (Gieryn, 2002: 38–39, emphasis added). We like to think of absent space as a critical tool to unearth those organizational interests, politics and power.

**Acknowledgements:** This study was supported by the Swiss National Science Foundation (SNSF) under grant numbers 138105 and 152272.

## Notes

1 In this chapter, conceived and planned spaces are equivalent: they indicate the practices and processes of space design.
2 Conceived and perceived space are critical developments of the Cartesian categories of *res cogitans* and *res extensa*, which Lefebvre had discussed earlier (Lefebvre, 1947). With the spatial triad, developed through the influence, amongst others, of French phenomenologists like Bachelard and Merleau-Ponty, "Lefebvre attempts consistently to maintain his dialectical materialist standpoint. In this way the epistemological perspective shifts from the subject that thinks, acts, and experiences to the *process of social production of thought, action, and experience*" (Schmid, 2008, pp. 40–41, emphasis added; cp. also Stanek, 2011).
3 To keep the discussion simple, we opt here for the comprehensive label of 'more-than-representational' (Lorimer, 2005), warning however that Lefebvre termed lived space also 'representational space' (to distinguish it from conceived space or 'representations of space') (Lefebvre, 1991), and that, related to affect-driven

practices and processual approaches to space, an influential 'non-representational theory' (Thrift, 2008) has started influencing organizational research on space (Beyes & Steyaert, 2012).

# References

Bateson, G. (1972). *Steps to an Ecology of Mind*. New York: Ballantine.

Benjamin, A. (2000). *Architectural Philosophy*. London: Athlone.

Beyes, T. and Steyaert, C. (2012). Spacing organization: Non-representational theory and performing organizational space. *Organization, 19*(1), 45–61.

Boje, D. M. (Ed.). (2011). *Storytelling and the Future of Organizations: An Antenarrative Handbook*. London: Routledge.

Callon, M. and Law, J. (2004). Introduction: Absence-presence, circulation, and encountering in complex space. *Environment and Planning D: Society and Space, 22*(1), 3–11.

Cooper, R. (2006). Making present: Autopoiesis as human production. *Organization, 13*(1), 59–81.

Cooper, R. (2007). Organs of process: Rethinking human organization. *Organization Studies, 28*(10), 1547–1573.

Cooper, R. (2014). Process and reality. In J. Helin, T. Hernes, D. Hjorth and R. Holt (Eds.), *The Oxford Handbook of Process Philosophy & Organization Studies* (pp. 585–604). Oxford, UK: Oxford University Press.

Crewe, L. (2011). Life itemised: Lists, loss, unexpected significance, and the enduring geographies of discard. *Environment and Planning D: Society and Space, 29*(1), 27–46.

Dale, K. (2005). Building a social materiality: Spatial and embodied politics in organizational control. *Organization, 12*(5), 649–678.

Dale, K. and Burrell, G. (2008). *The Spaces of Organisation and the Organisation of Space: Power, Identity and Materiality at Work*. Houndmills and New York: Palgrave Macmillan.

de Vaujany, F.-X. and Mitev, N. (2013). *Materiality and Space: Organizations, Artefacts and Practices*. Houndmills and New York: Palgrave Macmillan.

de Vaujany, F.-X. and Vaast, E. (2014). If these walls could talk: The mutual construction of organizational space and legitimacy. *Organization Science, 25*(3), 713–731.

Decker, S. (2014). Solid intentions: An archival ethnography of corporate architecture and organizational remembering. *Organization, 21*(4), 514–542.

Edensor, T. (2005). Waste matter—The debris of industrial ruins and the disordering of the material world. *Journal of Material Culture, 10*(3), 311–332.

Elden, S. (2004a). Rhythmanalysis: An introduction. In Lefebvre, H. (2004/1992), *Rhythmanalysis: Space, Time and Everyday Life* (pp. vii–xv). London: Continuum.

Elden, S. (2004b). *Understanding Henri Lefebvre*. London: Continuum.

Fleming, P. and Spicer, A. (2004). 'You can checkout anytime, but you can never leave': Spatial boundaries in a high commitment organization. *Human Relations, 57*(1), 75–94.

Ford, J. and Harding, N. (2004). We went looking for an organization but could find only the metaphysics of its presence. *Sociology, 38*(4), 815–830.

Ford, J. and Harding, N. (2008). Fear and loathing in Harrogate, or a study of a conference. *Organization, 15*(2), 233–250.

Gastelaars, M. (2010). What do buildings do? How buildings-in-use affect organizations. In A. Marrewijk and D. Yanow (Eds.), *Organizational Spaces. Rematerializing the Workaday World* (pp. 77–95). Cheltenham: Edward Elgar.

Gieryn, T. F. (2002). What buildings do. *Theory and Society, 31*(1), 35–74.

Giovannoni, E. and Quattrone, P. (2017). The materiality of absence: Organizing and the case of the incomplete cathedral. *Organization Studies*. First Published Online June 22, 2017, https://doi.org/10.1177/0170840617708005

Hancock, P. and Spicer, A. (2011). Academic architecture and the constitution of the new model worker. *Culture and Organization, 17*(2), 91–105.

Hetherington, K. (2004). Secondhandedness: Consumption, disposal, and absent presence. *Environment and Planning D: Society and Space, 22*(1), 157–174.

Jones, G., McLean, C. and Quattrone, P. (2004). Spacing and timing. *Organization, 11*(6), 723–741.

Kallinikos, J. (1995). The architecture of the invisible: Technology is representation. *Organization, 2*(1), 117–140.

Kingma, S. F. (2008). Dutch casino space or the spatial organization of entertainment. *Culture and Organization, 14*(1), 31–48.

Lefebvre, H. (1947). *Descartes*. Paris, France: Éditions Hier et Aujourd'hui.

Lefebvre, H. (1968). *Le droit à la ville*. Paris, France: Anthropos.

Lefebvre, H. (1970). *La Fin de l'Histoire*. Paris (France): Éditions de Minuit.

Lefebvre, H. (1975). What is the historical past? *New Left Review, 90*(27–34).

Lefebvre, H. (1980). *La présence et l'absence: contribution à la théorie des représentations*. Paris, France: Casterman.

Lefebvre, H. (1986). *Préface to the New Edition of La Production de l'espace* (3rd ed.). Paris, France: Anthropos.

Lefebvre, H. (1991). *The Production of Space*. Oxford: Blackwell.

Lefebvre, H. (2003). Key writings. In S. Elden, E. Lebas and E. Kofman (Eds.), *Key Writings*. London: Continuum.

Lefebvre, H. (2004/1992). *Rhythmanalysis: Space, Time and Everyday Life*. London: Continuum.

Lefebvre, H. (2014a). *Critique of Everyday Life*. London: Verso.

Lefebvre, H. (2014b). *Toward an Architecture of Enjoyment*. Minneapolis: University of Minnesota Press.

Lefebvre, H. (2014/1947). *Critique of Everyday Life*. London: Verso.

Lorimer, H. (2005). Cultural geography: The busyness of being 'more-than-representational'. *Progress in Human Geography, 29*(1), 83–94.

Meyer, M. (2012). Placing and tracing absence: A material culture of the immaterial. *Journal of Material Culture, 17*(1), 103–110.

Mitev, N. and De Vaujany, F. X. (2013). Conclusion: Back to long durée, materialism and management practices? In F. X. De Vaujany and N. Mitev (Eds.), *Materiality and Space: Organizations, Artefacts and Practices*. Basingstoke: Palgrave Macmillan.

Nicolini, D. (2013). *Practice Theory, Work, and Organization: An Introduction*. Oxford: Oxford University Press.

Orlikowski, W. and Scott, S. (2008). Sociomateriality: Challenging the separation of technology, work and organization. *The Academy of Management Annals, 2*, 433–474.

Petani, F. J. and Mengis, J. (2016). In search of lost space: The process of space planning through remembering and history. *Organization, 23*(1), 71–89.

Pettigrew, A. M. (1990). Longitudinal field research on change: Theory and practice. *Organization Science*, 1(3), 267–292.

Pettigrew, A. M. (1997). What is a processual analysis? *Scandinavian Journal of Management*, 13(4), 337–348.

Schatzki, T. R. (2006). On organizations as they happen. *Organization Studies*, 27(12), 1863–1873.

Schmid, C. (2008). Towards a three-dimensional dialectic. Lefebvre's theory of the production of space. In K. Goonewardena, S. Kipfer, R. Milgrom and C. Schmid (Eds.), *Space, Difference, Everyday Life: Reading Henri Lefebvre* (pp. 27–45). New York: Routledge.

Sebald, W. G. (2001). *Austerlitz*. London: Penguin.

Shanor, R. R. (1988). *The City that Never Was: Two Hundred Years of Fantastic and Fascinating Plans that Might Have Changed the Face of New York City*. New York: Viking.

Stanek, L. (2011). *Henri Lefebvre on Space: Architecture, Urban Research, and the Production of Theory*. Minneapolis: University of Minnesota Press.

Taylor, F. T. (1911). *The Principles of Scientific Management*. New York: Harper.

Taylor, S. and Spicer, A. (2007). Time for space: A narrative review of research on organizational spaces. *International Journal of Management Reviews*, 9(4), 325–346.

Thrift, N. (2008). *Non-Representational Theory: Space, Politics, Affect*. London: Routledge.

Tyler, M. and Cohen, L. (2010). Spaces that matter: Gender performativity and organizational space. *Organization Studies*, 31(2), 175–198.

Van de Ven, A. H. (1992). Suggestions for studying strategy process: A research note. *Strategic Management Journal*, 13(169–188).

Wapshott, R. and Mallett, O. (2012). The spatial implications of homeworking: A Lefebvrian approach to the rewards and challenges of home-based work. *Organization*, 19(1), 63–79.

Wasserman, V. and Frenkel, M. (2011). Organizational aesthetics: Caught between identity regulation and culture jamming. *Organization Science*, 22(2), 503–521.

Watkins, C. (2005). Representations of space, spatial practices and spaces of representation: An application of Lefebvre's spatial triad. *Culture and Organization*, 11(3), 209–220.

Zhang, Z. (2006). What is lived space? *Ephemera*, 6(2), 219–223.

Zhang, Z. and Spicer, A. (2014). 'Leader, you first': The everyday production of hierarchical space in a Chinese bureaucracy. *Human Relations*, 67(6), 739–762.

Zhang, Z., Spicer, A. and Hancock, P. (2008). Hyper-organizational space in the work of J. G. Ballard. *Organization*, 15(6), 889–910.

# 4 Lefebvre and Spacing Leadership

## From Power Over to Power With

*Perttu Salovaara and Arja Ropo*

### Introduction: Lefebvre and Leadership?

In this chapter, we discuss possible connections between Lefebvre and current leadership research. Although Lefebvre's writings on space have had a particularly significant impact on organizational thinking on spatiality, we do not go as far as to suggest that Lefebvre be forced into a category of leadership thinkers. However, borrowing Lefebvre's wording in his comment that 'Marx is not a sociologist . . . there is sociology in Marx' (in Elden, 2004: 129), we would like to say that Lefebvre is not a leadership researcher, but there is leadership in Lefebvre. His dissertation on rural peasant life in the Valley of Campan in the Pyrenees (2000, originally 1954), another more general book on the Pyrenees (1963) and his work on space (1991)[1] indicate a delicate understanding of how collectives become organized and of the relationship between humans and the natural and built environment, that is, between humans and materiality. This chapter introduces the concept of 'spacing leadership' that combines Lefebvre's writings on spatiality and rural culture to suggest that his work offers ways to conceptualize relationships between humans and spatial materiality in a way that informs and connects to leadership studies (cf. Ropo and Salovaara, 2018).

The interest in materiality shaping human (inter)action coincides with the recent focus on materiality in leadership studies. Instead of limiting leadership to human-human interactions, a number of authors claim that leadership takes place in human-material encounters as well; the material environment shapes and guides human action, for example, through physical resemblance to seafaring at the British Royal Navy training centre (Hawkins, 2015); through technological equipment, reports and protocols in healthcare policymaking (Oborn, Barrett, and Dawson, 2013); and through physical places and spaces (Ropo, Sauer, and Salovaara, 2013; Ropo, Salovaara, Sauer, and De Paoli, 2015; Zhang and Spicer, 2014). The chapter joins post-heroic and plural leadership approaches that extend the leadership concept beyond leaders to collectives, groups and communities with leaderless leadership (Crevani, Lindgren, and Packendorff, 2007, 2010; Denis, Langley, and Sergi, 2012; Edwards, 2015, b; Eslen-Ziya and Erhart,

2015; Sutherland, 2015). It is this line of thinking about leadership—how collectives work and cooperation and communities are organized—where Lefebvre's texts have the potential to inform leadership studies.

We develop our argument in relation to a university space renovation project that links Lefebvre's triadic, interrelated concept of space with ways of redirecting and organizing activities. Importantly for our argument, the project involved the end-users of the space in a particularly integral fashion in the planning and designing phase. The way the space becomes a lived experience for the end-users, including spatial atmosphere and mood, is something that is not commonly 'observed, analysed or theorized in architecture or planning', Pallasmaa notes (2014: 233), an architect himself. This implies that, although participation is rhetorically paid attention to, those running the spatial design process are often[2] not in possession of tools with which to facilitate more substantial engagement. In Lefebvre's terms, lived experience is typically not included in the design process.

To create a more nuanced image of how humans relate to space, we introduce the term 'spacing leadership'. It describes the emergent and ongoing nature of the relationship between a space and the end-users and how both gradually adapt to each other. Lefebvre's triad of conceived, perceived and lived space will be used as a conceptual device in explaining the social nature of this spatial production.

While attempting to connect Lefebvre with current leadership thinking, one must keep in mind, on the one hand, that Lefebvre lived and wrote his major texts between the 1930s and the 1970s in the French context, whereas leadership research is a predominantly North American endeavour that has flourished and expanded, particularly since the 1970s. On the other hand, we caution that leadership is very prone to a categorical mistake: when uttering the word leadership, people quickly and unreflectively think of leaders as individual human agents. This is fair enough, as mainstream leadership research has for the past century focused on leaders as strong individuals. However, in this paper we do not focus on leaders, but on leadership as a phenomenon that can take place between human and materiality.

Another categorical assumption is that leadership is about power, namely someone exerting power over someone else. The leader is seen in a power role as a subject, and the follower is seen as being in a subordinated object role. In contrast to this leader/power-centric tradition of leadership theorizing, an early 20th-century political theorist and philosopher of leadership, Mary Parker Follett (1868–1933), provides fitting terminology to describe the tension between vertical power structures and horizontal meaning-making processes. Leadership is not only a vertical *power over* others, but also a horizontal *power with* phenomenon. The power over reading of leadership is represented in the mainstream, leader-centric leadership literature, for instance, as Crevani, Lindgren, and Packendorff (2007) note, and in critical leadership studies (Alvesson and Sveningsson, 2003; Collinson, 2005; Fairhurst, 2007; Ford and Harding, 2007; Grint, 2010; Harding et al., 2011; Kelly, 2008). In critical leadership studies, leadership is literally described in terms of dominance and subservience, resistance, imbalance, hierarchy, omnipotence, inequality, gender or seduction. Leadership is seen to maintain and reinforce existing hierarchical and suppressive power structures that particularly disdain those in lower or poorer positions or who are otherwise disadvantaged. This (historically influenced) sociological reading of organizations, though meant to be liberating by making the repressive structures visible, still reproduces a power over divide between management and workers, capital and labour and leader and follower, thus reinstating 'old school' heroic, leader-centric and hierarchical constellations and enforcing ontologies based on dualisms.

But as power relations in Follett's terms can function and be divided horizontally between people, the 'new school' of leadership thinking does not associate leadership with power over structures in the first place but with leaderful and plural organizing (Denis, Langley, and Sergi, 2012; Raelin, 2005) where, potentially, we are all leaders (Ford and Harding, 2007). Recently, non-authoritarian and empowering relationships in societal and corporate structures have begun to emerge in various instances, ranging from mass political participation in social movements, social experiments in corporations and online production on the Internet to terrorist and anarchist organizations. (Aaltonen and Lanzara, 2015; Hatch and Cunliffe, 2006; Laloux, 2014; Margetts et al., 2013; Robertson, 2015; Salovaara and Bathurst, 2016; Sutherland, 2015; Sutherland, Land and Böhm2014).

It is in this spirit that we encourage the reader to step into the 'new school' of leadership thinking and to join post-heroic and sociomaterial leadership approaches that define leadership in two relatively novel ways. First, leadership is a collective quality that anybody can potentially contribute to, and it can take place even without designated or individual leaders. Second, leadership does not take place only in human-human relations but also between people and material objects, such as within social space. Discussing Lefebvre's writings from the traditional 'old school' leader-centric angle is indeed not very fruitful, but analysing his texts on rural peasants and space from the plural leadership perspective does provide the reader with interesting cues on how nature, culture and the built environment influence human interaction. In this respect, Lefebvre can be helpful in explaining the 'new school' of leadership.

The chapter proceeds as follows. First, we discuss features in Lefebvre's writings that have the potential to inform current plural and materially oriented leadership studies. We do this by relating Lefebvre to Follett's power over and power with terms. Second, we consider in more detail how human-material relations have recently been conceptualized as leadership. To signify the processual and performative quality of space, we introduce the concept 'spacing leadership'. Using the example of a university office space renovation, we show how Lefebvre's triadic concept of space—conceived, perceived and lived—and a sociomaterial approach to leadership constitute a dynamic phenomenon, spacing leadership.

## Lefebvre and Plural Leadership

In Marxist writings, 'leadership' typically has two meanings; it either refers to a hierarchical leader-centric concept (as in under the leadership of Lenin/ Stalin/Mao) or to an oppressive capitalist's power over workers (as in the labour process or industrial relations literature). The oppressive notion of power can be traced back to Hegel's (1986) dialectics of master and servant, where the master owns the land and the equipment, and the servant produces added value through his or her work because the master can later sell the products for a price that results in a surplus. This relationship constructs the identities of the master and the slave, as they and the surrounding society recognize these roles. Lefebvre's writing, however, is based on the assumption of oppressive power structures and 'differentiation between classes' (Lefebvre, 2003: 117). He also appreciates and studies the everydayness of rural communities, servants and their traditional life and feasts (e.g., 1963, 1971, 2000). Through his rural sociology, Lefebvre shows how everyday life is based on the collaboration of workers and collectives. Interestingly, it is this work on horizontal rather than vertical power structures that has the potential to inform the research on plural leadership (Denis, Langley, and Sergi, 2012), leaderless leadership (Sutherland, Land, and Böhm, 2014) and community as leadership (Edwards, 2015a).

Based on stays in the French Pyrenees during and after World War II and on archival materials he collected, Lefebvre wrote about local peasant communities and the Pyrenees landscape and cultural traditions. (cf. Brenner and Elden, 2009; Elden, 2004; Entrikin and Berdoulay, 2005; Merrifield, 2006) These writings (Lefebvre, 1963, 2000) and his texts on rural sociology (1971, 2004) reveal several cultural features about organizing, cooperation, communication and the relationship to nature and the built environment within traditional communities. Today, these texts, and secondary literature on Lefebvre, inform us how cooperation becomes directed toward common goals by the influence of material elements on human actions. As such, they offer guidance for analysing forms of current organizing, such as that in universities.

### Collectives

Lefebvre considered village communities as natural gatherings. Historically, rural peasantry gathered together to support and defend each other, to share tools and land and to harvest together. Although informal, for this purpose the peasant community was 'highly organized, held together by collective disciplines; it had collective characteristics, of widely varying types' (Lefebvre, 2003: 117). The post-heroic leadership approach (Crevani, Lindgren, and Packendorff, 2007) points out that leadership is not only one person's power over others (the great man theories) but also what collections of people do in practice. As this conceptualization defines leadership as collective actions across informal networks (Denis, Langley, and Sergi, 2012; Edwards, 2015b; Kuronen and Huhtinen, 2016), Lefebvre's interest in peasant groups serves as a contradiction to the model of industrialized society, where workers become alienated in various ways and used by oppressive power over structures. Although universities, for instance, are inherently hierarchical, collaboration forms through informal networks.

## From Rural to Industrial

The way production was organized in rural communities was based on the cooperation between local inhabitants. However, as cities and industrial workplaces began to attract people with the promise of a better livelihood, organizing in these new societies differed greatly from the rural setting. Workers' responsibilities in a rural setting were based on the understanding that things constantly change—such as the land, its fertility and the growth of crops; the weather and the seasons; what tools are available, such as animals or machinery—and on decision making that fluctuates according to these changes. In contrast, a factory organization is a more rigid, hierarchic, abstract constellation that follows pre-described hierarchies, processes and orders. Similarly, in today's offices, the connection to work is an abstraction in two ways. First, workspace has become subordinated to economy, and office space is measured as a means to an end rather than as an end in itself. It is a non-space, except for capitalist purposes. Second, at work, there is little connection to nature-type elements of physical materiality; these are replaced by products, instruments and software. However, Lefebvre's critique of urbanization does not imply a retreat to nature but rather signifies a way of reading and understanding current social conditions. (Elden, 2004, 2008) Commodification of everyday experience is observed today on a structural level in terms of corporations' determination to manage the whole work-life experience. A trend to build 'creative workspaces' (De Paoli, Sauer, and Ropo, 2017; Ropo et al., 2015) shows how managerial implications also take over the domain of leadership. The same commodification and urge for creative design applies to present day universities.

## Atomization

The shift from a rural to an urban environment also led to a 'transition to a new, individualistic morality, with the breakdown of the rural community and extended family, the transition to the city and the atomization of society' (Elden, 2004: 92). This social shift implicitly justified new forms of organizing. Whereas someone ploughing their field or selling products alone without any outside help would have been regarded as an anomaly in traditional peasantry, where organizing relied on the need for cooperation, industrial organizing depends on external management to bring separate individuals together. This shift can be observed in the leadership research; with the atomization of society from the 1950s onwards, modern leadership research concentrated on studying leaders as individuals and leadership as a rational intent (Grint, 2011). However, as Grint's (2011) overview of the history of leadership shows, leadership has occurred prior to overtly rational accounts. New interest in collectives as a form of leadership has emerged in the 2000s, yet it is not a return to pre-industrial times but a more sociological interest in forms of human organizing and in how leadership takes place in informal leaderless groups, such as in academic teams and knowledge-intensive project groups.

## Natural Frontiers and Space

One of Lefebvre's major observations was that, while the space defining a rural community used to be associated with its natural frontiers (rivers, forests, mountains), in emerging capitalism and Christianity nature, myths and first-hand experience became replaced by rational external reasoning (Elden, 2004: 92, 139). The limits and borders of rural landscape have been contested, as Lefebvre's historical studies show; but it is only recently that this historical struggle (to define who we as 'locals' are) has become overruled by a process of more reification, where cultural reasoning based on communal history, nature and its rhythms has become replaced by the culture of rationalism and capitalist market logic (Lefebvre, 2004).

## Rhythmanalysis

In observing the everydayness, *quotidien*, Lefebvre (2004) noted how rural communities were transformed during the process of modernization, industrialization and urbanization. The local feasts and everyday life followed the rhythms of nature, whether it was the sun rising and falling or time to seed or harvest. The social bonds within the community and the peasants who are affected by the rhythms of nature create an organic base for collective activities and inform everyday life (Butler, 2012: 35). As Christianity, capitalism and individualism began to replace the rural order and the rhythm of nature, this shift resulted in alienation from natural rhythms. This shift from natural rhythm to chronological, analytical time concepts also showed in the objectification of nature. Whereas nature used to be considered as an organic, unpredictable, performing and active force, in a capitalist context it becomes subsumed to calculation and rationalization of production forces. However, originally in Christianity the nature was to be cared and cultivated for, not exploited.

In line with Heidegger's critique of technology, Lefebvre also considers how technology comes to dominate over nature rather than being in harmony with it (Elden, 2004: 133). The performance of nature (space) for rural peasants was something that was in flux, and thus nature 'spoke' to the farmer (when to seed or harvest, when crops are ripe), whereas industrialized agriculture takes over from this natural order (for instance, by adding fertilizers) and expects it to produce ever more value. The same rational logic happens in present day universities by decreasing or increasing financial resources and expecting this to mechanically influence output.

### Mary Parker-Follett's Views On Power

As Edwards (2015b) and Sveiby (2011) describe in their anthropologically oriented leadership studies, hierarchies have always existed in human systems, but the pendulum has been swinging between 'strong men' and orientation to collectives. Lefebvre's examples are analogous to the historical accounts of collective leadership cultures and to understanding plural leadership in the form of collectives, networks and community formations (Denis, Langley, and Sergi, 2012; Edwards, 2015a; Sutherland, Land, and Böhm, 2014).

Mary Parker-Follett was particularly interested in organizing that took place through collaboration between various stakeholder groups searching for a meaningful existence. She insisted that in these kinds of organizations 'we find responsibility for management shot all through a business, that we find some degree of authority all along the line, that leadership can be exercised by many people besides top executives' (Follett, 1949/1987: 61). What is needed is a democratic horizontal approach for which 'the experience of all is necessary' (Follett, 1924: 38). From a knowledge economy perspective, this is a very contemporary observation, and from the perspective of leadership, this is what plural and leaderless leadership approaches also claim. In horizontally networked modes of organizing, the hierarchical top-down/bottom-up thinking is not the most adequate way of conceptualizing leadership. In criticizing extensive use of authoritative power (power-over) that characterizes modern capitalist societies, Lefebvre is clearly describing power with structures. This is one way to read his rural sociology from the plural leadership perspective.

As Elden (2004: 157) argues, Lefebvre's observations describe a shift from the rural agricultural communities to modern farming and urban industrialization. However, from the leadership perspective, the crucial difference is between voluntary or involuntary, self-determined or managed organizing. In industrialized society, the workforce became organized in a mechanistic and hierarchical power over fashion; but in pre-modern rural communities there were fewer external forces forcing the community to gather together. Rather, people became organized through the principle of power with, through an understanding of their own context. The same self-relying organizing originally applied to universities as well.

Traditionally, the power discussions on leadership convey leadership as a phenomenon that occurs in hierarchical human-human relations. However, leadership has lately been considered as also taking place in human-material relations, which is a more radical proposition. This conceptualization, associated with the power with view and horizontal organizing, provides a fitting framework for discussing how Lefebvre's insights on natural frontiers, space, and rhythmanalysis can become part of leadership analysis.

## Conceptualization of Spacing Leadership: Material, Processual and Embodied

Lefebvre's major contribution to conceptualizing space is *The Production of Space* (1991), which claims that space is socially constructed. Lefebvre argues that the dominant understanding of space refers to an empty area that in Euclidean geometrics became defined through mathematical formulations, such as angles, length, and height. Lefebvre points to two problems; first, this concept has widened the gap between abstract thinkers of space and the experience and language of those within the space. The second problem is that the abstract mental space is taken as equal to the social space that people inhabit. For a thinker deeply rooted in (Marxist) materialism and socialist thinking, an uncritical identification of mental space with social space and a neglect of material reality are not legitimate (Lefebvre, 1991: 6). This critique explains how Lefebvre formed his triadic space concept; the terms *conceived* (idealistic, abstract) and *perceived* (material, physical) space are equivalent to Descartes' distinction between *res cogitans* (mental substance) and *res extensa* (corporeal substance) (Lefebvre, 1991: 14). To overcome this dualistic dilemma, Lefebvre—in a dialectical fashion—constitutes a third element, synthesis; *lived space* is an imperative integrating condition between conceived and perceived space.

The conceived space of architectural drawings consists of abstract representations of space—of architectural blueprints and technical illustrations composed of lines, boxes, flowcharts and symbols. The material, perceived space is composed of walls, furniture and other materials and of employees' movements, workflow and practices. Neither of these entails an experiential element or emotions, while lived space is experienced through emotions, imagination and embodied sensations.

Lefebvre's triadic space concept was introduced to organization studies by Dale, (2005), Ford, and Harding (2004), Taylor and Spicer (2007), Watkins (2005), and Zhang (2006), and the adoption of Lefebvre among organization scholars can be connected to the material turn and sociomaterial approaches in organization studies (Barad, 2003; Carlile et al., 2013; Dale, 2005; Orlikowski, 2007) The material turn argues that material objects—such as water coolers (Fayard and Weeks, 2007), copy machines (Humphries and Smith, 2014) and smart phones (Orlikowski, 2007), material spaces and the built environment influence social actions (Clegg and Kornberger, 2006; Dale, 2005; Dale and Burrell, 2008; De Vaujany and Mitev, 2013; Taylor and Spicer, 2007; Van Marrewijk and Yanow, 2010; Zhang, 2006).

In leadership research, (socio)materiality has also been linked with leadership and particularly with spaces (Collinge, Gibney, and Mabey, 2011; Hawkins, 2015; Oborn, Barrett, and Dawson, 2013; Sergi, 2016; Ropo, Sauer, and Salovaara, 2013, 2015; Zhang and Spicer, 2014). However, following Lefebvre's triadic model, the influence of space is not a mechanical causal relation; there is no physical or mental structure that would 'produce a space with a perfectly clear understanding of cause and effect, motive and implication' (Lefebvre, 1991: 37). This idea is important in terms of leadership; although physical materiality influences social action, the lived experience cannot be 'managed' or manipulated for particular ends.

The noteworthy, even paradigmatic difference compared to the previous heroic leadership theories is that the (socio)materially inspired studies on leadership extend the definition of human-human relations to include human-material relations. But how exactly the connection between the social and the material should be conceptualized continues to be a subject of debate; the social and material are seen as intrinsically entangled (Barad, 2003; Orlikowski, 2007); intertwined (Jones, 2013); intertwined and mutually enacted (Dale, 2005); constitutively entangled (Orlikowski and Scott, 2008) or mutually constitutive (De Vaujany and Vaast, 2013; Van Marrewijk and Yanow, 2010). As Clegg and Kornberger (2006) describe it: 'we constitute space through the countless practices of everyday life as much as we are constituted through them' (144). In Lefebvre's terminology, the perceived space constitutes a lived experience, which in turn affects our practices (perceived space).

This mutual constitution shows in everyday work practices, where work is intimately linked to materials that give direction, guidance and meaning to work, for example, copy machine repair technicians being guided by the machine (Orr, 1995) or electricians working in a 200-year old building or a shipbuilder working with wooden materials (Salovaara, 2014). Material spaces also guide human action in a very mundane fashion; we follow corridors, take stairs and cannot walk through the walls; but we can listen to the walls talk (De Vaujany and Vaast, 2013), read the ruins (Dale and Burrell, 2011) and give voice to space (Yanow, 2010). As Hawkins (2015) states, British Naval practices on the ground were very much shaped by the forms and functions of actual ship spaces. Given the deeply rooted leader-centric views, these instances are not considered as leadership in the first place.

However, conceptualizing space through human experience the way Lefebvre does gives us a reason to view leadership as a sociomaterial phenomenon. What Lefebvre also brings to understanding leadership and space is the accounting of time. While noting that 'with the advent of modernity, time has vanished from social space' Lefebvre (1991: 95), observes that the social fabric in rural societies was greatly influenced by the rhythms of nature. Whereas spatiality can be accounted for visually, time needs to be grasped in terms of its historicity. It includes something that is not right now present but observable as an experience of the past. Time is accounted for through the horizon that connects the present with the past and the future. To borrow Shotter's (2006) distinction, this is no longer space in terms of 'aboutness thinking' but space approached from within and in terms of 'withness thinking'. A human experience from within, being a participant within the space, means to live in the space at the moment of its unfolding; it literally is a lived space. This take on space emphasizes its emergent, processual nature. Even the physical character of the space can change in a matter of minutes by adjusting existing furniture (as our illustration below will show). This dynamic nature of space we associate with the quality of space as 'performing' (Beyes and Steyaert, 2012); space is a carrier and enabler of various incidents and moments.

Conceptualizing space this way has prompted us to use the term 'spacing leadership': the experience of materiality at the moment of its unfolding makes space an active but not independent partner in that interaction. (Ropo and Salovaara, 2018) The material and processual nature of space are here linked with the 'new school' of thinking of plural leadership; human-material relations contribute to leadership in a complex network of interactions where events are emerging and constantly becoming (Crevani, Lindgren, and Packendorff, 2010; Denis, Langley and Sergi, 2012; Simpson, 2015; Wood, 2005).

When arguing for 'leadership in spaces and places' (Ropo et al., 2015; Salovaara, 2014), most people take this to mean that spaces can be designed to guide human action in an objective, mechanistic fashion, as if certain spatial configurations would lead to particular predictable social behaviours and organizational outcomes. However, according to Lefebvre, 'understanding of space . . . must begin with the lived and the body, that is, from a space occupied by an organic, living, and thinking being' (Lefebvre, 1991: 229; Simonsen, 2005). According to embodied and aesthetic notions, space is not an abstract, dead container, because the lived space is experienced through emotions, imagination and embodied sensations. As these experiences are personal, whatever the leadership influence of space as materiality is, it is an indirect one. Therefore, the same space can produce different and unintended consequences (Balogun and Johnson, 2005; Elsbach and Pratt, 2007). In leadership studies, the body was earlier considered an 'unwanted and unwelcome guest' (Ropo, Parviainen, and Koivunen, 2002: 22), and Lefebvre identifies a similar rejection of the body throughout the history of space, the 'decorporealization of space'. He describes this lack as a shift from 'the space of the body to body-in-space, from opacity (warm) to translucency (cold)' (Lefebvre, 1991: 201).

Lefebvre's lived space as an embodied experience resembles what recent leadership literature has called 'aesthetic' or 'felt sense' (Ladkin, 2008; Hansen, Ropo, and Sauer, 2007; Ropo, Parviainen, and Koivunen, 2002) parallel to the development of the literature on the aesthetics of organizations (Strati, 1999; Linstead and Höpfl, 2000 Wasserman and Frenkel, 2011, 2015). This resemblance is epistemological, as both Lefebvre and aesthetic epistemology define knowledge not only as something perceived 'out there' but as something understood primarily from within, as everyday experience. The relation between space and leadership is based on personal embodied, lived experience.

Lefebvre's triadic concept of social space and the material and spatial turns in organization studies provide an ample basis for developing a novel sociomaterial conception of leadership—spacing leadership. Spacing leadership is a material and embodied conception of leadership that connects the past with the present and even with the future. For example, in the office renovation process that we will illustrate next, one contemplates the past while engaging in packing things and tossing things away and at the same time anticipating what it might be like in the new office setting. Thus, spacing emphasizes the processual nature of lived space – an experience that includes senses, feelings and memories (Ropo and Salovaara, 2018).

In summary, work life in Lefebvre's and Follett's time was characterized by the great shift from agriculture to industrial work followed by various dualisms that reflect hierarchical asymmetries—worker/manager, blue collar/white collar, shop floor/top floor, low level supervisor/middle management/top management, among others. Here, we have introduced a sociomaterial notion of leadership that Lefebvre's triadic conceptualization of space greatly contributes to. The current work life and corporate situation have fundamentally changed since the industrial age and even from Lefebvre's time. Forms of work and forms of organizing are interdependent, and the changes in one impact the other (Barley and Kunda, 2001). Follett described plural leadership as 'collective creativeness' based on a 'circular theory of power' where employees, employers and other stakeholders collaborate and influence each other (Follett, 1918). Collective ways, also through material space, of leading and organizing have been increasingly developed and adopted both in theory and practice. Next, we will turn to an illustration of how this collaborative, human-material and emerging 'spacing leadership' might take place in today's modern office renovation.

## Illustration: Spacing Leadership in Action

While it may seem farfetched to link Lefebvre's rural communities to today's academic knowledge workers in their offices, we argue that the need to create more (knowledge) collectives and enhance cooperation in previously siloed university office spaces has made Lefebvre's thinking relevant in the current context. We wish to exemplify this by an illustration of a spatial renovation in a university building in Finland.

The materials were collected during a 12-month period in 2016–2017 from an actual renovation project, where the co-authors functioned as facilitators of the project workshops and aided architectural planning by including end-users' lived experience on the agenda. Two other researchers were involved in the material collection. The materials comprise interviews of all the space users (27 altogether), mapping of their spatial practices, video-tapes of four workshops, a survey at the end of the project and other official documents. As one of the authors worked in the space during the project and therefore interacted with the end-users, the construction company and the administration, participant and auto-ethnographic observations were also collected during the 12-month period. The objective of the following illustration is to 'explain our arguments rather than offer evidence for them' (Puranam, Alexy, and Reitzig, 2014: 163). Instead of an empirical valida-tion, the illustration primarily helps to create conceptual clarity.

Today, university buildings are increasingly redesigned to 'better meet the needs of academic work, such as teaching, research and community building' (a common discourse among the building owners and university administra-tion). Fostering collaboration, creativity and a better sense of community and allowing chance encounters were often mentioned in the interviews when discussing why the renovation was needed. As one of the interviewees said: *'These spaces support quite well the traditional view of doing research alone in social science. Doing things together they do not support.'* And another continued: *'It would be a start to get to know people better.'* At the same time, more efficient use of the space was sought after by the uni-versity administration. It is no coincidence that universities provide ample instances for applying the above Lefebvrian terminology; the buildings are typically based on atomization and industrialization of work experience, and within this architectural design natural forms are replaced by rational reasoning that takes less account of the embodied experience aspects. These aspects became something the end-users wanted to be changed. An often-heard characterization of the space was that *'it looked like a hospital, clini-cal, sterile, bureaucratic'.*

Architect Antti Katajamäki, who has an established reputation in public building architecture in Finland, planned the School of Management build-ing at the University of Tampere in Finland in the early 1990s. Novel at the time, the construction is of steel and concrete, and following the trend, the building has shiny metal surfaces and plenty of glass to give an airy atmo-sphere. The building is white outside and has a curvy shape (Figure 4.1).

The inside architecture includes nature-like elements resembling trees (green pillars), curvy paths in the forest (corridors that are not straight) and cloud formations on the ceiling, over the windows and by the office doors, all made of concrete or painted metal. The building reflects the views of the time (late1980s, early 1990s) of a university as a bureaucratic public organization, where the researchers work in individual offices (Figure 4.2).

Despite the strong architectural symbolism, the interpretations of which were not shared or even recognized among most of the users, the layout follows a traditional cubicle structure and long corridors where people sit in their private offices with glass doors half dimmed (Figures 4.3 and 4.4).

There are hardly any common spaces for spontaneous encounters. The coffee room is located in the middle of the office corridors, separated with

*Figure 4.1* The School of Management exterior design.

*Figure 4.2* Old corridor with individual offices (and closed doors).

a curvy glass wall (Figure 4.3, often covered with heavy curtains), and the toilets, separate for men and women (although the majority of the people working there were women), are 'for staff only'. The spaces are made to last and offer hardly any flexibility. The building and the office spaces were

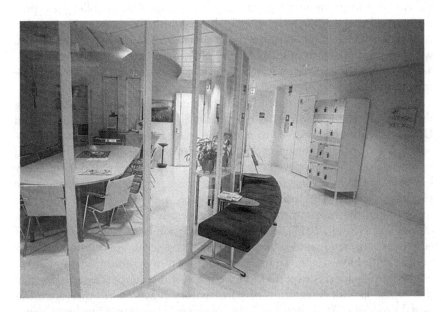

*Figure 4.3* Old café area with glass windows.

*Figure 4.4* New 'coffice' area.

not found to support communication, collaboration, knowledge sharing or community building, but for conducting independent work (alone) and seemingly to foster academic hierarchies as vividly described by an informant (Salovaara, 2014, 12:03). In addition, different sized offices were experienced to promote inequality and hierarchies among colleagues (professors and some lecturers having the biggest offices); walls and doors discourage socializing and corridors direct one to walk quickly past the offices, without stopping by to talk (Ropo and Höykinpuro, 2017). The offices are actively used for approximately 30% of the work time, while the administration struggles to assign workspaces to new recruits at the same time.

The DEMO project initiated by the project management team (including the authors) and the owner of the building (University Properties Finland UPF) had three objectives: 1) to make the space more transparent and democratic, and to provide spaces for collaboration, informal socializing, and private work; 2) to improve collaboration, communication and community building and 3) to involve the users of the space, faculty and students in the planning process. This user-centric approach and engaging the end-users to co-design the spaces throughout the process is quite unusual in projects (Stingl and Geraldi, 2017), although participation is a key issue in terms of employee satisfaction and achieving higher efficiency in organizations (Liverpool, 1990). However, he summarizes that even in organizational initiatives where participation is expected to take place, it does not necessarily happen due to the lack of integration of participatory practices in other organizational processes. As Pallasmaa (2014) observes, recognizing lived experience is not part of architectural processes. Therefore, it is highly likely that, even in cases where participatory practices are used, the input these provide is not necessarily substantial, which leads to an 'illusion of participation'. Based on Lefebvre's distinction (and interrelation) between the three spaces, we distinguish the 'illusion of participation' and 'engagement'. Engagement, as defined here, is based on embodied lived experience. Here, we join Shotter (2006), who draws a line between 'aboutness thinking' and 'withness thinking', the former representing a distanced, purely intellectual relation to the observed phenomenon and the latter describing 'our relations with living forms when we enter into dialogically structured relations with them' (Shotter, 2006: 585).

The renovation project was built on the Lefebvrian idea that space is a dynamic and evolving process that keeps changing as it is practiced and experienced over time. This, we think, is close to Shotter's description of dialogical relations in 'withness thinking'. In practice, the end-users of the space had a key role in planning and designing the spaces in workshops, theme groups and feedback sessions (Table 4.1). They adjusted their activities and interactions to the physical (changing) office design as the process unfolded over time.

This dialogical unfolding we term 'spacing leadership'; it does not describe the human relation to a momentary form of built environment but a process during which both parties change and evolve. This is how the process evolved:

The process started in January 2016 with preliminary interviews of the faculty and the first workshops. As an inspiration, examples of office

*Table 4.1* Examples of project activities in refers to Lefebvre's triadic space concept

| Renovation project activities | Lefebvre's triadic space |
|---|---|
| *First workshop* | |
| Examples from other workplaces | Conceived |
| Benchmarking | Stories of practices |
| Users' own examples | Lived |
| Crafting models | Conceived/imagined |
| *Interim task* | |
| Theme groups | Conceived |
| *Second workshop* | |
| Prioritizing | Conceived |
| *Physical construction project* | |
| Construction work | Conceived |
| *User-based redesign* | |
| Settling in | Perceived, lived |
| Experimenting with furniture | Conceived, perceived, lived |

re-design projects from around the globe were presented and discussed, followed by the participants crafting their own models of office layout using materials such as clay, small wooden bricks, paper, cardboard and Legos. The architect was present at the workshops, but his role was to carefully listen and observe rather than participate in the discussion.

After the first workshops, there was an interim task in which the end-users formed theme groups that concentrated on selected aspects of the design. In the theme groups, the participants reflected on their professional needs and then imagined future spaces based on these needs.

In May 2016, a second set of workshops was organized to further discuss the ideas. Here, through their design suggestions, the end-users functioned as 'lay-architects' when they adopted the conceived space perspective and also imagined the future uses (First workshop: 'Crafting models' in Table 4.1).

Only after these workshops and the theme groups' outcomes was the architect asked to draft his first sketches. This was the project's first deviation to adopting the abstract and geometrical thinking of space as conceived/planned (Lefebvre, 1991; Taylor and Spicer, 2007). The architect's drafts were then discussed, after which he created the next versions.

The actual construction work took place during the summer, and in August 2016 the end-users returned to the newly designed space. Table 4.1 describes the activities during the first phase of the project in relation to Lefebvre's triadic concept of space.

The next phase started in August 2016 when people tried to get settled in the new spaces, especially in the two open office spaces (where 13 out of 27 faculty members volunteered to move) and the new large communal space that was opened between the corridors by tearing down the walls of some offices. The following architectural sketches (Figures 4.5 and 4.6) illustrate the situation before and after the renovation.

During this phase, the furniture was moved back and forth several times within a few intensive weeks, and the spaces were shaped and reshaped constantly. As in Dale and Burrell (2015), the occupants of the open spaces took the initiative to physically reorganize the furniture by experimenting with different ideas, living with the arrangements for a few days or a week and then reorganizing things anew. This phase highlights Lefebvre's triadic and processual understanding of space. Conceived/planned, perceived/practiced and lived /experienced spaces (Taylor and Spicer, 2007) were in a very practical sense intermingled and simultaneously present. Following is an example of how it happened.

Old furniture (from university storage and leftovers from other renovations) was used in the newly built spaces. Based on the architect's understanding of the users' needs, the furniture was carried to the space after the construction phase, but people felt it was too cramped and congested, which nobody felt comfortable with. As a result, on the first day back in the office most of the tall closets were carried away. Desks were changed for smaller ones and moved to different locations. Instead of closets dividing the space, partitions of different types and heights were tried out. This first contact with the new spaces was intense and literally embodied. It describes how people's everyday lives and work were keenly entangled with the spatial arrangements, how their (un)usability was perceived and how the new spaces made people feel (Hansen, Ropo, and Sauer, 2007; Yanow, 2010). On the day of commissioning the open space areas, the administration insisted on receiving exact information on the location of individual desks, even though people were still negotiating and playing with ideas of how to locate themselves. This was seen as trying to exert power over (as was the case earlier when the administration assigned the workspaces). A clear uneasiness and frustration was sensed in the administration. '*We need to know where everyone sits. It cannot be that people move around between spaces*', one administrator lamented. Obviously, this process orientation was (and still is) at odds with the administration's purposes, thus being an example of the clash between the conceived space of the administration (they would like to see it as a planned entity, captured by numbers and measures) and the perceived, practiced and experienced space.

A week passed, and sofas found new places and drawers and closets were moved back and forth after experiencing what felt good and visually attractive. A former office newly designed as a living room style for smaller meetings and the communal space were decorated with pillows, throws, playful soft balls, plants (not officially approved) and candles (knowing that they could not be lit for safety reasons) after a spontaneous shopping spree at IKEA. This is how the workspaces were domesticated (Dale and Burrell, 2015; Wasserman and Frenkel, 2015: 1496, 1500). The occupants of the

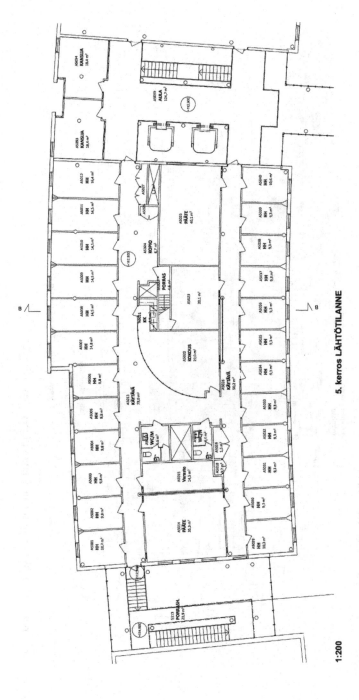

*Figure 4.5* Architectural sketch of the old layout.

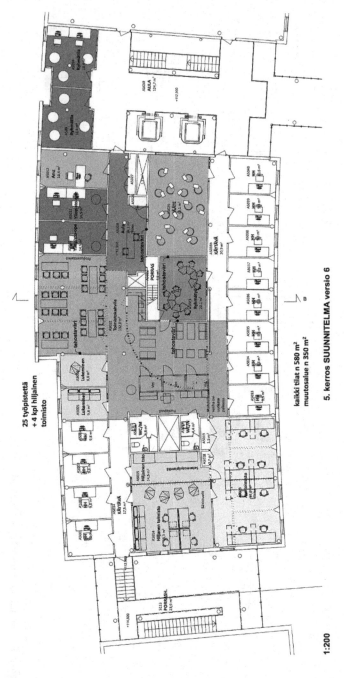

*Figure 4.6* Architectural sketch of the new layout (grey areas changed).

open spaces did all this by themselves, occasionally with the help of the university facility management if hammering was needed or heavy objects moved. The architect was not involved in this phase at all.

Figure 4.7 depicts how the new areas looked after the renovation; the area for communal space was increased but is now suitable for breaks, meetings and working. After the renovated space was handed over to the users in August 2016, a three-month period of observation, evaluation and experimentation followed to see how this and other areas would work. During this phase, the space was in a state of constant becoming as an open-ended, emerging outcome (Beyes and Steyaert, 2012). People working in the new spaces tried out different spaces for different activities and realized how important and enjoyable it was to actually see and meet people in the common areas, even if only walking through. This sentiment was shared by many in the feedback after the first round of renovation: '*I really like the setup and light. Every time I come to have lunch, there is someone to talk to or share lunch break with.*' Or: '*I often work by the stand-up table there since I like to see other people coming and going.*' Colleagues from the other floors started to find their way to the new spaces (*'We have moved our research group meetings to this space. It feels good to work here.'*). Also students had found the new spaces to do their teamwork or quiet reading. After the first few months in the renovated spaces, workshops were organized where the project's outcomes were evaluated and new ideas gathered. Based on user experiences, the floor carpet area was broadened, the copy machine

*Figure 4.7* New phone booths and meeting area.

was relocated to a specially designed noise-absorbing booth, separate phone booths were ordered and better lightning was installed.

After a new 'conversational furniture unit' was delivered, some tables and chairs were carried away and old sofas found new spaces, all in the spirit of experimentation: '*Let's try this out for now and we'll see how this works*'. People started to spend more time with each other, have coffee and lunch together, and even work around the communal table or on the cosy sofas and the 'Fatboy' beanbag seats (see Figure 4.8). Whereas the previous space prevented seeing anybody work, now people are more visible: '*I like to see people working here. It makes the whole floor feel more dynamic and alive.*' In this sense it is the comparison between the past (memory) and present (lived experience) space that makes the difference for the end-users so pronounced. Someone new to the space would be unable to make a such comparison.

## Discussion

An interesting feature of the project was that, as the reader can see in the figures, the end result itself is not that different from any modern office design. Part of the office space now has an open space design, updated furniture and contemporary functionalities such as phone booths and small meeting spaces. Looking on the surface, one might ask 'So what? Why is it relevant?' That is the key give-away of the paper: the point is not the

*Figure 4.8* Small meeting area and Fatboy bean bag seat in the open office space.

physical space, but the process of co-creation where humans and materiality influence each other. In Lefebvre's terms, the difference between the abstract plans (conceived space) does not explain the changes in the work environment and atmosphere. The figures—as sort of 'still life'—need to be appreciated in their broader context in order to depict the feel and the atmosphere in the space. The space was developed in relation to history and the earlier experiences in the old space, and it was just as much the human community that changed as the physical space. The space changed also for those who remained in private offices: they were not anymore part of the earlier context of corridors, but anytime they open the door or pass the 'coffice', the relations between people are changed as all are now more visible.

Therefore, to refer to space as pure materiality is to misunderstand the concept of 'spacing' in the first place. To highlight how physical space can be considered as dynamic and active *spacing*, we will now discuss three key features of the process—the power with approach, collective leadership and the role of embodied knowledge.

### Power with Approach

The power with approach in this project meant that the hierarchical power structures (university administration, space owner, architect, construction company) were balanced by introducing a new perspective to the space design—the rhythm of life of the end-users. This aspect is akin to Lefebvre's (2004) rhythmanalysis and draws attention to the geographical and historical limits of space (1963, 2000); the users interacted with each other and the space, and the new design was based on this lived experience. The main purpose of the participative, engaging design was to enable the renovated space to function more as a 'generative building' that, 'instead of being a merely passive container for actions happening in it contributes positively towards an organization's capacities' (Kornberger and Clegg, 2004: 1095). An office design that supports an organization's capacities would greatly benefit from engagement and witness thinking by those who act out the capacities, that is, the end-users of the space.

Figure 4.9 depicts the difference between being informed (knowledge), participating in the process and being bodily engaged in the co-design. We argue that the more fully the end-users are engaged in the project as co-designers, the better they understand and accept the project and the more it becomes their own. Being able to do so, their relationship with the space becomes an activity and process, and not a passive reception of something given from outside (cf. Shotter's (2006) witness thinking vs. aboutness thinking).

*Knowledge* that architects, designers or consultants, for example, possess and share can provide the end-users with some understanding and acceptance of the new space design (aboutness thinking, conceived space). Based on our materials and observations of the university illustration, we

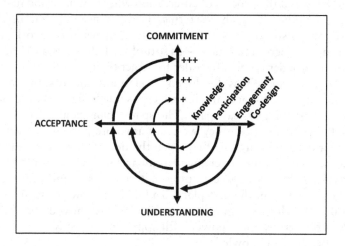

*Figure 4.9*  Degrees of involvement in the co-design process.

conceptualize in Figure 4.9 that being able to *participate* more concretely and develop ideas produces more understanding, acceptance and commitment. We conclude that if participants can become *engaged* in the project as co-designers, they will voice their issues, problems and solutions in a more practical fashion than when reacting to ready-made solutions by professionals. Having co-created the new design, they accept it, and there is much less 'change resistance', which can be attributed to the fact that they were change agents themselves (Ford, Ford, and D'Amelio, 2008). In Ryle's (1946) terms, there is a big difference between 'knowing that' and being able to implement one's know-how into the process (cf. Ropo, Sauer, and Salovaara, 2013). In summary, not only the space in itself but also the way the whole process was designed suggests a shift in the practice of power from power over relations towards power with relations.

## Collective Leadership

There was an ideological undercurrent in this project; the original physical layout of the spaces was experienced as hierarchical among the users, and the new spatial design implies a change towards more collective ways of cooperation. However, it would be a mistake to consider space—whether divided into closed offices or open—as doing anything by itself. Spacing, as pointed out earlier, is not a deterministic procedure but takes place through minor impacts, affects and mutual constitution (Beyes and Steyaert, 2012) and is fuelled by personal embodied experiences. A space cannot be designed to assert an ideology—hierarchical, collective or other—because it does not do anything by itself. Yet one should be reminded of the mutual constitution of space and people; neither takes over the agency on its own. At the core of the project is the process through which the space is moulded. The lived experience needed to be taken into account. Therefore, the process is more important than the outcome, as the process itself also changed people's interactions and activities. The material space is still 'just' a workplace, but the shared process and new ways of working changed the culture *('I like the atmosphere in the open office. I can see the others when turning my head and hear them working. People maintain a quiet, respectful conduct in the shared office')*. The end-users seem to show more ownership of the space now. Although the space is still formally owned by the UPF and managed by the university administration, the users experienced an empowering process where the space became what they wanted; it became 'their own'. For example, they take more responsibility for keeping the kitchen and table surfaces clean and organized. Furthermore, people who participated in the process are now used to adjusting the space, for example, by moving the furniture.[3] The process of re-design and its impact on attitudes and new ways of being in the space we associated with spacing leadership. We argued that spacing is fundamentally an embodied relation, and to conceptualize it thus requires the Lefebvrian concept of lived space that includes emotions, experiences and embodied relations to space.

In networks and leaderless organizations, leadership is not based on formal hierarchies or centralized command, but on collaboration that can emerge in an organic, improvised, needs-based fashion, as examples from informal organizing in social movements illustrate (Eslen-Ziya and Erhart, 2015; Sutherland, 2015) The same applies in our case; the spatial redesign was an outcome of constant reconfiguration and acting with the space. We suggest calling this form of plural power with organizing 'mass-driven', which indicates a collective of people formulating and following shared ideals. This does not necessarily happen in a traditionally organized, controlled fashion but when undefined and unpredicted impulses porously enter the leadership process.

### Embodied Knowledge

Once the physical construction work was finished, the embodied experiences and felt sense of the end-users were at the core of the process. When they entered the space, there were piles of boxes around the place and the furniture needed to be removed. To make sense of the totally changed space and the misplaced furniture, people relied on their aesthetic sensitivities, that is, their senses and feelings (Hansen, Ropo, and Sauer, 2007; Ropo and Parviainen, 2001): What kind of emotions, feelings and atmosphere does this space convey? Where do I want to sit and why? How should the furniture in the common space be arranged? How do we make the place look more attractive and feel good? Moving obstacles created a concrete physical-material touch to objects and furniture. This enhanced sensitivity towards the material objects, which had a direct impact on how the space 'became'. This was literally a first-hand experience, an experience from within the process in contrast to thinking about the space through architectural plans and miniature models (conceived space). The way perceptions through various senses advanced the project meant that spacing was based on sensible knowledge (Strati, 2007). The embodied experiences played a key role in defining how the space became designed and in the change process in general.

End-user engagement here implies that their perceptions of space and lived experience provided the primary guidelines for the re-design. They knew what works and what does not, which emphasizes a practice perspective on leadership (Sergi, 2016). This co-design allowed spatiality and human experience to influence each other in a more organic fashion. An organic relation to environment does not create a dualism between the human and material, but it reflects the same phenomenon Lefebvre's observed: how rural peasantry followed and was guided, even physically driven by the flows, rhythms and limits of their environment. They do not function in an architecturally designed space, but relate to the process in nature. Spacing leadership is meant as a reminder of this constant fluidity that in Beyes and Steyaert's (2012) terms can be defined as performative action. A similar approach was introduced in the renovation project: the end-users were encouraged to explore and investigate how they move around in the space, use it and relate to space and each other. As the illustration shows, this 'natural' fluidity was infiltrated into the spatial design.

In this respect, the project discussed was an exercise in relating to the work environment and developing new practices. Increased openness and visibility prompted socializing and led people to do things together and pay more attention to the overall atmosphere of the workplace. They learned to use the new communal space and new meeting rooms (*'The renovation of the seminar room, 'the terrible one', had unexpected outcomes: Now it is in high demand. I did not think it would be possible.'*) The process of trying out the new spaces and coming up with new ideas and implementing them continued; spaces construct leadership (give direction, guidance and support) not as dead materiality but through peoples' practices and experiences.

As noted above, prioritizing end-user experience is rather untypical in the mainstream project management world, and this is also seen in the Project Management Book of Knowledge (PMBOK, 2013), according to which the norm is that the architect plans, the constructor makes the physical changes and the end-users are given a ready-made space. In that pattern, the end-users of the space are clearly dominated by the power of other actors over them and the space. In contrast to this, our illustration shows that a space renovation process can be empowering to the end-users. We suggest that this is particularly the case if "the complexity and mutual dependencies of situated work activities" (Boell et al., 2016: 128) is integrated into the planning process. When this happens, the end-users and their relations with the space construct new work patterns and lead to new configurations and assemblages. This we consider as spacing leadership.

But just like getting to know a person takes time, so does getting to know a space. The space becomes known during a span of time, which means that the end-users began to get accustomed to it, while they also introduced further changes to it. The relation to space becomes dynamic and active, and from a theoretical perspective the relation to space turns into spacing. This shows in many ways. The new space brought a new meeting and discussion culture and even affected whom one meets. For example, the big communal table turned into a meeting place for people from other floors and even for students. The interview quotes above indicate that the sense of community and togetherness has changed. The former stable, walled and siloed space is reformed into a more open and multiple purpose space that allows more connections to various directions and activities than before. Because of this multiplicity, Beyes and Steyaert (2012: 48) call it 'and' space.

## Concluding Remarks

In this chapter, we have exercised a rather unorthodox reading of reading Lefebvre through the leadership lens. Leadership research has advanced from Taylorist managerialism and leader-centric approaches toward today's plural and sociomaterial theories. (Grint, 2011; Sergi, 2016) Confirming that, there is a trend in today's society and work life that organizing for a common goal can occur through collectives and mass movements that have no dedicated leaders. (Aaltonen and Lanzara, 2015; Denis, Langley, and Sergi, 2012; Esln-Ziya and Erhart, 2015; Margetts et al., 2013). Also large-scale organizations have been shown to function successfully through flat hierarchies, and by relying on self-management and informal organizing. (Getz, 2009; Hamel, 2007; Laloux, 2014; Salovaara and Bathurst, 2016) To conceptualize leadership in the current contexts calls for the inclusion of human-material relations, as well. Materiality is permeable in society in its various forms of technology, material artefacts, and physical spaces.

These new forms of organizing call for conceptualizing leadership in new ways, and it is in this context that Lefebvre's work on rural communities and space becomes relevant again. As he described it, during the process of industrialization, reification of nature also took place. Reasoning that used to be based on communal history, culture, and nature and its rhythms became replaced by rationalism and capitalist market logics.

At universities in the 20th century, the researchers' autonomy was preserved centrally by providing the same standard for all: individual offices. But according to Scotto (2014) the original intent of the university campus was the construction of collective life. In our case illustration, the researchers began to doubt the usefulness of the conceptual planning that increases separation. At the same time, with the advent of knowledge work and new ways of working, alternative office designs that emphasize lived experience have emerged. Compared to individual offices, the advantage of these alternative spaces is that they provide more room for interaction with others, and more chances for open communication and information sharing. The re-designed space of the management faculty now offers more common space that can be used for formal and informal meetings. As the space provides the chance for the construction of collective life, the whole lived experience of the space has changed.

Furthermore, there is an increasing awareness in Western societies of the ethical responsibility to conserve and preserve the environment (material surroundings) for the future, as was the case in Lefebvre's rural examples. Being in touch and in sync with one's physical environment and co-workers is what Lefebvre observed in the rural Pyrenees. Taking care of work environment and the spaces we live in is a central feature of spacing leadership, and in the university case, this relation was created by the communal planning process. This long-term relation of mutual influence, constitution and respect between human and material surroundings we call spacing leadership.

## Notes

1 Not all of Lefebvre's work has been translated into English, and we had to rely on secondary sources to some extent.
2 As architects' profession is not the key point of the paper, we will not delve further into this argument, but the reader is advised to, for instance, google 'what architects really' do. A lot of these descriptions are written by architects, and they seldom mention the client (except in terms of client presentations or communication) and almost never the term 'user experience' (or something similar). But, as said, this is a different conversation from the one we aim to have here.
3 However, as the space has started to be used by other than the occupants of the floor, these people do not know about this possibility.

## References

Aaltonen, A. and Lanzara, G. V. (2015). Building governance capability in online social production: Insights from Wikipedia. *Organization Studies, 36*(12), 1649–1673.

Alvesson, M. and Sveningsson, S. (2003). The great disappearing act: Difficulties in doing leadership research. *The Leadership Quarterly, 14*, 359–381.

Balogun, J. and Johnson, G. (2005). From intended strategies to unintended outcomes: The impact of change recipient sensemaking. *Organization Studies, 26*(11), 1573–1601.

Barad, K. (2003). Posthumanist performativity: Toward an understanding of how matter comes to matter. *Signs: Journal of Women in Culture and Society, 28*(3), 801–831.

Barley, S. R. and Kunda, G. (2001). Bringing work back in. *Organization Science, 12*(1), 76–95.

Beyes, T. and Steyaert, C. (2012). Spacing organization: Non-representational theory and performing organizational space. *Organization, 19*(1), 45–61.

Boell, S. K., Dubravka, C.-K. and Campbell, J. (2016). Telework paradoxes and practices: the importance of the nature of work. *New Technology, Work and Employment*, 31(2), 114-131.

Brenner, N. and Elden, S. (2009). Henri Lefebvre on state, space, territory. *International Political Sociology*, 3, 353–377.

Butler, C. (2012). *Henri Lefebvre. Spatial Politics, Everyday Life and the Right to the City*. New York: Routledge.

Carlile, P., Nicolini, D., Langley, A. and Tsoukas, H. (Eds.) (2013). *How Matter Matters: Objects, Artifacts and Materiality in Organization Studies*. Oxford: Oxford University Press.

Clegg, S. and Kornberger, M. (2006). Organising space. In S. Clegg and M. Kornberger (Eds.), *Space, Organizations and Management Theory* (pp. 143–162). Copenhagen: Liber and Copenhagen Business School Press.

Collinson, D. (2005). Dialectics of leadership. *Human Relations*, 58(11), 1419–1442.

Crevani, L., Lindgren, M. and Packendorff, J. (2007). Shared leadership: A postheroic perspective on leadership as a collective construction. *International Journal of Leadership Studies*, 3(1), 40–67.

Crevani, L., Lindgren, M. and Packendorff, J. (2010). Leadership not leaders: On the study of leadership as practices and interactions. *Scandinavian Journal of Management*, 26(1), 77–86.

Collinge, C., Gibney, J. and Mabey, C. (Eds.) (2011). *Leadership and Place*. New York: Routledge.

Dale, K. (2005). Building a social materiality: Spatial and embodied politics in organizational control. *Organization*, 12, 649–678.

Dale, K. and Burrell, G. (2008). *Spaces of Organization and the Organization of Space*. Basingstoke: Palgrave Macmillan.

Dale, K. and Burrell, G. (2011). Disturbing structure: Reading the ruins. *Culture and Organization*, 17(2), 107–121.

Dale, K. and Burrell, G. (2015). Leadership and space in 3D: Distance, dissent and disembodiment in the case of a new academic building. In A. Ropo, P. Salovaara, E. Sauer and D. De Paoli (Eds.), *Leadership in Spaces and Places* (pp. 217–241). Cheltenham and Northampton, MA: Edward Elgar.

Denis, J.-L., Langley, A. and Sergi, V. (2012). Leadership in the plural. *The Academy of Management Annals*, 6(1), 211–283.

De Paoli, D., Sauer, E. and Ropo, A. (2017). The spatial context of organizations: A critique of 'creative workspaces'. *Journal of Management & Organization*. https://doi.org/10.1017/jmo.2017.46 Published online: 18 September 2017

De Vaujany, F.-X. and Mitev, N. (Eds.) (2013). *Materiality and Space. Organizations, Artefacts and Practices*. New York: Palgrave Macmillan.

De Vaujany, F.-X. and Vaast, E. (2013). If these walls could talk: The mutual construction of organizational space and legitimacy. *Organization Science*, 25(3), 713–731.

Edwards, G. (2015a). *Community as Leadership*. Cheltenham: Edward Elgar.

Edwards, G. (2015b). Anthropological accounts of leadership: Historical and geographical interpretations from indigenous cultures. *Leadership*, 11(3), 335–350.

Elden, S. (2004). *Understanding Henri Lefebvre: Theory and the Possible*. London and New York: Continuum.

Elden, S. (2008). Mondialisation before globalization. In K. Goonewardena, S. Kipfer, R. Milgrom and C. Schmid (Eds.), *Space, Difference, Everyday Life: Reading Henri Lefebvre* (pp. 80–93). New York and London: Routledge.

100   *Perttu Salovaara and Arja Ropo*

Elsbach, K. D. and Pratt, M. G. (2007). The physical environment in organizations. *The Academy of Management Annals, 1*(1), 181–224.

Entrikin, J. N. and Berdoulay, V. (2005). The Pyrenees as place: Henri Lefebvre as guide. *Progress in Human Geography, 29*(2), 129–147.

Eslen-Ziya, H. and Erhart, I. (2015). Toward post-heroic leadership: A case study of Gezi's collaborating multiple leaders. *Leadership, 11*(4), 471–488.

Fairhurst, G. (2007). *Discursive Leadership: In Conversation With Leadership Psychology*. Thousand Oaks, CA: Sage.

Fayard, A. L. and Weeks, J. (2007). Photocopiers and water-coolers: The affordances of informal interaction. *Organization Studies, 28*(5), 605–634.

Ford, J. and Harding, N. (2004). We went looking for an organization but could find only the metaphysics of its presence, *Sociology, 38*(4), 815–830.

Follett, M. P. (1918). *The New State: Group Organization the Solution of Popular Government*. New York: Longmans, Green and Co.

Follett, M. P. (1924). *Creative Experience*. New York: Longmans, Green and Co.

Follett, M. P. (1949/1987b). Coordination. In L. Urwick (Ed.), *Freedom and Co-Ordination: Lectures in Business Organization* (pp. 61–76). New York: Garland Publishing.

Ford, J. D., Ford, L. W. and D'Amelio, A. (2008). Resistance to change: The rest of the story. *Academy of Management Review, 33*(2), 362–377.

Ford, J. and Harding, N. (2007). Mover over management: We are all leaders now? *Management Learning, 38*(5), 475–493.

Getz, I. (2009). Liberating leadership: How the initiative-freeing radical organizational form has been successfully adopted. *California Management Review, 51*(4), 32–58.

Grint, K. (2010). The sacred in leadership: Separation, sacrifice and silence. *Organization Studies, 31*(1), 89–107.

Grint, K. (2011). A history of leadership. In A. Bryman, D. Collinson, K. Grint, et al. (Eds.), *The SAGE Handbook of Leadership* (pp. 3–14). Thousand Oaks, CA: Sage.

Hamel, G. (2007). *The Future of Management* (With Bill Breen). Boston, MA: Harvard Business School Press.

Hansen, H., Ropo, A. and Sauer, E. (2007). Aesthetic leadership. *Leadership Quarterly, 18*, 544–560.

Harding, N., Lee, H., Ford, J. and Learmonth, M. (2011). Leadership and charisma: A desire that cannot speak its name? *Human Relations, 64*(7), 927–949.

Hatch, M. J. and Cunliffe, A. (2006). *Organization Theory: Modern, Symbolic and Post-Modern Perspectives*. Oxford: Oxford University Press.

Hawkins, B. (2015). Ship-shape: Materializing leadership in the British Royal Navy. *Human Relations, 68*(6), 951–971.

Hegel, G. W. F. (1986). *Phänomenologie des Geistes*. Werke 3. Frankfurt, a.M.: Suhrkamp.

Humphries, C. and Smith, A. C. T. (2014). Talking objects: Towards a post-social research framework for exploring object narratives. *Organization, 21*(4), 477–494.

Jones, M. (2013). Untangling sociomateriality. In P. R. Carlile, D. Nicolini, A. Langley and H. Tsoukas (Eds.), *How Matter Matters. Objects, Artifacts, and Materiality in Organization Studies* (pp. 197–226). Oxford: Oxford University Press.

Kelly, S. (2008). Leadership: A categorical mistake? *Human Relations, 61*(6), 763–782.

Kornberger, M. and Clegg, S. R. (2004). Bringing space back in: Organizing the generative building. *Organization Studies*, 25(7), 1095–1114.

Kuronen, T. and Huhtinen, A.-M. (2016). Organizing conflict: The rhizome of Jihad. *Journal of Management Inquiry*. DOI: 10.1177/1056492616665172.

Ladkin, D. (2008). Leading beautifully: How mastery, congruence and purpose create the aesthetic of embodied leadership practice. *Leadership Quarterly*, 19, 31–41.

Laloux, F. (2014). *Reinventing Organizations*. Brussels: Nelson Parker.

Lefebvre, H. (1963). *La vallée de Campan, études de sociologie rurale*. Paris: Presses Universitaires de France.

Lefebvre, H. (1971). *Everyday Life in the Modern World*. London: The Penguin Press.

Lefebvre, H. (1991). *The Production of Space*. Oxford: Blackwell.

Lefebvre, H. (2000). *Pyrénées*. Pau: Cairn.

Lefebvre, H. (2003). The country and the city. In S. Elden, E. Lebas and E. Kofman (Eds.), *Henri Lefebvre: Key Writings*. London: Continuum.

Lefebvre, H. (2004). *Rhythmanalysis. Space, Time and Everyday Life*. London: Continuum.

Linstead, S. and Höpfl, H. (2000). *The Aesthetics of Organization*. London: Sage.

Liverpool, P. R. (1990). Employee participation in decision-making: An analysis of the perceptions of members and non-members of quality circles. *Journal of Business and Psychology*, 4(4), 411–422.

Margetts, H., John, P., Hale, S. and Reissfelder, S. (2013). Leadership without leaders? Starters and followers in online collective action. *Political Studies*, 63(2), 278–299.

Merrifield, A. (2006). *Henri Lefebvre. A Critical Introduction*. New York: Routledge.

Oborn, E., Barrett, M. and Dawson, S. (2013). Distributed leadership in policy formulation: A sociomaterial perspective. *Organization Studies*, 34(2), 253–276.

Orlikowski, W. J. (2007). Sociomaterial practices: Exploring technology at work. *Organization Studies*, 28, 1435–1448.

Orlikowski, W. and Scott, S. (2008). Sociomateriality: Challenging the separation of technology, work and organization. *The Academy of Management Annals*, 2(1), 433–474.

Orr, J. (1995). *Talking About Machines. An Ethnography of a Modern Job*. Ithaca: Cornell University Press.

Pallasmaa, J. (2014). Space, place, and atmosphere: Peripheral perception in existential experience. In C. Borch (Ed.), *Architectural Atmospheres: On the Experience and Politics of Architecture* (pp. 18–41). Basel, Switzerland: Birkhäuser.

PMBOK (2013). *A Guide to Project Management Body of Knowledge*. Newtown Square, PA: Project Management Institute.

Puranam, P., Alexy, O. and Reitzig, M. (2014). What's 'new' about new forms of organizing? *Academy of Management Review*, 39(2), 162–180.

Raelin, J. (2005). We the leaders: In order to form a leaderful organization. *Journal of Leadership and Organizational Studies*, 12(2), 18–29.

Robertson, B. J. (2015). *Holacracy. The New Management System for a Rapidly Changing World*. New York: Henry Holt and Company, LLC.

Ropo, A. and Höykinpuro, R. (2017). Narrating organizational spaces. *Journal of Organizational Change Management*, 30(3), 357–366.

Ropo, A. and Parviainen, J. (2001). Leadership and bodily knowledge in expert organizations: Epistemological rethinking. *Scandinavian Journal of Management*, 17(1), 1–18.

Ropo, A., Parviainen, J. and Koivunen, N. (2002). Aesthetics in leadership. From absent bodies to social bodily presence. In J. Meindl and K. Parry (Eds.), *Grounding Leadership Theory and Research: Issues and Perspectives* (pp. 21–38). Greenwich CT: Information Age Publishing.

Ropo, A. and Salovaara, P. (2018). Spacing leadership as an embodied and performative process. *Leadership*. Published online: April 16.

Ropo, A., Salovaara, P., Sauer, E. and De Paoli, D. (Eds.) (2015). *Leadership in Spaces and Places*. Cheltenhamand Northampton, MA: Edward Elgar.

Ropo, A., Sauer, E. and Salovaara, P. (2013). Embodiment of leadership through material place. *Leadership*, *9*(3), 378–395.

Ryle, G. (1946). Knowing how and knowing that. *Proceedings of the Aristotelian Society, New Series*, *46*, 1–16.

Salovaara, P. (2014). Video: Leadership in spaces and places. *Organizational Aesthetics*, *3*(1): 79–79. Retrieved from http://digitalcommons.wpi.edu/oa/vol3/iss1/8/

Salovaara, P. and Bathurst, R. (2016). Power-with leadership practices: An unfinished business. *Leadership*. doi:org/10.1177/1742715016652932

Scotto, C. (2014). The principles of campus conception: A spatial and organizational genealogy. What knowledge can we use from a historical study in order to analyse the design processes of a new campus? In Francois-Xavier de Vaujany, N. Mitev, P. Laniryi and E. Vaast (Eds.), *Materiality and Time. Historical Perspectives on Organizations, Artefacts and Practices*. Basingstoke: Palgrave Macmillan.

Sergi, V. (2016). Who's leading the way? Investigating the contributions of materiality to the study of leadership-as-practice. In J. Raelin (Ed.), *Leadership-as-Practice: Theory and Applications* (pp. 110–131). London: Routledge.

Shotter, J. (2006). Understanding process from within: An argument for 'witness'-thinking. *Organization Studies*, *27*, 585–604.

Simonsen, K. (2005). Bodies, sensations, space and time: The contribution from Henri Lefebvre. *Geografiska Annaler: Series B, Human Geography*, *87*(1), 1–14.

Simpson, B. (2015). Where's the agency in leadership-as-practice? In J. Raelin (Ed.), *Leadership-as-Practice. Theory and Application* (pp. 159–177). New York: Routledge.

Stingl, V. and Geraldi, J. (2017). Errors, lies and misunderstandings: Systematic review on behavioural decision making in projects. *International Journal of Project Management*, *35*(2), 121–135.

Strati, A. (1999). *Organization and Aesthetics*. London: Sage.

Strati, A. (2007). Sensible knowledge and practice-based learning. *Management Learning*, *38*(1), 61–77.

Sutherland, N. (2015). Leadership without leaders: Understanding anarchist organising through the lens of critical leadership studies. In B. Carroll, J. Ford and S. Taylor (Eds.), *Leadership: Contemporary Critical Perspectives* (pp. 212–232). London: Sage.

Sutherland, N., Land, C. and Böhm, S. (2014). Anti-leader(ship) in social movement organizations: The case of autonomous grassroots groups. *Organization*, *21*, 759–781.

Sveiby, K.-E. (2011). Collective leadership with power symmetry: Lessons from Aboriginal prehistory. *Leadership*, *7*(4), 385–414.

Taylor, S. and Spicer, A. (2007). Time for space: A narrative review of research on organizational spaces. *International Journal of Management Reviews*, *9*(4), 325–346.

Van Marrewijk, A. and Yanow, D. (Eds.) (2010). *Organizational Spaces. Rematerializing the Workaday World*. Cheltenham: Edward Elgar.

Wasserman, V. and Frenkel, M. (2011). Organizational aesthetics: Caught between identity regulation and culture jamming. *Organization Science, 22*(2), 503–521.

Wasserman, V. and Frenkel, M. (2015). Spatial work in between glass ceilings and glass walls: Gender-class intersectionality and organizational aesthetics. *Organization Studies, 36*(11), 1485–1505.

Watkins, C. (2005). Representations of space, spatial practices and spaces of representation: An application of Lefebvre's spatial triad. *Culture and Organization, 11*(3), 209–220.

Wood, M. (2005). The fallacy of misplaced leadership. *Journal of Management Studies, 42*(6), 1101–1121.

Yanow, D. (2010). Giving voice to space: Academic practices and the material world. In A. van Marrewijk and D. Yanow (Eds.), *Organizational Spaces. Rematerializing the Workaday World* (pp. 139–158). Cheltenham and Northampton, MA: Edward Elgar.

Zhang, Z. (2006). What is lived space? *ephemera, 6*(2), 219–223.

Zhang, Z. and Spicer, A. (2014). 'Leader, you first': The everyday production of hierarchical space in a Chinese bureaucracy. *Human Relations, 67*(6), 739–762.

# 5 Between Institutional Theory and Lefebvre

## Sensemaking, Logics and Enactment of, and in, Space

*Gili S. Drori and Briana Preminger*

## Introduction

The paradigmatic breach by institutional theory into the field of organization studies, which resulted in its current domination over macro-analyses of organizations, was predicated on its reorientation of the field towards social constructivism and cultural analysis. Indeed, institutional theory's wide recognition is based on its reading of Weber, Schutz, Goffman, Berger and Luckmann, and on recasting their claims into a series of principles that emphasize, among other ideas, the centrality of symbolic systems, cultural scripts and discourse for institutionalization. Consequently, although institutions stand on regulative, normative and cognitive pillars and are formalized into structures, practices and behaviours, institutionalists devoted less attention to the material aspects of institutions. In other words, while institutionalists study formal aspects and structuration of organizations and empirically gauge such processes by a variety of organizational artifacts, the search for patterns of meaning obscured materiality. Most insistently, Friedland (2009: 24) declares that institutions have an "absent presence," claiming that whereas institutions are widely acknowledged as social constructs, they present themselves in material practices imbued with symbolic meanings. Friedland's call to make the invisible institutional substance visible (2009: 49) contributed to the recent "material turn" and "visual turn" in organization studies (see e.g., Carlile et al., 2013; Meyer et al., 2013; respectively). As summarized by Jones and Massa (2013: 1127):

> The cognitive bias in institutional theory casts institutions as malleable, prone to episodic fads and fashions. In contrast, materiality illuminates why some ideas persist in the face of competition and environmental shifts. Thus, the material instantiation of ideas is central not only to the durability of ideas but also to the social relations that form a community and underpin institutions. Materiality unites ideas and social actors through identification, enabling institutions to cohere and endure over time.

The "material turn" and "visual turn" in organization studies, however recent they may be, are already most prolific and rapidly gaining momentum. Still, although institutionalists now recognize aesthetics as one of the "nascent threads of research that hold strong potential for bringing institutional theory back to its core assumptions and objectives" (Suddaby, 2010: 14), space and spatiality often remain neglected. In this respect, the reorientation of institutional theory towards aesthetics of organizations, which enables a return of the theory to its grand concerns, regarding rationality, actorhood, and the construction and diffusion of ideas and practices, continues, on the whole, to neglect the sociability and institutional foundations of space. The aim of this chapter is to begin a dialogue between Lefebvre's theory of space and institutional theory, in order to expand discussions of materiality and specifically of spatiality.

This chapter is organized to start a dialogue between the Lefebvrian and institutionalist perspectives of space. Following a review of the recent turn of institutional theory towards materiality, visuality and multimodality, we expand on the need for including spatiality in institutional analyses. We then explore the parallels and the differences between the two perspectives, describing how the shared interest in material forms of social relations comes alongside an ontological divide between Lefebvrian and institutionalist perspectives of space. Building upon Lefebvre's tradition of the study of space and spatiality, we proceed to articulate propositions for institutionalist analysis of social space. Such propositions are inspired by a Lefebvrian theory of space and still draw on the institutionalist concepts of *logics, sensemaking, enactment, legitimacy* and *actorhood* as social devices for the scripting and use of space. Such an institutionalist reading of space situates space not only as a social product, but rather as primarily an *institutional sphere*: space allows for regulative, normative and cultural-cognitive institutional dynamics to construct and then assign meaning to social life. Most importantly, through such spatialized meanings, social space guides the construction of social actors and social action. We suggest points of dialogue between Lefebvre-inspired and institutionalist explorations of space through the illustration of Jerusalem's Western Wall.

## Materiality and Visuality Turns in Institutional Theory of Organizations: Preamble to a "Spatiality Turn"

The 1970s emergence of neo-institutionalism, which transformed organization studies, was predicated on several core principles. These principles, periodically précised by Scott (1987; 2008; and lately, 2014), include an emphasis (a) on the centrality of symbolic systems and cultural scripts for institutionalization, (b) on coercive, normative, and mimetic processes of institutional reproduction, (c) on diffusion, adoption and adaptation of institutional scripts, and (d) on the authority of professionals, professionalized knowledge and knowledge transfer and translation. These institutionalist principles came as a response to the rationalist and materialist theories that dominated organization studies; institutionalism grew out of a critique of theories that regarded organizations as rational, bounded and autonomous entities, as "closed systems," and as deliberative decision makers (see Krücken and Drori, 2009: 7–8; Scott, 2008, 2014). In that vein, foundational claims regarding ceremoniality and ritualistic isomorphism (Meyer and Rowan, 1977; Zucker, 1977; DiMaggio and Powell, 1983) expanded to emphases on the regulative, normative and cognitive pillars of institutions (Scott, 2014) and on the centrality of legitimacy as a social resource and strongly posit a cultural and constructivist viewpoint (Scott, 2008, 2014). This epistemic revolution of new institutionalism, which led it to become the strongest and most prolific paradigm in organization studies over the coming decades (see Greenwood et al., 2008; Greenwood, Lawrence, and Meyer, 2017), also caged new institutionalism in its own "institutional imperative" (Strang and Meyer, 1993: 495) of discursive analysis. As a result, institutions are noted to have an "absent presence" (Freidland, 2009: 24), meaning that the institution's so-called substance "exceeds its attributes and cannot be reduced to a thing's materiality" or other representations (Freidland, 2009: 41). As a result, until recently the institutionalist search for regulative, normative and cognitive patterns of meaning obscured, if not avoided, the materiality of institutions.

Over the past decade, when calls are made for the rejuvenation of institutional theory in light of its expansion and potential fragmentation, one such appeal is to turn its attention towards the materiality of organizational affairs. While heeding the linguistic turn and cultural turn in the social sciences and accentuating discursive aspects of organization, organizations and organizing (Alasuutari, 2015), the "material and visual dimensions of organizing tend to be absent or immaterial in the cognitive and cultural frameworks that dominate organizational theories" (Boxenbaum, Jones, Meyer and Svejenova, 2015: 133). Arguing for bringing matter back in, the compilation under the precise title "How Matter Matters: Objects, Artifacts, and Materiality in Organization Studies" (Carlile, Nicolini, Langley and Tsoukas 2013) starts by revealing the neglect of matter in organization studies. The editors refer to Orlikowski and Scott (2008, in 2013: 2) and claim that 95% of articles in leading management journals do not consider technology as affecting organizational processes; they continue and cite Barad's claim (2003: 801, in 2013: 2) that "Language matters. Discourse matters. Culture matters. There is an important sense in which the only thing that does not seem to matter anymore is matter." And de Vaujany and Mitev (2013: 2) heed the same call, claiming that "organizational theory must perform a 'spatial turn' to incorporate the voluminous analysis of objects and everyday spatial practices." Likewise, institutionalists identify the need for "bridging the current division of labour between studies of material and ideational aspects of institutionalization" (Zilber, 2007: 164). This is also relevant to the use of specific institutionalist concepts. For example, concerning institutional logics, "[w]hereas the more abstract aspects of institutional logics (i.e., cognitive, normative, and symbolic) have received ample attention in the literature, the material (practices) dimension has been surprisingly overlooked" (Jones, Boxenbaum, and Anthony, 2013: 52). As a result, discourse surpassed materiality.

Such a shortfall spurred the recent "materiality turn" (see Leonardi, Nardi, and Kalinikos, 2012) and subsequently the "visuality turn" and the "multimodality turn" in organization studies and among institutionalists (Meyer et al., 2013; Jones et al., 2017; respectively). These reorientations toward the various forms of matter—physical, visual, textual and any multimodal combination of these—share the commentary regarding materiality in general that ideas, values and norms have an embodied representation in artifacts, objects, instruments, technologies, bodies and space. These "turns," which are somewhat disjointed from the 20-year-old research on organizational artifacts as symbolic signifiers (Pratt and Rafaeli, 1997), also share a post-discursive outlook, claiming that language is only one form of content and meaning representation and the primacy of language is related to modern definitions of what is understood to be valid knowledge (see de Vaujany and Mitev, 2015). Such a claim is most notably represented in the compilation by Carlile et al., 2013) and in de Vaujany and Mitev (2013). In expanding institutionalist analyses of organizations in the direction of visuality, researchers analysed visual images in corporate reports (Höllerer et al., 2013), visual displays and practices in study rooms (de Vaujany and Vaast, 2016), and organizational logos (Drori, Delmestri, and Oberg, 2016). These iconographies encapsulate and deliver "imageries of organizing" (Jones et al., 2017), thus allow for sensemaking and sense-giving for organizations and for processes of organizing.

And still in spite of these recent "turns," space and spatiality remained largely overlooked by institutionalists. When analysed by institutionalists, space is conceived as a relational domain, professionalized domain, or a legitimation tool. First, much in line with the sociological approach to space (Löw, 2016), Kellogg's (2009) study of the implementation of a regulative change in two hospitals exemplifies how small-scale settings configure micro-institutional processes. Specifically, "relational spaces," where not only interaction but also inclusion occurs, drive relational mobilization, which constitutes opportunities for institutional change. In other respects, while institutionalists implicitly refer to space and spatiality as a defining dimension of an institutional field, hence recognizing that the web of relations that constitutes the field occupies a realm or social domain (see Scott, 2014: 232–234), such works focused primarily on matters of co-location or proximity, conceptualizing space as a matter of distance (see Bitner, 1992).

Second, as exemplified by Jones et al., 2012), space, much like other symbols and materials, is the outcome of a process of enactment by professional groups, struggling to mitigate the diverting institutional logics of their many constituents. Studying the emergence and theorization of the category "modern architecture" between 1870 and 1975, Jones and her colleagues "show that modern architecture," like the buildings and spaces it designed and constructed, "was shaped, from its inception, by fights over logics based on distinct client sectors and serviced by different groups of architects who enacted "modern architecture" (2012: 1539).

Third and most dominantly, much of the institutionalist analysis of space focused specifically on legitimation. For example, based on analysis of the form and use of the buildings of Paris Dauphine University, which resides in the building that originally served as the headquarters of the North Atlantic Treaty Organization (NATO), de Vaujany and Vaast (2014) coin the concept of "spatial legacies" and find that "the building's past—real or imagined—remains present in the thoughts and interactions of its current occupants" (2014: 725). Therefore, they conclude, while "space and organization [are] analytically distinct but interdependent" (de Vaujany and Vaast, 2014: 725), the spatial legacies construct and guide claims of legitimation by the organization and by its members. Likewise, Jones and Massa (2013), analysing Unity Temple by Frank Lloyd Wright in comparison with three other notable churches of the same period, note that "institutional evangelism" entangles space, institutional work and identity to gain legitimacy for novel ideas, or in this case also novel forms. They "demonstrate that when buildings engender identification, they become collective identity markers, spurring social actors to engage in institutional maintenance work to protect novel ideas and support the community instantiated by those novel ideas" (2013: 1101). In these institutionalist analyses of legitimacy and legitimation, space serves as an institutional carrier, imprinted by its social context and setting a context for institutional work: "Buildings embody the cultural meanings, material and technological practices, and identities of their time and place" (Jones and Massa, 2013: 1129).

Seeing institutional theory's emphasis on meanings and their social construction, the mode by which such meanings are symbolized is critical for understanding institutional dynamics. Indeed, for ideas and practices to diffuse, they get theorized and encoded (see Strang and Meyer, 1993; Strang and Soule, 1998) into organization artifacts, also into spatial arrangements. Yet, in the few institutitonalist studies of space-related materiality of institutions there is little echo of Lefebvre's (1991) iconic work. While discussions of space in organization theory draw heavily from Lefebvre's work and while many critical analyses of organization followed in his path (see Dale, 2005; Taylor and Spicer, 2007; Kingma, 2008; Wasserman and Frenkel, 2011; Wasserman, 2012), institutional studies of materiality in general and of space in particular overlooked Lefebvre. Our claim, developed over the course of this chapter, is that engagement with Lefebvrian tradition affords institutionalism—even contemporary institutional schools, such as those concerned with institutional logics (see Thornton, Ocasio, and Lounsbury, 2012) or institutional work (see Lawrence, Leca, and Zilber, 2013)—new paths for conceptual and empirical advances. Among such paths, two are particularly pertinent to the development of this chapter, which aims at linking institutional theory and Lefebvre's theory of space.

The first is a call for institutional theory to take social power and interest under serious consideration and thus to study how might power asymmetries affect processes of institutionalization. Therefore, in spite of institutionalism's constructivist and even phenomenological claims (see Meyer, 2010), still claims are made that "there are . . . limits to institutional theory's powers of critical illumination" (Willmott, 2015: 105). Likewise, Suddaby (2015) criticizes institutional theory for drifting away from its critical origins, which challenged the then-hegemonic economic and functionalist thinking, to itself became hegemonic and "as a result, lost its theoretical reflexivity" (2015: 94). Second, recognizing that "physical symbols, objects and artifacts form an important but relatively unexplored element in the chains of activities that constitute institutional work" (Lawrence and Suddaby, 2006: 245; see also Jones and Massa, 2013: 1103), institutionalism is at an exciting moment of a turn towards materiality and visuality and is primed also for acknowledgement of space as a unique yet complementary embodiment of institutions. In addition, institutionalist inroads into materiality and visuality, as well as the new work on space, are hopeful signals for identifying equilibrium between the materiality and discursivity of institutions and institutionalization. On both such accounts, institutionalist engagement with Lefebvrian tradition is potentially fruitful conceptually and empirically. The following section explores the links between institutionalism and Lefebvre, ontologically and specifically in regards to materiality and spatiality, with the goal of exploring common grounds and possibilities for cross-fertilization.

## Between Institutionalism and Lefebvre

Lefebvre broke new grounds in social theory by placing space at the centre of social analysis. Lefebvre's (1991; originally published in French in 1974) configuration of the conceived, perceived and lived spaces relies extensively on his neo-Marxist understandings and on the related emphasis on dynamics of power relations and interest-driven action (see Dale and Burrell, 2008). For Lefebvre, space is a reflection of relations of coercion, resistance and struggle. Lefebvrian theory of space also spurred a stream of empirical research in organization studies. Specifically, it inspired research on architecture as a power mechanism in various social sectors: entertainment (Kingma, 2008), academia (Hancock and Spicer, 2011; Peltonen, 2011), government (Wasserman, 2011; Wasserman and Frenkel, 2011) and international organizations (de Vaujany and Vaast, 2014). And such research identified the scheme for the ideal worker that is derived from such spatial arrangements, in terms of social class (Zhang and Spicer, 2013), production- or market role (Hancock and Spicer, 2011), gender category (Tyler and Cohen, 2010), or national identity (Wasserman, 2011) and thus identifies the spatiality of various social hierarchies. With this force, the philosophical

essays of Lefebvre on space penetrated and influenced organization studies. How may this Lefebvrian tradition of analysing space and organization
inform the recent turn in institutional theory toward the materiality of organizations? How may the concepts of "Lefebvrian space" and "institutional
space" relate to each other? In the following sections, we explore the potential for interchange between Lefebvrian theories of space in organization
and institutional theory of organizations.

*Ontological Divides*

The breakthrough of social studies of space—as a particular, however
broad, aspect of materiality—drives us to study the common and divergent
conceptual issues between Lefebvrian theories of space and institutional
theory of organization. The ontology that is at the root of each of the two
theories tracks each theory's analysis of space and organization follows a
unique path. Indeed, as described in the following section, Lefebvrian theory of space and institutionalism each offers a distinct definition for the
social character of space, for what are the sought-after social resources (the
"why?"), who are the social entities or parties engaged with and constituted
by space (the "who?") and what is the nature of the spatiality process (the
"how?"). Table 5.1 herein summarizes the comparison of the theories' distinct definitions and terminologies.

In a most fundamental way, Lefebvrian and institutionalist perspectives
of space, while sharing the claim that space is essentially social, diverge on
the definition of the underlying drive for social action. Lefebvrian analysis
of space revolves around power and the reproduction of hegemonic status:
"in the case of space, knowledge to be derived from analysis extends to the
recognition of the conflicts internal to what on the surface appears homogeneous and coherent—and presents itself and behaves as though it were"
(Lefebvre, 1991: 352). And while "space has no power 'in itself,' nor does
space as such determine spatial contradictions" (1991: 358), the contradictions of society—between elite and proletariat, producers and consumers,
haves and have-nots—"simply emerge in space, at the level of space, and
so engender the contradictions of space" (1991: 358). Space is, therefore, a
sphere of, and for, power relations and hierarchies (Dale and Burrell, 2008:
15). Institutionalists, on the other hand, draw heavily on Weberian emphasis on authority and the legitimation of power structures and on Berger
and Luckmann's description of legitimacy as a "second order" of meanings,
which provides cultural support and scripts the justification for structures
and action. Inspired by Geertz, institutionalists recast "muscular" power—
often drawn from political, economic and technological capacities—as
constituted by and transferred through cultural practices, ritual, and symbols. For example, de Vaujany and Vaast (2014: 728) show "how the characteristics and affordances of a space become intricately enmeshed not
only with what people can do, but also with an organization's legitimacy

*Table 5.1* Contrasting principal assumptions

|  | *Lefebvre* | *Institutionalism* |
|---|---|---|
| **WHAT is space?** | The monumentalizing of asymmetries of power among social groups or agents, which is produced and reproduced (through coercion, exploitation, exclusion, struggle, coercion, and resistance) at conceived, lived, and perceived spaces. | Spatially embodied meanings, which are assigned following relational processes of rationalization, sensemaking, translation, enactment, and contestation, which are anchored in the three pillars of regulative, normative and culture-cognitive, and which enable and constrain social action. |
| **WHY operate in space?** The sought-after resource | **Power** Control over resources of production and reproduction and hegemonic status. | **Legitimacy** Social acceptability and credibility, as prescribed within the relevant institutional context. |
| **WHO operates in space?** The parties | **Agents** Purposive and power-seeking social beings (individual or collective) that are identified and differentiated by their access to, or control over, power. | **Actors** Entities (individual or collective) constructed, or constituted, by the spatialized meanings and acting upon (carrying, reifying) the spatialized scripts. |
| **HOW do they operate in space?** The process | **Coercion and resistance** Struggles over, and manipulation of, power which instigate coercion, exploitation, exclusion, struggle, coercion, and resistance. | **Enactment and co-constitution** Institutional dynamics of sensemaking, translation, diffusion, enactment, isomorphism and contestation that recursively co-constitute meaning and meaning's materialized, here spatialized, form. |

claims. More specifically, diverse organizational stakeholders may perceive a space differently and associate it with more or less persuasive legitimacy claims." In these ways, legitimacy—distinct from the neo-Marxist concept of ideology—honours the embeddedness of action and of actors in a normative order and explains compliance and adherence as normative conformity and enactment—again distinct from a Lefebvrian reading of enactment (see Dale and Burrell, 2008).

Consequently, the two theoretical perspectives also diverge in their definition of the nature of social action and of social relations in and around space. From a Lefebvrian perspective,

Spaces are *produced*. The 'raw material' from which they are produced is nature. They are the products of an activity which involves the economic and technical realms but which extends well beyond them, for these are also political products, and strategic spaces.

(Lefebvre, 1991: 84; italics in the original)

Action—namely production and reproduction—is essential to a Lefebvrian understanding of space and such space-related action is described as segregating, exclusionary, and manipulating. This argument is loudly stated in all Lefebvrian-inspired research. For example, Kingma (2008: 46, 47) concludes, "the carefully designed divisions and variations in gambling areas within the casino facilitate a 'culture of difference'" and "confinement . . . euphemizes and softens gambling experiences, to gambling as a form of commercial entertainment." Likewise, Wasserman (2012: 21) concludes that

> The symbolic boundaries created by status markers thus form a key mechanism in the perpetuation of social inequality, direct exclusion and self-exclusion and camouflage the power relations underlying the creation of spatial-social significance. Architectural space imposes status differences on social relationships by the location of the worker's physical body within the space, the degree of surveillance the worker is subjected to and the degree of submissiveness needed to fulfil those imperatives.

And, in the face of such segregation and coercion, come struggle and disruption, where "workers' inter-subjective, deliberate and sometimes systematic attempts to transgress and ridicule management's aesthetic messages using aesthetic jamming" (Wasserman and Frenkel, 2011: 518). Overall, Lefebvrian analysis highlights struggles over, and manipulation of, power that instigate coercion, exploitation, exclusion and resistance. Moreover, the directionality of exploitative and manipulative action is from the conceived to the lived and perceived spaces, while acts of resistance, transgression, sabotage, or compliance are directed from the perceived and lived spaces towards the conceived space.

Institutionalist analysis highlights institutional dynamics of sensemaking, translation, diffusion, enactment and isomorphism, which recursively co-constitute meaning and its materialized form (or, as emphasized in this discussion, spatialized form). Therefore, the formal regulative pillar of institutions that is embodied in the conceived space is co-constituted by, and constitutive of, the normative and cultural-cognitive pillars of institutions; likewise, policy is co-constitutive of practice. That said, on this issue of social action, institutionalists split: The pioneering institutionalists, who accept phenomenological assumptions, define the actor as an imagined social entity and actorhood as a script of modernist agency (Meyer and Jepperson, 2000; Drori, Meyer, and Hwang, 2009), while others pursue the concept of "institutional work," attributing agency to individuals and organizations whose purposive labour creates, maintains, and disrupts institutions (Lawrence, Suddaby, and Leca, 2009; Lawrence, Leca, and Zilber, 2013). Furthering the agency school in institutional theory, Fligstein and McAdam (2011) define institutional fields as competitive arenas, emphasizing the differential power of institutional incumbents, and analysing the influence of challengers, who "[await] new opportunities to challenge the structure and logic of the system" (2011: 13). Overall, both institutionalist schools distinguish themselves from a neo-Marxist imagery of the social actor as rational, purposive and incentivized to pursue their goals. From this viewpoint, the actor, and actor's behaviour in space, embodies knowledge and social conventions. Rather, drawing on Weberian ideas of social roles and on Goffmanian ideas regarding the scripted actor, institutionalists argue that the "cultural system constructs the modern actor as an authorized agent" (Meyer and Jepperson, 2000: 101) and define social actors as "carriers" and "translators" more than as social agents.

In these ways, the ontological divides along the fault-lines of power-legitimacy and production/reproduction-enactment/institutional work also translate into the fault-line of agent-actor. While the constructed and manipulated nature of social space "does not mean that people are complete 'spatial dopes'" (Kingma: 2008: 46), some Lefebvrians nevertheless focus identity regulation, even of the body, by and through space. Wasserman and Frenkel, for example, reveal how workers interpret and disrupt the disciplining of behaviour and modes of thought that are conveyed through organizational aesthetics. Thus, while organizational aesthetics employ spatial terms to conceive of the image of the ideal worker, and while workers "located themselves in the organizational hierarchy in relation to this image" (Wasserman and Frenkel, 2011: 508), they also resist at the level of lived space. Institutional theory, on the other hand, remains focused on the concept of "embedded agency" that, as noted earlier, fuels the debate between phenomenological- and more agentic schools within the institutionalist camp. Indeed, the inherent tension within this idea of embedded agency again splits the institutionalist camps: On the one hand, the emphasis on context and cultural scripts as constructing also social actors (Meyer, 2010), while on the other hand, emphasis on institutional entrepreneurship, meaning on the agency of actors to constitute institutions (Battilana and D'aunno, 2009; also Zilber, 2007; Navis and Glynn, 2010).

In conclusion, the major ontological distinctions, herein accentuated, regarding the social character of actors and their relations, produce two distinct definitions of the sociability of space. From a Lefebvrian perspective, space is monumentalizing the asymmetries of power among social groups or agents, as determined through processes of exploitation, exclusion, struggle, coercion, and resistance. "The space hat homogenizes thus has nothing homogeneous about it," explains Lefebvre (1991: 308) and only an act holds its fragments together "like a fist clenched around sand" (1991: 320). From an institutionalist perspective, space embodies meanings, which are socially constructed and then assigned aspatialized form; space embodies relational processes of sensemaking, translation, and enactment within a particular institutional context.

## Foundations for Interchange

When it comes to the study of space and spatiality, can these two ontologies spur each other towards new realms of study? In the following section, we explore bases for fruitful dialogue, which while not undermining the onto-logical foundations of each theoretical tradition, would allow each theoreti-cal approach to respond to calls for regeneration.

First, Lefebvre's analytic theory of space, which explores a triad of social spaces, is an important foundation for institutionalist analyses of space and spatiality. While Lefebvrian definitions of the three spaces ("represen-tations of space" or "conceived space"; "spatial practice" or "perceived space"; and, "representational space" or "lived space") do not neatly map onto the pillars of institutions, both approaches hence highlight the mul-tidimensionality of social structure, action and artifact. In addition, like Lefebvre, institutionalists too would focus on the dynamic relations among the triad of spaces or among the pillars of institutions, thus acknowledg-ing the complexity of relations within each triad. From a Lefebvrian per-spective, "as a three part dialectic, the three dimensions work together, but can also contradict each other" (Kingma, 2008: 33). Watkins (2005: 220) adds: "All three aspects of the triad are continually and mutually informed and informing, and as such are essential in the successful negotiation of the social world. Furthermore, both approaches continue to spur empirical research. Lefebvre (1991: 40) writes, "The perceived-conceived-lived triad (in spatial terms: spatial practice, representations of space, representational space) loses all force if it is treated as an abstract 'model'." In inspiring and driving empirical research, Lefebvre's theory of space, like institutional-ism in general and Meyer's phenomenological institutionalism in particular (see Drori and Krücken, 2009), have been the most generative "theoretical research program." In these ways, Lefebvre's scheme of conceived-, per-ceived- and lived spaces inspires and drives institutional analysis of space-related phenomena.

Indeed, the conceptual import of Lefebvre's theory of space resonates with recent turns in institutional theory and impregnates institutionalism with further advances. First, seeing the recent material and visual turns in institutional theory, reaching out to a Lefebvrian theory of space expands the institutional analysis of organizational aesthetics to space. Emphasis on space and spatiality broadens the scope of aesthetic and materialized organizational dimensions to be deciphered with institutional terminol-ogy and considered as constructed through institutional processes. For example, as further elaborated on in the following section, by interjecting

Lefebvrian definitions of the three spaces onto the vocabulary of institutionalized logics, we coined the term "spatialized logic" to consider the conceived, lived and perceived—hence embodied and materialized—expressions of different interpretive scripts of Jerusalem's Western wall (Preminger and Drori, 2016).

Second, engaging with Lefebvrian tradition and focusing on space and spatiality gives institutional theory the opportunity to expand analysis beyond its traditional focus on discourse and textual configurations to consider additional aspects of institutionalization. First, as noted earlier, this is an opportune time for institutional theory, seeing that recent institutional research is increasingly cognizant of the material and the embodied and attuned to visual, emotional and spatial configurations. Second and furthering this research line, importantly drawing on Lefebvrian focus of spatiality, broadens multi-modal institutional analysis (see Jones et al., 2017). Third, seeing the recent turn of institutional theory towards the study of the microfoundations of institutions, thus redirecting towards agent-based and day-to-day institutionalization, links with Lafebvre's emphasis of the role of the body in activating social space. Because reaching out to a Lefebvrian theory of agency and space also challenges institutional analysis to consider matters of power and hierarchy, furthering institutionalist analysis in such direction would surely need to separate itself from traditional contingency theory, also by accentuating themes of the constructed character of social hierarchies, but such institutionalist accounts of social categories and differentiation mechanisms is already well developed (see, for example, Rao, Monin, and Durand, 2003; Navis and Glynn, 2010; Kennedy and Fiss, 2013). Last, the Lefebvrian analytic triad of spaces has already framed analyses of globalization (Crang, 1999) and of glocal organization (Höllerer, Walgenbach, and Drori, 2017) and is employed in the articulation of spatialized logics (Preminger and Drori, 2016). For such studies, Lefebvre's analytic work spurs institutionalism to address the multidimensionality of any material-, and specifically spatialized, phenomena.

Likewise, institutional theory is surely illuminating for a Lefebvrian analysis of space and spatiality. To date, there have been instances where institutional terminology has already been borrowed by some Lefebvrians for the analysis of space and organizational aesthetics. Wasserman (2011), for example, borrows DiMaggio and Powell's (1983) iconic work on isomorphism, which is one of the constitutive works of neo-institutionalism (Greenwood and Meyer, 2008), to analyse the similarity in architectural style between the iconic new buildings of two Israeli organizations. Likewise, in discussing the spatial dimensions of organizational identity, the language of scripting and re-scripting, which is central to institutional theory, is invoked to emphasize the role that workers and others living in organizations have in struggles over the character of the organization (Taylor and Spicer, 2007: 333). In these pioneering bridging studies, such borrowing of institutional terminology is without the underlying institutional assumptions. Most clearly, Wasserman's (2011) employment of the concept of "isomorphism" remains focused on mimicry itself, rather than on the institutional mechanisms that drive such similarity of form and processes of emulation.

Importantly, discussions and interchange between institutionalism and Lefebvrianism advance a more nuanced understanding of the reality of the material, acknowledging the material and spatial form is the product of social process. The neo-Marxist root of a Lefebvrian approach led to an emphasis on the spatial form of social struggles over "real" resources. For institutionalists, while the physicality of space makes space more tangibly real than verbal, textual or visual modes of meaning, space too is socially constructed and thus imprinted by its social context. Without resolving the "chicken-or-egg" dilemma regarding primacy of legitimacy over more material social resources, both approaches recognize that the physicality of space only veils the social processes—conflict or institutionalization—that constitute and validate its actuality. Obviously, social context, often described in terms of locale and epoch, into which space is born, invites engagement with Stinchcombe's widely acknowledged imprinting hypothesis. For example, Wasserman's (2011) analysis of two public buildings in Israel, specifically of a governmental ministry and a university, reveals that their spatial array reflects the socio-cultural context of Israeli society and that their spatiality "normalizes" the organizational identity in reference to Israeliness. These spatialized cultural meanings, which are imprinted into and carried by other structures, practices, and behaviours, constitute an institutional order. Likewise, seeing the principal interest of organization scholars in social construction, space emerges as a "site" for related processes. For example, both Petani and Mengis (2016), who study "lost spaces," and de Vaujany and Vaast (2014), who study "spatial legacies," consider the traces of history that are embodied in organizations' space and have a lingering constitutive impact on the organizations' trajectory.

Overall, both theories—Lefebvrian theories of space and institutional theory of organizations—have much to gain from conceptual cross-fertilization. Such bridging across the theoretical divide has been previously suggested. For example, in linking neo-institutionalist ideas of mimetic isomorphism with Lefebvre's three spaces, Wasserman (2011: 24) writes,

> For organizational aesthetics studies, this paper adds insights from neo-institutional theory, which is the most suitable theoretical framework for exploring managerial and architectural fashions and trends in designing organizational spaces.

For neo-institutionalism, this paper suggests the applying of symbolic isomorphism to spatial representations and to examine the diffusion of fashions and trends in organizational architecture.

*Propositions for Lefebvre-inspired Institutional Analyses of Space*

Building upon this foundation for cross-fertilization between Lefebvrian and institutional perspectives, further inroads into institutionalist analysis of space are warranted so as to recognize the social role of space as an important stage for institutional processes. In this spirit, and paraphrasing Meyer, Höllerer, Jancsary and Leeuwen's articulation of an institutionalist theory of visuality in organizations (2013: 494–496), we offer the following propositions regarding the institutional aspects of space and spatiality:

• The spatial mode of meaning construction materializes, organizes, communicates, stores and passes on social knowledge within particular communities; it both constitutes complex systems of symbolic signs and is able to build up and organize zones of meanings.
• The spatial mode of meaning construction contributes to a society's social stock of knowledge and, hence, is a part of an objectified social reality. The use of spatial means serves to create, maintain, and defend particular forms of practice, and the particular forms of knowledge that underpin them.
• The spatial mode of meaning construction is characterized by a prevalence of all-inclusive and immediate information, rather than linear and sequentially arranged information.

And, highlighting the uniqueness of the spatial as a mode of meaning that is distinct from verbal, textual or visual modes of meaning, we add that:

• The spatial mode of meaning materializes social arrangements and socially constructed realities through highly taken-for-granted physical and geographical area, its boundaries, and its dimensions of spread or congestion.
• Moreover, the spatial mode of meaning provides the "stage," or mise-en-scène, for the discursive performativity of other aesthetic artifacts and for the role performance of social actors. In this way, space's role as a mode of meaning is amplified through the situating of such artifacts and actors in its span.

These propositions—inspired by Lefebvre's tradition and anchored in institutionalism—could guide researchers of space and spatiality to seek the institutional order and institutional dynamics that underlie the existent physicality and presumed permanency of the space. From such an institutionalist perspective, relevant research questions are: What are the meanings expressed by, and in, the space? What are the regulative, normative and cultural-cognitive institutional dynamics to construct and then assign such meanings? How do such spatialized meanings guide the construction of social actors and social action? In the following section, we illustrate the potency of such a synergic perspective for site-specific research.

## Exemplar Analysis: Studying Jerusalem's Western Wall

Throughout this essay we set the foundation for formulating and articulating an institutionalist theory of space and spatiality in organizations, which is inspired by and engaged with Lefebvre's foundational conceptualization of space and spatiality. The basic premise for such an institutionalist perspective is the following definition of space as *spatially embodied meanings, which are (a) assigned following relational processes of rationalization, sensemaking, translation, and enactment, (b) anchored in the three pillars of regulative, normative and culture-cognitive, and (c) enable and constrain social action.* From this perspective, space is the taken-for-granted, namely institutionalized to the point of being socially invisible, that is all around us. Such taken-for-grantedness makes space into an important target for institutionalist analysis that would unpack the meanings attributed to space so to make it recognized as having certain attributes and ritualistically reaffirmed as having these attributes. Indeed, like all other theories of space, our attempt to formulate an institutionalist interpretation of social space aims at providing a better understanding of how social actors make sense (interpret, translate, and organize knowledge) of space and how such spatialized ideas co-constitute structures, practices, behaviours, ideas and feelings. Therefore, as institutionalists have argued about verbal, textual and, recently, visual material, we recognize space as a "central part of the strategic repertoire" that is available for use by "culturally skilled entrepreneurs" (Meyer et al., 2013: 492). The sociability of space is, therefore, the codification of space as a sign system that exhibits and communicates meanings. In other words, just as language, and lately also visuals and other artifacts, are used to identify discourse, so is space—its design, behaviour in it, and opinions of it—an embodied expression of culture and discourse. This approach is, obviously, rooted in the constructivist scholarly tradition that concentrates on the performativity of organizational structures, practices and also artifacts. Accordingly, space embodies institutions, carries institutional knowledge, and constructs institutional life; hence, space echoes its social context.

Change of the spatialized institutional order, like any change to institutions in general, comes from processes of sensemaking, translation, and recreation and diffusion. In regards to spatial reconstruction, top-down and bottom-up processes of institutional change map onto Lefebvrian spaces: top-down influences, which were the prime focus of early institutional sociologists, reflect the rules and regulations that prescribe institutional change, whereas bottom-up spurring of institutional change comes from actors' interpretation and innovation, which echo the lived space. Such institutional processes are prevalent in regards to space: industrial buildings are demolished and new buildings come in their place, reflecting new institutional meanings for, for example, the ideal worker; city streets are being redesigned to reflect new sensitivities towards, for example, environmental sustainability or citizenship; and ancient spaces are being preserved to convey a sense of heritage and to constitute a history to a contemporary identity. In these ways, space is both a *carrier* of the institutional order by giving a sense of the norms to those encountering and experiencing the space and an *outcome* of institutional processes by giving an embodied presence to institutional logics. Space is an arena for the enactment of the institutional order, as well as for contestation of the existing social order, while space is also itself such an enactment. In the following case analysis of Jerusalem's Western Wall, we provide an illustration of the potency of an institutional perspective of space and spatiality, which draws upon Lefebvrian concepts and tradition of research.

## The Site

The Western Wall in the Old City of Jerusalem, which is one of the most widely recognized sites in the world today, was erected as a part of the expansion of the Second Jewish Temple by King Herod, starting in the year 19 BCE. It served as the western supporting wall of the huge flat platform that was formed on top of Temple Mount, allowing for the expansion of the Second Temple and its surrounding compound. Since the destruction of the Temple by the Romans in the year 70 CE and the many wars over, and different rulers of, this area ever since, the Western Wall remains a holy monument to the sanctity of this mountain to the three monotheistic religions and, as such, it draws millions of visitors annually. Ever since the Israeli occupation of Jerusalem's Old City in 1967, the 500-metre long wall has progressively been partitioned into three zones, each formally designated for a specific functional use and uniquely governed (see Figure 5.1). First, the 60-metre-long section at the centre of the historic Wall is recognized as the Prayer Area and operates as a Jewish Orthodox synagogue (see Rabinowitz, 2009; Cohen-Hattab, 2010). Second, the southern end of the Wall, which has been the site of professional archaeological excavations between 1968–2000 (and obviously, even more sporadically, by European archaeologists since the late nineteenth century), is recognized as the Archaeological Park. This area was opened to the public in 2002 for self-guided tours for an entry fee, and entry may also include a visit to the Davidson Exhibition and Virtual Reconstruction Centre. Third, the northern section of the wall, which is buried under the buildings of the Muslim Quarter, was made accessible to the public in 1988. The Tunnels site offers hourly, guided tours, in various languages, and for a fee. The tours accentuate the historical connection of the Jewish people to Jerusalem and to the Wall. As neatly as the governance of the three sections is set, the demarcation among the uses is continuously contested. Notwithstanding the national and political fights swirling all around the Wall, the site of the Wall is itself a site for contestation: non-Orthodox Jewish groups use the Archaeological Park to protest Orthodox prayer conventions and the Tunnels' area is progressively encroached by

Temple Mount

Entrance
to Tunnels

Prayer
Area

Archaeological
Park

*Figure 5.1* Jerusalem's Western Wall, panoramic view.
Source: http://tomclarkblog.blogspot.com/2013_07_01_archive.html, accessed June 13, 2015.

Orthodox synagogues built alongside the route of the tour. In these various ways, the 2000-year-old Wall embodies and demonstrates social dynamics.

The partition of, and the contestation over, the uses of what is otherwise a consistently uniform 500-metre-long wall is evidence for the sociability of this space. On the one hand, the Wall is magnificent in the consistency of its material form: It has been built in accordance with the vision of a single monarch, within a short time period, by a steady set of builders, and of the same pale limestone huge "bricks" along its full span. On the other hand, this same spatial and material expanse has been treated very differently over its 2000-year history and by its different rulers and visitors, reflecting the many social meanings that came to be assigned to, and carried by, this stone wall. This juxtaposition—of a constant material form over several different socio-cultural spaces—makes the Western Wall ripe for analysis. For explicating the multiple sociabilities of a singular material space we restrict our analysis to the space that directly touches upon the Western Wall. In the following section we offer an institutional analysis of the Wall that marries Lefebvrian spaces with the institutional concepts of logics, sensemaking and enactment.

*Spatializing Logics*

Impressed by the variety of meanings attributed to the Western Wall and evident in the spatial arrangements of the Wall and its surroundings today, we coined the phrase of "spatialized logic" to capture the spatial embodiment of an institutional logic (Preminger and Drori, 2016). In an attempt to reorient institutionalism's "material turn" toward spatiality, we merged the widely acknowledged definition of *logics* as "the socially constructed, historical patterns of material practices, assumptions, values, beliefs, and rules by which individuals produce and reproduce their material subsistence, organize time and space, and provide meaning to their social reality" (Thornton and Ocasio, 1999: 804; Thornton, Ocasio, and Lounsbury, 2012) with the Lefebvrian definition of *space*. The dynamics of social action to conceive, perceive and live the meanings is captured in the idea of *spatializing* logics.

From this perspective, the three sections of the Western Wall embody three distinct spatializing logics, each reinforced and reproduced through the conceived, perceived, and lived spaces. First, the spatializing religious logic, which is embodied in the Prayer Area, conveys the holiness of the site and is carried by the Protection of Holy Places Law 1967 (conceived), the arrangement of this site in resemblance to an Orthodox synagogue (conceived), the modest dress code of visitors, bodily gestures of worshipers, and the placing of a personalized wish note within the Wall's cracks (perceived), and the opinions of visitors and governors alike describing this area as "a universal centre of spirituality" which "stirs the thoughts and emotions of Jew and non-Jew, and energizes the inner connection between the individual and G-d" (lived; source: on-site brochure). Second, the spatializing professional logic, which is embodied in the Archaeological Park, conveys professionalized meanings, initially (1968–2000) of archaeologists, historians and scientists and currently of curators and tour guides, of professional ethics and standards and the site's significance in the development of western, now global, civilization. This meaning is carried by the restriction of access to different zones, which is marked by designated visitation pathways (conceived), by visitors' behaviour that respects the prohibition of touching these displays (perceived), and by the site's naming as a Park, its self-description as "an exhibition," and the visitors' references to it as a mapping of history (lived). Third, the spatializing nationalistic logic, which dominates the Tunnels, specifically advocates and promotes Israeli-Jewish nationalism. This spatializing nationalistic logic is carried by the requirement of site-operated guided tours that follow a strict script (conceived), by involving visitors in demonstrations along the tour's route and encouraging the touching of the stone and experiencing of the site (perceived), and by textual and verbal expressions of the Jewish people's long and unbreakable relation with Jerusalem and the Temple Mount (lived). This spatialized nationalistic logic is distinct from the spatializing national logic, which celebrates Israeli statehood and citizenship and is indeed also spatialized in the open public square detached from the Western Wall. Lately, Jewish theological divisions are also receiving their spatialized embodiment in the allocation and then retraction of a fourth area along the Wall, called Ezrat Yisrael, for religious activities of reform Jews. This sectioning of additional and highly contested space, while conveying the religious logic that is also spatialized in the Prayer Area,

122 Gili S. Drori and Briana Preminger

and still demonstrates the intra-logic divisions, here between Orthodox and Reform Judaism, in their spatialized form.

This analysis produces three main insights. First, we identify that these three distinct spatializing logics recast the same physical site into three distinct social spaces and each such social space is defined by a particular meaning that gets translated into conceived, perceived and lived spatial expressions. Specifically, institutional logics get embodied in spatial arrangements at the conceived, perceived, and lived spaces, thus constituting distinct spatializing logics that segment what is otherwise a uniform physical site. Second, the principal force of spatialization is, therefore, meaning. In other words, individuals enact-conceive, enact-perceive and enact-live distinct assumptions, values, beliefs and rules, thus producing and reproducing three specific social spaces. Therefore, while we acknowledge the struggles, even wars, over control of this site, we consider this "turf war (Preminger and Drori, 2016) as a process of translation, contestation, co-construction and enactment. Third, this analysis recognizes the dynamics of relations among these three spatializing logics, thus revealing contestation over meanings and showing that such dynamics are specific to each conceptual space. Specifically, we identified patterns of bridging and leakage among the spatializing logics at the lived and perceived spaces, while at the conceived spaces the three spatializing logics were rather compartmentalized, bounded and impenetrable (see Preminger and Drori, 2016). Importantly, in accordance with Weberian analysis and with Weber and Glynn's (2006) claims, the three institutional orders that are captured here in the three spatializing logics—namely, religion, professionalism, and nationalism—are important mechanisms in the priming, editing and triggering of sensemaking.

*Spatializing Sensemaking*

The spatialization of each of these logics results from sensemaking processes. Sensemaking is defined as "the process through which people work to understand issues or events that are novel, ambiguous, confusing or in some other way violate expectations" (Maitlis and Christianson, 2014: 57). Such sensemaking may be prospective, hence done in anticipation of events or issues, or may be "the on-going retrospective development of plausible images that rationalize what people are doing" (Weick, Sutcliffe, and Obstfeld, 2005: 409). Either way, it "is about the interplay of action and interpretation rather than the influence of evaluation on choice," thus linking between sensemaking and action and revealing the "micro-mechanism[s] that produce macro-change over time" (Weick, Sutcliffe, and Obstfeld, 2005: 419). Drawing Weber and Glynn's (2006) claim that sensemaking is embedded in social context, we extend the claim to space. We argue that interpretations of the site of Jerusalem's Western Wall get spatialized, thus defining spatializing sensemaking as the spatial expression of the process by which issues and events take meaning. Therefore, not only is space the target of sensemaking (sensemaking of space) but space is also a means for sensemaking (sensemaking through space).

The spatial demarcation between the three sections of the Western Wall— the Prayer area, the Archaeological Park and the Tunnels—is an act of sensemaking. Each site is organized uniquely to declare its distinction from the others. For example, an admission fee is charged at the entrance to both the Tunnels and the Archaeological Park, whereas the Prayer Area is open to all and at all times, even if under formal restrictions regarding dress and behaviour; likewise, in the Prayer Area and in the Tunnels visitors are encouraged to be intimate with the stones, whereas in the Archaeological Park the site's artifacts are literally put on display, namely staged, separated by rope, and tagged with explanation signage. Therefore, while all three sections draw upon the holiness and history of the overall site, they each make a different sense, or spatially encapsulate a specific meaning, of it. This demarcation is a reaction to the multiplicity of logics and, with that, to the institutional complexity of this site. Therefore, spatiality here also conveys the sense of commensurability among the logics. We find that in the Western Wall the religious and the nationalistic logics co-exist (see Reay and Hinings, 2009), if not hybridize (see Battilana and Dorado, 2010; Pache and Santos, 2013), and do so also spatially. For example, the Tunnels are formally open only to paying visitors who go on the site operator's tour and thus participate in the site's nationalist performance, yet informally Jewish worshipers are admitted without entry tickets to use the site's "hidden" synagogue or worship by the point closest to the ancient Holy of Holies. At the section of the Archaeological Park, on the other hand, the religious and professional logics come into competition (see Lounsbury, 2007), igniting political debates and civic action. In such competition, it is sensemaking that defines power, since it "is expressed in acts that shape what people accept, take for granted, and reject" (Pfeffer, 1981 in Weick, Sutcliffe, and Obstfeld, 2005: 409).

*Spatializing Enactment*

Enactment, which is one of the key micro-mechanism of institutionalization (Powell and Colyvas, 2008: 284), is activated by institutional entrepreneurs, namely by agents of institutionalization. At times of change, the new or renewed institutional order is framed, justified and made legitimate though the accounts given by people, thus making stories into powerful sensemaking tools (Zilber, 2007). And yet, because "individuals and environments are mutually constitutive" (Powell and Colyvas, 2008: 284), enactment delivers the complex models of the modern actor, be it an individual, an organization, the state, or even a generalized other (Meyer and Jepperson, 2000: 111). The term 'enactment' is not, by any means, exclusively used by institutionalists; rather, the term is also employed in the Lefebvrian tradition (see Dale and Burrell, 2008). Still, the institutionalist use the term is anchored in Goffmanian and phenomenological traditions, therefore orienting the term towards the construction of meaning and of the actor alike. Seeing that "[e] nactment represents the reciprocal interaction of the material and the cognitive world" (Powell and Colyvas, 2008: 284), the concept of spatialized enactment captures the acting of the appropriate social roles and identities in and through space. Therefore, again, not only is space an arena for the enactment of such diverse social roles and identities (enactment in space) but space is also a form of enactment (enactment through space).

Jerusalem's Western Wall is an obvious arena for the spatializing enactment of various social roles and identities. In this area, people publically enact their gender, national, ethnic, familial, religious and political identities; they also play out the social roles of a devout believer, an archaeologist, or a tourist. Moreover, the spatializing enactment of distinct social roles and identities is highly nuanced along Jerusalem's Western Wall. For example, Orthodox Jews would not worship in the Archaeological Park, although the stones in this section are no different than in the Prayer Area, thus the Archaeological Park violates their spatialized sense of identity; meaning, enactment of their religious identity is tied with the prayer area, and now also with specific places within the Tunnels, because of the historic significance poured into these specific social spaces. Likewise, gender identities are enacted in the spatial segregation of male and female worshipers in the Prayer Area; meaning, identity enactment of Jewish Orthodox women is tied with gender segregation of the space in the Prayer Area and identity enactment of Jewish Reform women is currently constructed through linkages with a newly demarcated (and recently revoked) area called Ezrat Yisrael. These enactments follow the scripts of contemporary actorhood, which is highly constructed, legitimate, and steeped with the themes of the individual, choice and preferences. Therefore, while "[m]odern actors are seen as autonomous and natural entities, no longer really embedded in culture, . . . [o]ut of the unspecified core of actorhood emanate the utilities and preferences said to produce the entire social world" (Meyer and Jepperson, 2000: 100). Seeing that contemporary actorhood is defined and organized in terms of individual choice, the Western Wall too gives a sense of choice: one can choose to worship in the central Prayer Area yet also in the Tunnels or the Archaeological Park. Yet, the spatializing logics that dominate each of these three sections of the Wall prescribe the form of spatializing enactment that is appropriate, formally and informally, at each section. This confirms the institutional embeddedness and institutional boundaries of spatializing enactment.

## Summary

Our analysis here includes a series of examples, where institutional vocabulary interjects with theory of space to constitute an institutional theory of space that, in turn, would interpret various spaces and locations. Additional institutional concepts could illuminate the spatiality of Jerusalem's Western

Wall. Some, such as *translation* and *diffusion*, would illuminate the processes of spatial institutionalization, deinstitutionalization and reinstitutionalization. Others, such as *loose coupling*, would describe the characteristics of spatialized institutional order. And others yet, such as *field or network*, would describe the institutional context of such space or location, while terms such as *embeddedness* would describe the relations between the spatializing institution and its context. Institutional analysis of space has much to mull on, also seeking examples of spaces and places that challenge the conceptual premises of institutionalism.

## Concluding Comments: Spatiality Between Lefebvrianism and Institutionalism

Any visitor to Jerusalem's Western Wall would be awed by security arrangements in, and all around, it: armed soldiers, security check points, surveillance cameras, and watch towers are a matter of security routines in this physical space. How, we are asked by colleagues, can institutional analysis ignore the role that state power plays in this locale, when we concentrate on spatialized logics, sensemaking and enactment? Power, and particularly the security capacities of the state, is indeed an obvious marker of control and hegemony. Institutional analysis, such as we propose here regarding the ignitable locale of this holy site in Jerusalem, diverts attention away from muscular power and towards consideration of how institutional forms and dynamics shape what people accept as legitimate or as taken for granted. Therefore, the research puzzle regarding Jerusalem's Western Wall is not the mere capacity of coercive power to shape this space, but rather the institutional processes that frame the options for the exercise of power and constitute the exercise of power as it is. In this suggestive analysis of Jerusalem's Western Wall, which we pose as a provocation for further development of a Lefebvre-inspired institutional perspective on space and spatiality, we highlight the importance of culture and institutions for the analysis of space.

Our call for institutional analyses of space is inspired by the recent turn in organizational institutionalism towards the material, visual and multimodal aspects of organization, organizations, and organizing. Such recent institutionalist turn towards materiality, visuality and multimodality, demands expanding the scope of institutional analysis of space and spatiality. Space—as a principal domain of action and enaction, rather than as mere "background" for other organizational aesthetics—deserves specific institutional attention and space needs to be integrated into institutional discussions. And, obviously, any discussion of space in organization theory would draw upon the iconic work of Lefebvre (1991) and the many critical analyses that followed in his path (see Kornberger and Clegg, 2004; Dale, 2005; Taylor and Spicer, 2007; Kingma, 2008; Wasserman and Frenkel, 2011; Wasserman, 2012). And still, as outlined in this chapter, the ontological gulf between Lefebvre and institutionalism spurs us to follow

Wasserman (2011) in proposing a research-based bridge. Without evading the ontological differences between the two theories, we propose that engagement between institutionalism and Lefebvrianism is potentially fruitful conceptually and empirically. The goal of this chapter is to relate—compare and engage—the two theoretical approaches as they refer to space. We claim that our proposed Lefebvre-inspired institutional readings of space, and our institutional analysis of the site of Jerusalem's Western Wall, serve as first steps in this direction. We suggest that accounting for spatializing aspects of institutions and institutionalization—specifically spatializing logic, spatializing sensemaking and spatializing enactment—rests upon regarding the Lefebvrian conceived-lived-perceived as *tangible* dimensions of the spatialized institution. Much work remains, obviously, to fully act upon the institutionalist impulse to seek the embodied, materialized, visualized and spatialized dimensions of institutions to create a dialogue between the two theoretical traditions as they come to analyse materiality, visuality and spatiality.

**Acknowledgement:** We thank Tammar Zilber and the editors of this compilation for their most sensible and helpful comments on earlier drafts of this manuscript.

## References

Alasuutari, P. (2015). The discursive side of new institutionalism. *Cultural Sociology, 9*(2), 162–184.
Battilana, J. and D'aunno, T. (2009). Institutional work and the paradox of embedded agency. In T. Lawrence, R. Suddaby and B. Leca (Eds.), *Institutional Work: Actors and Agency in Institutional Studies of Organizations* (pp. 31–58). Cambridge: Cambridge University Press.
Battilana, J. and Dorado, S. (2010). Building sustainable hybrid organizations: The case of commercial microfinance organizations. *Academy of Management Journal, 53*(6), 1419–1440.
Bitner, M. J. (1992). Servicescapes: The impact of physical surroundings on customers and employees. *The Journal of Marketing, 56*(2), 51–71.
Barad, K. (2003). Posthumanist Performativity: Toward an understanding of how matter comes to matter. *Journal of women in culture and society, 28*(3), 801-831.
Boxenbaum, E., Jones, C., Meyer, R. E. and Svejenova, S. (2015). The material and visual turn in organization theory: Objectifying and (re)acting to novel ideas. *Organization Studies, 36, 133-138.*
Carlile, P. R., Nicolini, D., Langley, A. and Tsoukas, H. (Eds.) (2013). *How Matter Matters: Objects, Artifacts, and Materiality in Organization Studies.* Oxford, UK: Oxford University Press.
Clegg, S. and Kornberger, M. (Eds.) (2006). *Space, Organization and Management Theory.* Copenhagen: Copenhagen Business School Press.
Cohen-Hattab, K. (2010). Struggles at holy sites and their outcomes: The evolution of the Western Wall plaza in Jerusalem. *Journal of Heritage Tourism, 5*(2), 125–139.
Crang, M. (1999). Globalization as conceived, lived and perceived spaces. *Theory, Culture & Society, 16*(1) 167–177.

Dale, K. (2005). Building a social materiality: Spatial and embodied politics in organizational control. *Organization, 12*(5), 649–678.

Dale, K. and Burrell, G. (2003). An-aesthetics and architecture. In A. Carr and P. Hancock (Eds.), *Art and Aesthetics at Work* (pp. 155–173). New York: Palgrave Macmillan.

Dale, K. and Burrell, G. (2008). *The Spaces of Organization and the Organization of Space.* New York: Palgrave Macmillan.

DiMaggio, P. J. and Powell, W. W. (1983). The iron cage revisited: Institutional isomorphism and collective rationality in organizational fields. *American Sociological Review, 48*(2), 147–160.

Drori, G. S., Delmestri, G. and Oberg, A. (2016). The iconography of universities as institutional narratives. *Higher Education, 71*(1), 163–180.

Drori, G. S. and Krücken, G. (2009). World society: A theory and research in context. In G. Krücken and G. S. Drori (Eds.), *World Society: The Writings of John W. Meyer* (pp. 1–32). Oxford, UK: Oxford University Press.

Drori, G. S., Meyer, J. W. and Hwang, H. (2009). Global organization: Rationalization and actorhood as dominant scripts. *Research in the Sociology of Organizations: Institutions and Ideology, 27,* 17–43.

Fligstein, N. and McAdam, D. (2011). Toward a general theory of strategic action fields. *Sociological theory, 29*(1), 1–26.

Freidland, R. (2009). Institution, practice, and ontology: Toward a religious sociology. *Research in the Sociology of Organizations: Institutions and Ideology, 27,* 45–83.

Greenwood, R. and Meyer, R. E. (2008). Influencing ideas: A celebration of DiMaggio and Powell (1983). *Journal of Management Inquiry, 17*(4), 258–264.

Greenwood, R. Oliver, O., Lawrence, T. and Meyer, R. E. (Eds.) (2017). *Sage Handbook of Organizational Institutionalism* (2nd ed.). Los Angeles: Sage Publications.

Greenwood, R., Oliver, C., Suddaby, R. and Sahlin-Andersson, K. (Eds.) (2008). *The Sage Handbook of Organizational Institutionalism.* Los Angeles: Sage.

Hancock, P. and Spicer, A. (2011). Academic architecture and the constitution of the new model worker. *Culture and Organization, 17*(2), 91–105.

Höllerer, M. A., Jancsary, D., Meyer, R. E. and Vettori, O. (2013). Imageries of corporate social responsibility: Visual recontextualization and field-level meaning. *Research in the Sociology of Organizations: Institutional Logics in Action, 39*(b), 139–174.

Höllerer, M. A., Walgenbach, P. and Drori, G. S. (2017). Consequences of globalization for organizations and institutions. In R. Greenwood, C. Oliver, T. Lawrence and R. E. Meyer (Eds.), *The Sage Handbook of Organizational Institutionalism* (2nd ed.). Los Angeles: Sage Publications.

Jones, C., Boxenbaum, E. and Anthony, C. (2013). The immateriality of material practices in institutional logics. *Research in the Sociology of Organizations: Institutional Logics in Action, 39*(A), 51–75.

Jones, C., Maoret, M., Massa, F. G. and Svejenova, S. (2012). Rebels with a cause: Formation, contestation, and expansion of the de novo category 'modern architecture,' 1870–1975. *Organization Science, 23*(6), 1523–1545.

Jones, C. and Massa, F. G. (2013). From novel practice to consecrated exemplar: Unity temple as a case of institutional evangelizing, *Organization Studies 34*(8), 1099–1136.

Jones, C., Meyer, R. E., Jancsary, D. and Höllerer, M. A. (2017). The material and visual basis of institutions. In R. Greenwood, C. Oliver, T. Lawrence and R. E. Meyer (Eds.), *The Sage Handbook of Organizational Institutionalism* (2nd ed.). Los Angeles: Sage Publications.

Kellogg, K. C. (2009). Operating room. Relational spaces and microinstitutional change in surgery. *American Journal of Sociology*, *115*(3), 657–711.

Kennedy, M. T. and Fiss, P. C. (2013). An ontological turn in categories research: From standards of legitimacy to evidence of actuality. *Journal of Management Studies*, *50*(6), 1138–1154.

Kingma, S. F. (2008). Dutch casino space or the spatial organization of entertainment. *Culture and Organization*, *14*(1), 31–48.

Kornberger, M. and Clegg, S. (2004). Bringing space back in. *Organization Studies*, *25*(7), 1095–1114.

Lawrence, T. B., Leca, B. and Zilber, T. B. (2013). Institutional work: Current research, new directions and overlooked issues. *Organization Studies*, *34*(8), 1023–1033.

Lawrence, T. B. and Suddaby, R. (2006). Institutions and institutional work. In S. R. Clegg, C. Hardy, T. B. Lawrence and W. R. Nord (Eds.), *The Sage Handbook of Organizational Studies* (2nd ed., pp. 215–282). London: Sage.

Lawrence, T. B., Suddaby, R. and Leca, B. (2009). *Institutional Work: Actors and Agency in Institutional Studies of Organizations*. Cambridge, UK: Cambridge University Press.

Lefebvre, H. (1991). *The Production of Space*. Oxford: Blackwell.

Leonardi, P. M., Nardi, B. A. and Kalinikos, J. Eds. (2012). *Materiality and Organizing: Social Interaction in a Technological World*. Oxford, UK: Oxford University Press.

Lounsbury, M. (2007). A tale of two cities: Competing logics and practice variation in the professionalizing of mutual funds. *Academy of Management Journal*, *50*(2), 289–307.

Löw, M. (2016). *The Sociology of Space: Materiality, Social Structures, and Action*. New York: Palgrave Macmillan.

Maitlis, S. and Christianson, M. (2014). Sensemaking in organizations: Taking stock and moving forward. *The Academy of Management Annals*, *8*(1), 57–125.

Meyer, J. W. (2010). World society, institutional theories, and the actor. *Annual Review of Sociology*, *36*, 1–20.

Meyer, J. W. and Jepperson, R. L. (2000). The 'actors' of modern society: The cultural construction of social agency. *Sociological Theory*, *18*(1), 100–120.

Meyer, J. W. and Rowan, B. (1977). Institutionalized organizations: Formal structure as myth and ceremony. *American Journal of Sociology*, *83*(2), 340–363.

Meyer, R. E., Höllerer, M. A., Jancsary, D. and Van Leeuwen, T. (2013). The visual dimension in organizing, organization, and organization research: Core ideas, current developments, and promising avenues. *The Academy of Management Annals*, *7*(1), 489–555.

Navis, C. and Glynn, M. A. (2010). How new market categories emerge: Temporal dynamics of legitimacy, identity, and entrepreneurship in satellite radio, 1990–2005. *Administrative Science Quarterly*, *55*(3), 439–471.

Orlikowski, W. J. and Scott, S. V. (2008). Sociomateriality: Challenging the separation of technology, work and organization. *Academy of Management Annals*, *2*(1), 433-474.

Pache, A. C. and Santos, F. (2013). Inside the hybrid organization: Selective coupling as a response to competing institutional logics. *Academy of Management Journal*, *56*(4), 972–1001.

Petani, F. J. and Mengis, J. (2016). In search of lost space: The process of space planning through remembering and history. *Organization*, *23*(1), 71–89.

Peltonen, T. (2011). Multiple architectures and the production of organizational space in a Finnish university. *Journal of Organizational Change Management*, 24(6), 806–821.

Pfeffer, J. (1981). *Power in organizations*. Pitman, Marshfield, MA.

Powell, W. W. and Colyvas, J. A. (2008). Microfoundations of institutional theory. In R. Greenwood, C. Oliver, K. Sahlin and R. Suddaby (Eds.), *The Sage Handbook of Organizational Institutionalism* (pp. 276–298). Los Angeles: Sage.

Pratt, M. G. and Rafaeli, A. (1997). Organizational dress as a symbol of multilayered social identities. *Academy of Management Journal*, 40(4), 862–898.

Preminger, B. and Drori, G. S. (2016). How institutions get materialized in space: 'Spatialized logics' along Jerusalem's Western Wall. In J. Gehman, M. Lounsbury and R. Greenwood (Eds.), *Research in the Sociology of Organizations: How Institutions Matter?*, 48(A), 101–136.

Rabinowitz, S. (2009). *The Western Wall: Laws and Customs*. Jerusalem: The Western Wall Heritage Foundation.

Rao, H., Monin, P. and Durand, R. (2003). Institutional change in Tocque Ville: Nouvelle cuisine as an identity movement in French gastronomy. *American Journal of Sociology*, 108(4), 795–843.

Reay, T. and Hinings, C. R. (2009). Managing the rivalry of competing institutional logics. *Organization Studies*, 30(6), 629–652.

Scott, W. R. (1987). The adolescence of institutional theory. *Administrative Science Quarterly*, 32(4), 493–511.

Scott, W. R. (2008). Approaching adulthood: The maturing of institutional theory. *Theory and Society*, 37(5), 427–442.

Scott, W. R. (2014). *Institutions and Organizations: Ideas, Interests and Identities* (4th ed.). Los Angeles: Sage.

Scott, W. R. and Meyer, J. W. (1994). *Institutional Environments and Organizations: Structural Complexity and Individualism*. California: Sage.

Strang, D. and Meyer, J. W. (1993). Institutional conditions for diffusion. *Theory and Society*, 22(4), 487–511.

Strang, D. and Soule, S. (1998). Diffusion in organizations and social movements: From hybrid corn to poison pills. *Annual Review of Sociology*, 41, 265–290.

Suddaby, R. (2010). Challenges for institutional theory. *Journal of Management Inquiry*, 19(1), 14–20.

Suddaby, R. (2015). Can institutional theory be critical? *Journal of Management Inquiry*, 24(1), 93–95.

Taylor, S. and Spicer, A. (2007). Time for space: A narrative review of research on organizational spaces. *International Journal of Management Reviews*, 9(4), 325–346.

Thornton, P. H. and Ocasio, W. (1999). Institutional logics and the historical contingency of power in organizations: Executive succession in the higher education publishing industry, 1958–1990. *American Journal of Sociology*, 105(3), 801–843.

Thornton, P. H., Ocasio, W. and Lounsbury, M. (2012). *The Institutional Logics Perspective: A New Approach to Culture, Structure and Process*. Oxford, UK: Oxford University Press.

Tyler, M. and Cohen, L. (2010). Spaces that matter: Gender performativity and organizational space. *Organization Studies*, 31(2), 175–198.

de Vaujany, F. X. and Mitev, N. (2013). Introduction: Space in organizations and sociomateriality. In N. Mitev and F. X. de Vaujany (Eds.), *Materiality and Space: Organizations, Artefacts and Practices* (pp. 1–21). London: Palgrave Macmillan.

de Vaujany, F. X. and Mitev, N. (2015). The post-Macy paradox, information management and organising: Good intentions and a road to hell? *Culture and Organization, 21*(5), 1–29.

de Vaujany, F. X. and Vaast, E. (2014). If these walls could talk: The mutual construction of organizational space and legitimacy. *Organization Science, 25*(3), 713–731.

de Vaujany, F. X. and Vaast, E. (2016). Matters of visuality in legitimation practices: Dual iconographies in a meeting room. *Organization, 23*(5), 763–790.

Wasserman, V. (2011). To be (alike) or not to be (at all): Aesthetic isomorphism in organizational spaces. *International Journal of Work Organisation and Emotion, 4*(1), 22–41.

Wasserman, V. (2012). Open spaces, closed boundaries: Transparent workspaces as clerical female ghettos. *International Journal of Work Organisation and Emotion, 5*(1), 6–25.

Wasserman, V. and Frenkel, M. (2011). Organizational aesthetics: Caught between identity regulation and culture jamming. *Organization Science, 22*(2), 503–521.

Wasserman, V. and Frenkel, M. (2015). Spatial work in between glass ceilings and glass walls: Gender-class intersectionality and organizational aesthetics. *Organization Studies, 36*(11), 1485–1505.

Watkins, C. (2005). Representations of space, spatial practices and spaces of representation: An application of Lefebvre's spatial triad. *Culture and Organization, 11*(3), 209–220.

Weber, K. and Glynn, A.N (2006). Making sense with institutions: Context, thought and action in Karl Weick's theory, *Organization Studies, 27*(1), 1639–1660.

Weick, K. E., Sutcliffe, K. M. and Obstfeld, D. (2005). Organizing and the process of sensemaking. *Organization Science, 16*(4), 409–421.

Willmott, H. (2015). Why institutional theory cannot be critical. *Journal of Management Inquiry, 24*(1), 105–111.

Zhang, Z. and Spicer, A. (2013). 'Leader, you first': The everyday production of hierarchical space in a Chinese bureaucracy. *Human Relations, 67*(6), 739–762.

Zilber, T. B. (2007). Stories and the discursive dynamics of institutional entrepreneurship: The case of Israeli high-tech after the bubble. *Organization Studies, 28*(7), 1035–1054.

Zucker, L. G. (1977). The role of institutionalization in cultural persistence. *American Journal of Sociology 42*(5), 726–743

Part II

# Spaces of Organization— Everyday Work Life, Embodiment, Rhythms, Boundaries

# 6 Managing Tensions in an English Cathedral—An Embodied Spatial Perspective

*Sarah Warnes*

## Introduction

> *It's a Christian foundation which finds itself more and more involved in the commercial world, and having to think commercially to exist.*
>
> (Shop Manager, St Michael's Cathedral)

In this chapter, I share with readers my experiences of spending time with the employees and volunteers at St Michael's Cathedral (a pseudonym), a small cathedral in England. Ecclesiastical organizations such as cathedrals and churches are hitherto underexplored in the organization space literature and yet they provide a compelling site for exploration. Providing the conceptual framework underpinning the chapter is Henri Lefebvre's (1974/1991: 196) notion of the 'spatial body' where space and body are "intertwined in mutually constitutive ways that need to be engaged jointly." The body to which Lefebvre conceptualizes is a "total body" (Lefebvre, 1974/1991: 200), made up of its mental abstracts, movements and gestures capable of infusing prescribed space with a different space, a lived space. To gain a deeper, more holistic understanding of the lived experience of space a phenomenological approach is required. An approach which shifts from a representational understanding of workspace toward an experiential understanding. For before we start thinking and representing our spaces of work we embody them, we perceive them through the rhythms of our body which sees, hears, touches, smells and feels. As Lefebvre notes, we listen first to our body where we "learn rhythm from it, in order consequently to appreciate external rhythms" (1992/2004: 19). It is through our bodies that we are able to sense the rhythms of the workspaces we inhabit (Edensor and Holloway, 2008). The organizational space literature does contribute to our understanding of the lived experience of space through an experiential lens, but lacks a focus on the rhythms of the body. To begin to address this lacuna I suggest that it is worthwhile paying greater attention to bodily actions in the context of how, through an embodied spatiality taking into account the 'total body' (Lefebvre, 1974/1991), competing value claims are being managed within such organizations as cathedrals.

The contributions to the extant organizational space literature that this chapter makes are threefold. The first contribution draws on Lefebvre's ideas concerning Rhythmanalysis. Currently, rhythmanalysis has not been widely explored in the organizational space literature, for exceptions see Beyes and Steyaert's (2012) work which explores a performative approach to spatial understanding; Toyoki, Spicer and Elliot's (2006) work who use the concept of rhythms as a way of understanding the social reproduction of organizations and Verduyn (2015: 641) who applies the concept of rhythm-analysis to the process of entrepreneuring. I argue that there is value to the spatial study of organizations in considering Lefebvre's work on rhythm-analysis in terms of its role in furthering our understanding of the embodiment of space. For from this perspective, we can learn how organizational members are managing organizational pressures, reconciling organizational value clashes and resisting organizational change through the rhythms of their body.

The second contribution, linking to the first, builds on the body of knowledge which explores an embodied spatiality. That is literature which has moved on from focusing on calculable, external space to the complexities and tensions of the embodied lived experience of space (Beyes and Steyaert, 2011; Dale, 2005; Dale and Burrell, 2010; Halford, 2004; Kim and de Dear, 2013; Petani and Mengis, 2016; Wapshott and Mallett, 2012; Wasserman and Frenkel, 2010; Wasserman and Frenkel, 2015; Watkins, 2005; Zhang, Spicer, and Hancock, 2008). This body of literature contends that exploring bodily lived experience is a key means to understanding organizational space. Dale (2005), for example, draws on Lefebvre, shedding light on how organizational control operates through gestures, movements and the "ways of engaging our bodies with a certain materiality" (Dale, 2005: 657). In an organizational context, embodied spatiality has been explored in a number of ways, for example, the materialization of gender in the workplace (Tyler and Cohen, 2010; Wasserman and Frenkel, 2015); the spatial embodiment of sexuality (Riach and Wilson, 2014); the lived and embodied experience of working in sex shops (Tyler, 2011); the embodied dimension of organizational culture (Flores-Pereira, Davel, and Cavedon, 2008); ethics and embodiment (Dale and Latham, 2015; Pullen and Rhodes, 2015); embodied leadership (Bathurst and Cain, 2013); organizational gestures (Bazin, 2013) and organizational wellness (Dale and Burrell, 2014). Whilst research conducted within this embodied spatial perspective has increased, there remains an aspect that warrants further exploration. That is research which examines an embodied spatiality, with a particular focus on the way competing value claims are being managed through the conceptual notions of dwelling (Shortt, 2015) and dressage (Lefebvre, 1992/2004), that is, through bodily actions and the rhythms of the body.

The third and final contribution presents my interpretations based on empirical research, of the idea of cathedrals as organizations. Typically, cathedrals are studied from a theological perspective (Cameron et al., 2005;

Hopewell, 1987), from an architectural perspective, namely the cathedral building and its sacred symbols (Maddison, 2000) and on the cathedral as a tourist destination (Francis, Mansfield, and Village, 2010; Gutic, Caie, and Clegg, 2010; Shackley, 2001, 2002; Voase, 2007). These studies do not focus on the everyday lives of those moving through the spaces of the organization and do not explore how value clashes are being negotiated and contested through the embodiment of space. In taking the idea of the cathedral as an organization, we can learn how tensions in organizations more broadly are being managed by the employees who inhabit a workspace. These three contributions support the main arguments of this chapter, which is to explain how, through an embodied spatiality, focussing on the rhythms of the body, the tensions associated in dealing with conflicting organizational value claims, are being managed through the body entwined with organizational space.

Following this introduction, the chapter presents the literature pertaining to the lived experience of space, which specifically draws on an embodied spatial view providing important links with Lefebvre's spatial concepts. The methodology of Gadamer's (1975/2004) hermeneutic phenomenology and the research site are then presented, followed by the methods of data collection and analysis. The chapter then continues with the presentation of the empirical findings, which are situated within the theoretical concepts of Dwelling and Dressage. The chapter closes with a discussion of the ways that the three contributions outlined in the introduction are realized in the empirical findings.

## Conceptualizations of Space

A key reason for adopting a Lefebvrian analysis in this chapter is Lefebvre's (1974/1991) clear epistemology of space and the body. This epistemology sees space not as a fixed, stable, homogeneous entity which is external to the body, but instead sees space as fluid, irrational, dynamic and importantly entwined with the body. In the context of organizational space and in agreement with Lefebvre, there has to be a rejection of a "Cartesian split between mind and body" (Dale, 2001: 11). The idea of the body as an object needs to be replaced with "the body as experience" (Flores-Pereira, Davel, and Cavedon, 2008: 1011). From this perspective, there is no knowing outside of the body; we come to know the world through our body and its movements. For Lefebvre (1974/1991: 201), this is how space is produced, through the "body of space." In order to gain an understanding of the embodied lived experience, the body in terms of its perceptions, senses and its movements must be considered as *of* space or *through* space, as opposed to *in* space.

Scholars seeking to conceptualize the lived experience of organizational space based on a Lefebvrian epistemology, include Dale and Latham (2015); Tyler and Cohen (2010); Wapshott and Mallett (2012), all of whom recognize that in order to understand space as lived we must start from the body, as, following Lefebvre (1974/1991: 405), "the whole of space proceeds from the body." As such, conceptualizations of lived space necessarily imply an embodied dimension. Studies of organizational space from this experiential perspective explore the ways in which organizational space is being socially produced through the embodied actions of individuals. It is the space of human agency, where embodied experience has the potential to alter conceived or planned space (Lefebvre, 1974/1991) and is where "alternative imaginations of space" (Simonsen, 2005: 7) arise. Whilst workspace is imposed upon us by the organization, the literature here shows that employees seek to recreate the space, so that space "is at once a becoming of expression, and a becoming of our being" (Bachelard, 1964/1994: xxiii). Simply put, space becomes an expression of who we are, and we become an expression of the space we inhabit. These forms of expression emerge through the different ways that individuals seek to inhabit their workspace. For example, artefacts are being used by employees as a way to 'manage' workspace as opposed to being managed by their workspace. Imposed organizational space is challenged and an alternative space emerges, which takes on new meanings and which represents a spatial form of spatial ownership.

Through the appropriation of space, individuals are able to seek ownership of their workspace, assert their identity and reconcile organizational tensions, such as the feeling of 'alienation' or of being forgotten. Although the meaning of artefacts is often discussed in the organizational space literature, interestingly, artefacts have not been discussed in relation to liminal organizational space. In organization space studies, liminal space and liminality are typically studied from two differing perspectives. For example, Czarniawska and Mazza (2003), Garsten (1999) and Sturdy, Schwarz, and Spicer's (2006) study applies the concept of liminality on people who are temporarily part of an organization, for example, consultants. Providing an alternative view is where liminal space is considered as the forgotten and taken for granted spaces of the organization. Such spaces are often cited as cupboards, doorways, 'secluded corners', toilets, backrooms and stairwells (Iedema, Long, and Carroll, 2010; Shortt, 2015). These studies of liminal space do not consider how personal artefacts can play a role in 'crafting' moments of liminality or respite from daily work pressures. Analysing artefacts from this perspective is of particular interest, for I consider that they have a role in producing liminal states of being within organizational space. This space does not have to exist amongst the previously mentioned forgotten spaces of the organization; it can appear in the ordinary space of work, for example, in the office. Liminal space considered alongside artefacts and the feelings they evoke provides a view of organizational space which accounts for how individuals need more than a functional space for work. They need a space where they can dwell, a space where they have a sense of belonging.

The applications of Lefebvre's (1974/1991) spatial concepts in organizational space studies provide a significant body of literature. The most drawn upon is his spatial triad; Conceived Space (representations of space), Perceived Space (spatial practice) and Lived Space (representational space). Whilst this body of work contributes significantly to our understanding of the lived experience of space, it highlights a lacuna in the literature. This lacuna pertains to a lack of focus on understanding the habits and routines of the body as it moves through and coexists with space. To illustrate this lacuna, we can say that existing literature commonly applies the triad to explore aspects of power, including the controlling and ordering of employees placed within particular organizational spaces. In such works, instead of interpreting the meaning of embodied behaviours through the lived experiences of the employees, the focus is from the point of view of an observer looking in and reporting on spatial behaviours. For example, in Hancock and Spicer's (2011) study of the Saltire Centre, observed were the outcomes of the spatial ordering by designers and managers who sought to dictate desired behaviours in the centre. The different floors of the centre were designed in order to elicit expected spatial practices. As in Peltonen's (2011) study, there was resistance to this enforced ordering by students who wilfully contested the spatial design, with the researchers observing "students sleeping on beanbags . . . and instances of students using . . . hairstraighteners and razors at the table power points" (Hancock and Spicer, 2011: 103). These observations recognized that spaces are interpreted differently by users who become the "unofficial architects of space" (Hernes, 2004: 67). These 'unofficial architects' through their embodiment of space, produce a different space to the one imposed upon by the organization. It is understanding and interpreting this embodiment through the rhythms of the body, that present the previously referred to lacuna in the literature. A lacuna which can be filled through Lefebvre's work on Rhythmanalysis entwined with the spatial triad, a coupling hitherto underexplored in the study of organizational space.

In his text *Rhythmanalysis*, Lefebvre presents two types of rhythms linear and natural. The linear rhythms impose themselves on the body and stem "from human activity: the monotony of actions and of movements, imposed structures" (1992/2004: 8). Lefebvre here is referring to the repetitive and routine nature of daily life, where actions are repeated day in and day out. These actions in an organizational context are often structured by imposed external factors. For example, work schedules and the following of stipulated procedures in stipulated workspaces are all deemed necessary in order to comply with organizational rules. These rhythms align with clock time, are quantitative in character and represent the imposed order which measures everyday life at work. Lefebvre and Régulier (1986: 73) consider these rhythms to be a "desacralisation" of time, a kind of disenchantment where any form of pleasure or spontaneity experienced in daily life has been sacrificed through a twenty-four-seven focus on work. However, this is not the only time, nor the only rhythms we experience, for they are in constant contact with "what is least rational in human being: the lived, the carnal, the body" (Lefebvre, 1992/2004: 9): namely, the natural rhythms of the body as irrational and full of personal expression. Natural rhythms produce a certain kind of organizational space, a lived embodied, unpredictable space, which at times can display a "victory . . . over the linear, integrating it without destroying it" (Lefebvre, 1981/2008: 131). Linear and natural rhythms cannot be separated; they intermesh in everyday life. They are "multiple interrelated rhythms, functioning independently, but influencing each other" (Verduyn, 2015: 641).

We can link Lefebvre's rhythmanalysis to his spatial triad, and do so through the empirical data presented later in the chapter. This data shows and explains how lived and perceived space contests and disorders conceived space through bodily action and rhythm, where natural rhythms seek 'victory' over the imposed and linear rhythms of the organization. Through the fieldwork conducted in the cathedral, the spatial triad is taken from its abstract form to something that is dynamic and real. This is achieved through observing and questioning the embodied actions of the employees as they move within the conceived, perceived and lived space. I claim that the triad along with the rhythms of the body, provide a conceptual framework which enables an understanding and interpretation of the ways in which value clashes are being managed through the daily experiences of the employees at St Michael's Cathedral.

## Methodology

Empirical studies of the lived experience of organizational space most commonly adopt a qualitative based analysis. The research undertaken for this chapter is no exception and brings together phenomenology (lived experience) with Gadamer's (1975/2004) hermeneutics (interpretation). This was considered most suitable for the aim was "to understand an experience as it is understood by those who are having it" (Cohen, Kahn, and Steeves, 2000: 3). For Gadamer, understanding the experience requires a temporal focus in that experience is influenced by both the past and the present. Aligned with this, Lefebvre (1974/1991: 48) states that the history of a space forms "the basis of representational spaces [lived space]." Therefore, the temporal aspect of the embodied experience of space cannot be ignored, for we are at once situated in both present and past time, where past traditions join with and make up the lived experience in the present. At the heart of Gadamer's hermeneutics is the art of conversation, and his approach to data analysis provides the 'tools' to interpret the lived experience, for example, through his notion of the hermeneutic conversation. For Gadamer, conversation and its analysis thereof is about language. For Lefebvre (1974/1991), language must include not only words, but also the interpretation of the 'total body' experience, including its mental abstracts, movements and feelings. Drawing together both Gadamer and Lefebvre's conceptualizations enables an embodied interpretation of the lived experience which considers the impact of both the past and the present in its analysis.

## The Research Context

To situate the cathedral in a wider context, it is important to understand the current challenges and tensions that this sector is having to manage. The last report published by the Archbishop Council (2014) shows that, over the last ten years, cathedrals have seen a steady rise in visitor numbers, which have increased from 9.7 million in 2012 to 10.2 million in 2013 (Ibid.). Two reasons are given for these growing numbers. The first rests in the nature of worship, where a more individualized practice of worship is desired, one not characterized by the communal experience of a tightly knit local parish church. The second reason is the versatility afforded by the size of the cathedral, allowing for a welcome that embraces and extends to those beyond worshippers. In acknowledgement of the different purposes that cathedrals serve today, research into the contemporary use of the cathedral was commissioned on behalf of the Association of English Cathedrals and the Foundation for Church Leadership. The research published by Theos (2012) entitled 'Spiritual Capital' reported a key finding: the tension between managing the pilgrims' expectations and the expectations of the tourists. The root of the tension can be found in the popularity of the cathedral, which according to Engel (2011) can be explained as follows:

> Cathedrals are especially popular, with good reason. And their services have actually become more popular in recent years—why go to the local am-dram if you have the ecclesiastical equivalent of West End theatre only a short drive away?

Engel strikingly likens the cathedral to a London West End production, which brings forth associations of entertainment, a spectacular staging, and marketization. Such framings of the cathedral highlight its juxtaposition of being a place of worship and a place of cultural interest. This co-existence of two different purposes and experiences in one space reinforces a perceived dualism which characterizes the contemporary cathedral. Whilst there has been a rise in visitor numbers, the cost of running cathedrals is high. For example, it costs some £60,000 per week to run Durham Cathedral and the average donation is only 32p per visitor (Kasprzak, 2012). This has meant that the raising of income levels through enterprise activities is now a fixed feature of the management of cathedrals. Indications of how cathedrals are responding to this demand can be seen in the news media. For example, on the Church of England vacancy page, with a closing day of May 24 2018, there is an advert for a Finance Director for the Diocese of Winchester and Portsmouth with a salary of £62,000—£64,000. The advert states the

Diocese want to recruit a "strong leader with a proven track record of change management and strategic financial planning" (The Church of England 2018). Here we are seeing a 'professionalization' of cathedrals.

Modernization programmes are taking place within broader economic and social contexts, which affect the management of the organization and drive the need for change. For example, visitors now expect to have such facilities as lavatories, a shop and a refectory, satisfying the needs of consumption. In conjunction with managing the expectations of its different visitors, cathedrals are also faced with the challenge of negotiating a path between innovation and tradition. The sacred space of the cathedral is increasingly being used in commercially orientated ways, for example, Christ Church Cathedral in Oxford was used as a location for the Harry Potter films and Ely Cathedral, an established filming and recording venue, for the production of the Netflix drama *The Crown*. These, along with general events such as art exhibitions, concerts and dinners, all contribute to generating much needed income. Innovation in the form of technology is increasingly being used in cathedrals. Most cathedral websites now offer Twitter, Facebook and news feeds. Other technology-driven initiatives is the use of touchscreen multimedia tours at St Paul's Cathedral and online shops. Such practices do not only furnish the traditional cathedral space with modern technology, but also serve to extend the cathedral space into virtual space.

The changes in the cathedral sector, which sees cathedrals increasingly having to be managed in a commercial way, can be clearly seen at the research site—St Michael's Cathedral. Here we are able to see the co-existence of the sacred and the commercial through the organization's structure. At the most senior level sits the Dean of the cathedral with line management responsibility for the Cathedral Administrator; the Canon Precentor responsible for worship, liturgy (the order and performance of services) and music; the Canon Pastor responsible for the pastoral care of the congregation, visitors and wider community; the Canon Curate responsible for theological education, and the Cathedral Chaplain. The organization has seven departments, each led by a manager who oversees their teams. Managerial positions include the Finance Manager; the Public Relations Manager; the Refectory Manager; the Shop Manager; the Education Officer, the Head Verger responsible for preparing the cathedral for service and an IT Manager. In the managers' titles we see typical organizational roles which point to a division between the sacred and the secular. For example, the Refectory Manager, Shop Manager and Finance Manager are roles with a greater commercial orientation than the Education Officer and Head Verger who share a greater focus in upholding the sacred values of the organization. In order to manage the commercial side of the organization, 'St Michael's Cathedral Enterprise Ltd' was set up in 1973. Today the enterprise comprises a board of volunteer members from local businesses, who advise and support the cathedral's commercial operations, for example, the shop and the refectory. These enterprises are significant income generators for the organization and are as such treated as economic units in terms of having to manage budgets and meet financial targets. All are charged a rental fee and administration costs by the Cathedral Chapter. There are four full-time Clergy, nine lay staff who are full-time and sixteen part-time lay staff. In addition to these paid staff there are approximately 250 volunteers (figures confirmed 11th July 2014). This large number of volunteers is typical of cathedrals, which rely on volunteers to ensure that the organization can serve all of its visitors, sacred and secular, every day of the year. The hierarchical structure of the organization and the key roles within it, point to an organization which is attempting to manage competing value claims. These claims are associated with having to meet the commercial needs of the organization, the sacred needs and expectations of the pilgrim and the secular needs and expectations of the tourist. In addition, it has to manage a team of employees who have different understandings of the organization. What became clear during the fieldwork was a perceived separation between the cathedral as sacred and the organization as secular. These differences in perception exemplified key tensions associated with the inevitable bringing together of the sacred and the secular and it is this that presents the organization's problematic—its value clashes. These clashes are caused by the differing needs and demands of its key stakeholders driven by the commercial pressures facing the organization. These contrasting needs inevitably lead to tensions which are present due to the particular expectations of the organization, which in this case are overtly based on Christianity. Without the secular activities of, for example, ticket sales from concerts hosted in the cathedral, along with the purchases being made in the cathedral shop and refectory, the longevity of the cathedral is at risk. It is the income generated from these commercial enterprises which are contributing significantly to the running of the cathedral. From this perspective, the secular actually upholds the sacred. What is having to happen is a reconciliation of the fact that the secular is becoming as equally important as the sacred.

## Data Collection

The fieldwork at St Michael's Cathedral took place between June 2011 and October 2011. A focal point of the research was to observe the routine and mundane aspects of the everyday organizational lives of the employees of the cathedral, as they moved through their workspaces. Following the interpretive nature of the research, the sample was selected purposively. The level of detail required in order to understand individual lived experiences meant that, intentionally, the research sample was small, considered to be typical of hermeneutic phenomenological research (Symon and Cassell, 2012). The ten employees making up the sample represented a cross-section of departments and roles: the Refectory Manager; the Education Officer and Administrator; the Public Relations Manager; the Canon Pastor; the IT Manager and the Shop Manager. Completing the sample were three volunteers who represented the cathedral flowers, the cathedral tour guides, and a retired chaplain.

The first phase of data collection was observation through shadowing, considered to be a suitable way to understand and represent employees' embodied experience of organizational space. Through the process of shadowing, rhythmanalysis is made possible, for, as Lefebvre (1992/2004: 27) states, for those wishing to analyse rhythms there is a need to "situate oneself simultaneously inside and outside." In other words, instead of immersing oneself in the field carrying out the same tasks as the employee, rhythmanalysis researchers need to observe from a point of distance. This allows a level of objectivity enabling researchers to become aware of the different aspects of rhythms, such as sounds, repetition, habits and pace, along with how these respond to one another through the actions of the body. Some distance enables researchers to observe, for example, the way the pressures of deadlines increase pace and reduce the sounds of chatter, or a spontaneous encounter with a colleague, slows the rhythms of the body down and increases the sounds of chatter. Whilst we need a level of exteriority when analysing rhythms, at the same time, there has to be closeness whereby we can be *grasped* (ibid.) by the rhythm, where we can, as far as is possible, experience the rhythms others are experiencing as they embody workspace. Each employee was shadowed across three working days, spanning a seven-day week. Detailed fieldnotes were taken of everything observed, and whilst acknowledging that it is not possible to observe 'everything', it enabled an exploration into the employees' "role in, and paths through the organization" (McDonald, 2005: 457). The detailed fieldnotes were transcribed and shared with each employee. This was part of the methodological process of joint interpretation. In being given the transcripts, they had the opportunity to re-acquaint themselves with their daily habits and routines.

The second chosen research method was photo-elicitation, whereby employees were given a simple brief to take photographs of spaces in the organization which were significant to them. This method is complementary to shadowing, as it puts the participant in control of the data being produced. Participant-led photography followed by conversation "provides a direct entry into [the participant's] point of view" (Radley and Taylor, 2003: 79). This helps to ensure that the photograph is the participant's representation as opposed to the researcher's representation. When discussing the taken photographs, the employees' narratives extended beyond the visual representation, suggesting that the "intention behind taking the photograph may be more relevant to the research than the actual product" (Barker and Smith, 2012: 94). Whilst the visual image alone cannot be said to represent the 'reality' of experience, when interpreted alongside our conversations, the photograph does and did provide a way of accessing embodied experience.

The third and final phase of the research was the hermeneutic-based conversations. Like shadowing and the use of photographs, conversations provide an opportunity for the researcher to "enter the participant's life-world" (Smith, Flowers, and Larkin, 2009: 58). The conversations focused on the transcribed fieldnotes and the employees' taken photographs. When constructing how these conversations would evolve, a two-way flow of communication following a conversation style was essential. The key aim of the conversation was to co-construct the interpretation of the transcribed fieldnotes and the taken photographs until consensus in terms of what represented a momentary truth of the embodied experience emerged.

*Data Analysis*

By the end of the fieldwork, the data corpus comprised of fieldnotes totalling 182 pages of typed text and 105,709 words. A total of ninety-six photographs had been taken and ten hours of conversation were recorded. In line with the taken methodology, the approach for analysing the field data followed elements of Interpretive Phenomenological Analysis (IPA). Typical of IPA, once fieldnotes for each employee had been typed, they were read and re-read as a way of re-immersing oneself with the original data (Smith, Flowers, and Larkin, 2009). Through the reading and re-reading of fieldnotes, coding the data followed a manual process advised by Saldaña (2009), of first, second and third cycle coding. Away from the field, the photographs were analysed following a similar coding process. The conversations taking place in the field were later subjected to formal analysis, following the same process of coding. The conversations were recorded and transcribed and later re-listened to alongside the fieldnotes and photographs, providing further interpretive analysis. Each phase of the research represented a different aspect of the employees' embodied experience. This was a form of data triangulation which, when viewed in its totality, led to the identification of a number of themes centred on dwelling and movement. These conceptual themes provided a way of understanding the embodied experiences of workspace and are discussed in greater detail in the following section of this chapter.

## Active Bodies at Work

This section of the chapter presents some of the findings taken from the fieldwork in St Michael's Cathedral. The theoretical notions of dwelling and dressage provide the lens through which the findings are presented. The presented data and accompanying discussion show that the 'total body' (Lefebvre, 1974/1991) entwined with space, emerges as the agent which manages the competing value claims taking place within the organization.

Dwelling in the context of this chapter is considered as a concept which can be used to explain how employees seek to belong in their place of work. The theoretical heritage which the concept of dwelling acknowledges is Heidegger's (1971) perspective according to which, dwelling is considered as centred on our very being. It is a key feature of human existence: "to be a human being means to be on the earth as a mortal, it means to *dwell*" (Heidegger, 1971: 147, my emphasis). Dwelling, then, is considered as a mode of being; a spatial expression of 'feeling at home' in one's immediate workspace. Dwelling, then, is more than an occupation of space, it is a representation of the way we are, a representation of being in the world. What this means is described well by (Ingold, 1995: 76), who says that "the forms people build, whether in the imagination or on the ground, arise within the current of their involved activity, in the specific relational contexts of their practical engagements with their surroundings." Our being is thus intertwined with the 'forms' that we build. To dwell is born from a subjective knowing and an embodied engagement with a given space. Making workspace a dwelling necessitates the undertaking of labour and in the following empirical examples we see the crafting of dwellings within the workspaces of the cathedral.

## Dwelling at Work

Two participants are presented, first Valerie, the Administrator to the Education Officer, responsible primarily for helping to co-ordinate educational events both inside and outside of the cathedral. Valerie's narrative revealed that her immediate workspace was a space she had appropriated in order to be able to dwell and escape the pressures of work. Our conversation began with Valerie talking me through the artefacts she had placed in and around her desk area:

> Right, okay this one on the computer screen [she points, Figure 6.1], this one is a labyrinth . . . and when I go on retreat, I go to a place called St Beunos in North Wales and they have a copy of this labyrinth that I walk, it's a big one in the grounds. . . . It is here [at work], because I do find myself getting really, really pressured and under pressure a lot.
>   It is supposed to be there to help me think about it [laughs] and I don't know whether you noticed but at something like 12.45 everyday a little reminder will pop up on my screen that will say take a labyrinth break. What I'm then supposed to do and what I decided would be good for me, would be to take 10 minutes to actually, with my finger, walk the labyrinth. I came back in February and set that up and now it is September and I've not done it yet.
>   *Why?*
>   Because I've always been in the middle of something that I've felt I couldn't leave. So that is interesting that I can't somehow make myself do it, it doesn't work in this environment. But having it there reminds me, and this image here, yeah, this image [points at the PC screen-saver], that is where I sit when I'm on retreat; I'm looking out across the valley there to North Wales.

*Figure 6.1* Computer screen and artefacts.
Picture by author.

Valerie's narration of the paper copy of the labyrinth at a well-known place of pilgrimage, and the image taken at her annual retreat, which she had set as her screen-saver, is set in the context of work pressures. Her narrative can be examined through the notion of rhythm, more specifically the juxtaposition of Lefebvre's (1992/2004) different rhythms, linear and natural. While organizational pressure can be understood as an intensification of the imposed linear rhythms required of the body to meet required deadlines, the alternative more natural bodily rhythm is a slower pace, here symbolized through the labyrinth and image of the retreat. Through these artefacts the body can, as it needs, seek respite from the pressures of the daily grind. This deliberate placement of pictures enables Valerie to create lived space by bringing the rhythms of the retreat into her office.

Following a similar theme, Valerie explained the paintings positioned above her computer screen (Figure 6.1):

> That painting there is Iona in Scotland [. . .]. I just love the beaches there, the colours are stunning, the white, sand and the sea because it's so clear, like really deep blues and greens which are just amazing. Again that's a place where I feel really at peace and really calm. That's one of

my own paintings again with blues and greens. My paintings come out of when I meditate and that has a real feeling of depth and peace for me. I just like it there because again it's something that I can look at and take a deep breath.

Like the labyrinth and picture of the retreat, the paintings evoked feelings in Valerie which enabled her to momentarily escape the pressures of the working day. Regulating and monitoring her breath in a natural way allowed a slowing down of her body, providing her with a liminal space for moments of reflection and calm. In this way, Valerie is able to humanize the space to meet her own needs; it enables an embodiment of workspace, which resists the hurried linear rhythms of work. Valerie, through her pictures, was crafting a dwelling space where her personal values could be expressed and where her spatial practices could be slowed. This notion of dwelling was enabled by an appropriated overlaying of the physical conceived space (Lefebvre, 1974/1991) of work, whereby her embodied responses stemming from her carefully placed pictures, produced a way for her to 'be' in her workspace. Valerie was able to express herself through her immediate workspace by the connections that she had created with the retreat and her meditative practice.

Much of Valerie's time was spent conforming to the organizational norms that seek to order and control her spatial behaviours in the conceived space of her office. However, through her pictures, Valerie showed that this ordering is shot through with potential difference, a difference stemming from her body which has "the capacity to open out experience and even sketch out alternative ways of being" (Obrador Pons, 2003: 55). This alternative way of being for Valerie shows a body in moments of peacefulness and calm, following the natural rhythms of her body, within the hurried space of work.

The second example of dwelling at work was provided by David, the IT Manager, whose remit is to provide IT support to all departments and employees. Known widely as 'the hovel', David's office is located beneath the body of the cathedral. David's narration below presents the tensions between how the organization values his work and how he values his work. These value clashes are depicted through the montages of two photographs (Figures 6.2 and 6.3):

Right, this represents the cathedral, but it sort of a little more represents in a very broad sense the management of the cathedral.

The Chapter, the management hierarchy of the cathedral, and this is the invisible hovel [pointing to the bottom half of the picture]. Now, what I wanted to do in here, if you look really hard you can see it and that's the really bad thing about here, is that it is not visible.

*What, you are not visible?*

The place isn't visible, work required down here isn't visible, but I try to make myself visible, as you've noticed I slip out of the office when I can. This isn't a big gloomy thing really, but what I don't like about

*Figure 6.2* The invisible 'hovel'.
Picture by author.

it, it's not about actually being down here, it's what this [the picture] represents.

*And you say in this Picture that the Cathedral is more about representing did you say the chapter?*

Yes that is the governance and the senior management of the cathedral. And I feel this room [his office in the photograph] is very symbolic of that, its position is very symbolic—almost in the unconscious of the cathedral. It's there, it's expected that occasionally it causes problems, but most of the time it's taken for granted, and it all ticks along. I did sort of want to do a break in there [pointing to the split in the picture], I would probably put like an earthquake line in there—sort of a disconnect. So I've got the invisible office and I feel it's almost like 'crossing the Styx' to get down here. I am in the underworld in more ways than one.

In this image, David comments that the cathedral represents "the management of the cathedral, the Chapter, the management hierarchy." The cathedral characterizes the business-orientated realities of the organization, reflective of a calculative and at times political organization. When viewed from this perspective, there is a clash with the Christian values which disappear and are replaced with managerial values, which David feels disconnected from. In his account of the image, David portrays himself and his work as being invisible and detached from the organization; his office is not considered as a space in which he can dwell. Through the image, David expresses an experience of a manifestation of organizational power which spatially structures and controls its workforce and provides an order of ranking. The assigning of David to an office beneath the cathedral signifies to him that the importance of his work is questionable; his work is taken for granted and hence made invisible.

In contrast, David then showed me a second montage he had created using the same two photographs as the ones above (Figure 6.3). This time, the photograph shows his office as a space of dwelling, a lived space (Lefebvre, 1974/1991). The office is now made visible and through his narration of the image, we can learn how David reconciles his place in the 'underworld' through his physical connection to the cathedral:

> Right, this is the good thing about where I work. So this is my hovel, supporting the work of the cathedral, both physically just underneath it and also mentally in terms of my mental space.

*Figure 6.3* The visible 'hovel'.

Picture by author.

For the good part it is yellow at the bottom, it's warm, it's a nice warm place.

*Have you put that colour in?*

It was me, so I have yellowed it at the bottom so it's a warm place and it's a cosy place.

*Why is it a warm and cosy place for you?*

Obviously it's a physically warm place, but it also sort of wraps around me, shall we say it's like home, it's not like home per se, but it's warm, cosy and secure like home.

In this image, David defines his position as one of support, shown in his representation of the organizationally connected, warm, embracing office. The hovel is now represented as literally physically supporting the structure of the cathedral and this is aligned with how David views his role as supporting the continuation of the daily life of the cathedral. David's narrative mirrors the twofold organizational representations of his two montages. The first representation is of the cathedral as a rational-logical, economically driven organization and the second as an ecclesiastical organization encompassing Christian values which he fully supports. This dual representation reflects tensions and value clashes which he seeks to manage through the embodiment of his workspace. The hovel becomes a way of spatially expressing the values of the cathedral as a sacred organization to which he is supporting, as opposed to an economically driven organization, to which he feels an outsider.

The hovel is now imbued with personal meaning and whilst still being considered as physically disconnected from the organization, his appropriation of the space has ensured it is connected to home and therefore creates a feeling of belonging:

Where I live at home and here [referring to his office] are both homes to me. This [his office] isn't so much a home per se, but here and my house are a home both inside of me.

For David, his home and his office were viewed as a space existing inside of him. This representation of the space transcended the physical conceived space (Lefebvre, 1974/1991), for home and work become a part of his body. By doing this, David is able to experience the space in a personal way. The physical space remains a part of his spatial understanding and informs his spatial behaviours, but this is not the only way in which the space is being understood and experienced. Like Valerie, David's lived space (Lefebvre, 1974/1991), is being produced through the exterior physical space, but is also being produced through the space existing on the 'inside', the felt experience of space. The interior and exterior are entwined producing a space for David to dwell, a space which allows him to experience the intermeshing of both the linear rhythms of the organization and the natural rhythms associated with the sense of being at home. Dwelling, then, is more than just occupying a space; it is about being at one with the space, bringing together the outside and the inside, the interiority of the body with the exteriority of the physical space.

David's production of his organizational space described as intimate, cosy, warm, secure can be seen in the light of Bachelard's (1964/1994: 91) imagery of the nest. Bachelard describes the nest as a refuge, a shelter, somewhere we retreat to, a place in which we can "withdraw." Through shaping the conceived space of work through his body, David created a lived space "a personal house of his own, a nest for his body padded to his measure" (Bachelard, 1964/1994: 101). He produced a space to dwell in, along with a way to be and belong in his space of work. This crafting of a dwelling through overlaying the conceived space of work with lived space and its associated spatial practices (perceived space), enabled David to reconcile the negativity he associated with his role's being rendered invisible by the placement of his office underneath the body of the cathedral.

## Organizational Dressage: Pace and Action

The second theoretical notion I would like to share is the concept of organizational dressage. Dressage is applied in this chapter as a way to explore the ways employees of the cathedral were 'playing out' conflicting organizational value claims through their embodied actions in workspace. Lefebvre (1992/2004: 49), defines dressage as the action where "one breaks-in another human living being by making them repeat certain acts, a certain gesture or movement." We can say that dressage in an organizational context is a form of training, of learning, imposed by the organization onto the body. It is a form of organizational power that is inscribed on the body and is observed through the actions of the body. Dale and Burrell (2014: 170), can be said to provide a contemporary conceptualization of dressage as "the organizational shaping of the body," whereby our bodies are being shaped through our occupations (Ibid.). While dressage occurs in any organization to some extent, cathedrals provide a particular example of how the organization seeks to control bodily movement. For example, dressage is clearly on display through the regimented way of the daily service where we are instructed where to sit; when to sit; when to stand, when to bend in prayer and when and how to exit. Here the body is conforming to and orientated towards a sacred mode of being which stipulates the spatial behaviours expected in the conceived space (Lefebvre, 1974/1991) of the cathedral. Such bodily conforming is aligned to Lefebvre's linear rhythms (1992/2004), where the body follows expected organizational norms which "embody ideology and bind it to practice" (Lefebvre, 1974/1991: 215) and, in so doing, help to ensure that organizational norms and traditions are upheld. The daily experiences shared in this section present a more complex view of dressage. That is a view which observes actions which both challenge and uphold the competing organizational tensions of preserving sacredness whilst increasing income levels. Actions are presented which can be argued as benefiting the organization on a sacred level *or* a commercial level. Not observed are actions which successfully uphold both the sacred values *and* the commercial needs.

In the data presented below, dressage is viewed specifically through an awareness of pace and bodily action. The first example is provided by Robert, the shop manager. Robert shows how the body can resist the linear rhythms of the organization, resist the conforming to new organizational ideals, refusing to 'perform' in certain ways, and thereby challenge organizational progress and change. The shop plays a key role in terms of revenue generation, and is therefore an important part of the organization, whilst also being the object of some contention. Robert's narrative of what it is like to work in the shop portrays feelings of frustration caused by competing value claims which affect the ways in which he is required to manage the shop:

> Previously, I and the volunteers were absolutely and completely left on our own in the shop, there was really no support or interest from other people within the cathedral management. Then about a year ago the acting dean decided that the cathedral needed some additional money and so decided that the shop and the refectory should come under the umbrella of St Michael's Cathedral Enterprises Ltd. Since then there has been increasing pressure to increase income. But if you took a look at the bigger picture of what the shop is all about, you will see that to me the shop is not just a shop, a commercial enterprise, there is also this ministry of welcome and that is what is being forgotten. . . .
>
> (Interview 26th October 2011)

Robert was anxious that a particular valued past was vanishing amongst the required practices of the present. His past was a past which stood in contention to the modern organization. Observing Robert, it became clear that he was resisting attempts to modernise the working practices taking place in the shop:

> Robert has a book where he notes his invoices, he crosses out when they are paid with a ruler. Robert photocopies the paid invoices and stamps 'copy' on it, and then chooses the correct folder to file them in. All quite laborious, I am not sure why he does not do it on the computer after all they have been printed from the computer.
>
> (Fieldnotes, 21st July 2011)

> Robert goes back to the filing cabinet and retrieves a file, returns to his desk and goes through the document. He has been asked to do a reference and is finding out a start date for a volunteer, he pulls out relevant papers then puts the file back together and returns to the filing drawer. He then proceeds to hand write the reference, this is very unusual to see nowadays. His pace is steady but slow compared to others observed.
>
> (Fieldnotes, 8th September 2011)

I watch him handwriting an internal memo in a triplicate book—very dated.

(Fieldnotes, 23rd September 2011)

Robert's resistance was directed at new ways of working, in the face of increasing commercial pressure he was, through the rhythms of his body, hanging on to old values. He was seeking to uphold what he considered to be the Christian values of the organization, namely the 'ministry of welcome'. In so doing, his working behaviours and routines deviated from the required purpose of the space, which was primarily to increase income. Robert's traditional ways of working resist the linear rhythms (Lefebvre, 1992/2004) of the organization, which require ways of working aimed at enhancing efficiency and productivity. Through Robert's pace and spatial practices, we are able to see the appropriation of or the reconfiguring of conceived space (Lefebvre, 1974/1991).

In contrast to Robert's movements is Maggie the PR manager. Whereas Robert's working practices were slow, Maggie's were fast, and this was seen in the pace that she moved around the organization. Maggie's key purpose was to be productive. Her pace was always fast and purposeful and when she could she would plan her routes so that she could complete other tasks on the way:

*Is there any reason as to why you select the different routes that you do?*
   I think if I'm going into the cathedral I would go along the route at the back [shown in the picture]. If I'm going just to the shop I think I would tend to go along the front [road side] and enter in through the door opening onto the pavement. I rarely go anywhere for a single reason. If I'm going to walk out the door [of her office] I'd save up a whole list of things to do while I'm there [in the cathedral]. So I probably have got a load of leaflets in my hand, or a poster or something, so I will have a reason for going on a route.

Maggie's routes to the shop and the cathedral were chosen for their efficiency, for they met her criteria of being able to perform the greatest number of tasks en route. Maggie's body, unlike Robert's, was performing in such a way that was reflective of the organizations need for change, that is, moving toward a more efficient, productive and commercial direction. The route to the shop took Maggie outside, onto a public pavement and in so doing meant that she was unlikely to bump into work colleagues which would slow her down. Whilst the routes she chooses to take help her to manage her time, they do provide Maggie with a dilemma:

Maggie informs me that she put up all the signs around the cathedral which direct people where to go; "I usually come in this way but I feel sad as I put the sign up saying to go that way round, [a longer route], so I always have a dilemma but for me and my time management this way is quicker."

(Fieldnotes 28th July 2011)

Time management for Maggie overrides the official guidelines of the signs, which represent a way of ordering people. Signs are a form of dressage, an expectation that the body will move in a certain direction. However, Maggie performs a circumventing of organizational rules, a disregard of a prescribed path and in doing so Maggie ensures that she is more efficient at work and therefore produces greater value for the organization. Maggie's body was a productive body being put to work for the benefit of the organization.

Maggie's rapid movements continued in the spaces of the cathedral, the fast pace changed the atmosphere of the space and challenged the sacred values inscribed in the space. Instead of the space imposing its ideals on Maggie's body, for example, through the slowing of pace, her body resisted such prescribed conformity, refusing to be shaped by it. This resistance of the body conforming to the ideals of sacred space, was also observed with Jill the education officer:

> "Right I'm going into the cathedral to lay out the treasure hunt" (Jill). She goes down to the cathedral taking the shortest route into the quire area, she places treasure on the quire stalls, then into the nave area, she moves very quickly, cuts across the nave by the pulpit, takes the short cut into the office via the door which connects her office to the cathedral—I struggle to keep up.
>
> (Fieldnotes, 23rd August 2011)

In my observations with Maggie and Jill, the aisles of the cathedral became the connecting corridors of the organization; they symbolized action and movement, as opposed to the conceived ideals of the space namely stillness and reflection. Like Maggie, Jill created shortcuts which enabled her to be more productive at work. They both present a form of bodily resistance which, whilst it did not serve to negatively disrupt the running of the organization, could be viewed as serving to disrupt the sacred values of a Christian organization. Their bodies were not orientated towards a sacred mode of being; their bodies were orientated toward a work mode of being. Whilst their pace contested the sacred space of the cathedral, it mirrored organizational goals in terms of *movement* always heading somewhere; *speed* in terms of deadlines and time pressures and *direction*; purposeful and ever changing.

Providing a final example of dressage were the actions of Richard, the cathedral tour guide who described his tour as 'formulaic'. Richard had clear limitations imposed on him throughout his tour. He was controlled physically, spatially and temporally, expected to follow a prescribed path around the cathedral, follow a set script and given a set time by which to complete the tour. At times, Richard's body obeyed these orders and at other times he challenged them. For example:

> This time he climbed over the cord barrier which prohibited access to the high altar to read the inscription on the gold cross . . . He climbs back over and says "this space is for Priests and Bishops they are the only people that get in here."
>
> (Fieldnotes, 21st July 2011)

By entering this space, Richard is displacing the conceived meaning of the space, like Jill's and Maggie's fast pace around the cathedral, the act of crossing the boundary can be interpreted as reducing the sacredness of the space. The boundary is momentarily not observed resulting in the experience of the tour group being heightened. In another observation, Richard entered a door to the cathedral which is not meant for use on tours and said to his tour group, "we will go in this entrance, we are not meant to, but we will." This was similar to Maggie's use of prohibited entrances in order to shorten her walking route. The reason for Richard was to improve the experience of the tour. On both occasions that Richard crossed the boundary into a prohibited space, he was actively making decisions which increased the spaces of the tour, but which conflicted with the prescribed tour guidelines. Whilst seen as bodily contesting the spatial order, this defiance, like Maggie's and Jill's, ultimately serves the organization that benefits from the likelihood of increased visitor donations. Whilst Richard was trained to adhere to the rules of the tour, his movements on the tour were being shaped by conflicting forces, both economic and sacred. His role as a guide was, first, to preserve the sacredness of the cathedral, second, to share the history of the cathedral and, third, to contribute to visitor donations. For Richard, meeting these competing value claims was challenging, and at times sacred values were compromised.

What we can observe through this data are the complexities of managing the conflicting values of the organization. For whilst we can see differing value claims in terms of the movements of the body in the sacred spaces of the cathedral, such movements served to benefit the commercial needs of the organization both in the sense of money and time. For example, adopting a pace reflective of time pressures and deadlines, Maggie and Jill were seen to be in rhythm with the commercially orientated organization, but were observed as being out of rhythm with the organization's sacred values. And in contrast, Robert's actions can be seen as being out of rhythm with the commercial needs of the organization but in rhythm with the sacred values of the cathedral. The organization dilemma presented here is that, whilst conflicting in nature, Robert, Maggie, Jill and Richard, through their spatial embodiment, were all producing and re-producing the conceived spaces (Lefebvre 1974/1991)of the organization in ways which served their own needs, and in some way, also the needs of the organization.

## Discussion

The aim of this chapter has been to explore, explain and interpret through a Lefebvrian lens how competing organizational value claims associated with meeting the commercial needs of the organization, along with upholding the sacred expectations associated with being a Christian organization, are being played out through the embodied spatial experiences of employees at St Michael's Cathedral. Three contributions were promised at the beginning of the chapter, the first contribution rests with the application of Lefebvre's work on rhythmanalysis along with his spatial triad, which provided a way of exploring organizational value clashes, interpreting how these value clashes are being played out through Lefebvre's (1974/1991) notion of the 'total body of space'. The second contribution was in adding to the body of literature on organization space and, in particular, literature that focuses on an embodied spatiality. To do this, I applied the concepts of dwelling and dressage to assist with our understanding of how, through the embodiment of space, competing value claims facing the organization are being reconciled. The final contribution rests in the taking of the cathedral as a compelling site for organization studies. The cathedral is a modern organization, and, like many organizations today, it is an organization in transition. Based on the research presented, I suggest that what makes the site particularly interesting to organization studies is its key challenge of managing the competing value claims imposed upon it in modern times, value claims which the employees of the cathedral have shown are difficult to reconcile, due to the differences being so great.

The findings presented raise the importance of two key issues to organization studies. The first is *why* there is a need to dwell in organizations, along with *how* we dwell in organizations. Valerie and David both showed a need to dwell in their workspace, and this was evident through their spatial appropriation of their workspace. I conclude that their appropriation enabled them to just 'be' in their space of work, to be able to feel at home at work. How this sense of being at work was produced is of great interest and I contend that this was assisted by the entwining of the exterior physical space with the interior felt experience of space. This brings Lefebvre's (1974/1991) notion of the total body from the abstract to something that is real and experienced. Valerie and David's appropriation of workspace meant that they could, through their body *of* space, adopt bodily strategies which enabled them to cope with the conflicting representations of the organization. How Valerie did this was through alternating the rhythms of her body through her strategically placed pictures, enabling liminal moments in the day to pause and reflect, thereby escaping the pressures of work. For David, crafting a workspace that evoked feelings of home, provided him with a clear reminder of the purpose of his work, to support the cathedral as an ecclesiastical organization, as opposed to the economically driven organization to which he felt alienated. Valerie and David's spatial appropriation created a sense of intimacy at work, transforming workspace into a deeply felt, embodied space which provided a way of reconciling organizational value clashes, associated with managing the tensions with trying to marry the sacred and the secular.

The concept of dwelling at work in terms of *why* we seek to dwell and *how* we enable a sense of dwelling, provides organizational researchers with a further way to explore ways that conflicts in organizations are being experienced and managed. It takes the concept of spatial appropriation a step further by requiring the interior experience of space to be considered as entwined with the physical experience of space. There is no separation. In organization studies research pertaining to how artefacts and the appropriation of space are being explored goes some way toward bringing the exterior and the interior together. For example, when artefacts are viewed as expressions of identity construction (Elsbach, 2003; Tian and Belk, 2005) or from an aesthetic perspective (Warren, 2002, 2006). In these studies, the felt experience is certainly not ignored, and is considered *alongside* physical workspace, but there remains a separation; there is not a sense of body *of* space, but instead a sense of body *in* space (Lefebvre, 1974/1991). This idea of space and body as one is difficult to express, but I hope that I have gone some way in doing so through the concept of dwelling and the embodiment there of. From this perspective, physical space is not only appropriated through artefacts; entwined with this is a form of internal appropriation. That is, there is a recognition that feelings, emotions and behaviours are changing at the same time as the physical appropriation of space, showing that space and the body are both shaping and being shaped by the other.

The second key issue raised in the chapter observes the significance to organization space studies of exploring bodily action and pace through the Lefebvrian lens of dressage. Through the bodily actions of the participants presented in this chapter, we are able to appreciate the different ways the body can assist in understanding organizations and in particular interpret how conflicting organizational values are being spatially enacted. What the data presented highlights is the complexity of managing and reconciling the cathedral's two distinct and contentious value claims, namely the sacred and the secular. How Lefebvre's (1992/2004) notion of dressage is applied in the context of the cathedral contributes to the organizational space literature, in that it affords a different perspective to the more common view of the body being placed in a designated space, conforming to the conceived ideals of the space. Instead, in this chapter I have conceptualized dressage from the embodied experience of being entwined with space, according to which dressage is viewed as both "the organizational shaping of the body" (Dale and Burrell, 2014: 170) and the bodily shaping of the organization. This perspective of dressage is one which is explored through an awareness of pace and bodily action, without necessarily attending to it as a means to an end in terms of maximizing levels of production. From this view, we see the inhabitants of workspace not passively accepting the imposed spaces of the organization, but instead orientating their bodies in ways which meet their own needs and values and which uphold either one or other of the organization's competing value claims.

Through the concept of dressage, we are able to see the reason for the complexity of reconciling these two differences. For whilst bodily action may be showing a resistance to one value claim, it is at the same time, showing an upholding of the other value claim. For example, we were able to see from Robert's bodily actions a resistance to the increasing need to raise income levels. His spatial practices mirrored the slow pace of halcyon days which were considered to be out of rhythm with the values of the commercially driven organization. By holding on, through his bodily actions, to traditional values he was able to deal with the changes going on in the organization which he did not fully agree with. For others, we see further incongruities at play. Maggie, Jill and, at times, Richard performed bodily actions more aligned with upholding the commercial needs of the organization whilst embodying the sacred spaces of the cathedral. This showed a bodily resistance to conforming to the conceived space of the cathedral, but a body conforming to the values of the commercially orientated organization.

So whilst the participants' bodies were actively orientated towards upholding the particular values that they considered to be most important, interestingly the desired goals of bodily resistance or conformity were the same—ensuring the longevity of the cathedral as a space where all visitors are welcomed every-day of the year. So, rather than viewing the different value claims as competing, through the interpretation of the bodily actions of the participants, we can instead conclude that, whilst indeed different, the upholding of both is essential. So, rather than competing against one another, these organizational value claims can be reconciled by viewing them as supporting one another.

# References

Archbishop Council. (2014). *Research statistics Church statistics.* https://www.churchofengland.org/sites/default/files/2017-10/2013cathedralstatistics.pdf

Bachelard, G. (1964/1994). *The Poetics of Space.* Boston: Beacon Press.

Barker, J. and Smith, F. (2012). What's in focus? A critical discussion of photography, children and young people. *International Journal of Social Research Methodology, 15*(2), 91–103.

Bathurst, R. and Cain, T. (2013). Embodied leadership: The aesthetics of gesture. *Leadership, 9*(3), 358–377.

Bazin, Y. (2013). Understanding organisational gestures: Technique, aesthetics and embodiment. *Scandinavian Journal of Management, 29,* 377–393.

Beyes, T. and Steyaert, C. (2011). The production of educational space: Heterotopia and the business university. *Management Learning, 42*(5), 521–536.

Beyes, T. and Steyaert, C. (2012). Spacing organization: Non-representational theory and performing organizational space. *Organization, 19*(1), 45–61.

Cameron, H., Richter, P., Davies, D. and Ward, F. (2005). *Studying Local Churches a Handbook*. London: SCM Press.

Cohen, Z., Kahn, L. and Steeves, R. (2000). *Hermeneutical Phenomenological Research: A Practical Guide for Nurse Researchers*. London: Sage.

Czarniawska, B. and Mazza, C. (2003). Consulting as a liminal space. *Human Relations*, 56, 267–290.

Dale, K. (2001). *Anatomising Embodiment and Organisation Theory*. Hampshire: Palgrave MacMillan.

Dale, K. (2005). Building a social materiality: Spatial and embodied politics in organizational control. *Organization*, 12(5), 649–678.

Dale, K. and Burrell, G. (2010). All together, altogether better': The ideal of 'community' the spatial reorganization of the workplace. In A. van Marrewijk and D. Yanow (Eds.), *Organizational Spaces Rematerializing the Workaday World* (pp. 19–40). Cheltenham: Edward Elgar Publishing Limited.

Dale, K. and Burrell, G. (2014). Being occupied: An embodied re-reading of organizational 'wellness'. *Organization*, 21(2), 159–177.

Dale, K. and Latham, Y. (2015). Ethics and entangled embodiment: Bodies—materialities—organization. *Organization*, 22(2), 166–182.

Edensor, T. and Holloway, J. (2008). Rhythm analysing the coach tour: The Ring of Kerry, Ireland. *Royal Geographic Society*, 33, 483–501.

Elsbach, K. (2003). Relating physical environment to self-categorizations: Identity threat and affirmation in a non-territorial office space. *Administrative Science Quarterly*, 48, 622–654.

Engel, M. (2011). British Institutions: The Church of England. *FT Magazine*.

Flores-Pereira, M., Davel, E. and Cavedon, N. (2008). Drinking beer and understanding organizational culture embodiment. *Human Relations*, 61(7), 1007–1026.

Francis, L., Mansfield, S., E., W. and Village, A. (2010). Applying psychological type theory to Cathedral visitors: A case study of two Cathedrals in England and Wales. *Visitor Studies*, 13(2), 175–186.

Gadamer, H. (1975/2004). *Truth and Method*, Vol. 2. London: Continuum.

Garsten, C. (1999). Betwixt and between: Temporary employees as liminal subjects in flexible organizations. *Organization Studies*, 20(4), 601–617.

The Church of England (2018) Our Vacancies. Retrieved May 9, 2018, from https://pathways.churchofengland.org/jobs/job/Finance-Director-for-the-Dioceses-of-Winchester-and-Portsmouth/657.

Gutic, J., Caie, E. and Clegg, A. (2010). In search of heterotopia? Motivations of visitors to an English Cathedral. *International Journal of Tourism Research*, 12, 750–760.

Halford, S. (2004). Towards a sociology of organizational space. *Sociological Research Online*, 9(1).

Hancock, P. and Spicer, A. (2011). Academic architecture and the constitution of the new model individual. *Culture & Organization*, 17(2), 91–105.

Heidegger, M. (1971). Building dwelling thinking. In M. Heidegger (Ed.), *Poetry, Language, Thought* (translated by A. Hofstadter, pp. 140–160). New York: Harper and Row.

Hernes, T. (2004). *The Spatial Construction of Organization*. Amsterdam: John Benjamins.

Hopewell, J. (1987). *Congregation Stories and Structures*. Philadelphia: Fortress Press.

Iedema, R., Long, D. and Carroll, K. (2010). *Corridor Communication, Spatial Design and Patient Safety: Enacting and Managing Complexities*. Cheltenham: Edward Elgar Publishing Limited.

Ingold, T. (Ed.). (1995). *Building, Dwelling, Living: How People and Animals Make Themselves at Home in the World*. London: Routledge.

Kasprzak, E. (2012). Concern over funding for upkeep of England's cathedral. Retrieved July 28, 2014, from http://www.bbc.co.uk/news/uk-england-17432028.

Kim, J. and de Dear, R. (2013). Workspace satisfaction: The privacy-communication trade-off in open-plan offices. *Journal of Environmental Psychology, 36*, 18–26.

Lefebvre, H. (1974/1991). *The Production of Space*. Oxford: Blackwell Publishing.

Lefebvre, H. (1981/2008). *Critique of Everyday Life From Modernity to Modernism*, Vol. 3. London: Verso.

Lefebvre, H. (1992/2004). *Rhythmanalysis*. London: Continuum.

Lefebvre, H. and Régulier, C. (Eds.) (1986). Attempt at the rhythmanalysis of Mediterranean cities. In H. Lefebvre (Ed.), *Rhythmanalysis* (pp. 73–84). London: Continuum.

Maddison, J. (2000). *Ely Cathedral Design and Meaning*. Suffolk: Ely Cathedral Publications.

McDonald, S. (2005). Studying actions in context: A qualitative shadowing method for organizational research. *Qualitative Research, 5*(4), 455–473.

Obrador Pons, P. (2003). Being-on-holiday tourist dwelling, bodies and place. *Tourist Studies, 3*(1), 47–66.

Peltonen, T. (2011). Multiple architectures and the production of organizational space in a Finnish university. *Journal of Organizational Change Management, 24*(6), 806–821.

Petani, F. and Mengis, J. (2016). In search of lost space: The process of space planning through remembering and history. *Organization, 23*(1), 71–89.

Pullen, A. and Rhodes, C. (2015). Ethics, embodiment and organizations. *Organization, 22*(2), 159–165.

Radley, A. and Taylor, D. (2003). Images of recovery: A photo-elicitation study on the hospital ward. *Qualitative Health Research, 13*(1), 77–99.

Riach, K. and Wilson, F. (2014). Bodyspace at the pub: Sexual orientations and organizational space. *Organization, 21*, 329–345.

Saldaña, J. (2009). *The Coding Manuel for Qualitative Researchers*. London: Sage.

Shackley, M. (2001). *Managing Sacred Sites*. London Thomson.

Shackley, M. (2002). Space sanctity and service the English Cathedral. *International Journal of Tourism Research, 4*, 345–352.

Shortt, H. (2015). Liminality, space and the importance of 'transitory dwelling places' at work. *Human Relations, 68*(4), 633–658.

Simonsen, K. (2005). Bodies, sensations, space and time: The contribution from Henri Lefebvre. *Human Geography, 87*(1), 1–14.

Smith, J., Flowers, P. and Larkin, M. (2009). *Interpretive Phenomenological Analysis, Theory, Method and Research*. London: Sage.

Sturdy, A., Schwarz, M. and Spicer, A. (2006). Guess who's coming to dinner? Structures and used of liminality in strategic management consultancy. *Human Relations, 59*, 929.

Symon, G. and Cassell, C. (2012). *Qualitative Organizational Research Core Methods and Current Challenges*. London: Sage.

Theos. (2012). Social capital the present and future of English Cathedrals. Retrieved January 10, 2013, from https://www.theosthinktank.co.uk/research/2012/10/12/spiritual-capital-the-present-and-future-of-english-cathedrals.

Tian, K. and Belk, R. (2005). Extended self and possessions in the workplace. *Journal of Consumer Research, 32*(2), 297–310.

Toyoki, S., Spicer, A. and Elliot, R. (2006). Beyond old horizons: Theorising the rhythms of social reproduction. *Tamara Journal of Critical Organisation Inquiry, 5*(1), 96.

Tyler, M. (2011). Tainted love: From dirty work to abject labour in Soho's sex shops. *Human Relations, 64*(11), 1477–1500.

Tyler, M. and Cohen, L. (2010). Spaces that matter: Gender performativity and organizational space. *Organization Studies, 31*(2), 175–198.

Verduyn, K. (2015). Entrepreneuring and process: A Lefebvrian perspective. *International Small Business Journal, 33*(6), 638–648.

Voase, R. (2007). Visiting a Cathedral: The consumer psychology of a 'Rich Experience'. *International Journal of Heritage Studies, 13*(1), 41–55.

Wapshott, R. and Mallett, O. (2012). The spatial implications of homeworking: A Lefebvrian approach to the rewards and challenges of home-based work. *Organization, 19*(1), 63–79.

Warren, S. (2002). Show me how it feels to work here': Using photography to research organizational aesthetics. *ephemera, 2*(3), 224–245.

Warren, S. (2006). Hot-nesting: A visual exploration of the personalization of work space in a hot-desking environment. In P. Case, S. Lilley and T. Owen (Eds.), *The Speed of Organization* (pp. 119–146). Liber: Copenhagen Business School Press.

Wasserman, V. and Frenkel, M. (2010). Organizational aesthetics: Caught between identity regulation and culture jamming. *Organization Science* (1–19).

Wasserman, V. and Frenkel, M. (2015). Spatial work in between glass ceilings and glass walls: Gender-class intersectionality and organizational aesthetics. *Organization Studies, 35*(11), 1485–1505.

Watkins, C. (2005). Representations of space, spatial practices and spaces of representation: An application of Lefebvre's spatial triad. *Culture and Organization, 11*(3), 209–220.

Zhang, Z., Spicer, A. and Hancock, P. (2008). Hyper-organizational space in the work of J. G. Ballard. *Organization, 15*, 889.

# 7 City Rhythms
## Walking and Sensing Place Through Rhythmanalysis

*Louise Nash*

## Introduction

This chapter considers the value to organizational scholars of Lefebvre's *Rhythmanalysis* (2004), and, specifically, how it can be used as a methodological tool for empirical investigations into organizational life. I start by arguing that, whilst Lefebvre's (1991) theories of space as socially produced have been applied to organizations and their spatial configurations (Beyes and Steyaert, 2012; Dale, 2005; Dale and Burrell, 2007; Ford and Harding, 2004; Taylor and Spicer, 2007; Wasserman and Frenkel, 2015), his later work on rhythms, originally published in France in 1992, later translated into English, has had less impact in this field (notable exceptions will be explored below).

The background to the research that is described here is concerned with organizational place and setting. I had a particular interest in studying how a setting dominated by one industry sector was experienced by those working within it. Whilst the spatial turn in organization studies has resulted in many rich explorations and analyses of organizational life over the last twenty years (Halford, 2004; Kornberger and Clegg, 2003, 2004, Tyler and Cohen, 2010), there has been less of a focus on work settings. What can a study of setting tell us about organizational life? Is it the scene of collective experiences and behaviours? As Tyler (2011: 5) describes:

> Work clearly does not take place—it is not enacted, experienced or made meaningful—within a social or material vacuum, yet we know comparatively little about how *where* work is carried out shapes its lived experience, and of course vice versa; that is, how a close association with a particular sector of work shapes a locale.
>
> (original emphasis)

The research was conducted in the City of London, also known by its metonym the Square Mile, the heart of the UK financial services industry. It is a city within a city, forming a geographical part of, but administered by a separate body to, greater London which encircles it, and is the site of

Roman Londinium. The City is widely recognized as a distinct and bounded place. It is architecturally recognizable, due to its mix of soaring skyscrapers and British imperial–era architecture, medieval streets and Roman ruins, and maintains historical traditions which set it apart from many other work settings. It exists in the public imagination as a particular geographical location, with a distinctive materiality, a distinctive culture and where distinctive behaviours are manifested. Today, the City employs approximately 400,000 people and contributes £45 billion, or 3% of the UK's entire economic output to the economy of the United Kingdom (Cityoflondon.go.uk, 2017).

Researching the City as an organizational setting allows an exploration of how meaning, materiality, sector and place come together, and what this means for the people who work there. My interest in the City was initially ignited by the years I spent working there, in a variety of different organizations and roles. I became interested in its history and the narratives of resilience and endurance which permeate much writing about the City, but also by its distinct geographical boundaries, its architecture and its sense of particular culture; you simply *know* when you are in the City, even if you do not consult a map or a guidebook. Some years later, and pursuing the idea of a research degree in Organization Studies, I vividly remembered my City days, and began to wonder why this sense of the City as such a particular locale endures, and what this might mean to people working there. I wished, in essence, to explore what Thrift (1996: 238) describes as its 'distinctive patina'. The etymology of patina is from the Latin for a shallow dish, referring specifically to the green film formed on copper or bronze from exposure, and is often used to mean the surface appearance of something grown beautiful with age and use, or the appearance or aura of something derived from long association or habit. Thrift's use of the concept is a reminder not only of the distinctiveness of the City, both materially and culturally, but of its age and history and long association with finance and trade. The City can be read as a palimpsest, with diverse layers and meanings apparent beneath the surface, all of which add to the rich patina of the City.

The chapter will explain the use of rhythmanalysis to uncover the patina of the City, describing why it was used, how it was developed, and what it can add to studies of organizational life. In addition, I will acknowledge its limitations as well as its potential. In the section below, I explore the City as a place of work, before moving onto Lefebvre's engagement with the urban, and specifically with urban rhythms, before presenting more detail on the methods and a discussion of the findings.

## Exploring the City

My leading questions are, then, that if setting and locale can shape the lived experience of work, how can they be empirically explored? And what can the rhythms of place tell us about how the place itself is perceived and experienced, and how they contribute to the patina of the City?

Building upon emerging insights, this chapter emphasizes that understanding the relationship between space, place and work is important because, as McDowell (1997: 5) has noted, in one of the few studies focusing exclusively on the City of London, more critical attention needs to be given specifically to *where* things take place'. Through its focus on the City as a particular organizational sector and setting, the study set out to emphasize the symbolic and material significance of place to understanding organizational life.

Lefebvre, (1991), using the concept of space as socially produced, theorizes that space is fundamentally bound up with social reality and with our lived experience of the world; as Watkins (2005: 211) puts it, he moves space 'from the realm of the mental to become the foundation of our engagement with the world'. Lefebvre claims that spatial practices can 'only be evaluated empirically' (Lefebvre, 1991: 38); thus it is only through an empirical analysis that the spatial practice of a society can be deciphered. Contextualizing his theories into a particular setting is not necessarily straightforward, particularly since he does not specifically relate his theories to organizational space, yet his work is highly applicable to discussions of urban spaces where day to day activities are carried out. An additional benefit of Lefebvre's theorization of space in this regard is his insistence on the importance of representations of bodily, lived experiences of space. This emphasis on the body and its relationship to place will be central to the methodological approach of this study.

How to undertake the empirical study presented several challenges. Whilst the research setting, the City, is a relatively small space, with distinct and historic boundaries and borders, it was difficult to decide on the best mode of analysis for understanding how people treat, move within, and use the space. My own memories of working within the City, of the fast pace of life and demands of the place, were strong, and I was interested to see if it was possible to recreate the sense of urgency that was often felt in the City, whilst simultaneously being able to observe and analyse the street life and to see what findings might emerge in relation to how the City is experienced as a work place. Lefebvre's work on rhythms (Lefebvre, 2004) became a methodological key which helped to unlock a very specific sense of place. In developing what he described as a nascent science, Lefebvre analyses time and its effect on places; more particularly, he focuses on the conjunction of time and space which, he argues, both results in and occurs through rhythm.

This space has its own history outside of the greater city of which it forms part, as well as its own cultural norms (McDowell, 1997; Thrift, 1996). These spaces have become partially detached from other cities in their nation states, and have become truly 'global' in that they are spatially dispersed yet globally integrated (King, 1990). London, along with Tokyo and New York, is pre-eminent among them, with elite workers typifying the individualist attitudes and lifestyles celebrated since the 1980s (Coakley, 1992; Corbridge, Thrift, and Martin, 1994; Zukin, 1991). Nonetheless, it can be argued that the City is still in many ways a territorially bounded culture with a local 'flavour' which makes it simultaneously both like and unlike other financial centres.

At the time of writing, the effects of the most recent financial crisis, which started in 2007, are still being felt by Western economies, which poses ongoing questions for the future of the Square Mile; are its skills and history, its networks of firms and the liquidity of its markets enough to keep it as the world's pre-eminent international financial centre? This anxiety and loss of confidence, though less acute than at the time the crisis erupted, is still relevant to understanding the lived experience of those working in this place. Although there is a great deal of commentary and analyses both academically (French, Leyshon, and Thrift, 2009; Reinhart and Rogoff, 2008; Sikka, 2009) and within the media about the most recent financial crisis, and many written histories of the City (Porter, 1998; Roberts and Kynaston, 2002), which document the various failures and crises of its history, there is little that connects these with the lived experience of those working within the setting and subject to recurring cycles of disorder and chaos. Cycles of crisis have played their part in the ongoing history of the City, from the South Sea bubble crisis of 1720 to the more recent banking collapses in the late twentieth and early twenty-first century. How the experience of such cycles is expressed rhythmically will be explored in the section of the findings discussing the City as a site of both order and disorder.

In addition to cycles of crisis, the increasing number of areas in the City which are owned by developers or corporations, but open to the public, mean that the line between public and private is being blurred. Walking in the space, therefore, can become a contested act where access can be denied, causing unexpected deviations.

The chapter, therefore, makes a methodological contribution to studies using Lefebvre's theories to researching organization, by using rhythmanalysis to explore and analyse a shared communality of performance in a work setting. The research described here also makes an empirical contribution to the literature on organizational place and setting by applying an urban level of analysis to the City, developing an understanding of it as both global and local and shaped by both global and local rhythms. Below, I illustrate how Lefebvre's theories pertain to the City of London.

### Lefebvre, Space and the Urban

Lefebvre explains that just as everyday life has been colonized by capitalism, so too has its location; social space is produced and experienced through a conceptual triad of spatial practice, representations of space, and spaces of representation, or, in other words as perceived, conceived and lived (Lefebvre, 1991). Lefebvre describes how particular space may be conceived, designed and produced in a particular way, but the meaning of the space, and the space itself, is adapted and transformed as it is perceived and lived by social actors and groups, for example a city park. In

Lefebvre's writing on the urban, he explains that the effects of industrialization on a capitalist society of production and property have produced their results: a programmed everyday life which is carried out in a predominately urban setting (Lefebvre, 1971 [1968]). Such a process has been enabled by the disintegration of the traditional town and the endless expansion of urbanism. Thus, the urban is accorded a central place in Lefebvre's philosophy and politics; his understanding of urban space is infused with time and history.

Lefebvre's engagement with the urban ranges from questions of planning and design, the importance of movement, mobility and rhythms, to the relationship of space and time, particularly with regard to the proliferation of capitalism, which is embedded and internalized in the urban. Lefebvre relates the dominance of the spatial directly to the reproduction of capitalism. In terms of financial centres, processes of capitalist enclosure lead to the intensification and extension of the urbanization process, directly connecting accumulations of finance capital with the rise of urban agglomeration (Lefebvre, 2003). He argues that a new understanding of the urban is required (Brenner and Schmid, 2015). As Prigge (2008) explains:

> It is no longer the industrial and its disciplines focusing on capital and labor, classes and reproduction that constitute the episteme (the possibility of knowing the social formation), but the urban and its forms focused on everydayness and consumption, planning and spectacle, that expose the tendencies of social development in the second half of the twentieth century.

It is in urban studies and geography that the influence of Lefebvre has been most strongly developed, for example Brenner, (2000), Brenner and Elden (2009), Elden, (2004), McCann (1999), Merrifield (2006, 2011), and Soja (1998), inter alia. World city theorists suggest that the urban scale operates as a locally organized node within globally organized flows (Brenner, 2000). This has particular relevance for the City of London, which retains a very local character and socio-cultural traditions, but which is entangled not only with the greater city which surrounds it, but with other global cities and webs of global finance. Suggestions that the urban can no longer be understood as a bounded spatial unit, but instead saturates modern life, lead to questions about the implications for the City. On the one hand, the City maintains its ancient boundaries and is a geographic spatial unit. On the other hand, its temporal rhythms are dictated by global markets, and it can therefore be said to have a unique spatio-temporal character, or a 'patina' (Thrift, 1996: 238). It is this 'patina' which in this study will be explored in relation to its rhythms.

Previous studies of financial districts have examined the relationship between location and industry sector (Allen and Pryke, 1994; Amin and Cohendet, 2003; Beunza and Stark, 2003; Ho, 2009; Thrift, 1996). In these studies, financial centres are both constructed in and through global connectivity, but also through their particular geographical location.

Thrift (1996) explores how the City was historically reproduced by an interrelated web of time and space, for example, the various temporal routines associated with the management of money, such as the historic cheque clearing systems, along with rules on spatial regulation of the City; for example all Stock Exchange members had to maintain an office within 700 yards of the Exchange building. These traditions, rhythms and materiality all combine to form what he calls 'a coherent City space . . . confirming the identity of place and person' (Thrift: 241). The network of contacts, always so vital to professional life in the City, has been focused by the City's small spatial extent, so ensuring that the City, was, in effect, kept in the City. Allen and Pryke (1994) use Lefebvre to help disentangle the social spaces which constitute the City. As they point out, the City is synonymous with finance, and anything not pertaining to this dominant sector is sidelined. They point to the production of a dominant coding in the City, and to the way in which it has been secured by the repression of differences, and point to its 'cohesive clubbiness, its dress codes, its web of gentleman's agreements' (Allen and Pryke, 1994: 460) as evidence of its legacy of social practices which help cement tradition and which derive from its spatial history, with its roots in the small members-only coffee houses.

Extending this concept of a cultural legacy deriving from the spatial history of the place, McDowell's (1997) ethnography of the City focuses particularly on the gendered practices within investment banks, and examining the multiple ways in which masculinities and femininities are constructed therein. Exploring the places and spaces within which City workers spend their time, McDowell argues that these affect as well as reflect acceptable ways of performing gender in a highly stylized way. For example, she identifies both the patriarchal, cerebral, almost disembodied masculinity of the 'old' City and its private, exclusive boardrooms and the noisy, sweaty, 'carnivalesque' masculinity of the trading floors. She emphasizes how the built environment of the City and its symbolic meanings are entwined with its social practices, leading to a tradition of inclusion and exclusion based primarily on gender.

The research undertaken here builds on the insights from these studies by exploring the ways in which what the City is and does is materialized in what and where it is; in other words, exploring the relationship between the lived experience of work and the setting within which it takes place. As I wished to understand how the City was both sensed and made sense of, I was looking for a method that would allow me to understand the 'lived space' of the City, and to sense it in the way that City workers sense it. What can an analysis of the spatial and temporal flows and shifts of the City tell us about the lived experience of working there? What can be added to our knowledge of how people experience their working lives in a setting that is historically, architecturally and culturally distinctive? These questions led

me to an exploration of how the rhythm and movements of urban space
might be researched.

## Lefebvre and the Rhythms of Everyday Life

In *Rhythmanalysis* (2004), Lefebvre turns again to the everyday and urban
life, but through the notion of rhythm in an attempt to analyse the coming
together of space and time. Rhythmanalysis is the study of spatio-temporal
rhythms and the dynamics that these rhythms create, at the bodily, urban,
regional national and global scale.

In his essays on rhythm, Lefebvre pays particular attention to urban
rhythms, in order to extend his understanding of how space is produced to
how we are able to understand it; in other words, how by listening and analysing the rhythms of place, we can better understand their particular character and the effects they create. Rhythmanalysis is an attempt to use the
body to understand the rhythms of space. The rhythmanalyst perceives the
whole of the space, not just visually, but with all her senses, and by using her
bodily responses in order to analyse them. Lefebvre uses the masculine form
of the third-person pronoun when describing a rhythmanalyst. In order to
provide balance, I have used 'she':

> He tries to hear the music that the city plays and to understand its com-
> position. He heeds the tempo, the beat, the repetitions of the tune and
> the rhythms. He hears the functional interruptions and the arrhythms.
> His is an attempt to keep the scientific and the poetic apart as little as
> possible.
>
> (Meyer, 2008: 156)

Lefebvre writes of time, space and an expenditure of energy colliding as
rhythm in particular spaces, and of the importance of observing these
rhythms in order to fully understand the place:

> Concrete times have rhythms, or rather are rhythms—and all rhythms
> imply the relation of a time to a space, a localised time, or, if one pre-
> fers, a temporalized space. Rhythm is always linked to such and such a
> place, to its place.
>
> (Lefebvre, 2004: 96)

For Lefebvre, rhythms are never fixed and stable, but are by their nature
fluid, susceptible to changes and based on difference—repetition in itself
does not, cannot, produce a rhythm, but as soon as difference appears, a
rhythm begins to form. So, in the quotation above, Lefebvre is explaining
that rhythms belong to, and are shaped by, a particular place, but, at the
same time, are always in a process of becoming, like a wave, because they
are dependent on time.

His aim is to encourage the observer to listen to a space, to recognize that there is nothing inert in the world—only diverse and multiple rhythms which characterize a particular place or a particular time. To analyse rhythms successfully means becoming 'more sensitive to times than to spaces, to moods than to images, to the atmosphere than to particular events' (Lefebvre, 2004: 94). Lefebvre identifies both cyclical rhythms and linear rhythms. The former are rooted in nature and the physiological rhythms of the body, which, broadly, involve repetitive rhythms which take place after specific and naturally occurring intervals of time, for example the sun rising or the changing of the seasons. In contrast, linear rhythms, again broadly, are exterior and imposed by humans (although these two may coincide, for example news bulletins which occur at regularly punctuated intervals throughout the day).

Rhythms are fundamentally based upon repetition, yet repetition inevitably produces difference, in that it is only by the insertion of difference that a rhythm can be perceived. It is these differing rhythms which he asks us to observe and analyse. The only way we can do this is through bodily engagement, to use a multiplicity of the senses: 'he thinks with his body, not in the abstract, but in lived temporality' (Lefebvre, 2004: 94) Indeed, he posits that the only way to analyse rhythms is to use our own bodies and their rhythms as reference points.

What differentiates rhythmanalysis from more straightforward observations of urban rhythms is the stress on the body as the mode of analysis. For Lefebvre, the body proportions the rhythms we sense; therefore, it is critical that they are experienced with and through the body, and not only understood in the abstract, or through visual observation alone. Rhythmanalysis therefore becomes a multi-sensory, embodied and immersive method of researching organizational life. As Lefebvre explains, the rhythmanalyst 'listens—and first to his body; he learns rhythm from it, in order consequently to appreciate external rhythms. His body serves him as a metronome' (Lefebvre, 2004: 29). Lefebvre does highlight a methodological concern, however; 'in order to analyse a rhythm, one must get outside it' (ibid: 95). What Lefebvre is drawing attention to here is the difficulty of grasping the relationship between rhythms that constitute a whole, particularly within our own body. We do not, for example, pay attention to individual bodily rhythms except when one of them is in a state of pathology, i.e. when we are suffering. He relates this to the sensation of immersion in music and dance; we feel these sensations within our bodies, but in order to understand the experience we must also be able to detach ourselves from it and to observe the effects on others. What he is recommending is both observation and immersion, for we cannot experience rhythms unless it is through our body, and we cannot analyse our experience unless we observe; we need to be therefore both inside and outside, participant and observer.

Geographers have been interested in rhythms for some time (Edensor, 2010; Edensor and Holloway, 2008; Matos Wunderlich, 2008), particularly as a tool to reveal how they 'shape human experience in timespace and pervade everyday life and place' (Edensor, 2010). Delyser and Sui (2013: 293) point out that conceptually, rhythmanalysis 'may enable a shift in geographic focus from one ocularcentric to one more auditory', following Lefebvre's observation that a rhythmanalyist is 'capable of listening to a house, street, a town as one listens to a symphony, an opera' (Lefebvre, 2004: 87). Rhythmanalysis has also been used for empirical explorations of, for example, festival spaces (Duffy, Waitt, Gorman- Murray and Gibson, 2011), and street performance (Simpson, 2008, 2012).

Lyon (2016), in one of the few studies which uses rhythmanalysis to explore organizational life, in this case Billingsgate Fish Market in London, notes that it is not just temporal patterns which structure a place, but also the activity and movement of people within it. For Lyon, drawing on Lefebvre, rhythm can be seen to operate at different scales and beats, creating a distinctive space-time. Lyon shows how rhythmanalysis can be an important and insightful tool to examine the interrelations between the body and urban organizational life, and can be situated within a methodology that explores work setting.

These studies of rhythms, both bodily and institutional and their relationship, demonstrate a method of analysis which explores the concrete lived experience of place. My particular interest was in how actors navigate the material setting in which they work and how their bodily rhythms are attuned to the space around them. The methodological imperative, therefore, of this study was to place the fieldwork directly in the streets of the research setting, to foreground the connection between bodies, space, materiality and culture and how rhythms can help us understand this. The next section will outline how I deployed rhythmanalysis in order to explore the City.

## Walking as Rhythmanalysis

I will explain and evaluate the methodology in this section, and I will also further explore some of the methodological contributions and limitations in the conclusion to this chapter.

The fieldwork took place over a period of five months and represents ten full days of observations in the City. Most of the field days took place during the week, at different times of day. I used the ancient boundaries of the City to plot the walks (Figure 7.1).

Given the City's relatively small spatial extent, and the fact that most City workers arrive via various transport termini and then walk through the space, both to and from their individual place of work and during the day (visiting cafes, parks, shops and travelling between office locations), walking the City was chosen as a method of rhythmanalysis. Walking both replicates the experience of most City workers, and enabled me to sense the rhythms of the streets and bring my sensory and embodied understanding

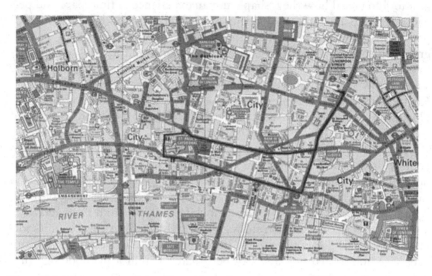

*Figure 7.1* Master map of the City with an example of a walk mapped onto it.

into the research, in order to be able to fully analyse the rhythmic effect of place.

An embodied methodological approach such as walking within a given setting is not novel within sociological and organizational studies, although it is still relatively rare. Various forms and practices of walking have been used as methodologies by authors for understanding city life and modern urbanity (Edensor, 2010, 2012; Elkin, 2016). Most recent scholarly contributions have originated from the discipline of geography and are loosely bound by a shared understanding that seeks to uncover a nuanced and immersed sense of place (Edensor, 2010, 2012; Matos Wunderlich, 2008; Simpson, 2012, inter alia.) In addition, there are alternative ways of creatively representing the rhythms of place, for example 'walking with video,' i.e. filming and recording participants whilst walking alongside them (Pink, 2007), spatial shadowing, where the interviewer walks alongside the participant who is encouraged to describe what they perceive and experience throughout the walk (Raulet-Croset and Borzeix, 2014, Thibaud, 2013), and soundwalks, or recording the auditory experience of moving through a soundscape (Hall, Lashua, and Coffey, 2008; Paquette and McCartney, 2012).

The aim was to use my own body to immerse myself within the research setting, noticing the rhythms of my body and those of the wider setting, and observing and recording my sensory perceptions and emotional reactions as I moved through the space. This helped to make strange the familiar, and uncover what had previously been unnoticed by me (when I worked in the setting).

The subjective nature of this approach, however, does mean that the research lacked the perspectives of others. The study also involved research participants, in order to emphasize the depth of insight and understanding from those spending their working lives there. Interviews were carried out with eighteen City workers, recruited via a snowball sample, consisting of a roughly equal number of men and women, from a wide range of occupations, and representing a range of ages and time spent working in the City. Each interview lasted between one and a half to three hours. The aim of the interviews was to gain an understanding of how they sensed and experienced the rhythms of their wider workplace, and how they responded to them. During the interviews, my own status as interviewer was never fixed, but continually re-made through a process of negotiation; my personal history of having worked in the City for a period of time, and of familiarity with some of the financial services terminology, helped establish me as someone who was not there to be prurient or in some way critical about the post financial crisis City. A degree of anxiety was expressed by all participants with reference to how they might be viewed by the 'outside' world. At other times, however, my status as a university researcher who has not worked in the City for ten years made it easier to express a naivety and interest in their working lives, and helped them to see the need to offer fuller explanations or descriptions of their daily lives.

The first part of the fieldwork was carried out mainly over a period of five months and represents ten full days of observations in the City. Each of those ten walks was mapped onto a master map of the City (see Appendix A for an example). I walked armed with a notebook and pen for field notes and a phone for taking photos. I took regular coffee stops to be able to make notes whilst observations were still fresh in my mind. The walks lasted anywhere between three hours and six hours, and often included visits to museums and historic places of interest in the City, for example the Museum of London, which specializes in the history of London, the Guildhall, the ceremonial and administrative centre of the City of London Corporation, and the Tower of London.

The observational framework was structured around the external environment, noting both the physical characteristics of the setting and the human use of the space, as well as the time of day, the season, the weather and their relation to the setting. Particular attention was paid to the materiality: the architecture, and the placing of objects which impacted the flows and rhythms of the space and the behaviour of human actors. I also listened to background noise (often very intrusive), traffic noise, human speech and language, the tones of voices, as well as observing the physical characteristics of human actors—their gender, age, clothing and behaviour. I wished to observe and analyse the relationship between corporate space and public space on the City, particularly from a walker's perspective. Paying attention to the rhythms of place also meant observing the order in which events unfolded, such as sequential patterns of behaviour. Following Lefebvre's insights into the polyrhythmic body as the mode of analysis, internal responses were also noted, including sensory perceptions, for example temperature, bodily (dis)comfort, as well as feelings and emotions, reflections and interpretations.

I also collected data by means of photographs taken during the walks. The purpose was to help develop a richer understanding of the setting and to capture data that illustrate the environment in a way that written accounts cannot do in isolation. In line with the observational fieldwork, the aim was to capture the street life of the City, the way that people moved within the space, architectural points of interest, transport termini and the streets at different times of day.

Within the written accounts of my walks I referred to my own history as a worker in the City, particularly in relation to memories which were evoked as I walked. This is a space that I am very familiar with, yet engaging with it as a researcher was very different to engaging with it as someone who works there every day. For example, although in one sense I was immersed in the setting and therefore 'within', I was also free to 'dip in and out' as I wished, finding dates and times for research which accommodated my other responsibilities. I was not wearing business attire; this sometimes marked me out as an 'outsider', albeit one who is familiar with the geography of the place.

## The Patina of the City

Themes emerged from the data collection, which can broadly be grouped into three main headings. Firstly, a sense of the City as a rarefied place shaped by performative rhythms was identified. Secondly, the corporate nature of the City is represented beyond the boundaries of individual organizations to encompass the space outside; the lived space of the City is often privatized with a sense of exclusion present when attempting to navigate the space. Thirdly, whilst the linear rhythms of the City are partly imposed by the temporal rhythms of global finance, they are also local, shaped by its particular history, and influenced by the recurring cycles of crisis. These themes will be discussed and analysed below.

### The City as a Performative Workplace

The linear rhythms of the City are intense and purposeful. At Liverpool Street station, whilst dithering as to which direction I should head towards, I found myself walking against the flow and being almost knocked sideways by the crowd. My hesitancy was contrary to the purposive sense of early morning commuters all around me, as this quote from my field notes shows:

*The sense of purpose is already apparent—very few people are stopping to get their bearings or consult maps, most move swiftly towards the tube entrance or to the main exits. I can't hear the jumble of languages and differently pitched voices that you hear at an airport or other railway stations—the background noise is footsteps and automated announcements, there is little audible conversation.*

> (Liverpool Street station, 8am on a Tuesday
> in March 2015; the rhythms are fast and
> staccato with a sea of bodies moving
> purposefully at the same pace).

On another occasion I travelled in at the end of the working day, arriving just as the rush hour was starting, with workers heading home in the opposite direction to me:

*It's really busy, people everywhere, which I expected, but I'd forgotten how intent and focused rush hour crowds can be when the purpose is focused in one direction . . . it is physically hard work moving against the flow, I am weaving in and out of people. The rhythm is purposeful and directional.*

> (Liverpool Street station, 5pm on a Friday
> in May 2015; again the rhythm is fast and
> builds to a crescendo as people arrive in
> the main concourse and onto the platforms).

All participants vividly described the rhythms of the City. Adjectives used included busy, stressful, and urgent, but by far the most common was purposeful. This sense of rhythms that are, 'not sort of chaos busy, like the West End' (the shopping and entertainment district of London)', but 'intense, fast and focused' (Dave, a business development manager in his thirties with a very positive view of the City). Claire says, 'you have no place here unless you are here to work, and to be seen to be working'. Claire is a woman in her forties, an ex-investment banker who left the City several years ago and found returning to it to carry out our interview to be a stressful experience, full of bodily discomfort; as soon as she started walking alongside me, she was reminded of the intense rhythms which to her were all about performing work. For her and the other participants, the rhythms of the City were not like any other place, because of their focused intensity of purpose, and because they were so acute at certain times of day, and so different when the City is at rest; there is no sense of twenty-four hour nightlife or weekend downtime here.

Many mentioned the stress of walking around such a dense and compact space; Ian, a financial consultant in his forties who enjoys the fast pace of the City, says, 'You just need to know where to go. You need to be able to find your way around.' This sense of navigational confidence was seen to be characteristic of what might be described as 'eurythmia', to use Lefebvre's terminology; in other words, a sense that the rhythms are in harmony with the body. When a sense of 'arrythmia' (a sense of irregularity between the body and the rhythms) takes hold, it is because of a sense of not being able to keep up with the rhythms:

> Certainly you've got to prove yourself, to always be able to keep up . . . I'm not like that, I'm very passive . . . I'm not like that at all . . . I'm past all that now, to be honest. I've just had enough of the place.
>
> (Rob, an insurance broker in his forties)

Rob's feelings about the City are characterized by a sense of weariness. When I asked if his fatigue was caused by his current job or employer, he replied that, no, it was caused by 'the whole place, the City itself'. The concepts of euryhmia and arrhythmia in relation to place will be further discussed in the conclusion to this chapter.

As explained above, the fundamental emphasis with rhythmanalysis is the foregrounding of the body as a means of experiencing rhythm. Whilst walking the City streets, I had to often stop and remind myself to consciously record how my body was feeling as I walked. Once I started to consciously think about and record my bodily responses, I started to notice rhythms everywhere; the way the traffic moved, the way that people moved in and out of buildings, the pace of walking on different streets. Lefebvre links rhythms to repetition (Lefebvre, 2004: 18) but makes the point that repetition in itself does not produce a rhythm—it is the insertion of *difference* which does that. So the noticeably fast rhythms of the morning and evening rush hours, and lunch times when the buildings disgorge hundreds of workers onto the streets at the same time, are created by also witnessing the slower rhythms of mid-afternoon, when only a few people rush up and down the streets, and the strangely tense and silent Sundays.

This sense of the City as dystopian 'after hours,' is attributed to the intense performativity that is expressed during the working week. For Claire, it is brutally exclusive: 'It's a place where you come if you've got a purpose and that's for work—otherwise you don't fit in, you shouldn't be here.'

I was conscious of the way that I walked speedily in this space, my heart often beating fast, my head down. This is magnified at stations, particularly at Liverpool Street, which was my arrival and departure point. On weekdays, especially at rush hour but at other times as well, it is a sea of bodies moving towards the exits. There is little chatter or noise such as you might expect at an airport of other rail destination. The most audible sound is train announcements and the tapping of shoes on the concourse. On a Sunday, however, the scene is both visually and rhythmically transformed, as these photographs (figures 7.2 and 7.3) illustrate:

*Figure 7.2* Liverpool Street station concourse, weekday; business suits and a lack of colour.

Picture by author.

Outside on the streets on a Sunday, the rhythms continued to be different. Tourists stood waiting for buses to take them out of the City, as a contrast to weekday mornings when very few people are waiting for buses but some straight out of the rail terminus and walk to their City destination. People were waiting around, not rushing, heads down, as is the norm on weekdays (as seen in Figure 7.4):

*Figure 7.3* The same view on a Sunday; colour and suitcases.
Picture by author.

With Lefebvre's foregrounding of the body in mind, the body can be used not only as a metronome for sensing the rhythms of place, but metaphorically as well. The main thoroughfares of the City are like the main arteries of the body; you feel the blood flowing, sense the energy and the impatience, the activity. The quieter side roads are like the smaller veins, still carrying the blood, but quieter, calmer and emptier, with a slower rhythm. The linear rhythms of the City are temporal and attuned to commerce, and more specifically finance—the busy early mornings, the days punctuated by flows of people at lunchtime and in the early evening, the rest of the time more or less empty streets, with workers treating them like internal corridors. There

*Figure 7.4* Bishopsgate on a Sunday afternoon; people waiting, not rushing purposefully. Picture by author.

is a sense that the dominant rhythms are creating a place where anything not connected to patterns of intensity and focus is only 'on show', not to be used; participants talked about the particular 'atmosphere' of the City, and connected it with an unusually focused intensity on performing work in a stylized and visible way.

## The Corporate City—Both Inside and Outside

The rhythms are noticeably slower and less frantic in the enclosed spaces in which the City abounds—the pretty gardens, the squares, but all too often these places are locked and inaccessible. It is as if the City discourages attempts to slow down, and let your body rest, as I recorded in my field notes:

> *Even on a sunny evening in May the parks and gardens are empty, and sometimes inaccessible; they seem to be created to be looked at, not to use.*
> (6pm on a June evening, 2015, walking down Camomile Street)

Wandering through the streets posed a very real problem of access, which both interrupted my attempts to stroll through the space, and both annoyed and unnerved me. As well as omnipresent construction work, many streets were blocked off for no apparent reason, and attempting to take short cuts through side streets and alleyways proved frustrating and usually unsuccessful, as can be seen (figure 7.5 and 7.6) in the photographs below:

*Figure 7.5* Access denied.
Picture by author.

On one occasion, I was asked to stop taking photographs of the interior of the Royal Exchange; I was attempting to capture the stunning architecture of the interior. On another, I was prevented from accessing the ruins of a Roman Temple on a busy road by a security guard who explained that

*Figure 7.6* A reminder that the City is often a private space.
Picture by author.

the land was private. Participants also described the sense of frustration that was experienced when trying to walk through the City, with many complaints about the endless construction and the privatization of public spaces such as parks and squares.

For Sasha, a sales executive in her twenties, what she describes as the 'exclusive' and gendered nature of the City space is a mirror of what happens within her organization, describing how 'it's like there's a club of City men which women are not part of'. She describes how it is men who demonstrate spatial confidence on the streets, connecting this to the men who seem to know the 'shorthand' and banter which allows them to successfully network in their organizations, reminding us of Allen and Pryke's (1994) description of the cohesive clubbiness of the City. This reflects my personal experience of working in the City, since one of my most vivid memories is the feeling of claustrophobia, in that I could never escape the sense that I was in a male bastion. This was not only because I was working in an organization where the senior positions were held by men, but because when I left the building, at lunchtimes and in the evenings, I seemed to be immersed in crowds of men, particularly in bars and restaurants. Women accounted for about 40 per cent of employees where I worked (mainly in support roles), but simply were not visible in the space in the same way as men were.

Most participants, whilst feeling that no firm would risk its reputation by not adhering to diversity regulations, did agree that women were far less visible on the City streets. Some had not consciously notice this until I asked what they thought in the interviews:

> 'It's not something I would have picked up on, to be honest, but when you ask, well, yes. It's just men outside',
> (Tim, a software development engineer in his twenties)

The rhythms of the global financial markets do instil a culture of long hours for which financial districts such as the City and Wall Street are infamous. When I worked in the City, it was common to hear people bragging about working the 'banker 9–5' (defined as 9 am until 5 am the following day). This demanding culture was described by all participants, even though many did not work in finance and some were 'back office' staff or support staff rather than traders or investment bankers. For most, the City is brutally exclusive:

> It is a place which is very demanding of staff. In that respect it is a hard place in which to work, it's not a place in which you can last if you don't come up to scratch . . . you can't afford to slack off, ever, because your career will be over.
> (Philip, an actuary in his sixties)

Ian describes the type of person who 'fits' in the City as being: 'young, energetic, ambitious, prepared above all to work really *really* hard.' Drive, ambition and the capacity for working hard were universally cited as 'City attributes' for all roles in the Square Mile.

According to Phillip, the demands are endless: 'There are no soft options in the City. No padding. You can't just sit there filling your days, you'd be exposed. So much is demanded of you'. This idea that to earn—and keep—your place is linked to how you are seen to be filling your days was raised by many, 'presenteeism' being viewed as a key characteristic of City life. As Pete, an insurance specialist says: 'You know, it goes down well if you've got in early and gone late, and . . . that certainly gets noticed. Not so much what goes on in between,' and for others, it is associated with being a game that you have to play:

> In the City it's like everyone is parading, saying look at me, I'm so important, I have to be in early, work late and so on . . . in reality outside of traders I don't think people need to be at their desks as often as the prevailing culture seems to demand they should be. There's a lot of posturing.
>
> (Neil, IT consultant in his forties)

Anna, a Communications Director for an investment bank in her thirties, agrees that women are less visible on the streets, but she relates this to the pressures placed upon women to be visible inside the office, and to not leave their desks for fear of being seen as less committed than men, although she considers this directly in relation to working mothers. As she explains:

> I am always apologising, feeling bad, hoping nobody will notice if I sneak away to pick up the children . . . but this is the last place on earth you can do that. It's like there's a bloody alarm goes off outside or something if you dare to look towards the door. And you just know that all the men are raising their eyes while they roll their sleeves up and keep working and someone else picks up all their domestic responsibilities.

Jennifer, a chartered surveyor in her fifties, agrees that 'you still need to be seen to be working twice as hard as the men, and always look like you're keeping up'.

In this way, the sense of the City acting as a private organization is reinforced on the streets and through the ability to keep up with its rhythms; to exhibit spatial rhythmic confidence is a symbol of belonging to the City club. The temporal rhythms are equally demanding. But at the same time, the comments above relate the lack of women in the space *outside* to the 'presenteeism' faced by women (or some women) *inside*, and the need to keep up with the demanding pace. In this way, both the inside and outside space are organized in a gendered way.

### The City as a Site of Order and Disorder

Most participants expressed a defensive reaction when asked about how they felt the City was perceived by those not working there. Whether their perceptions were positive or negative, fifteen of the eighteen respondents articulated a sense that 'outsiders can't understand' when talking about the most recent financial crisis; this was raised spontaneously in interviews. Most conflated the place with a sense of urgency and with repeated cycles of crisis. As Nigel, an insurance broker in his forties says, 'It's so pressurized here—you can only ever understand if you work here'.

Rob connected the performative nature of the City with excessive behaviour for which the world of finance is well known. This perhaps explains the nervousness that interviews expressed when talking about this; they all felt tainted or judged in some way for the excesses of the City, and were keen to explain that they weren't 'like that'. Yet many acknowledged the extent to which that culture does still exist. Jennifer argued:

> Because it is a pressured environment, some people have to let off steam. But they let off steam in such a way that they don't know how to come down. You know, they just come strutting into work and they're wide eyed, and you think, oh, you've been up all night . . . it's accepted, rewarded even.

Jennifer also believes that the build-up and then release of pressure is a rhythmic characteristic of the City, one which is played out on the streets:

> You go home at night and you see people fallen over in the gutter . . . and you know that they'll scrape themselves up, go and buy a new suit, shirt, tie and be back again the next day bright and early.

She describes the 'underbelly' of the City as being 'not what it looks like on the surface. There's a lot of, you know, unhappiness, and certainly where I worked there was a lot of drug abuse'.

This excessive behaviour seems to be at odds with the serious, focused, hard-working ethic of the City that was cited by so many as being its key characteristic. Yet this sense of it being a pressure cooker which needs to explode from time to time, and which forces, and even rewards, this type of performance, was also accepted. This coexistence of order and disorder was experienced as a rhythm by many participants; Jennifer and Rob both felt that the endless cycles of boom and bust, and the way that the intensity of City life builds to a crescendo, pauses, and then starts again, was a characteristic City rhythm. This was perceived not only as part of a wider global rhythm (the City will always be influenced and affected by the shockwaves of the global economy) but also as a very situated spatial rhythm, in that the intensity builds on the streets in the way that people move speedily and purposefully, and then 'let off steam' in a way that is played out on the streets. Certainly a view of masculinity as being at times out of control in the City was prevalent amongst participants. Many talked about the most recent financial crisis, and were uncomfortably aware of the public perception of the City as being about 'loads of City boys doing dodgy deals and wrecking everything . . . they were out of control weren't they?' (Anna). Although most felt that post-crisis regulation had controlled some of this excess, as Rob says:

> Scratch the surface, it's still there, you know, it's still there . . . People saying, you know, we haven't got the money but people still do go out. . . . I mean, it's not as bad as it was, but, you know, it's still there.

Lorraine, a personal assistant in her twenties, agrees that the public rejection of the excesses of the City has merely pushed this behaviour into the background: 'It might have changed a little, but I think under the surface it's still there. They probably feel that they can't be too in your face yet, but it will go back to that, I bet.'

For Claire, it has always been this type of masculinity—loud, excessive, all about money, competition and status—which defines the City: 'The predominant masculinity was always the hands-dirty traders who were grudgingly respected by everyone else' as she describes.

Rob agrees that it is this behaviour which is not only accepted but rewarded here, and that is can never disappear entirely:

> You know, if the company recognises it, they reward you. And sometimes I think, are they rewarding them for the wrong attitude because that's what got the City in the problems in the first place, let's face it. But there is so much pressure to keep being like that.

From these observations, we can see a connection between the world of finance as represented in popular culture, for example, the movies *Wall Street* (Pressman and Stone, 1987) and *The Wolf of Wall Street* (Scorsese, 2013), where masculinity is excessive, priapic and out of control. As McDowell (1997) described, ideas about potency dominate modern mythologies of men in the City. Characteristics such as being tough and ruthless, aggressive and explicit in terms of language are highly valued and inherently masculine.

From the participants' accounts, it is the rhythms of place that force a strict performativity, which rewards periods of excessive behaviour, as long as profit is achieved and maintained, and which forces behavioural norms based upon dominant versions of masculinity. There is a rhythmic connection perceived, then, between the rhythms of global financial crisis and the situated spatial rhythms of the City streets. Again, the boundaries between what happens inside the organizations which make up the City, and what happens outside, become fluid.

The observational findings show that there is, therefore, a disconnect between the City as conceived space—abstract, rational, ordered—and the lived experience, or perceived space, which history demonstrates is about cycles of crisis and disorder. Lefebvre (2003 [1970]) argues that a central component of the overall dynamic of capitalist development lies in the production of the built environment and the process of city building. He conceptualizes cities as subject to implosion and explosion (see also Amin and Thrift, 2002; Thrift, 2005); their destructive social and environmental characteristics lead to cycles of instability and crisis.

## Conclusion

The aim of this chapter has been to show how the foregrounding of the body can illuminate how place is used and sensed. Lefebvre reminds us that the human body lives polyrhythmically, but that bundles of rhythms from the immediate environment penetrate it. A rhythmanalysis is able to show how this interplay of rhythms is experienced and sensed, and through it a shared communality of performance, of situated and particular rhythms, can be described. Through its rhythms, therefore, the sense of how the City coheres as a space can be seen and how its distinctive patina (Thrift, 1996), which I conceptualize as performative, exclusionary and subject to cycles of disorder, is created. In this way, then the 'patina' of the City, it would seem, is shaped by performative, intense, focused rhythms, which are cyclical in terms of the temporal connections with global markets, with the linear rhythms of the working day, and in terms of the particular history and culture of this place, which is characterized by tension between order and disorder.

The fieldwork undertaken has enabled a view of the City as operating rhythmically on many levels—as a global financial centre, as a local 'district' within the larger city of greater London, as a historic setting which maintains its distinctive cultural and spatial traditions, and as a public space which often operates as a private space.

Methodologically, it is important to avoid privileging any one particular sensory perception, but to pay attention to ocular, auditory, and muscular sensations, as well as to the patterns of movement which unfold, so that a multi-sensory understanding of the rhythms can be experienced. Drawing upon Lefebvre's (2004) concepts of eurythmia and arrhythmia, eurythmia in the City is characterized by navigational and spatial confidence and an ability to 'keep up' with the rhythms and to belong. Arrhythmia, on the other hand, is characterized by feelings of anxiety, fatigue and a sense of displacement and exclusion. In this research, feelings of eurythmia and arrhythmia emerged as analytical tools to help understand how feelings of gendered inclusion and exclusion can be expressed spatially.

The sense of both immersion within the rhythms, and an occasional detachment from them, in order to observe, is a difficult but important balance to maintain; in this study, time taken out from walking to pause in a coffee shop or similar public space helped to achieve this balance. This also helps with cultivating a reflexive approach; familiar places are the settings for rhythmically apprehended routines, but habitual processes and routines become unreflexive, so even in a situation or, in this case, geographical place which is familiar, Lefebvre's cues to listen to it as if it were a symphony, or to watch it as a ballet, is useful. Understanding the rhythms of the City, and how they are experienced, extends our understanding of how work settings influence the lived experience of organizational life, and vice versa.

### Methodological Reflections

Since the focus of this chapter has been on the application of rhythmanalysis for empirical explorations of workplaces, it is worth considering both its methodological limitations and its potential.

Using rhythmanalysis as a starting point allowed me to develop a sensory method of navigating and understanding the research setting. Through its application, I have been able to observe how the place is sensed and experienced, and how patterns of inclusion and exclusion are present, in a way that it would not have been possible to uncover merely through interviewing City workers, who are aware of the frenzied rhythms but do not, in general, have the time to step outside them. Observing the flows of crowds and developing notions of rhythm provide a means of engaging with how time, space and place interrelate. Lefebvre insists that to be a successful rhythmanalyst, you must experience the rhythms with your whole body in the same way that those you are observing do. As Lefebvre informs us, the researcher 'must arrive at the concrete through experience' (Lefebvre, 2004: 31). Experiencing the rhythms subjectively, and foregrounding my bodily responses and senses of bodily eurythmia and arrhythmia, which as explained above are key analytical tools when carrying out a rhythmanalysis, allowed a deeper understanding than would have been possible through interviews alone. The interviews added to this sensory methodology, however, by helping me to understand how City workers 'make sense' of the place cognitively. Whilst a case study or an in-depth ethnography would have yielded rich insights into the rhythms of a particular organization, my interest was in the setting as a whole and how the rhythms 'outside' interrelate with, and sometimes replicate, the lived experience of 'inside', particularly in relation to gendered practices on the streets and inside the buildings.

Whilst the practice of walking was both relevant in this setting, since it is representative of how City workers move around the setting, and generated rich data, there are other methods of analysing rhythms which could be explored as complementary methods. Whilst the participant interviews generated rich accounts of the experience of working life in the City, only one interview (with Claire) was conducted as we walked together through the streets, following the spatial shadowing method described in the methodology section. The rhythms of the City were emphasized during our interview with an emotional intensity that was stronger during this interview than any other. Kusenbach (2003), whilst discussing lived experiences of place, argues that sedentary interviews discourage context sensitive reactions of the interviewer and interviewee, and separate participants from their routine experiences and practices. Evans and Jones (2011) argue that walking interviews generate richer data because participants are prompted by meanings and connections to the surrounding environment, and claim that it is intuitively sensible for researchers to ask interviewees to talk about the places that they are interested in while they are in that place. My experience with Claire suggests that walking with an interview participant allows the narrative to evolve spatially rather than temporally, and produced more spontaneous and emotional data as the surrounding environment prompted discussions of place, and her bodily discomfort was evident as she became immersed once again in the rhythms of place.

To conclude, a Lefebvrian rhythmanalysis can furnish organizational scholars with an embodied, immersive way of exploring the subjective and cultural experiences of place. This is important as it adds to our understanding of how organizational settings are sensed and lived. The rhythms of place are not just individual, but collective. Analysing rhythm can show how this communal experience manifests in a particular place. Organizational setting can therefore be depicted, sensed and experienced through its ensemble of rhythms.

## References

Allen, J. and Pryke, M. (1994). The production of service space. *Environment and Planning D: Society and Space, 12*(4), 453–475.

Amin, A. and Cohendet, P. (2003). *Knowledge Practices, Communities and Competences in Firms.* Oxford: Oxford University Press.

Amin, A. and Thrift, N. (2002). *Cities: Reimagining the Urban.* Cambridge: Polity Press.

Beunza, D. and Stark, D. (2003). The organization of responsiveness: Innovation and recovery in the trading rooms of lower Manhattan. *Socio-Economic Review, 1*(2), 135–164.

Beyes, T. and Steyaert, C. (2012). Spacing organization: Non-representational theory and performing organizational space. *Organization, 19*(1), 45–61.

Brenner, N. (2000). The urban question: Reflections on Henri Lefebvre, urban theory and the politics of scale. *International Journal of Urban and Regional Research, 24*(2), 361–378.

Brenner, N. and Elden, S. (2009). Henri Lefebvre on state, space, territory. *International Political Sociology, 3*(4), 353–377.

Brenner, N. and Schmid, C. (2015). Towards a new epistemology of the urban? *City, 19*(2–3), 151–182.

CityofLondon.gov.uk (2017). *Statistics About the City.* Retrieved July 12, 2017, from www.cityoflondon.gov.uk/business/economic-research-and-information/Pages

Coakley, J. (1992). London as an international financial centre. In L. Budd and S. Whimster (Eds.), *Global Finance and Urban Living: A Study of Metropolitan Change* (pp. 52–72). London: Routledge.

Corbridge, S., Thrift, N. J. and Martin, R. (1994). *Money, Power, and Space.* Oxford: Blackwell.

Dale, K. (2005). Building a social materiality: Spatial and embodied politics in organizational control. *Organization, 12*(5), 649–678.

Dale, K. and Burrell, G. (2007). *The Spaces of Organisation and the Organisation of Space: Power, Identity and Materiality at Work.* London: Palgrave Macmillan.

DeLyser, D. and Sui, D. (2013). Crossing the qualitative-quantitative divide II: Inventive approaches to big data, mobile methods, and rhythmanalysis. *Progress in Human Geography, 37*(2), 293–305.

Duffy, M., Waitt, G., Gorman-Murray, A. and Gibson, C. (2011). Bodily rhythms: Corporeal capacities to engage with festival spaces. *Emotion, Space and Society, 4*(1), 17–24.

Edensor, T. (2010). Walking in rhythms: Place, regulation, style and the flow of experience. *Visual Studies, 25*(1), 69–79.

Edensor, T. (Ed.). (2012). *Geographies of Rhythm: Nature, Place, Mobilities and Bodies*. London: Ashgate Publishing, Ltd.

Edensor, T. and Holloway, J. (2008). Rhythmanalysing the coach tour: The Ring of Kerry, Ireland. *Transactions of the Institute of British Geographers*, 33(4), 483–501.

Elden, S. (2004). *Understanding Henri Lefebvre*. London: A&C Black.

Elkin, L. (2016). *Flaneuse: Women Walk the City*. London: Chatto & Windus.

Evans, J. and Jones, P. (2011). The walking interview: Methodology, mobility and place. *Applied Geography*, 31(2), 849–858.

Ford, J. and Harding, N. (2004). We went looking for an organization but could find only the metaphysics of its presence. *Sociology*, 38(4), 815–830.

French, S., Leyshon, A. and Thrift, N. (2009). A very geographical crisis: The making and breaking of the 2007–2008 financial crisis. *Cambridge Journal of Regions, Economy and Society*, 2(2), 287–302.

Halford, S. (2004). Towards a sociology of organizational space. *Sociological Research Online*, 9(1). Retrieved from www.socresonline.org.uk/9/1/halford.html

Hall, T., Lashua, B. and Coffey, A. (2008). Sound and the everyday in qualitative research. *Qualitative inquiry*, 14(6), 1019–1040.

Ho, K. (2009). *Liquidated: An Ethnography of Wall Street*. Durham, NC: Duke University Press.

King, A. D. (1990). *Global Cities: Post-Imperialism and the Internationalization of London*. Abingdon: Taylor & Francis.

Kornberger, M. and Clegg, S. (2003). The architecture of complexity. *Culture and Organization*, 9(2), 75–91.

Kornberger, M. and Clegg, S. R. (2004). Bringing space back in: Organizing the generative building. *Organization Studies*, 25(7), 1095–1114.

Kusenbach, M. (2003). Street phenomenology: The go-along as ethnographic research tool. *Ethnography*, 4(3), 455–485.

Lefebvre, H. (1971). *Everyday Life in the Modern World* (translated by Sacha Rabinovitch). London: Blooomsbury.

Lefebvre, H. (1991). *The Production of Space* (translated by Donald Nicholson-Smith). Oxford: Blackwell Publishing.

Lefebvre, H. (2003). *The Urban Revolution*. Minneapolis: The University of Minnesota Press.

Lefebvre, H. (2004). *Rhythmanalysis: Space, Time and Everyday Life*. London: A&C Black.

Lyon, D. (2016). Doing audio-visual montage to explore time and space: The everyday rhythms of Billingsgate Fish Market. *Sociological Research Online*, 21(3), 12.

Matos Wunderlich, F. I. L. I. P. A. (2008). Walking and rhythmicity: Sensing urban space. *Journal of Urban Design*, 13(1), 125–139.

McCann, E. J. (1999). Race, protest, and public space: Contextualizing Lefebvre in the US city. *Antipode*, 31(2), 163–184.

McDowell, L. (1997). *Capital Culture: Money, Sex and Power at Work*. Oxford: Blackwell.

Merrifield, A. (2006). *Henri Lefebvre: A Critical Introduction*. Abingdon: Taylor & Francis.

Merrifield, A. (2011). The right to the city and beyond: Notes on a Lefebvrian reconceptualization. *City*, 15(3–4), 473–481.

Meyer, K. (2008). Rhythms, streets, cities. In K. Goonewardena, S. Kipfer, R. Milgrom and C. Schmid (Eds.), *Space, Difference, Everyday Life: Reading Henri Lefebvre* (pp. 147–160). London: Routledge.

Paquette, D. and McCartney, A. (2012). Soundwalking and the bodily exploration of places. *Canadian Journal of Communication, 37*(1), 135.

Pink, S. (2007). Walking with video. *Visual Studies, 22*(3), 240–252.

Porter, R. (1998). *London: A Social History.* Cambridge, MA: Harvard University Press.

Pressman, E. (Producer) and Stone, O. (Director). (1987). *Wall Street* (Motion Picture). United States: 20th Century Fox.

Prigge, W. (2008). Reading the urban revolution: Space and representation. In K. Goonewardena, S. Kipfer, R. Milgrom and C. Schmid (Eds.), *Space, Difference, Everyday Life: Reading Henri Lefebvre* (pp. 46–61). London: Routledge.

Raulet-Croset, N. and Borzeix, A. (2014). Researching spatial practices through commentated walks: "on the move" and "walking with." *Journal of Organizational Ethnography, 3*(1), 27–42.

Reinhart, C.M. and Rogoff, K.S., (2008). Is the 2007 US sub-prime financial crisis so different? An international historical comparison. *American Economic Review, 98*(2), 339–344.

Roberts, R. and Kynaston, D. (2002). *City State: A Contemporary History of the City of London and How Money Triumphed.* London: Profile.

Scorsese, M. (Producer and Director). (2013). *The Wolf of Wall Street* (Motion Picture). Hollywood, California: Paramount Pictures.

Sikka, P. (2009). Financial crisis and the silence of the auditors. *Accounting, Organizations and Society, 34*(6), 868–873.

Simpson, P. (2008). Chronic everyday life: Rhythmanalysing street performance. *Social & Cultural Geography, 9*(7), 807–829.

Simpson, P. (2012). Apprehending everyday rhythms: Rhythmanalysis, time-lapse photography, and the space-times of street performance. *Cultural Geographies, 19*(4), 423–445.

Soja, E. W. (1998). Thirdspace: Journeys to Los Angeles and other real-and-imagined places. *Capital & Class, 22*(1), 137–139.

Taylor, S. and Spicer, A. (2007). Time for space: A narrative review of research on organizational spaces. *International Journal of Management Reviews, 9*(4), 325–346.

Thibaud, J. P. (2013). Commented city walks. *Wi: Journal of Mobile Culture, 7*(1), 1–32.

Thrift, N. (1996). *Spatial Formations*, Vol. 42. London: Sage.

Thrift, N. (2005). But malice aforethought: Cities and the natural history of hatred. *Transactions of the institute of British Geographers, 30*(2), 133–150.

Tyler, M. (2011). Tainted love: From dirty work to abject labour in Soho's sex shops. *Human Relations, 64*(11), 1477–1500.

Tyler, M. and Cohen, L. (2010). Spaces that matter: Gender performativity and organizational space. *Organization Studies, 31*(2), 175–198.

Wasserman, V. and Frenkel, M. (2015). Spatial work in between glass ceilings and glass walls: Gender-class intersectionality and organizational aesthetics. *Organization Studies, 36*(11), 1485–1505.

Watkins, C. (2005). Representations of space, spatial practices and spaces of representation: An application of Lefebvre's spatial triad. *Culture and Organization, 11*(3), 209–220.

Zukin, S. (1991). *Landscapes of Power.* Berkeley and Los Angeles: University of California Press.

# 8 Lunch Beat, Lefebvre and the Politics of Organizational Space

*Tuomo Peltonen and Perttu Salovaara*

## Introduction: Lefebvre's Triad and Its Interpretation in Organization Studies

Research into organizational space has advanced notably in recent years (e.g. Beyes and Steyaert, 2011; Clegg and Kornberger, 2006; Dale, 2005; Dale and Burrell, 2008; Hernes, 2004; Kingma, 2008; Taylor and Spicer, 2007; Watkins, 2005), and Henri Lefebvre's writings on space, particularly his 1991 book *The Production of Space*, offer a comprehensive framework for the field. In particular, Lefebvre's triadic model of social space—comprising conceived, perceived and lived space (Lefebvre, 1991a)—has been widely used for spatial analysis in organization studies.

However, the theoretical and philosophical commitments informing Lefebvre's work have not yet received the same level of attention as the triad (for exceptions, see Dale and Burrell, 2008; Beyes and Steyaert, 2011; Zhang, 2006). As a consequence, the spatial triad has largely become detached from the critical societal analysis with which his larger oeuvre is engaged (Elden, 2001, 2004a; Merrifield, 2000). The surge in interest in Lefebvre's work is cause for both celebration and concern, as Elden (2001, 2004b) warns. There is a risk that his background in philosophy and Marxism may remain unnoticed, causing him to be categorized as, for instance, a 'postmodern thinker' or 'philosopher of space'. This may result in 'his political edge [being] blunted and his philosophical complexity [being] denied' (Elden, 2001: 810).

The aim of this chapter is to situate the triadic model in its wider context and reconsider the meaning of this in terms of spatial analysis. Reevaluation is necessary to address the concern that the triadic model may be too easily used as a 'tool' for spatial analysis without consideration of the more broad social, economic and cultural aspects of spatial production. The chapter studies how everyday life, even its emancipatory aspects, is constructed by the capitalist modes of control and production. For this purpose, we examine 'Lunch Beat', a 2010 fad in Scandinavia in which people were offered a chance to disco dance during their lunch break.

The chapter begins by providing the broad intellectual background of Lefebvre's social and political thinking. This is followed by an overview of the current use of Lefebvre's spatial triad in organization studies. Using the case of Lunch Beat, we then show how Lefebvre's spatial triad allows for not only analysing space and movement within a place but also obtaining insights into the 'organized society of controlled consumption' where 'everyday life has become an object of consideration and is the province of organization' (Lefebvre, 1971: 72). We conclude by arguing that the Lunch Beat movement 'failed' because it did not stop re-affirming the conceived space of work; a lunch disco mirrors the canteen work tradition and occurs within the given one-hour lunch period. In its dual opposition to the workplace, it remained defined by the cultural and political discourses attached to work.

## The Philosophical, Political and Social Context of Lefebvre's Work

The literary output of Lefebvre is vast and varied, comprising 72 books, numerous articles, and writings on the works of Marx, Hegel and Lenin (Elden, 2004a: 4). In 1975, Lefebvre said, 'I write a lot, a lot more than I publish, but I do not consider myself as a writer' (Lefebvre, 1975: 9). Maybe because he processes his ideas through writing and continues to think throughout the work, his texts seldom speak for themselves; one has to understand the background, context, audience and French influences in order to understand Lefebvre's work.

Lefebvre was a practicing Marxist. He was not only a professional academic devoted to publishing papers on capitalism, social critique and social change but also a member of the French Communist Party and a socialist and revolutionary in many forms and contexts (Merrifield, 2000; Elden, 2004a: 3). Lefebvre's Marxism is evident in the way he aimed to incorporate traditional concepts such as exchange value and the capitalist mode of production into a nascent spatial analysis (Lefebvre, 1979, 1980). Space, for him, was not merely a site or context for establishment of relations of production, but something produced according to the logic of capitalist accumulation. Lefebvre (1991a: 104) writes about a 'political economy of space', suggesting that spatial dynamics constitute a central political issue in industrialized societies, where 'space has taken on . . . a reality . . . much like . . . money and capital' (Lefebvre, 1991a: 26).

For Marx, money 'serves as a *universal measure of value*' (Marx, 1887: 67), and it thus provides a means for assessing the value of various commodities. For Marx, the value of a commodity corresponds with the amount of labour it took to produce the commodity. Therefore, the exchange value of a commodity does not depend on it as an object, but on the process of production and the way this production is economically organized and societally governed. Marx emphasizes that the exchange value of a commodity—its value in money—is misleading; production comprises various conditions required to produce the commodity. When raw materials and distribution—including branding, marketing and sales—are considered, the social nature of value creation becomes more explicit.

Lefebvre adapts Marx's value creation theory to space, conceptualizing space as a social production. For Lefebvre (1991a), it would be too simplistic to assume 'correspondence between social actions and social locations, between spatial functions and spatial forms' (p. 34) as the value of a space, place or building is not determined only by its physical form. Rather, in general, conceptualizing space requires consideration of the social context that brought it forth. Any space—Lefebvre uses a courthouse and a cathedral as examples—is a product of its time and of the politics that gave birth to it. These buildings depend on 'the creative capacity . . . of a community or collectivity, of a group' (Lefebvre, 1991a: 115) that is capable of investing in and providing resources for construction. Even the countryside, as a (human) cultural production, relies on 'peasants to give it form' (Lefebvre, 1991a: 115). Space is a social production in which a set of ideas, values, principles and practices are moulded into action. 'The analysis of any space', Lefebvre (1991a: 116) writes, 'brings us up against the dialectical relationship between demand and command, along with its attendant questions: "Who?," "For whom?," "By whose agency?," "Why and how?"' These questions indicate that space is not non-historic since its production is related to history, politics and society. Thus, space cannot be analysed within the triad as a non-historic entity either. Through discussing the case of 'Lunch Disco' in relation to its social production, we hope to create a new, more complex interpretation of the event.

Lefebvre (1991a: 116) is interested in the 'history of space' as a 'social reality' and as 'a set of relations and forms'. This implies a Marxist undercurrent in Lefebvre's thinking, according to which understanding space requires articulating the political and social context of that space and the capitalist nature of its value creation. Acknowledgement of these interests, which underlie spatial projects, creates limits for what is new and for what should diverge from the ordinary. Our study of Lunch Disco below shows a case that failed to realize a space that served as an alternative to dominant modes of capitalist spatial production.

## Domination and Control Through Spatial Organization

In the history of organization, one of the most prevalent ideas about control involves bringing a workforce together and binding them within planned spatial arrangements, such as farms, fields, factories, work sites and offices. In his early work, Lefebvre (1957/2000, 1963) discussed natural boundaries and how regions used to be divided according to mountain ranges, rivers and lakes, forests or other natural signs as well as how this system in advanced modernism was replaced by the rational calculations of the capitalist era. This distinction between natural and rational boundaries reflects the difference between the phenomenological experience of lived space and the conceived, more abstract representation of space. The way in which a space is perceived has an impact on social formations; practices that occur in the space, that is, the way in which people relate to a space and interact with it, are constructed over time as routines and cultural habits (cf. Dale, 2005: 656–657).

Applied to today's context, this means that workplaces such as offices as well as city planning are, in contemporary Western society, not something that emerges organically or that is designed along natural boundaries, but is planned on an architect's drawing board. The interests of various stakeholders; politics, managerial and administrative discourses; and current concepts regarding organization and productivity influence the planning process. Yet, these discourses highlight that the planning process is dominated by rational and abstract terminology. This creates a constant tension between the abstract space of regulation and control and perceived—lived spaces. Merrifield (2000: 175) observes that

> Lefebvre knows too well . . . that the social space of lived experience gets crushed and vanquished by an abstract conceived space. In our society, in other words, what is lived and perceived is of secondary importance compared to what is conceived. (. . .) Conceptions, it seems, rule our lives, sometimes for the good, but more often—given the structure of society—to our detriment.

Lefebvre seems to suggest that, particularly in the context of Western modernity and capitalism, the contestation between the conceived and the lived space might characterize critical dynamics regarding the production of space. This tension reveals the dialectics of power and control that affect the production of space. Although it is theoretically possible for the lived space to take a leading role in the performance of a social space, this is less typical in Western societies and institutions than in, for example, Eastern cultures (Lefebvre, 1991a). This interpretation reflects that societal control mechanisms are not value-neutral since abstract conceptualizations are preferred over embodied experiences in the context of societal decision-making in Western cultures.

Lefebvre is neither a straightforward analyst of contemporary structures and ontologies of the political economy similar to, for example, Baran and Sweezy (1966) or Braverman (1974) nor a pure theorist of alienation and cultural hegemony in the tradition of Frankfurt Critical Theory (Held, 1980). Instead, it is good to remember that his early work on peasant life in Pyrénees shows his engagement with rationalized capitalism as sociopractical, aesthetic and highly philosophical. As useful as the triad seems to be for providing a wide context for spatial analysis, we argue that the model tends to be used as a tool for adding multiple perspectives to organizational analysis, although this instrumentalization may neglect the larger space-external social, political and economical environment. Following Lefebvre's main argument, any space—an office space, home, governmental structure or cityscape—is a product of its time and can be best contextualized by the circumstances, questions and needs of the time that produced it. Analysis of a space without such consideration may be incomplete and possibly even misleading, as we suggest below.

In Lefebvre's critique, abstract spaces, no longer adjusted or unique to a situated community of practice, conceptualize space as a commodity in global networks of power and control. However, the term 'lived space' expands the conceptualization of space towards a more processual and fluid ontology. As Beyes and Steyart (2011) describe, lived space is not only an embodiment, representation or entity, but conveyed in 'intensities, capacities and forces; rhythms, cycles, encounters, events, movements and flows; instincts, affects, atmospheres and auras; relations, knots and assemblages' (p. 47). Considering organizations and space as processual, evolving concepts and able to be re-produced through, for example, scholarly work, offers a reason to suggest that space is performative and name this quality 'spacing'. The performative homogeneity of capitalist space—where spaces represent consumption and control—undermines the social effects of space.

The presentation of lived and perceived spaces alongside dominant abstractly conceived spaces needs to be understood as a political act in Lefebvre's work. He wants to overcome the separation between 'institutional' and 'everyday' meanings of space, pointing to the possibilities inherent in the dialectics between the two. Lived and perceived spaces are forms of resistance, akin to de Certeau's (1984) practices of consumption enacted within the micro-moments of everyday life. According to Merrifield (2000: 176), Lefebvre's analysis of social space focuses on the informal moments of spatial doing and imagining; 'everyday life . . . internalizes all three moments of Lefebvre's spatial triad'. In this politicized sense, Lefebvre's theory of triadic space represents a critical attempt to address the inherent shortcomings of institutionalized description of spaces as the standardized 'managed spaces' of capitalist institutions.

## Festival: Spatial Emancipation

If conceived space aligns with attempts to control, lived space can be connected with life and experience and, as said above, with resistance. Yet, an understanding of the triad as a contestation between the conceived and lived space should be tempered with the argument Lefebvre makes in *The Production of Space*: that the three aspects of space are inseparable, and all are needed to inform what he calls a 'unitary theory' of space (Lefebvre, 1991a: 11). He makes an analogy to the human body, illustrating how bodily operations (perceived), knowledge and ideology related to human sciences (conceived) and partly unconscious symbolizations and emotions—the 'heart' of the body (lived)—are all needed for a complete, functioning subject. The three dimensions are ontologically interconnected, yet not equally present;

they are fluctuating constellations: 'it is reasonable to assume that spatial practice, representations of space and representational space contribute in different ways to the production of space according to their qualities and attributes, according to the society or mode of production in question, and according to the historical period' (Lefebvre, 1991a: 46). When there is an aspect of control to the triad, it takes place in a fluctuating fashion. This applies to the emancipatory aspect, too.

Taking into account Lefebvre's intellectual background in Surrealism and Situationism (Ross and Lefebvre, 1997), it is plausible to deduce a considerable normative emphasis in his work on the subversive potential of lived space to serve as the realm of fantasy, symbolism and the unconscious. The Surrealist movement tapped into Freud to inform a Marxist method of exploring and discovering the transformative powers of the collective subconscious (Carr and Zanetti, 2000). Untamed inner fantasies and irrational dream-like visions offer a reservoir of potential resistance to the alienating powers of capitalist representations and normalizations, even though the two are always relationally unified.

The *festival* is a concrete manifestation of the absent potential of subliminal moments in Lefebvre's work (Grindon, 2013). To him, the rural festival represents a joyful 'taking of the space' that celebrates the release of suppressed passions and desires as a form of resistance and upheaval. He thought that the excess of the festivals could be transported to urban and industrial contexts, where it might subvert the bureaucratic order and control associated with the hegemony of the conceived space. A festival for peasants 'is a day of excess (le jour de la démesure). Anything goes. This exuberance, this enormous orgy of eating and drinking—[has] no limits, no rules' (Lefebvre, 1991b: 202). Festivals emancipate the oppressed by revealing the absurdity of everyday life and space (Merrifield, 2000). In terms of production of space, they could be seen as subversions of the capitalist divisions inherent in articulations of the conceived space through the collective performance of a carnival. In a broad sense, this could result in the transformation of subjects of capitalism (peasants, workers) from products to producers of sociality and space (Grindon, 2013).

Research emerging from these reflections should examine the power relations inherent in the dialectics between the spatial appropriations of architects, administrative planners and capitalists on the one hand (conceived space) and the symbolizations that users attach to space through sensemaking and signified meaning (perceived and lived space) on the other hand. Overall, however, the main focus would not be on space as an abstraction from the society by which it is surrounded but on the way in which it results from and is a product of historical conditions and reflects societal dynamics. The tension to be observed is whether lived space can challenge and subvert the flattening powers of abstract representational space. To illustrate this approach to space, the next section presents a case study of the Lunch Beat movement, which has the potential to challenge the capitalist, normative production of workspace reality.

## Lunch Beat Movement in Scandinavia

Lunch discos emerged as a movement fuelled by media hype in the early 2010s. Originating in Sweden under the title 'Lunch Beat', the purpose was to momentarily disrupt the normal workplace discipline in terms of both time and space. Basically, it is a lunch break that is spent dancing in a disco-like environment (Lunch Beat, 2011).

Lunch disco is an attempt to reclaim the time spent in the office from abstract conceptualizations of managerial administration. Dull office routines are replaced, even if for just one hour, by dancing and connecting to the bodily knowledge 'that will make you create magic during the rest of your day too' (Lunch Beat, 2011). It was claimed to be a parallel to the spontaneous street parties or occupations that affirm urban space for festive activities and free-flowing celebration of the communal carnival. It is designed to blur the lines between work and leisure, order and disorder, discipline and creative embodiment. In Lefebvre's work, it is analogous to the festival, where roles and duties become reversed; work time anarchistically shifts into dance time.

The lunch disco phenomenon in Scandinavia relates to the official societal role of the lunch break. In Finland, the modern conception of workplace lunch originated in military canteens. Feeding soldiers as well as workers in national war production factories required efficient techniques and facilities. Later, in peacetime, civilian companies, hospitals and schools adapted the canteen concept (Vicky, 2014), and the workplace lunch tradition was established by former members of a women's defence organization (*Lotta Svärd*) that had operated military canteens during the war (Fazer Group, n.d.).

The canteen could be analysed in terms of the triadic model, but the narrative presented above links the officiated lunch break to its societal and political context and thus is more complete. Analysis of the work canteen would be incomplete if it were not connected to the Finnish system of school lunch breaks, including a full hot meal. This reading underlines the societal and political conditions the canteen springs from—its social production.

The development of the workplace canteen in the UK in the 1920s reflected the growing interest in efficiency, rationalization and discipline in relation to the managerial discourses of the time (Barley and Kunda, 1992; Vicky, 2014). Lunch spaces were designed to foster efficient flow of employees through the various stages of the eating process. Also, since they limit harmful employee behaviours such as alcohol consumption, canteens could be seen as having a disciplinary function (Foucault, 1977). While aspects of well-being related to human relations ideology were introduced later, originally the canteen format followed the principles of scientific management and disciplinary institutional orders (Vicky, 2014). These types of canteens can be observed in Finland, where school, office and workplace canteens are now outsourced to private companies.

Although modern office cafeterias and canteens are aesthetically diverse, they still tend to operate similar to an assembly line from which the users collect their portions. Queuing, assembling one's lunch and taking a seat in a familiar group are relatively programmed actions, representing the military's commanding power over soldiers (Dale and Burrell, 2008). Lunch is a quick accomplishment that involves minimal amounts of spontaneous interaction or movement. In a canteen, bodies move along pre-scripted paths, reproducing the dominant rules and subject-positions prevailing elsewhere in a rationalized organizational regime. This is a spatial workplace practice of disciplined movements within an efficient context of programmed actions. The dominance of order and control reflect Lefebvre's concept of conceived space. The dominance of this over lived experience is evident in how little room is left for the characteristics of festival—spontaneity, chaos and disorder. The canteen is business as usual.

Canteens are rarely objects of rich or subversive symbolism as the lived space of lunch experience leans towards bureaucratic or disciplinary images. In literature and film, lunch breaks are absent, even from works of fiction that depict subversive aspects of working life or business. Intense drama or high-level intrigue is typically located in corridors, cabinets or restaurants. For example, the acclaimed TV series *House of Cards* depicts the workplace cafeteria in the US Capitol predominantly as a zone dedicated to efficient eating, reserving political scheming and interpersonal dynamics for offices, corridors and bars. Canteens are not interpreted as sites for transgression or subconscious dreams.

Against this constellation of the spatial triad, the Lunch Beat movement could be viewed as an attempt to interrupt the relational emergence of the canteen as a site for disciplined and normalized space. It is seemingly outside the abstract space of work organizations and yet is intimately integrated within the bureaucratic order of the office in the capitalist relations of production. The Lunch Beat movement, echoing the subversive features of the early disco phenomenon (Mcleod, 2006), could be seen as an attempt to carnivalize a culture with a collective embodied experience of rhythmic swing and a hint of fantasy and non-conformism (Echols, 2010). This type of intervention broadly corresponds to Lefebvre's notion of the festival as a dis-alienating performative event involved in the production of space (Grindon, 2013). A brief study of actual interpretations, symbolizations and practices related to lunch disco events sheds light on the ways in which the movement unfolded and the extent to which it managed to challenge the dominant triad associated with the spatiality of workplace lunch breaks.

## Method

The empirical study presented in this the paper is intended to serve as an illustrative analysis of a movement aiming to subvert the prevailing production of organizational space. The main function of the analysis is to examine the perceived and lived spaces related to the lunch disco phenomenon. The analysis relies on publicly available sources obtained from the

Internet: 1) the manifesto of the Lunch Beat movement, 2) media articles about Lunch Beat (26 in total), including interviews with and comments by organizers and participants, and the responses of online readers, 3) videos of Lunch Beat events (12) as well as 4) a sample of related news stories about dancing in the workplace (12). Newspaper articles were used to study information about the spatial practices of participants of lunch discos and about the lived experiences and symbolic representations of space. The Lunch Beat manifesto provides information about the initial motives and cultural inspirations of the movement. The videos were viewed to assist in making sense of the spatial practices.

The main function of the analysis is to explore the lived experiences and symbolizations of the lunch disco event. As suggested by Peltonen (2012), this aspect of the production of space was studied with an interpretative approach focusing on metaphors (Morgan, 2006), symbols (Morgan, Frost, and Pondy, 1983) and phantasms (Gabriel, 1995) in the newspaper articles and user comments on the media articles and videos. Spatial practice was another part of the triad analysed in this paper. This dimension of analysis concentrated on the actual routines and movements that participants of the disco events were enacting. Here, the method involved more direct observation of people's bodily actions and interactions (Pavis, 2003). The main source for this dimension of the analysis was videos depicting live scenes at Lunch Beat gatherings.

## Lunch Beat, the Lived and the Perceived Space

### Lived Experiences and Symbolizations

The founders of the Lunch Beat movement have explained in media interviews that they were inspired by *Fight Club*, a 1999 film directed by David Fincher (Olson, 2012). The film tells a narrative about an underground circle of men who meet to fist-fight in an attempt to reclaim some of the masculinity they have lost as subjects of late modern society. As it turns out, the fight club phenomenon and its champion, Tyler Durden, are just mental projections of the narrator, a blue-collar everyman suffering from consumptionist emptiness.

In videos available on YouTube, the originators of Lunch Beat re-imagined dance events as clandestine gatherings of a secret order, like *Fight Club*. However, the film's social critique of capitalism (Ta, 2006; Lizardo, 2007) is not present in the fantasies informing the lunch discos; the founders of the movement primarily concentrated on the idea of a secret underground cult. The selective actualization of Fight Club implies a particular spatial imagery: lunch discos are associated with abandoned or eccentric spaces, such as garages, car parks or cellars. This way, lunch disco spaces are set in direct opposition to sanctioned, formal workplaces and thus (politically and ideologically) oppose managerial control.

Lunch Beat is as much about fun as it is about the release of fatigue and frustration through extreme bodily interactions. There is also a rationalized use of time and space as the movement's manifesto guides all participants to use the lunch disco break exclusively for dancing: 'if you are getting too tired to actually dance at Lunch Beat, please have your lunch at some other place' ("Lunch Beat," 2011). In this sense, the founders of the Lunch Beat movement present the worktime disco experience as a normatively regulated dance performance that is spatially separated from organized places such as work or the canteen. This opposition, however, also ties the two spaces together as one (disco) is defined as the antithesis of the other (workplace). As a consequence, the disco place becomes defined in Lefebvrian terms as a conceived, abstract space instead of offering more festival-related or anarchist motives for participation. Interrelating disco and the workplace may counter the original aims of disco's emancipation.

*Fight Club* portrayed the underground cult as a way for Generation X men to reclaim their lost agency through physical fighting and the associated embodied experience of pain (Ta, 2006). A central theme is the alienation of the service worker class in late modern capitalism and the commodification and diminishment of political subjectivity associated with this phenomenon (Lizardo, 2007). The clandestine fight club is a fantasy of the protagonist— an imagined place where he can revolt against the consumptionist hegemony and reclaim, with the group, a sense of class consciousness. The social production of the 'club' is intimately tied to the extreme bodily practice of fighting. In Lefebvre's terms, the social production of a new space, of the fight club, demonstrates the potential for producing an alternative space for work and consumption. Yet in the Lunch Beat movement, this social production of space and the original Marxist and psychological themes of the film are somewhat sidelined. There seems to be little awareness of the societal context of consumptionist capitalism that informs the *Fight Club* narrative and of the imagined, fantasy-like nature of the clandestine cult, which is vital for portrayal of the club's events. In particular, the Lunch Beat movement is lacking juxtaposition of the role of the workplace canteen in the maintenance of capitalist discipline and subversion of the production of organizational space through lunch disco events.

Turning to the interpretations and symbolizations of actual participants, some of the aims of the original organizers are successful. Firstly, there is a focus on the affirmative aspects of the physicality of the dance act. As an organizer in New York notes, the purpose of the event is to 'get off the couch, get away from your computer and go have experiences' (Marikar, 2013). Another article noted that one participant 'usually spends her lunch hour in front of her computer, munching on a baguette, surfing the internet. But on Thursday lunchtime, she wasn't browsing—she was boogieing' (Manzoor, 2012). Dancing over lunch is seen as a gateway that allows participants to return to the real, embodied experience of being and move away from the inert or artificial experience of working in digital reality.

In addition, using the lunch break for disco can be justified as an act promoting wellness (cf. Cedeström and Spicer, 2015). Disco dancing is likened here to a workout, 'gym with fun' or an *escape*. But without the typical features of a disco nightclub, such as alcohol service, the one-hour Lunch Beat was interpreted as an oxymoron. According to several commentators, this was, however, the charm of the event. 'It's been surreal', said one participant of the London event, 'I'm dancing but, at the back of my mind I know it's daytime and I know that I have to go back to work' (Manzoor, 2012).

Related to the idea of escape, the event was also described as 'de-embodying', not heightening one's physicality. One of the initiators said, 'you can allow yourself to be absorbed completely by the present and not worry about work or your next meeting' (Manzoor, 2012). A similar feeling of escape is reported by Biehl-Missal (2016) and Ropo and Sauer (2008) in regard to the embodied experience of dancing, particularly disco, rave and techno. The disco dance experience of Lunch Beat was associated with meditation and mindfulness exercises that help to create a sense of distance from office life. That is, Lunch Beat was imagined as a form of spiritual sanctuary or retreat rather than an opportunity for physical exercise. This perspective relates to Cohen and Taylor's (1992) notion of 'escape attempts', where resistance allows a respite from the conditions of labour but does not fundamentally challenge them.

Although our analysis focuses on the European and Scandinavian experience, we acknowledge a difference in reactions to the lunch disco phenomenon across the Atlantic. Whereas in Finland newspaper articles and Twitter reactions were positive, commentators on newspaper web sites in the US voiced concerns about the morality of spending part of the workday dancing. It was argued that the lunch break is embedded into the workday and thus should be used responsibly in service of the employer. The very idea of a lunch disco was considered impossible given the high demands for employees: 'people can party after work, on the weekends, on their days off. If someone's job is that bad that they have to party at lunch, I would submit they're in the wrong line of work' (Marikar, 2013). In this comment, there is an underlying assumption that the lunch break is part of the formal hours spent under employer control and that the spatial boundary between work and life is determined primarily by temporal markers. Locating the Lunch Beat event outside the office space is considered a threat to the unity of the spatial context of work.

However, proponents of lunchtime dancing argued that time spent at the disco is not time wasted; the following tweet was associated with the Twitter hashtag devoted to lunch disco, #lounasdisko: 'Lunch disco [is] the new best practice from the Finnish Tax Administration' (Pajunen, 2017). It is argued that dance events help to energize employees, consequently raising productivity and creativity beyond any costs incurred. In Scandinavian commentaries, Lunch Beat events were associated with goal-oriented wellness practices such as walking, exercising or engaging in community building.

The analogy to well-being and motivation programs therefore makes the time spent at Lunch Beat valid.

### Spatial Practice

What about spatial practices, perceptions, performances and practices enacted in relation to the Lunch Beat phenomenon? In keeping with the image of Lunch Beat as a secret cult, the locations of events are in closed, remote locations. In Sweden, participants had to go through a series of corridors to enter the basement or to queue in order to be admitted into a conference hall that was adequately isolated and dimmed for the gathering. In a video depicting the first Lunch Beat event in 2010, the cameraman illustrates the spatial practice of entering the space of the dance event by shooting the complex journey from the street to the underground garage. He shows the heaviness of the door and the steep ascent of the ramp leading to the actual location, which serve as stages to pass as one transitions from the outer world to the internal reality of the club (Karlsson, 2010).

The transition from the outside world of work, order and consumption is also marked by practices such as changing clothes for dancing and refusing to talk about job-related matters. In the dance venue, participants seem to behave as instructed in the movement's manifesto (www.lunchbeat.org). There are no groups of static spectators; all try to join the collective 'groove'. Unlike the early gatherings, at which dance acts were more individualistic and personalized, footage from more recent lunch discos shows a scene that is more reminiscent of a standard nightclub, with anonymous mass swaying to the tempo of music (Karlsson, 2010)

In general, the spatial practice of Lunch Beat tends to sustain a well-defined boundary between the workplace and the experience of dancing. The setup of the Lunch Beat venue typically resembles a hideout in line with the image of a clandestine fight club or a conventional nightclub with a darkened hall and disco lights. The hidden, secretive nature of the event underlines the specificity of the space and the context: the event primarily acts as a site-specific performance (Biehl-Missal, 2016). Thus, this place is distinct from the formal working spaces of organizations emphasizing orderliness, division of labour and hierarchy. At the same time, the otherness of a lunch disco venue may be limiting: like a corporate luncheon, the Lunch Beat event is time-bound, effective and wholesome.

Recently, there have been individual cases in Finland in which the disco is arranged within the workplace, in the midst of the everyday routines of the office. Although these events strengthen the value of spatial *practices* (perceived space) compared to planning (conceived space), their shorter duration (15 minutes) and smaller audio equipment make the event feel like a short break aimed to improve employees' well-being rather than a movement emerging from outside corporate structures. Lunch disco may be different, but it is not dangerous.

## Discussion

What is the value of the Lunch Beat events in light of Lefebvre's analysis of the contested production of space? The lunch disco has been described as an isolated location offering either affirmation of an individual's authentic existence via an experience of physical embodiment or escape from the office atmosphere in the form of a mindful bodily exercise. It is possible to applying Lefebvre's triad to analyse the physical space in which Lunch Beat takes place, but we suggest that there are two aspects to such an analysis. On the one hand, organizational spaces can be analysed in isolation in terms of their physical materiality; the experience of dancing can be detached from its societal context. As Pallasmaa (201e), a renowned architect, confirms, architecture and planning tend to focus on physical and visual structures, which can lead to neglect of the lived experience and the mood and atmosphere of the space. This exemplifies the above-mentioned tension between the conceived and lived space—in the capitalist production of space, abstract, planned structures are typically prioritised over users' lived and perceived experience (cf. Connellan, 2013). On the other hand, the analysis can include the phenomenon's political, philosophical, psychological and societal context. These two options are not contradictory, but complementary. Here, we want to discuss the Lunch Beat from the combined perspective that, in addition to space-internal analysis, includes sociological and political aspects.

The link between dance and space has been analysed by Biehl-Missal (2016). In her study of techno dance movement, she connects dance and space with its context, including the particular time, cultural space and physical place in which dancing occurs. The techno events in the old turbine hall, Berghain, in Berlin are clearly not ruled by corporate structures, neither in terms of time nor space (it operates from midnight until dawn in a dimly lit old industrial space, allowing sexual and drug-related behaviour). In contrast, to account for the emergence and effects of Lunch Beat, one must understand it in the context of officiated lunch breaks and the spread of the news by mainstream media. Following from this, one can argue that Lunch Beat is less about analysing the space in itself through the triad and more about a phenomenon that we can interpret using the Lefebvrean political economy of space.

The spatial practice of the lunch disco seems to reinforce the interpretation of the disco as an egalitarian space in which one's only duty is to dance, emphasizing the non-hierarchical nature of the event. Workplaces are increasingly crossing the boundaries between work and private life in the form of remote work and 24/7 access to workers. It can be argued that this invasion of privacy invokes a counter-movement that shifts away from the domestication of workplace (Dale and Burrell, 2008) to spaces where one can escape top-down manipulation during the workday. Based on the above comments, Lunch Beat shares features of such an escapist space.

The boundary between workspaces and spaces for dancing and embodied expression is regulated insofar as the lunch disco is temporally tied to the one-hour lunch break. There is also a lack of the more subversive elements of nightlife, such as alcohol. Lunch Beat reminds us of and remains within the regimes of workplace discipline in its rules, which direct the participants to use the available time solely for dance. Also, some 'power arrangements' (Dale and Burrell, 2008: 171) are prioritised over other options. Descriptions of the event focus on the duality of working spaces, which have a dulling, normalizing effect on workers, and the lunch disco space, which allows for physical invigoration or mindful concentration. In this respect, Lunch Beat can be interpreted as a reaction against the normalization of work practices (Dale and Burrell, 2008). Thus, Lunch Beat appears to be more concerned with helping employees endure the alienating spatiality of the office than with reclaiming the organizational space through creative movement and underground phantasms. As depicted in a TV documentary on Lunch Beat in Sweden, participants are mindful about the temporariness of the disco and their need to return to work: 'I feel sweaty. I feel filled with energy. I feel happy. Actually I'm longing to go back to my office as well. This fills me with a lot of energy and lot of ideas' (DW English, 2012).

Similar to Shortt's (2015) study of liminal spaces in hairdressing and Biehl-Missal's (2016) work on embodied space in techno dancing, our analysis emphasizes the need to study the embodied aspects of work and organization. The understanding of space, Lefebvre (1991a) notes, is initially an embodied experience.

## Conclusions: Lunch Disco 'Fails'

While all of the elements in the triad are involved in the production of space, this paper argues that the tension between the conceived space of institutional logic and the everyday enactment of the perceived and lived space is central to the political nature of the social space. In hegemonic closures of space, the logics and structures of the dominant dimension—the conceived space—are reproduced through the performance of distinct spatial practices and symbolic representations of space.

A critical approach to space becomes relevant especially when analysing the actual transformative consequences of cultural interventions that aim to destabilize the dominant forms of social space. As Lunch Beat demonstrates, the impact of a seemingly liberating practice of embodied expression (disco dance) in the middle of the working day depends on the subsequent practices and symbolizations surrounding the intervention.

In line with what Lefebvre calls a 'festive' occasion (Grindon, 2013), celebrating lunch with collective dancing might have a transgressive potential to break the capitalist divisions between the actor and the spectator with its primordial sensual energy. While Lunch Beat could be considered a countermovement to industrialized society's regressive, even manipulative tendencies, there is not much evidence that the event affects domains outside of the disco space; rather, lunch disco seems to re-affirm the division between work and dance. The actual production of a larger social space around lunch disco falls short of the type of collective carnival Lefebvre was seeking by emphasizing the role of collective artistic events in transcending the existing capitalist order. In a nutshell, according to our reading of the Lunch Beat movement in terms of Lefebvre's politically expanded triadic model, the movement had the potential for a larger emancipatory effect but did not fulfil it. We conclude that this failure is due to the fact that the lunch disco remains within the realm of the social production of capitalist space: even its escapist and emancipatory element is ultimately directed towards more productivity and experienced within the context of well-being at work. It socially re-produces capitalist modes of consumption and joins the dominant discourse in which escape from work is, paradoxically, acted out during the institutionalized setting of lunch break within the framework of work.

The lunch disco movement's failure to challenge the discipline of the 'canteen' in the workspace mirrors the fate of the original disco movement. As, for example, McLeod (2006) has noted, disco first developed in the early 1970s as an underground movement comprised of marginalized groups of African Americans, gays and Latinos. It offered an embodied experience of collective aesthetic empowerment that the mainstream expressive culture was suppressing or limiting at the time. Disco culture allowed for an aesthetic and sensual extravaganza where racial and class distinctions melted away through rhythmic trance and the loosening of bourgeoisie moralities (Echols, 2010).

Yet, as the movement became commercialized, the transgressive properties of the disco event started to wane. In *Saturday Night Fever* (1977), the male protagonist and his nightlife is pictured as a series of escapist experiences that do little to alter his working-class identity beyond the closed world of the club (Steven, 1980). Disco, originally a revolutionary underground movement, was represented as a site for affirming rather than challenging the divisions and distinctions of capitalist formations.

In a similar vein, Lunch Beat's promise to offer an underground experience that transgresses the spatial boundaries and hegemonic logics of the modern office was not properly realized due to the tempered nature of the seemingly transformative imageries and practices. Lunch Beat was symbolically interpreted as a place for an escape or clandestine gathering instead of as a site for enacting subversive phantasms in the midst of the workplace. Ultimately, it could not challenge the established spatial triad that performed and reproduced the disciplined space of work lunch as a regulated and functional 'canteen'.

However, Lunch Beat's failure to challenge established workplace, organizational and societal norms may not be wholly negative. Rather, its assumed revolutionary nature might be a function of the lenses we used for looking at the phenomenon (of Lefebvre's triadic model), not necessarily something Lunch Beat was attempting to achieve. The event's apparently hidden (Marxist) aims may arise only when applying the triad, with its complex political, social and philosophical underpinnings. This is not a demerit of the model, but a reminder of how our methods and their origins may influence our interpretations. On the other hand, the tension between conceived and lived space points to implicit and inherent societal power relations that, from a critical perspective, are too easily taken for granted. Lefebvre's philosophical background led him to not dismiss these underlying tendencies for capitalist and managerial normative control that characterize our everyday experiences, even today.

## References

Baran, P. A. and Sweezy, P. M. (1966). *Monopoly Capital: An Essay on the American Economic and Social Order*. New York: Monthly Review Press.

Barley, S. and Kunda, G. (1992). Design and devotion: Surges of rational and normative ideologies of control in managerial discourse. *Administrative Science Quarterly, 37*, 363–399.

Beyes, T. and Steyaert, C. (2011). Spacing organization: Non-representational theory and performing organizational space. *Organization, 19*(1), 45–61.

Biehl-Missal, B. (2016). Filling the 'empty space': Site-specific dance in a techno club. *Culture and Organization*, DOI: 10.1080/14759551.2016.1206547

Braverman, H. (1974). *Labour and Monopoly Capital: The Deregulation of Work in the Twentieth Century*. New York: Monthly Review Press.

Carr, A. N. and Zanetti, L. A. (2000). The emergence of a Surrealist movement and its vital estrangement-effect in organization studies. *Human Relations, 53*(7), 891–921.

Cederström, C. and Spicer, A. (2015). *The Wellness Syndrome*. Cambridge: Polity Press.

Clegg, S. and Kornberger, M. (Eds.) (2006). *Space, Organizations and Management Theory*. Copenhagen: Copenhagen Business School Press.

Cohen, S. and Taylor, L. (1992). *Escape Attempts. The Theory and Practice of Resistance to Everyday Life*. London and New York: Routledge.

Connellan, K. (2013). The psychic life of white: Power and space. *Organization Studies, 34*(10), 1529–1549.

Dale, K. (2005). Building a social materiality. *Organization, 12*(5), 649–678.

Dale, K. and Burrell, G. (2008). *Spaces of Organization and the Organization of Space*. Basingstoke: Palgrave Macmillan.

De Certeau, M. (1984). *The Practice of Everyday Life*. Berkley, Los Angeles, and London: University of California Press.

DW English. (2012). *Lunch Beat—Midday dancing in Stockholm*. Retrieved November 11, 2017, from www.youtube.com/watch?v=mjR0FyFAQu0

Echols, A. (2010). *Hot Stuff: Disco and the Remaking of American Culture*. New York and London: W. W. Norton & Company.

Elden, S. (2001). Politics, philosophy, geography: Henri Lefebvre in recent Anglo-American scholarship. *Antipode, 33*(5), 809–825.

Elden, S. (2004a). *Understanding Henri Lefebvre*. London and New York: Continuum.

Elden, S. (2004b). Between Marx and Heidegger: Politics, philosophy and Lefebvre's *The Production of Space. Antipode, 36*(1), 86–105.

Fazer Group. (n.d.). *Fazer's Know-How in Food Services Was Inherited From Women Who Served as Caterers During the War.* Retrieved from www.fazer group.com/about-us/history—heritage/fazer-and-lotta-svard/

Foucault, M. (1977). *Discipline and Punish: The Birth of the Prison* (translated by A. Sheridan). New York: Random House.

Gabriel, Y. (1995). The unmanaged organization: Stories, fantasies and subjectivity. *Organization Studies, 16*(3), 477–501.

Grindon, G. (2013). Revolutionary romanticism: Henri Lefebvre's revolution-as-festival. *Third Text, 27*(2), 208–220.

Held, D. (1980). *Introduction to Critical Theory: Horkheimer to Habermas* (Vol. 261). Berkeley: University of California Press.

Hernes, T. (2004). *The Spatial Construction of Organization.* Amsterdam: John Benjamins.

Karlsson, P. (2010). *Lunch Beat Stockholm #1* [Video]. Retrieved November 7, 2017, from www.youtube.com/watch?v=WlLRGy_1Y5k&feature=youtu.be&list=PLVWEwN391vOeyghk1ny4S20fBZNWakdFq%29

Kingma, S. (2008). Dutch casino space or the spatial organization of entertainment. *Culture and Organization, 14*, 31–48.

Lefebvre, H. (1957, reprinted 2000). *Pyrénées.* Pau: Cairn.

Lefebvre, H. (1963). *La vallée de Campan, études de sociologie rurale.* Paris: Presses Universitaires de France.

Lefebvre, H. (1975). *Hegel, Marx, Nietzsche, Ou, le Royaume des Ombres.* Paris: Casterman.

Lefebvre, H. (1979). Space: social product and use value. In: Freiberg, J. W. (Ed.). *Critical sociology: European perspectives* (pp. 285-295). Irvington, NY: Halsted Press.

Lefebvre, H. (1980). Marxism exploded. *Review (Fernand Braudel Center), 4*(1), 19-32.

Lefebvre, H. (1991a). *The Production of Space.* Oxford: Blackwell.

Lefebvre, H. (1991b). *Critique of Everyday Life.* London and New York: Verso.

Lukács, G. (1971). *History and Class Consciousness: Studies in Marxist Dialectics* (Vol. 215). Cambridge, MA: MIT Press.

Lizardo, O. (2007). *Fight Club,* or the cultural contradictions of late capitalism. *Journal for Cultural Research, 11*(3), 221–243.

Lunch Beat. (2011). *If It's Your First Time at Lunch Beat, You Have to Dance.* Retrieved November 7, 2017, from www.lunchbeat.org

Manzoor, S. (2012, May 31). Lunch Beat entices office workers to mid-day 60-minute boogie. *The Guardian.* Retrieved November 7, 2017, from www.theguardian.com/

Marikar, S. (2013, May 8). It's lunchtime: Let's dance. *New York Times.* Retrieved from www.nytimes.com/

Marx, K. (1887). Capital. A critique of political economy. Moscow: Progress Publishers. Retrieved November 7, 2017, from www.marxists.org/archive/marx/works/download/pdf/Capital-Volume-I.pdf

McLeod, K. (2006). "A Fifth of Beethoven": Disco, classical music, and the politics of inclusion. *American Music, 24*(3), 347–363.

Merrifield, A. (2000). Henri Lefebvre: A socialist in space. In M. Crang and N. Thrif (Eds.), *Thinking Space* (pp. 167–182). London and New York: Routledge.

Morgan, G. (2006). *Images of organization* (updated edition). Thousand Oaks: Sage.

Morgan, G., Frost, P. J. and Pondy, L. R. (1983). Organizational symbolism. *Organizational Symbolism, 3*, 35.

Olson, P. (2012, May 16). Meet the woman behind Europe's new lunchtime dance craze. *Forbes*. Retrieved November 7, 2017, from www.forbes.com/

Pajunen, J. (2017). Lunch disco- the new best practice from the Finnish Tax Administration. Retrieved November 7, 2017, from https://twitter.com/JenniPajunen/status/903266378492239874

Pallasmaa, J. (2014). Space, place and atmosphere. Emotion and peripheral perception in architectural experience. Lebenswelt – experience and philosophy in architecture, 4, 230-245. https://doi.org.10.13130/2240-9599/4202

Pavis, P. (2003). *Analyzing Performance, Theater, Dance, and Film*. Ann Arbor: University of Michigan Press.

Peltonen, T. (2012). Exploring organizational architecture and space: A case for heterodox research. *International Journal of Organizational Analysis, 20*(1), 68–81.

Ropo, A. & Sauer, E. (2008). Corporeal Leaders. In D. Barry & H. Hansen (Eds.), *New Approaches in Management and Organization* (pp. 469-478). London: Sage.

Ross, K. and Lefebvre, H. (1997). Lefebvre on the situationists: An interview. *October, 79*, 69–83.

Shortt, H. (2015). Liminality, space and the importance of 'temporary dwelling places' at work. *Human Relations, 68*(4), 633–658.

Steven, P. (1980). *Saturday Night Fever* just dancing. *Jump Cut, 23*, 13–16.

Ta, L. M. (2006). Hurt so good: *Fight Club*, masculine violence, and the crisis of capitalism. *The Journal of American Culture, 29*(3), 265–277.

Taylor, S. and Spicer, A. (2007). Time for space: A narrative review of research on organizational spaces. *International Journal of Management Reviews, 9*, 325–346.

Vicky, L. (2014). Situating the factory canteen in discourses of health and industrial work in Britain (1914–1939). *Le Mouvement Social, 2*(247), 65.

Watkins, C. (2005). Representations of space, spatial practices and spaces of representation: An application of Lefebvre's spatial triad. *Culture and Organization, 11*(3), 209–220.

Zhang, Z. (2006). What is lived space? *ephemera, 6*(2), 219–223.

# 9 Cake and the Open Plan Office
## A Foodscape of Work Through a Lefebvrian Lens

*Harriet Shortt*

## Appetizer: An Introduction to Food, Work, Space and Place

This chapter is about food and eating in the workplace. In fact, as I write I have opened a packet of biscuits and made a coffee and, perhaps, before you continue to read you might want to pause here, put the kettle on and open the biscuit tin.

It has been argued that eating is a necessary, mundane and routine activity (Sobal and Wonsink, 2007: 135) and this would indeed be a reasonable point of view if we considered food simply as a fuel with which to nourish our bodies—we need food and water to survive. Yet food can shape who we are, our lifestyle choices, our bodies, our identities (see Caplan, 1997; Abbots and Lavis, 2013; Dejmanee, 2016), and our eating behaviours can differ according to sexuality and gender (see Conner, Johnson, and Grogan, 2004; Nath, 2011). Food and eating is also an inherently social activity and is one that is bound up with social, religious, cultural and ritualistic traditions and symbols. The act of cooking and eating brings families and friends together, it unites us in our homes and in public spaces[1] and as Throsby (2012: 7) suggests, it is the very currency of sociality. From formal wedding feasts with symbolic wedding cakes (see Charsley, 1997) to the milieu of carnival street food, from ceremonial military mess dinners to mingling by the cake stand at the village fête, food brings people and communities together. In addition, and more broadly, food and drink are core to far wider social issues including globalization, agriculture and farming, political agendas and the environment. Over the past decade or so, researchers and journalists have examined the politics of food and raised key questions about the contents of our plates and kitchen cupboards (see Klein, 2002). And we only need look as far as recent reports in the media, such as Jamie Oliver tackling childhood obesity and sugar (both in the UK and the US), Hugh Fearnley-Whittingstall confronting food waste in UK households and organizations, and the report from the Royal Society for Public Health discussing the impact of rush hour commuting on our health and wellbeing (2016), to conclude that food is far from mundane or routine and is very much a concern on the social menu.

Specifically, however, this chapter puts food on the *workplace* menu and explores the interconnectedness of food, work, people and space using Lefebvre's spatial triad framework (1991) and considers how the social production of space and the micro-geographies of the workplace influence food consumption, social interactions and relationships at work. There is no doubt that food and eating in the workplace is a common occurrence for most of us; we might frequent a coffee shop on our way to work in search of the first caffeine fix of the day, we might take sandwiches from home to the office for lunch or take advantage of hot meals in our workplace canteens, and we might enjoy after work drinks and dinners with colleagues or clients. Food and drink are an integral part of daily working life but what this chapter seeks to do is raise questions about the nexus of food and *space* at work; in what ways does space influence where we eat, what we eat and with whom?; what is the role of food in our organizational environment and how does it impact everyday spatial practices?; how might formal and informal eating practices alter our lived experiences of space at work?

To investigate these sorts of questions, I combine Lefebvre's spatial triad framework (perceived, conceived and lived space), and his discussions around dominated and appropriated spaces, dialectics and embodiment (1991; Shields, 1999) with insights from food studies in a range of disciplines including public health, geography, sociology, anthropology, and organization studies. This chapter begins with an overview of food and eating at work and considers the attention researchers have paid to food in factories and offices thus far. The subsequent discussion presents insights from foodscape studies to highlight the important connections that have already been made between food, people and *space*. Foodscape studies (see for example Mikkelsen, 2011; Swinburn et al., 1999; Brembeck and Johansson, 2010; Goodman, Maye, and Holloway, 2010) specifically explore the food environments that people, communities and societies are exposed to and offer frameworks that help us 'analyse how food, places and people are interconnected and how they interact' (Mikkelsen, 2011: 209). I then argue that it is only by overlaying Lefebvre's spatial triad framework and analysis onto a foodscape of an organization that we gain a more complex, comprehensive, multifaceted understanding of food, people and work space.

The following section discusses the research setting on which this chapter is based and the methodological approach: a qualitative, interpretive three-month field study in a large Government agency in the UK that adopted participant-led photography and photo-elicitation interviews. The findings and discussion explore the formal and informal eating habits of employees, how and where food is shared, and how such eating/ spatial practices are manifestations of both power and resistance, and in turn, produce and transform space (Lefebvre, 1991: 343; Wapshott and Mallett, 2011: 68). Specifically, I argue that Lefebvre's spatial triad provides an analytical tool with which we might enrich and further develop the foodscapes literature by highlighting how a) foodscapes are transformed by inhabitants and their eating practices, b) that foodscape boundaries are permeable and somewhat fluid, and c) that foodscapes are imbued with complex and ambiguous social, political and cultural meanings. As such, the contributions of this chapter are threefold: this Lefebvrian analysis of a foodscape specifically highlights the dialectical and contradictory nature of our social/spatial encounters at work and thus draws out a wider understanding of the domination and appropriation of space; in using Lefebvre's framework, this chapter strengthens the understanding that foodscapes are both physically and socio-culturally produced—it is both concrete, as well as lived and embodied; and it aims to contribute to foodscape studies in an organizational/institutional context and attend to the call for a more micro-level view of foodscapes (see Mikkelsen, 2011).

## Starter: A Recipe for Food, Work and Space

### Food and the Workplace

As noted above, food and eating have long been of interest to sociologists, anthropologists and those in cultural studies who, in this interdisciplinary field, have explored food from perspectives of production to consumption, from individual eating habits to family meals and ritualistic eating. Indeed, the social aspects of food and eating and how and why food connects us has drawn much attention from scholars and includes a wide variety of concerns; food and eating out (Beardsworth and Keel, 1997); eating on holiday (Williams, 1997); health and identity (Caplan, 1997); rituals and customs of eating and the social significance of the meal (Visser, 1991); diets and our bodies (Beardsworth and Keel, 1997; Abbots and Lavis, 2013); the ethics of food consumption (Johnston, Rodney, and Szabo, 2012; Cairns, Johnston, and MacKendrick, 2013); and food, social status and class (Elias, 1969; Douglas and Isherwood, 1979). What is common to many of these studies is the sociality of food and eating: food connects people, and what we eat and how we eat it highlights the complexities around communities, cultures and identities.

Yet despite this rich and complex field offering fruitful areas of research, the study of food and eating in organization studies is still rather neglected, with only around two dozen or so key studies over the past six decades contributing to our understanding of workplace eating. Those in organization studies who have sought to explore the cultural dimensions of food in the workplace have included studies of workplace canteens (Cook and Wyndham, 1953; Poulsen and Jørgensen, 2011), food orientated workplace rituals (Roy, 1959; Domenico and Phillips, 2009; Plester, 2015; Kiffin et al., 2015) which has included breakfast meetings and office Christmas parties (Rosen, 1985, 1988) and business dinners (Sturdy, Schwarz, and Spicer, 2006), and the aesthetic appearance of restaurants and bars and the influence on emotions and behaviour (Wasserman, Rafaeli, and Kluger, 2000). A variety of studies surrounding food and drink at work can also be found in the *Human Relations* special issue 'Food, Work and Organization' edited by Briner and Sturdy (2008), where authors discuss food, self and embodiment at work (Driver, 2008), and eating with the Mafia (Parker, 2008). More recently, food has been understood as a social construction of memory and connections made between food, work, and nostalgia in Strangleman's article on the former Guinness brewery at Park Royal, London (2010). And Kniffin et al. explore the organizational benefits and improvement in work-group performance when teams eat together (2015). Of course, we might consider other studies in the wider field of business and management research that have also contributed to an awareness of food in organizations; Underhill's studies of sensory marketing and retailer and consumer behaviour and the influence of food smells and food courts on shopping habits (2000, 2004; see also Blythman, 2004), and the role of food and eating in servicescapes and the design of food retail outlets (see Bitner, 1992; Ritzer, 1993).

Albeit a relatively small field of research there are perhaps some useful commonalities between some of these studies that should be drawn out here. Indeed, most worthy of note in the context of this chapter are the hints and traces of links being made between food, eating and *space*. For example, Sturdy et al.'s paper (2006) '*Guess who's coming to dinner?*' discusses the liminal space of the restaurant in the working relationships between organizations and management consultants, suggesting that liminal spaces allow for different, often more creative, open conversations between colleagues. Although not the key focus for other studies, organizational spaces appear to provide important field study locations for some researchers: workplace canteens, formal dining halls, the firehouse, and factory floors. Space, it seems, has some social, cultural and historical significance in these studies but for the most part it is side-stepped in favour of alternative theoretical investigations. These explorations do not, therefore, sufficiently or explicitly consider the relationship between food and space. For more comprehensive links between these concepts, we must turn to other disciplines and perhaps a good place to start might be the study of 'foodscapes'.

## Food, People and Space

A core literature that specifically focuses on the relationships between food, space and people and how they interact, are 'foodscape studies'. At the heart of what have become known as 'foodscape studies' are key questions around eating practices, where food and drink are consumed, how we encounter food in our built environments, and the notion that the design of the built environment influences people and their eating behaviours. Much of the foodscape literature is based on concerns for public health and often discusses, for example, the location and physical placement of fast food outlets in busy shopping centres, and how this contributes to rising levels of obesity in western society (see Brembeck and Johansson, 2010; Goodman,

Maye, and Holloway, 2010). Indeed, for the most part this literature focuses on macro-level issues surrounding food and health, urban design and wider national and international communities.

However, Mikkelsen's (2011) paper on foodscape studies and 'out-of-home' eating neatly highlights the significance of food in other spaces such as schools and, most relevantly here, institutions, and presents a typology of foodscapes where a more micro-level of analysis is considered. In collaboration with the Royal Society for Public Health, Mikkelsen's paper focuses on how these foodscapes impact on our health and wellbeing and argues for future research to include the analysis of the institutional foodscape, which he defines as, 'the physical, organizational and sociocultural space in which clients/ guests encounter meals, food and food-related issues, including health messages' (2011: 215). Certainly, this call is acknowledged in a report by the Royal Society for Public Health, where food and the eating habits of workers during their rush hour commute is examined in some detail. Key findings highlight that commuting increases the likelihood of snacking, consuming fast food and less time spent preparing healthy meals (2016: 8). The report calls for 'greater restrictions on unhealthy food and drink outlets in stations' (2016: 12) to tackle the increasingly unhealthy 'foodscapes' at many train stations, through which millions of UK workers pass each day.

Broadly, then, the foodscape literature is useful in the context of this chapter because it raises the important connections we should be making between our physical environment and how it impacts what we eat and when. Certainly, it is worth considering how foodscape studies might have applications in organization studies and, as Mikkelsen (2011) suggests, how we might pay more attention to the micro level foodscapes within our institutions. Indeed, this would be a useful framework with which to assess the eating behaviours of the workforce. However, there are currently several gaps in this literature and opportunities for further research to give strength to this emerging discipline. Given that we know that food and eating is not just a health concern and is one inextricably linked to socio-cultural concerns, it would be appropriate to seek further frameworks to inform the analysis of a *socially produced* institutional foodscape. Indeed, much of the foodscape studies literature appears focussed on how the food environment shapes people and their behaviour, and seems to give little detailed attention to the notion that people and their behaviour shape the food environment. There is a sense in the literature that people are somewhat passively 'managed' and influenced by their foodscape rather than playing an active role in what might be considered a more dynamic, dialectic and complex relationship between food, people and place. Indeed, what seems lacking in some of these studies is the exploration of the 'unmanaged', informal and subjective *lived* experiences of food in the spaces and places we inhabit.

Therefore, to shed further light on such complexities, I propose Lefebvre's theoretical conceptualizations of space—that which is socially produced and socially producing (1991). Specifically, I propose Lefebvre's spatial triad as an analytical tool that will help inform and deepen our understanding of an institutional foodscape. Lefebvre's spatial triad (1991) is a valuable theoretical framework that provides us with a critical understanding of space and acknowledges that it is both physical and material as well as imaginary and social. Lefebvre offers three useful perspectives on space: perceived space (or spatial practice)—the daily routines, habits and physical movements we engage in. In this chapter, a useful example might be the mid-morning walk we take across the office to make a cup of coffee and how we habitually know where and when to negotiate desks and stairs along the way; conceived space (or representations of space)—the space 'as planned and executed by planners, designers, architects' (Dale and Burrell, 2008: 9) that is ultimately connected to the manipulation of space to control and organize. An example in this case might be the deliberate design of a canteen-style restaurant in the workplace (by architects and managers) to manipulate employee behaviour and promote a collaborative culture; and finally, lived space (or representational spaces)—the subjective experience of space that 'gives it life, animation, and makes it occupied' (Taylor and Spicer, 2007: 333). An example here might be an office worker using her own coffee mug from home because she feels it represents something about her identity, rather than using the company branded coffee mugs made available by the organization.

Importantly, Dale and Burrell remind us that the three elements of this triad are somewhat conflicting and overlap and that Lefebvre himself 'recognises that there are contradictions within and between these elements of social space' (2008: 10). Lefebvre's work reveals the 'dialectical relationship that exists within the triad of the perceived, the conceived and the lived' (1991: 39) and thus helps to further draw out the tensions, for example, between power and control that is established through and with space on the one hand (dominated space), and the adaptation of space on the other hand (appropriated space).

Thus, if we embrace Mikkelsen's definition of an institutional foodscape as the 'physical, organizational and sociocultural space in which clients/guests encounter meals, food and food-related issues, including health messages' (2011: 215), whilst acknowledging that despite recognizing foodscapes as physical and social sites, the foodscapes literature could do more to explore the meaningful ways these perspectives inform each other, we should look to Lefebvre's framework in order to develop an understanding of foodscapes as a 'dynamic social construction that relates food to specific places, people and meanings' (Johnston and Bauman, 2010: 3). The marriage of both foodscape studies and a Lefebvrian lens offers us a sound set of conceptual tools for understanding the social/spatial encounters we have with food and exploring the contested terrain of spatial practices of eating at work.

## Amuse Bouche: Field Study and Research Method

The data presented in this chapter are drawn from a wider three-month study that explored the newly built offices of a large Government organization's headquarters in the UK (for the sake of this study, I will refer to the name of the agency as *Davenupe*). Specifically, this interpretive, qualitative study focussed on an in-depth, post-occupancy examination (18 months after re-location) of how workers felt about their new building, their subjective experiences of the space, and how they felt the new space had impacted on their everyday work practices, wellbeing, and interactions.

Re-locating to this new building was particularly significant for this organization since workers had previously been in many separate offices and employees had worked in discrete, single offices in dated buildings with limited facilities. The new office represented a large cultural shift for the organization with new working practices including hot-desking, open-plan office spaces, and bookable break-out meeting rooms. Due to the dramatic changes to working life associated with re-locating, the organization began a new build campaign two and a half years before the move, and worked with teams across the organization to promote the up-coming benefits to employees. These included more flexible working opportunities, being better placed to work with the local community, and the ability to all work under one roof. Davenupe's building now consists of a light-filled atrium with a central staircase reaching up four levels to large roof lights complete with solar panels and a roof terrace provides wide-reaching views over the city skyline.

Within this study, the sample included 18 employees in total, both male and female, aged between 25 and 55 years old and incorporated junior managers, senior managers and administrative staff across a variety of functions within the organization. An important part of this study was the use of visual methods—namely participant-led photography (Warren, 2002, 2005; Shortt and Warren, 2012; Shortt, 2015), and was chosen since it aligned with the ontological and epistemological foundations of the wider study; the concern being with the participant's subjectivity and individual experience of work space (Ray and Smith, 2012). Each participant was given a disposable camera (although some chose to use their own digital camera-phones) and asked to capture six to eight images of spaces that they felt were important to them at work and spaces that were meaningful in relation to their everyday work practices and sense of wellbeing. The participants had three working days in which to capture their photographs. After the photographs had been taken, developed and printed (or in the case of those who had captured images on their camera-phones, emailed and printed) photo-elicitation interviews were arranged and conducted. These interviews comprised one-to-one, face-to-face, interactions with each participant, where their images were discussed and conversations recorded (Collier and Collier, 1986; van

Leeuwen and Jewitt, 2001; Harper, 2002). The ethics and confidentiality of this study were addressed using participant consent forms for the use of quotes and images for research purposes and with the agreement that pseudonyms would be used both with regards to the name of the organization and the names of participants involved.

These data were then subject to qualitative analysis from which key themes were established. Specifically, the analytical process started within the interview setting; participants ascribed meanings to their photographs and talked about why they had captured these images. Transcripts from each interview were then produced and initial memos were recorded as part of the preliminary reading of these texts (Saldaña, 2012). Codes were grounded in the data to preserve the inductive participant-centred character of the research. This coding process finally led to the development of key themes (for more on visual analysis see van Leeuwen and Jewitt, 2001; Pink, 2007). As noted above, this field-study set out to explore staff experiences of the new building and examine how the new open-plan, shared offices impacted on daily working practices and wellbeing. However, it was only after participants had taken their photographs, and photo-elicitation interviews and analysis had taken place, that themes around food and eating at work emerged as particularly significant.

## Main—the Contested Terrain of Spatial Practices of Eating at Work

The staff at Davenupe took an array of photographs that were connected to food, drink and eating in the office. They took photographs of food in the canteen, homemade cakes on desks, tins of biscuits on locker tops, and where they made tea and coffee. They talked to me about what meanings these held and why they were important in their everyday working lives. What is particularly evident in the images and the subsequent discussions are that food is experienced and encountered in a multitude of ways across the organizational terrain. The consumption of food in this office highlights tensions that exist between the planned and designed spaces for eating (Lefebvre's notion of conceived space), and the workers' routines and experiences of eating elsewhere (perceived and lived space). The foodscape of this office is both physically produced but importantly *socially* produced through the lived experiences of workers, their symbolic associations with food, where it is consumed and with whom it is eaten. Indeed, food encounters meant one thing in the canteen, another at one's desk, and yet another standing at a colleague's locker. The following analysis and discussion draws on the findings from the field study and reveals how a) foodscapes are transformed by inhabitants and their eating practices, b) that foodscape boundaries are permeable and somewhat fluid, and c) that foodscapes are imbued with social, political and cultural meanings. Most significantly, this analysis reveals a previously underexplored context in which we are able to witness the very contradictions of organizational space; from the 'forces that aspire to dominate and control space . . . [to] the forces that seek to appropriate space' (Lefebvre, 1991: 392). I present this discussion under four themes; *table talk*; *private dining*; *can you smell what's cooking?*; *health and well-being*.

## Table Talk

Conversations with the agency workers uncovered the importance of being able to talk over food; being able to converse over a meal or a snack was part of everyday life in the office and a fundamental factor in bringing people together. This is perhaps unsurprising since we already know that food is the currency of sociality and collaboration (Throsby, 2012; Kiffin et al., 2015) and that eating and drinking together at work contributes to personal and social well-being (Stroebaek, 2013). Yet these conversations varied according to the type of food or drink that was being consumed and most significantly here, the space in which it was consumed.

Formal, designated spaces for eating and drinking, such as the canteen and tea stations, proved to be popular with many workers. Eating lunch in the canteen with groups of friends became a daily ritual for some and provided an opportunity to talk about personal lives, gossip, and a time and space to share hobbies and interests—'cake . . . creates . . . a time and space away from "work" ' (Valentine, 2002: 6):

> *We meet each lunch time in the canteen or at one of the tea stations and have our sandwiches and do the crossword together. We just like puzzling things out together. Sometimes we don't do much of it because we're gossiping and eating instead!*
>
> (Yvonne, see Figure 9.1)

> *So, we have a knitting group. Once a week on a Wednesday we meet in the canteen, have lunch and bring our knitting. It's great because it makes me leave my desk. We talk about all sorts really . . . birthdays, weddings, what we're making. People bring their latest projects with them and later in the year we all make stuff for our office charity craft sale at Christmas.*
>
> (Dana)

The tea stations, designed by the architects and planners to provide a space in which workers could meet whilst making a hot drink, were identified by many as *'nice chatting areas'*;

> *The tea area is just a, well you get just a small bit of engagement. It's nice to chat there but you've got to be careful because obviously now we are open plan, everyone near that area can hear what you're saying!*
>
> (Dana)

*Figure 9.1*
Picture taken by participant, Yvonne.

*Figure 9.2*
Picture taken by participant, Kerry.

*It's not obviously where, well, you wouldn't have a personal chat there y'know. It's not personal stuff or work really, it's just . . . like this morning, I had a conversation about mugs and left-handed people, nothing to do with work or anything really.*

(Kerry, see Figure 9.2)

Just as Stroebaek (2013) discusses in her paper on coffee and coping communities, the tea stations in this office provide a space to make a drink, share a few words with colleagues and allow for chance meetings with others. However, due to their central location in the open-plan office, conversations here appear to be somewhat brief and inhibited by the visible and audible nature of the space. Participants noted that these drinking spaces were suitable neither for private *nor* for work-related discussions.

It is the sharing of food at desks and on locker tops in walkways and corridors across the office space that was most prevalent during the interviews. During these discussions, employees reflected on their new open-plan, hot-desking environment and discussed how they felt this new workplace design impacted rather negatively on teams and working practices;

*We just don't get to have the banter around the office . . . not social banter but sort of y'know, asking for advice on what we're doing . . . now it can be very isolating and we just can't do that in here because there's too many other people around.*

(David)

However, it is the ability to share *food* across the office space that most employees identified as key to bringing people back together and reconnecting conversations;

[at your desk] *it can be quite a lonely, isolating experience but when you've got food on offer . . . and if it goes up higher* [Lauren points to the top of the lockers pictured in her photograph] *where people can see it . . . it's like come and see us, we have food! It gets people talking that might not otherwise talk. It connects teams and you find out what stuff other people are working on.*

(Lauren, see Figure 9.3)

It is worth reflecting here on the notion that, as Hatch (1990) suggests, open-plan offices are often designed with collaboration, togetherness and teamwork in mind and as Lefebvre (1991) would argue, such planned spaces are manifestations of power and control, attempting to ensure workers engage and interact. Yet here we see the word 'isolating' being used to describe how this new open-plan space is experienced by its users. It is somewhat ironic that workers feel isolated with '. . . *too many other people around*'.

*Figure 9.3*
Picture taken by participant, Lauren.

Taking a Lefebvrian perspective here highlights the contradictory nature of social space—that on the one hand the logical, rational design of such a space allows for inclusion and connection with others, yet on the other hand, those situated within it experience a sense of exclusion due to its proximity to others (1991: 294). Indeed, it could be argued further that although open plan, flexible work spaces might be considered 'neutral spaces' which are open to all, they are far from devoid of the 'subdivisions of space' (1991: 294) that create pockets of power for some and create vacuums of isolation for others. It is worthy of note here that several women who work flexible hours in the organization identify the new hot-desking arrangements in the office as somewhat exclusionary. An example of what Wasserman and Frenkel (2015) discuss as the role of space in the doing of gender in the workplace, these women described themselves as *'nomads'*, *'wandering around the office to find a desk'* because they have come in *'late'* after the school run. There are insights here into the female bodily practice of searching for a hot-desk in an open-plan office and how this might affect women and their 'gender work' in organizations (Wasserman and Frenkel, 2015: 1487). The very use of the word 'nomad' is telling given its connection to migration and having no fixed sense of place or belonging.

> *Cake . . . cake is a really big feature of our team. We take it in turns. That's my tin—in the picture—so I had made cake that day. It's really important for lots of reasons—it breaks up the day, gives us a treat, but it really is all about morale, it impacts on morale in a big way.*
>
> (Eve, see Figure 9.4)

Thus, it seems it is the combination of both open-plan space *with food* that produces a collaborative working environment for these workers. Indeed, one participant described the placement of food on locker tops as how people *'display their wares and encourage people to talk more'* and how this *'encourages passers-by to stop, talk a bit of shop, eat and move on'*.

*Figure 9.4*
Picture taken by participant, Eve.

This workplace sharing of food is not simply the currency of sociality as Throsby (2012) has noted, but for these workers it is the currency of team relations and the edible facilitator of their office networking and work collaborations, just as Kiffin et al. (2015) suggest in their research on the enhanced team performance of firefighters who eat together.

This also mirrors Di Domenico and Phillips's (2009) discussion around Oxbridge dining rituals where they find such eating behaviours in formal halls assist in politicking, relationship-building and information exchange. Yet of course, here we see workers' spatial practices and eating practices around the open-plan office as far more informal and somewhat ad-hoc. It seems it is the combination of open-plan offices (and thus, visibility), food 'displayed' in unprescribed ways, and the informal wandering of the office that truly creates a collaborative working environment in this case.

Furthermore, although Di Domenico and Phillips highlight the importance of relationship-building, their study draws out the hierarchical, inclusion and exclusion in formal dining practices, whereas here, we might liken spatial and eating practices to more informal 'reception drinks' or the chance encounter at a cocktail party. Visser notes that in social eating and drinking contexts 'dining-room furniture limits numbers, prevents mobility, and promotes unwanted intimacy . . .' (1991: 344) but reception drinks allow people to 'stand and move about' and 'break away from a talking group' and it is these sorts of practices we witness in this office.

More broadly, the lived experience of this space is quite different from the planned space (Lefebvre, 1991; De Certeau, 1984), and regardless of the organization's formal rules discouraging employees to eat at desks and in the office space (all eating, they suggest, should be done in the canteen or at tea stations), these workers are subverting such regulations 'in 'deviant' ways' (Taylor and Spicer, 2007: 331). As Lefebvre reminds us, 'human beings situate themselves in space as active participants' (1991: 294) and it is the users that produce and transform space. So, our understanding of power here is served only when we consider its opposite concept, appropriation and resistance and as Lefebvre notes, the appropriation of space produces new spaces that temporarily suspend domination (1991: 167–168). Workers resist the intended use of office spaces and the expectations of planners and architects regarding where they eat—for workers their locker tops are not for storing folders or for organizational ephemera, they are for food displays and the presentation of edible symbols of collegiality and conversation.

Through our Lefebvrian lens, then, we see the social construction of eating practices in this open-plan space affording workers the opportunities to both approach and escape conversations and the informal, casual nature of eating on the move, as they transition through and around the office talking and eating. This clearly provides vital moments for making contact with others without some of the social and political rules of more dominant 'structured' canteen dining settings. In addition, through this analysis we can observe the dialectics of space that emerge from these practices (Shields, 1999). Lefebvre suggests that space embodies its own contradictions (1991: 129) where complex inconsistencies arise and so might be the case in this context. Simultaneously, we see how management re-appropriate the sociality around food, with controls 'from above' regarding expectations that workers socialize in the canteen, and yet 'from below' we see eating practices as part of informal interactions in liminal spaces (see Turner, 1982; Shortt, 2015). Indeed, the dialectical nature of space, food and the workplace continues in the following theme, where workers discuss dining alone.

### Private Dining

Despite all the talk of talk, social interactions and connecting over cake, paradoxically, workers also identified the inability to eat *alone* as somewhat problematic in their everyday working lives. The very sociality of eating posed privacy issues for some and the new open-plan, hot-desking environment presented particular challenges in this regard.

Some identified the canteen as a space where the *'pressure to talk'* was often unwelcome. As highlighted above, the canteen has been designed and is used by many as social space where bench seating and long tables promote conversation and create a setting where meals can be eaten together. Yet, for example, Bob talked about wanting to *'just go and sit, eat my lunch and get back to work'* and appeared frustrated that there was no opportunity, or rather no space in which he might dine alone. The spatial and therefore social expectations in the canteen were such that *talking* over lunch was almost seen as a prerequisite; as we saw above, another example of Lefebvre's conceived space 'that attempts to control, to dominate, the spatial practices' (Wapshott and Mallett, 2011: 68) of workers. Indeed, a number of workers deliberately choose to eat lunch at alternative times to avoid eating with others:

> *I usually go to the kitchen area at any time but lunchtime, it's quite empty then. You can just sit there, eat . . . and if you want to take five minutes to yourself, gather your thoughts . . .*
>
> (Pauline)

> *Sometimes I say to my team that I'm just going to go downstairs to eat now, like at 2 o'clock, and that's it. Then I can have a quick sort of fifteen minutes on my own and that's fine . . . so you can get away when you need to.*
>
> (Eve)

Consequently, it seems, alternative spaces for *private* dining were frequently sought out. Almost half the participants I spoke to took photographs outside the office, at various locations in the nearby city centre that captured

*Figure 9.5*
Picture taken by participant, Graham.

where they liked to eat, including cafes, parks, and benches by the river (see Figure 9.5):

> *I can just have a little wander at lunchtime . . . sit on the . . . green and have a bit of peace and quiet and eat my sandwich . . . y'know, get away for a bit. There's often loads of people out in the sun if the weather's nice . . . I can just people watch without talking.*

(Hannah)

Others talked about finding alternative meeting and eating spots in cafes so they could *'talk about sensitive materials'* over lunch or *'have a bit of a gossip'* As we heard from Dana previously, the tea stations offer a nice chatting area, but *'you've got to be careful because obviously now we are open plan, everyone near that area can hear what you're saying!'* Thus, it seems only certain sorts of conversations can be had over food in the office and if privacy is required, alternative eating spots are pursued. Perhaps one of the most poignant examples of this was Martin's story of finding a private place for a cup of coffee;

> *I'd just gone for an internal job, a promotion and I was told by my manager that I didn't get it. I came back up the stairwell and thought I've got to go back to my desk, but I just didn't want to. She [Martin's manager] could see from my face I was upset. I wanted a coffee and to find a corner y'know? So, I went out, went to the café at the end of the road around the corner and sat there for a bit . . . just had a coffee and came back.*

(Martin)

Given these stories of eating and drinking *outside* the office space we might argue that this organizational foodscape is not one that is fixed to formal or 'typical' encounters with food, it is one with permeable boundaries and is negotiated and renegotiated by its users' everyday spatial and eating practices. Thus, with the help of Lefebvre's perceived and lived perspectives on space we can widen our understanding of foodscape boundaries in the workplace. Understanding better the lived experience of food in the office and the 'unmanaged' informal subjective experiences of workers' eating and drinking habits has shifted the boundaries to include far more than simply the office building itself. These office workers cite the social aspects of eating together in the canteen as problematic when seeking privacy and thus the city and the built environment *around* the workplace becomes part of their foodscape. As such, we should perhaps not be limited in our thinking when considering the micro-geographies of organizational foodscapes (Sobal and Wonsink, 2007) and instead appreciate that the boundaries encompass other environments as well.

Furthermore, it seems the foodscape of this workplace and its 'influences on our food behaviour' (Mikkelsen, 2011: 210) is centred around the social aspects of eating—be it formally or informally—and does not consider the need for people to find solace when eating, nor does it consider the rather more contemplative, reflective setting that eating alone can offer. Indeed, there seems to be growing consensus that we live and work in increasingly transparent workplaces where walls and privacy have given way to surveillance, display and the disciplinary gaze (Foucault, 1991) and as such, workers here find alternative routes to private spaces in which to eat and drink alone. There appears to be little in the food literature that discusses dining alone and of course our Western sociocultural norms still suggest eating alone is rather unusual (see Burkeman, 2015).

Lefebvre's thoughts on the dialectics of space (Shields, 1999) can extend this analysis further. There are perhaps several examples in this case; firstly we see how the pressures of work, technology and organizational expectations of instant communication might encourage workers to stay at their desks through a lunch break, as Altman and Baruch note, we might 'grab(s) a sandwich, consuming it alone at [our] workstation while keeping up . . . high-paced work' (2010: 130), yet at the same time, the organization might prohibit such food-based activities at workstations based on the argument workers' must take appropriate breaks; secondly, to eat alone is considered unusual (certainly given the discourse in much of the sociological and anthropological research on the sociality of eating), yet spaces for eating alone are actively sought out by workers in this organization for moments of solace and reflection; and finally, Lefebvre's acknowledgement of space being both exclusionary at the same time as inclusionary (1991: 294) is also evident in that we might consider this canteen space as one that both excludes those who wish to be alone, and includes those who wish to socialize. The workers' attempts to seek alternative private eating spaces demonstrates Lefebvre's argument that space creates conflict between different groups and although organizations wish to create cultures of collaboration, workers will always attempt to 'transcend political institutions' (1991: 392).

In addition, although the focus of this study is not a gendered one, we might reflect on the nature of eating alone and further reasons as to why food might be consumed privately since there are echoes here of Wasserman and Frenkel's findings where women feel uncomfortable eating in public spaces (2015: 1499). It may not just be a sense of solace and quiet that workers seek, it may indeed be linked to the wish to conceal food choices from the gaze of others; when talking about eating chocolate where she can be seen, a participant in Wasserman and Frenkel's study notes 'it's especially problematic at my status, because it might be interpreted as a lack of self-control' (2015: 1499). Certainly, links can be made here to the recent rather disturbing social 'trend' of 'food-shaming'; the act of judging someone else's food choices and 'shaming' them into feeling guilty about those choices (see for example, Bates, 2014). Indeed, the Metro recently ran an article in

June 2017 titled 'Stop Food-Shaming in the Office' in which they discuss co-workers observing each other's food choices and openly negatively commenting on them and the impact of such commentary on body image issues and eating practices (Lindsay, 2017).

More broadly, then, this raises important questions about the design of contemporary workplaces that embrace open-plan, collaborative working and the foodscapes within them—if foodscapes are inherently social spaces and food encounters are always with *others*, are we marginalizing and excluding those who wish to eat without conversation, or indeed, observation? We might consider how and when we make space to reflect on our work or indeed just take ten minutes out of our day, and what role food and drink plays in these activities. If food and drink are associated with taking a break, yet these moments are constructed and mediated as social interactions with the accompanying social norms of chit-chat and discussion, arguably, are these 'breaks' at all? And in what ways does food consumption in public, private or liminal spaces shape and influence the construction of the gendered body at work?

## Can You Smell What's Cooking?

Food smells were also discussed as part the workers' everyday experience of food in the office. Working in an open-plan office such as this means the smell of food can easily permeate the air and creep across desks and between floors and unlike the sweet smells of baking bread that are deliberately wafted through supermarkets by sensory marketers (Underhill, 2000; Hultén, 2009), these food smells were not always welcome:

> *I use the microwave to warm up my hot wraps and people are like God, what's that smell? It's a bit embarrassing really, then everyone knows it's you and you go back to your desk and it's like, yep, here I am with my stinky food!*
>
> (Kelly)

> *When people use the microwaves downstairs, the smell can really travel right up the atrium. But it happens anyway, y'know, the canteen preparing for lunch and you can smell all the food—sometimes it's a nice smell, other times it's like I just don't want to smell that whilst I'm trying to work.*
>
> (Gav)

> *Yeah, you have to be careful what you bring in to put in the microwave— you can end up stinking the whole place out!*
>
> (Lauren)

Indeed, these olfactory accounts are somewhat reminiscent of the findings in Warren and Riach's (2017) exploration of smell in the workplace, the 'sensory signifiers' that permeate one's surroundings, and the complexities associated with wanted and unwanted food smells (Visser, 1991). Furthermore, workers discussed the auditory routines of the office and noted that 'you know when it's lunchtime because the bloody noise from the canteen comes right up through the middle of the building' and 'there's a real hubbub downstairs when it's lunchtime and people are queuing to get into the canteen . . . it can be quite off putting if you're still at your desk working'.

These are examples of how food encounters at work are *embodied* experiences (Plester, 2015; Flores-Pereira, Davel, and Cavedon, 2008; Driver, 2008; Valentine, 2002). Lefebvre draws on embodiment in his understandings of space and emphasizes links between the corporeal and the social, particularly with regards to both lived space and perceived space. Dale and Burrell usefully discuss Lefebvre's perspectives noting 'how the materiality of the world influences and shapes us as irreducibly embodied and spatial social beings' (2008: 217). Yet it seems our lived, embodied experiences of space are often discussed in relation to the material, or notably here, food as object—Plester (2015) discusses eating food as 'ingesting the organisation' and Valentine (2002) uses actor network theory to explore eating practices and food as 'things' consumed by and unified with employee bodies. Here however, it is *smell* that is ingested and incorporated into the employee body. What is significant here is that these workers cannot shut the sensory door on the smell (or noise) of food and food preparation, given the design and spatial layout of the building. To some degree, the very air in the office becomes part of how food is encountered and much like the sharing of food on locker tops or the seeking of external private dining spaces, these sensory phenomena disrupt the formal, planned foodscape of the workplace. This careful examination of space, as Lefebvre reminds us, must 'not only be with the eyes . . . but also with all the senses, with the total body' (1991: 391).

Arguably we might also consider how smells construct and reconstruct our lived experiences of space. We might have different sorts of embodied, lived experiences of space when we start to pick apart the sensory elements of workers' lives. If we mapped the physical, material lived space against a map of the smells of lived space, we might get two very different pictures (Riach and Warren, 2015); on the one hand, our bodies dictate how we experience space, we move around and see things—we have heard how workers sit in the canteen, stand at tea stations and wander the office space—but on the other hand, the smells (and sounds) we experience do not respect those boundaries that we create—smells are unrestrained and here we have heard how the smell politics (Warren and Riach, 2017) of the office, including having a smelly lunch, can influence the cultural and social practices of workers.

Lefebvre's suggestion that space embodies both inclusion and exclusion can be reflected upon again here; his discussion argues that some spaces are prohibited and other spaces, for some, are accessible (1991: 294), yet this is predominantly based on material space, a dwelling or a vicinity. In the context of smell, as an aspect of the embodied experience of space, it is more complex to consider how smells influence and control such lived experiences (Warren and Riach, 2017) and how, without physical boundaries we might experience a different sense of inclusion or exclusion. Lauren tells us, '*Yeah, you have to be careful what you bring in to put in the microwave—you can end up stinking the whole place out!*'—on the one hand, her material experience of space and food consumption could be seen as accessible or encouraged (able to bring food from home, use the office microwaves and so on), yet, on the other, with regards to the smelliness of her food, her experience is redefined as unacceptable or perhaps an unwanted, unwelcome 'inclusion' to the office space. We can see this as an 'unequal struggle' (Lefebvre, 1991: 391) whereby the examination of space, through and with all the senses (or at least the eyes and nose), becomes distorted and the conflicts between groups shifts 'homogenized space to their own purposes' (p. 391), desires, judgements and impressions.

In addition, this analysis might also help us delve deeper into the sociocultural nature and makeup of institutional foodscapes. How and where we encounter food is so far in the foodscapes literature dominated by the physical, material and visual encounters with food and food-related messages. In future research, both conceptually and methodologically, it would be pertinent to acknowledge and consider the rather more sensory aspects to our encounters with food and think more about how we might problematize embodiment, space and food at work.

## Health and Wellbeing

Finally, an important part of the new building for most of the participants was the canteen and the provision of healthy snacks and food. In stark contrast to many of the participants' previous workplaces, where no canteen space was provided and only small kitchenette style facilities were available, Davenupe's new canteen space had been designed with social interaction in mind, but importantly with the health of employees;

> *it's such a nice open plan canteen and it's open all day with accessible healthy refreshments. When I look at this photo it makes me feel relieved that it's here and I feel energised!*
>
> (Hannah)

> *healthy snacks are always available on the ground floor and it means I start my day in the right way. I feel like I have more energy and*

*Figure 9.6*
Picture taken by participant, Rana.

*motivation at work now and I'm probably more productive too. I can kit myself out and I am ready for the day ahead.*

(Rana, see Figure 9.6)

From many workers, there was a positive response to the type of food served in the canteen. Some of the participants in this study cycle to work and took pictures of the food in the canteen as well as photos of the new showers and cycle storage spaces provided, and noted that they felt together these elements of their new workspace were a positive message from the organization, that they *'care about our health and how active we are being . . . they are promoting a healthy workforce'*. Indeed, others reflected on the paradoxical experience of eating cake and sweets at their desks;

*We have a cupboard full of food—Celebrations [a brand of chocolates] and all sorts . . . we have lots of food around, and I'm sort of slightly a bit surprised that we don't share more fruit or something! We should really. It's hard . . . it's kind of important because it gets people together but I guess it's not that healthy really.*

(Lauren)

There is a sense here that health is on the workplace agenda, be it through the organization's efforts in the canteen, through to the recognition that cakes and sweet treats across the rest of the office might not always fit with a wider sense of well-being. Such findings highlight the tensions between the organization's wish to impose a healthy, ethical foodscape (Mikkelsen, 2011) and to some extent control the health of the workforce, and the appropriation of space and the food within it by workers.

This further reiterates Lefebvre's notions of dialectics and embodiment. There is evidence to suggest the management and control of employee bodies through the promotion of workplace health (Thanem, 2009), where the organization can be seen to construct, limit and reappropriate food and what, where and how it is placed in the canteen space. Juxtaposed to and somewhat at odds with this is the 'bottom up' reappropriation of food at desks and on lockers through employees' sharing of sweet treats and cakes in the liminal spaces of the office. The boundaries between the management of the 'healthy' employee body and what might be defined by Thanem as bodily resistance practices on the part of employees (2009) are blurred. Indeed, it could be argued there is a sense of oscillation between how space is practiced in the office and the food encounters that are negotiated there; for example, as Rana suggests above, she can start the day *'in the right way'* with healthy snacks provided by the organization, but once situated within the office space the socio-cultural aspects of eating create quite a different set of 'unhealthy' but seemingly vital food encounters with colleagues.

## Dessert: Conclusions and Future Considerations

This research argues that the social production of space influences the consumption of food and the consumption of food influences the social production of space. As such, we have seen that where we eat, what we eat and with whom we eat is an embodied and conflicting experience that is both planned and controlled, resisted, lived and practiced—it is Lefebvre's spatial framework and his conceptualization of social space that has drawn attention to what is described here as the contested terrain of spatial practices of eating at work.

These findings highlight the complex and multifaceted nature of an organizational foodscape. If we define a foodscape as the actual sites where people find food (Freidberg, 2010) and understand foodscapes as the study of how and where people encounter and interact with food, this study sheds light on the many and varied sites of food consumption in the everyday lives of office workers. However, by drawing on Lefebvre's work we can make better sense of these complexities and in doing so, further our knowledge of food encounters in an organizational environment and extend our socio-cultural understanding of foodscapes more broadly.

Significantly though, it is through this Lefebvrian analysis of food and eating practices in an open-plan office that we have seen how the contra-dictions of space dissolve what 'on the surface appears homogeneous and coherent' (Lefebvre, 1991: 352). In using Lefebvre's triad, (perceived, con-ceived, and lived), the dialectics of this office space have been foregrounded and the discussions around the sharing of food, eating alone, the sensory nature of food, and healthy eating practices have all served to demonstrate the subdivisions that exist within this space. Lefebvre's work enables us to not only recognize the dominant ways in which our organizations manipu-late and control space (and our food encounters and what we eat and where we eat it), but throws new light on the appropriation of space in the office, re-defined by workers as, for example, informal eating locations and spaces for informal munching and chatting. Lefebvre's perspectives on space high-light how foodscapes are not passively experienced or stood before like a 'picture . . . or a mirror' (1991: 294), but are constructed and engineered by those living and practicing the spaces in which they eat, and are shaped by and embedded within social, political, embodied, cultural and contradictory meanings. The meanings of food and eating at work here have enriched our understanding of the ambiguous nature of space, particularly in relation to an open-plan, hot-desking environment. We have seen how space includes and excludes, how it is controlled and at the same time resisted, how we continually see, hear (and smell) the 'unequal struggle, sometimes furious, sometimes more low-key, [that] takes place between the Logos and the Anti-Logos' (Lefebvre, 1991: 391).

Furthermore, this analysis of food unearths some important considerations for those exploring new, open-plan spaces and the process of working in those spaces. For example, food in an open-plan office shapes and re-shapes (informal) communications and interactions and, as the dialectics of space show here, this redraws the hierarchical lines inside the workplace. These shifting boundaries of interaction and territory are not just office politics at play, they are the politics of cake and space, and as Lefebvre might argue, open-plan offices, with their all-embracing, collaborative, (theoretically) 'unrestricted' ethos are indeed far from such spaces—neutral, they are not.

Organizational spatial theorists might reflect further on making compari-sons between (informal) interactions in spaces with and *without* food—such as toilets, the lifts and at the printer—or office versus *non-office* spaces and food related dynamics at pubs or restaurants as part of after-work socializ-ing or client entertainment. In comparing such spaces in this way, we might further understand broader politics at play in organizations, surrounding gender, ethnicity or cultural diversity and where the difference in public/ private eating practices may be examined in more depth. In this study we have seen how the lack of space in which workers can eat privately, and the demands made on workers to avoid eating food that emits strong odours, limits and prohibits eating practices and potentially the loss of personal, social, and cultural identities. We might reflect on how certain eating and drinking practices at work therefore undermines the needs of some workers or marginalizes and excludes their food choices and behaviour.

In addition, we have seen how cake culture in an open-plan office has prompted more informal eating practices, such as eating in public spaces and *transitory* spaces, like corridors and walkways. It may be pertinent to consider how the boundaries and attitudes around food practices are changing in today's working world and how our social rituals and embodiment of social identities are shifting. In the future, we might thus consider the eating practices of workers on the move or flexible workers without desks or offices—eating practices in cars, trains or in doorways and fire exits.

Finally, we might consider the wider implications of this research and what these findings might mean for organizations in the future. For example, in the current climate of health and well-being programmes and the drive for a healthy workforce, organizations might wish to take heed of the complex meanings of food across the landscape of work before implementing such programmes. Growing levels of obesity and dental problems (see Thanem, 2009; Gallagher, 2016), wider concerns about obesogenicity (see Glanz et al., 2005), and with the growing 'cake culture', reported by the Royal College of Surgeons, are all seen as dangers to our health and our waistlines. Other discourses around health and eating at work promote messages that food should only be consumed in designated eating spaces, and not at one's desk. This comes from a health and safety perspective where workers are encouraged to take 'proper breaks' (Shaw, 2016), as well as organizations who demand a clean and tidy office, with clear rules 'not to eat at your desk' or 'not to eat food that emits strong odours' (Calligeros, 2011). If organizations are serious about understanding the eating habits of their employees, they should understand that food matters at work, but not just in the canteen and not just in relation to health. Food plays a vital social, cultural and political role in office life and organizations should be considerate of the relationships and interactions that are centred on food.

It is with these reflections in mind that I end this chapter and ponder over the future of food in the workplace, over a coffee and an after-dinner mint.

## Note

1 Indeed, our homes can opened up as public spaces for eating and sharing food with others and, for example, unite us in learning about different cultures and ethnic diversity (see the work of Flowers and Swan, 2012, 2013). See also the work of www.91ways.org that uses food and cooking to build more diverse, united and sustainable cities.

# References

Abbots, E. and Lavis, A. (Eds.) (2013). *Why We Eat, How We Eat: Contemporary Encounters Between Foods and Bodies*. Farnham: Ashgate.

Altman, Y. and Baruch, Y. (2010). The organizational lunch. *Culture and Organization, 16*(2), 127–143.

Bates, L. (2014, July 24). 'Are you really going to eat that?' Yes, and it's nobody else's business. *The Guardian*. Retrieved August 7, 2017, from www.theguard ian.com/lifeandstyle/womens-blog/2014/jul/24/women-meal-choices-control-female-bodies-food-policing

Beardsworth, A. and Keel, T. (1997). *Sociology on the Menu: An Invitation to the Study of Food and Society*. London: Routledge.

Bitner, M. J. (1992). Servicescapes: The impact of physical surroundings on customers and employees. *Journal of Marketing, 56*, 57–71.

Blythman, J. (2004). *Shopped: The Shocking Power of British Supermarkets*. London: Fourth Estate.

Brumbach, H. and Johansson, B. (2010). Foodscapes and children's bodies. *Culture Unbound, 2*, 797–818.

Briner, R. B. and Sturdy, A. (2008). Introduction to food, work and organization. *Human Relations, 61*(7), 907–912.

Burkeman, O. (2015, April 28). You're the only person who notices you are dining alone. So, enjoy it. *The Guardian*. Retrieved December 19, 2016, from www.theguardian.com/commentisfree/oliver-burkeman-column/2015/apr/28/dining-alone-enjoy-yourself

Cairns, K., Johnston, J. and MacKendrick, N. (2013). Feeding the 'organic child': Mothering through ethical consumption. *Journal of Consumer Culture, 13*, 2 97–118.

Calligeros, M. (2011, August 23). No smelly lunches: BHP's strict staff rules. Retrieved December 19, 2016, from www.executivestyle.com.au/no-smelly-lunches-bhps-strict-staff-rules-1j7dg

Caplan, P. (Ed.). (1997). *Food, Health and Identity*. London: Routledge.

Charsley, S. (1997). Marriages, weddings and their cakes. In P. Caplan (Ed.), *Food, Health and Identity*. London: Routledge.

Collier, J. and Collier, M. (1986). *Visual anthropology: Photography as a research method*. Albuquerque: University of New Mexico Press.

Cook, P. H. and Wyndham, A. J. (1953). Patterns of eating behaviour: A study of industrial workers. *Human Relations, 6*, 141–160.

Conner, M., Johnson, C. and Grogan, S. (2004). Gender, sexuality, body image and eating behaviours. *Journal of Health Psychology, 9*(4), 505–515.

Dale, K. and Burrell, G. (2008). *The Spaces of Organisation and the Organisation of Space—power, identity and materiality at work*. Hampshire: Palgrave Macmillan.

De Certeau, M. (1984). *The Practice of Everyday Life*. Berkeley: University of California Press.

Dejmanee, T. (2016). 'Food Porn' as postfeminist play: Digital femininity and the female body on food blogs. *Television and New Media, 17*(5), 429–448.

Di Domenico, M. and Phillips, N. (2009). Sustaining the ivory tower: Oxbridge formal dining as organizational ritual. *Journal of Management Inquiry, 18*(4), 326–343.

Douglas, M. and Isherwood, B. (1979). *The World of Goods*. London: Routledge.

Driver, M. (2008). Every bite you take . . . food and the struggles of embodied sub-jectivity in organizations. *Human Relations, 61*(7), 913–934.

Elias, N. (1939/1969). *The Civilizing Process: The History of Manners Volume 1.* Oxford: Blackwell.

Flores-Pereira, M. T., Davel, E. and Cavedon, N. R. (2008). Drinking beer and understanding organizational culture embodiment. *Human Relations, 61*(7), 1007–1026.

Flowers, R. and Swan, E. (2012). 'Teaching People to Suck Eggs': Pedagogies of food activism. *Australian Journal of Adult Learning*, Special Issue: 'Food Pedagogies,' *52,* 3.

Flowers, R. and Swan, E. (Eds.) (2013). *Food Pedagogies.* London: Ashgate Publishing.

Foucault, M. (1991). *Discipline and Punish: The Birth of the Prison.* London: Penguin.

Freidberg, S. (2010). Perspective and power in the ethical foodscape. *Environment and Planning A, 42,* 1868–1874.

Gallagher, J. (2016, June 24). Office cake culture is 'danger to health'. *BBC News.* Retrieved December 19, 2016, from www.bbc.co.uk/news/health-36608269

Glanz, K., Sallis, J., Saelens, B. and Frank, L. (2005). Healthy nutrition environ-ments: Concepts and measures. *American Journal of Health Promotion, 19,* 330–333.

Goodman, M., Maye, D. and Holloway, L. (2010). Ethical foodscapes? Premises, promises and possibilities. *Environment and Planning A, 42,* 1782–1796.

Harper, D. (2002). Talking about pictures: A case for photo elicitation. *Visual Stud-ies, 17*(1), 13–26.

Hatch, M. J. (1990). The symbolics of office design: An empirical exploration. In P. Gagliardi (Ed.), *The Symbolics of Organizational Artefacts* (pp. 129–146). Ber-lin: de Gruyter.

Hultén, B., Broweus, N. and van Dijk, M. (2009). *Sensory Marketing.* London: Palgrave Macmillan.

Johnston, J., Rodney, A. and Szabo, M. (2012). Place, ethics and everyday eating: A tale of two neighbourhoods. *Sociology, 46*(6), 1091–1108.

Kiffin, K. M., Wansink, B., Devine, C. M. and Sobal, J. (2015). Eating together at the firehouse: How workplace commensality relates to the performance of firefighters. *Human Performance, 28*(4), 281–306.

Klein, N. (2002). *Fences and Windows: Dispatches from the Frontlines of the Glo-balization Debate.* London: Harper Perrrenial.

Lefebvre, H. (1991). *The Social Production of Space.* Oxford: Blackwell.

Lindsay, J. (2017, June 28). Stop Food Shaming in the Office. *Metro.* Retrieved August 7, 2017, from http://metro.co.uk/2017/06/28/stop-food-shaming-in-the-office-6740630/

Mikkelsen, B. (2011). Images of foodscapes: Introduction to foodscape studies and tier application in the study of healthy eating out-of-home environments. *Royal Society for Public Health, 131*(5), 209–216.

Nath, J. (2011). Gendered fare? A qualitative investigation of alternative food and masculinities. *Journal of Sociology, 47*(3), 261–278.

Parker, M. (2008). Eating with the Mafia: Belonging and violence. *Human Rela-tions, 61*(7), 989–1006.

Pink, S. (2007). *Doing Visual Ethnography.* London: Sage.

Plester, B. (2015). Ingesting the organization: The embodiment of organizational food rituals. *Culture and Organization, 21*(3), 251–268.

Poulsen, S. and Jørgensen, M. (2011). Social shaping of food intervention initiatives at worksite: Canteen takeaway schemes at two Danish hospitals. *Royal Society for Public Health, 131*(5), 225–230.

Ray, J. and Smith, A. (2012). Using photographs to research organizations: Evidence, considerations and application in a field study. *Organizational Research Methods, 15*(2), 288–315.

Riach, K. and Warren, S. (2015). Smell organization: Bodies and corporeal porosity in office work. *Human Relations, 68*(5), 789–809.

Ritzer, G. (1993). *The McDonaldization of Society*. London: Sage.

Rosen, M. (1985). Breakfast at Spiro's: Dramaturgy and dominance. *Journal of Management, 11*, 31–48.

Rosen, M. (1988). You asked for it: Christmas at the bosses' expense. *Journal of Management Studies, 25*, 463–480.

Roy, D. (1959). Banana time: Job satisfaction and informal interaction. *Human Organization, 18*(4), 158–168.

Royal Society for Public Health. (2016). *Health in a Hurry: The Impact of Rush Hour Commuting on Our Health and Well-Being*. London: Royal Society for Public Health.

Saldaña, J. (2012). *The Coding Manual for Qualitative Researchers*. London: Sage.

Shaw, D. (2016, March 6). Office Etiquette: Five rules for eating at your desk. Retrieved December 19, 2016, from www.bbc.co.uk/news/business-35717493

Shields, R. (1999). *Lefebvre, Love and Struggles: Spatial Dialectics*. London: Routledge.

Shortt, H. (2015). Liminality, space and the importance of 'transitory dwelling places' at work. *Human Relations, 68*(4), 633–658.

Shortt, H. and Warren, S. (2012). Fringe benefits: Valuing the visual in narratives of hairdressers' identities at work. *Visual Studies, 27*(1), 18–24.

Sobal, J. and Wonsink, B. (2007). Kitchenscapes, tablescapes, platescapes, and foodscapes: Influences of microscale built environments on food intake. *Environment and Behaviour, 39*(1), 124–142.

Strangleman, T. (2010). Food, drink and the cultures of work: Consumption in the life and death of an English factory. *Food, Culture and Society, 13*(2), 260–280.

Stroebaek, P. S. (2013). Let's have a cup of coffee! Coffee and coping communities at work. *Symbolic Interaction, 36*(4), 381–397.

Sturdy, A., Schwarz, M. and Spicer, A. (2006). Guess who's coming to dinner? Structures and uses of liminality in strategic management consultancy. *Human Relations, 59*, 1–32.

Swinburn, B. Egger, G. and Raza, F. (1999). Dissecting obesogenic environments: The development and application of a framework for identifying and prioritizing environmental interventions for obesity. *Preventive Medicine, 29*, 563–570.

Taylor, S. and Spicer, A. (2007). Time for space: A narrative review of research on organizational spaces. *International Journal of Management Reviews, 9*(4), 325–346.

Thanem, T. (2009). 'There's no limit to how much you can consume': The new public health and the struggle to manage healthy bodies. *Culture and Organization, 15*(1), 59–74.

Throsby, K. (2012). *Dreaming of Jelly Babies: English Channel Swimming and the Challenges and Comforts of Food.* BSA Food Study Group Conference, Food and Society, British Library.

Turner, V. (1982). *From Ritual to Theatre: The Human Seriousness of Play.* New York: Performing Arts Journal Publications.

Underhill, P. (2000). *Why We Buy: The Science of Shopping.* New York: Touchstone.

Underhill, P. (2004). *The Call of the Mall: How We Shop.* London: Profile Books Ltd.

Valentine, G. (2002). In-corporations: Food, bodies and organizations. *Body and Society, 8*(2), 1–20.

Van Leeuwen, T. and Jewitt, C. (Eds.). (2001). *Handbook of Visual Analysis.* London: Sage.

Visser, M. (1991). *The Rituals of Dinner: The Origins, Evolution, Eccentricities, and Meaning of Table Manners.* London: Penguin.

Wapshott, R. and Mallett, O. (2012). The spatial implications of homeworking: A Lefebvrian approach to the rewards and challenges of home-based working. *Organization, 19*(1), 63–79.

Warren, S. (2002). Show me how it feels to work here: Using photography to research organizational aesthetics. *ephemera: Theory and Politics in Organizations, 2*(3), 224–245.

Warren, S. (2005). Photography and voice in critical qualitative management research. *Accounting, Auditing and Accountability Journal, 18*(6), 861–882.

Warren, S. and Riach, K. (2017). Olfactory control, aroma power and organizational smellscapes. In V. Henshaw, G. Warnaby, K. McClean and C. Perkins (Eds.), *Designing With Smell: Practices, Techniques and Challenges.* London: Routledge, forthcoming/ in print.

Wasserman, V. and Frenkel, M. (2015). Spatial work in between glass ceiling and glass walls: Gender-class intersectionality and organizational aesthetics. *Organization Studies, 36*(11), 1485–1505.

Wasserman, V., Rafaeli, A. and Kluger, A. (2000). Aesthetic symbols as emotional cues. In S. Fineman (Ed.), *Emotion in Organisations.* London: Sage.

Watkins, C. (2005). Representations of space, spatial practices and spaces of representation: An application of Lefebvre's spatial triad. *Culture and Organization, 11*(3), 209–220.

Williams, J. (1997). 'We never eat like this at home': Food on holiday. In P. Caplan (Ed.), *Food, Health and Identity.* London: Routledge.

## Part III

# Organization of Spaces— Capitalism, Urban and State Relations

# 10 Exploring the Spatial Dynamics of the City

## A Case Study in China

*Zhongyuan Zhang*

## Introduction

Lefebvre's reflections on social space have profoundly changed the ways scholars think about the physical environment of organizations. As researchers start from their own perspectives to engage with Lefebvre's thinking and develop research agendas for organizational space, new questions also arise that require closer scrutiny. One such question concerns the dynamics of social space. Earlier seminal works (Dale, 2005; Dale and Burrell, 2008) recognize organizational space as *social materiality*; more recently, a body of literature points to the direction that organizational space may be seen as *social processes*. For instance, Beyes and Steyaert (2012) invite us to view organizational space as undergoing an ongoing process of making and remaking. A number of empirical works use Lefebvre's triad of conceived, perceived and lived spaces to understand and trace changes in organizations' spatial formations and their underlying power rationales (Beyes and Michel, 2011; Wasserman and Frenkel, 2011; Zhang and Spicer, 2014). So far, however, little is known about how the conceived, perceived and lived elements of Lefebvre's triad inform, affect and perhaps transform one another during the ongoing processes of spatial production. I think that knowledge of this kind is important as it would allow us to further register organizational space as a social process, which is one of the central ideas laid out in *The Production of Space* (Lefebvre, 1991). This chapter makes an effort in this direction.

The chapter is based on the assumption that investigations into the dynamics of organizational space can learn from investigations of the dynamics of urban space. My reasoning is that, since Lefebvre's spatial thinking is closely related to his earlier writings on urban space (Shields, 1999), by reading Lefebvre's urban writings and applying some of his frameworks to the analysis of empirical urban space, we may gain some lessons of how future research on organizational space, in particular the dynamics of social space, may proceed.

To this end, the chapter first reads *The Right to the City* (RtC) and borrows from this work the logic frame of exchange-value/use-value. The chapter then uses the logic frame to analyse the urban space of Hangzhou, a Chinese city. It presents an autoethnographic case study that looks deeply into some examples of everyday lives in Hangzhou: redesigning roads, using the sidewalk and practising square-dancing. In doing so, the study reveals the city's space as an ongoing dynamic process that is played out among the interactions of the conceived, perceived and lived moments of space as these moments inform, affect and transform one another. Based on these findings, in the concluding part the chapter raises some suggestions concerning future research on the dynamics of social space in the organizational setting. The chapter makes a two-fold contribution to organizational studies. It contributes a case study that invites researchers to think of organizational space as social processes, and some advice on how this might be done in future research.

## *The Right to the City* and Organization Studies

In RtC, Lefebvre used a powerful set of Marxist concepts—exchange-value and use-value—to read urban reality. The city is related to exchange-value (city-as-product) in that it can be traded and consumed just like any other product in the market. The city is also related to use-value (city-as-oeuvre) in that people can use it in non-economic ways such as meeting others and visiting places. The city is at once a 'beautiful' work of art and a not-so-beautiful piece of commodity (Lefebvre, 1996: 67).

In the West, the exchange and use values of the city were balanced out against each other until the arrival of industrialization. Since then, 'exchange value is so dominant over use and use value that it more or less suppresses it' (*ibid.*: 73). For instance, in Paris, public gardens were increasingly replaced by shops and private estates, and slums were demolished to make room for shopping boulevards. The poor who, up till then, used the city non-economically were banished from the city centre; their return to the city was justified on economic grounds (e.g. paid tours and shopping). The rich who owned and traded estates in central Paris hardly ever used the city as oeuvre, for they lived in country villas. The city of Paris became predominantly exchange-value.

Lefebvre found this situation highly problematic. 'Urban consciousness will vanish . . . *consciousness of the city and of urban reality is dulled* for one or the other, as to disappear' (*ibid.*: 77, 80, italics in original). When the city is informed only by economic thinking, which is typical of 'the ruling class or fractions of ruling class' (*ibid.*: 74) such as technicians, city planners, and key decision-makers, our consciousness of the city is rooted in a network of signifiers that refer to one another, disconnected from the vital—and, in the sense of the signified, also real—insights that the city-as-oeuvre can offer. The result is that our once 'warm' sense of the city as the founding base of humanity's meaningful social existence is gone: 'the *urban* remains in a state of dispersed and alienated actuality' (Lefebvre, 1996: 148, italics in original).

The restoring of the city-as-oeuvre is thus at the centre of urban revival. For Lefebvre, this task cannot be achieved without the participation of the working class: 'a new humanism' connected to the best heritage of pre-industrial rural traditions (i.e. of festivity and boundless creativity). Hence Lefebvre's famous pledge 'the right to the city'—the right for the working class to participate in everyday urban activities, not simply as tourists or shop-goers, but in 'a transformed and renewed *right to urban life*' (*ibid.*: 158, italics in original). Our urban consciousness would be rescued from its alienated actuality once the city-as-product and the city-as-oeuvre start to interact, to talk to and inform each other, and the closed (and in a way empty) thinking of the 'ruling elites' torn open by myriad alternatives that the working class may offer.

Lefebvre's urban thinking—that through everyday practices, the spontaneity of the ruled class would call into question the symbolic fabrication of the ruling class, and in so doing set a spatial system of alienation into one of open and recurring evolution—would reappear, in the form of the conceived/perceived/lived spatial triad, in his magnum opus *The Production of Space*. This book, which since the publication of its English translation in 1991, has inspired a growing body of literature on organizational space (Clegg and Kornberger, 2006; Kornberger and Clegg, 2004; Beyes and Michels, 2011; Beyes and Steyaert, 2012; Dale, 2005; Dale and Burrell, 2008; Ford and Harding, 2004; Hernes, 2004; Spicer, 2006; Taylor and Spicer, 2007; Wapshott and Mallett, 2012; Wasserman and Frenkel, 2011; Watkins, 2005; Zhang, Spicer, and Hancock, 2008; Zhang and Spicer, 2014). These writers follow Lefebvre in viewing the physical space of organizations as a phenomenon of power, though they focus on different aspects of Lefebvre' spatial thinking. Some dig into power rationales that are materialized in and hidden under organizational spatial forms (Dale, 2005; Dale and Burrell, 2008), others build up connections between the logics of space and those of organizing (Clegg and Kornberger, 2006; Kornberger and Clegg, 2004), while still others try to unravel the dynamic processes of the production of social space in organizations (Beyes and Michels, 2011; Wasserman and Frenkel, 2011; Zhang and Spicer, 2014).

This last body of work turns to Lefebvre's spatial triad to understand the becoming of organizational space. It shows that organizational space shapes and reshapes as it is informed by representations of space (the conceived space), representational space (the lived space) and spatial practices (the perceived space). What is less clear, however, is how the elements of the triad affect and perhaps transform one another in the process. I think that it is important to address this challenge if we are to understand social space as intrinsically processual and dynamic, as Beyes and Steyaert (2012) point out, and to locate social space firmly in its own history, as Lefebvre (1991) insisted.

Reading Lefebvre's urban writings makes me think that perhaps we could learn something about the dynamics of organizational space by observing the dynamics of urban space. To this end, below, the chapter presents a case study that investigates the spatial dynamics of Hangzhou, a big second-tier city of China situated in the nation's economically developed coastal regions. The author of the chapter is very familiar with the city as this is where he was born and raised, and where he has been living and working for the last seven years.

The case study starts with an introduction of the urbanization project of China, citing Hangzhou as an example. This part of the study relies on archival documents collected from newspapers, the internet and government websites. The study then reads into Hangzhou's urban space in more details, focusing on some particularly telling examples of everyday city lives and using autoethnography as the main research method. This method is chosen for two reasons. First, since unearthing spatial dynamics inevitably involves engaging space in its history of changes, close observations of the mundane aspects of spatial practices, and intimate encounters of lived experiences, autoethnography seems a good choice (Boyle and Parry, 2007). Secondly, although risking triangulated validity, autoethnography generates crystal imageries from the vantage point of the researcher's own political situatedness (Jones, 2005). This is suited to the study since the researcher—being unable to drive and having commuted by walking and biking for years—can look at the use-value/exchange-value rationale through the unusual angle of a non-consumer.

## The Case of Hangzhou

### Urbanization in China

Urbanization occupies a very important position in the Chinese government's development strategy. Specifically, the *Thirteenth Five-Year Plan 2016–2020* reads that 'the key of the urbanization project is to accelerate the transformation of rural citizens into urban citizens' (*State Council Report*, 5 March 2016, www.gov.cn).[1] To this end, a particularly noticeable change in China's urban space is the fast expansion of major cities' geographic boundaries. Take my hometown, Hangzhou, as an example. For a very long time, the city consisted of just six administrative districts (designated as districts 1 to 6 in Figure 10.1 below). Among these six, only districts 2 (the Lower District) and 3 (the Upper District) were quintessential urban areas in the traditional sense. Districts 1, 4, 5 and 6 remained relatively underdeveloped until around 2000. For instance, the Lake District (district 5) consisted largely of tea farms and fishing villages that were isolated from one another by the Westlake—a UNESCO heritage site—and its surrounding hills. Until quite recently, 'city-folks' of Hangzhou typically considered it beneath them to marry 'tea-leaf pickers and fishermen' from the Lake District who were under-privileged rural citizens. However, with the expansion of urban boundaries, things have taken a dramatic turn. Today, Lake

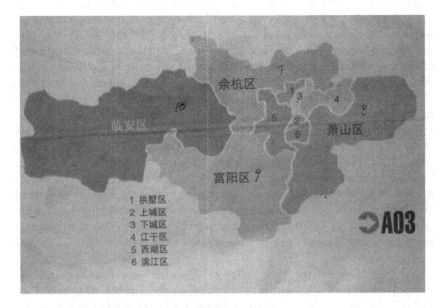

*Figure 10.1* The ten districts of Hangzhou.
With courtesy of *Metropolitan Express* 12 August 2017.

District residents find themselves not only proper urban Hangzhounese, but also the wealthiest of all urban Hangzhounese, almost overnight, for as peripheral fishing villages became the centre of Hangzhou's urban landscape their market values skyrocketed.[2] In 2001, districts 7 and 8 (previously rural townships) were added to Hangzhou's geographic map. This is followed by district 9 in 2014, and district 10, very recently, on 12 August 2017. In just ten years from 2006 to 2015, the registered urban population of Hangzhou rose from 6.6 million to over 9 million.

The 'transformation of rural citizens to urban citizens' draws from another important source: immigrant workers. Two issues, it seems, weigh heavily on the minds of policy makers in terms of urbanization. The first is regulated mass production. An article at the official website of the Chinese People's Political Consultative Conference reads, 'big cities are effective in pooling together resources, taking advantages of economics of scale, reducing emission waste, and positively impacting on surrounding rural regions' (2005, http://cppcc.people.com.cn/). Making effective use of resources is key to industrialization, and the crucial resource that adds value to raw materials is the human resource. Urbanization creates jobs that are attractive to the rural populations. In 2015, immigrant workers contributed another 2.23 million to Hangzhou's registered urban population. These immigrant workers are referred to as 'new Hangzhounese', a kindly gesture from the local media to give immigrants a new welcoming urban identity. Many new Hangzhounese work on jobs that a rapid urbanization process gives rise to: infrastructure constructor, real-estate salesperson, automobile servicer, taxi drivers and logistic workers. The last of these is perhaps most revealing of China's urbanization: the need for consumer items to be delivered at the doorstep increases as the city grows bigger and less convenient. In 2016, the top five logistic firms in China employed some 820,000 people, most of whom are immigrant workers, to work as warehouse keepers, deliverers and customer managers, and the industry is growing at an annual rate of 40% (*Chinese Industrial Information*, 14 December 2016, www.chyxx. com). A local Hangzhou newspaper cited a food deliverer: 'It is a hard job, but I love it!' (*Metropolitan Express*, 16 August 2017) This deliverer makes 8,000 CNY a month after tax; this is over four times the average income of his place of origin and well above the salary of an average Hangzhou citizen (about 5,400 CNY in 2017). By attracting the rural population to work in cities, urbanization has control over a labour force that is crucial to 'the economies of scale'.

The second issue that I think policy makers of urbanization have in mind is regulated mass consumption. According to the *Twelfth Five-Year Plan 2011–2016*, 'expanding the domestic basis for consumption' is the second most important strategy of twelve strategies all together (*State Council Report*, 29 October 2010, www.gov.cn). Such an expansion is achieved, partly, through giving immigrant workers not only well-paid city jobs that make consumption possible, but also a new city life that makes consumption necessary. In recent years, the local governments of major Chinese cities are increasingly lowering the criteria for the application for urban citizenship. The once pronounced differentiation between rural and urban citizenships is quickly diminishing.[3] In Hangzhou, for instance, the basic criterion is 'a labour contract that lasts more than two years, a legal residence (purchased or rented), and a record of social security payment of the last six months' (*Hangzhou Immigration Household Policy 2017*, www.hzpolice. gov.cn)—hardly a demanding one for anyone who seriously considers life and work in the city. The urban citizenship, however, marks only the initial step for immigrant workers to access the city's superior medical, educational and financial services. For instance, all public schools (which have better teaching quality) in Hangzhou require that enrolled students have a registered private residence, which is only possible with a purchased (not rented) apartment in the city. It is not a mere coincidence that Hangzhou's urban expansion is at the same time a process whereby the city's real estate price skyrocketed: the average market price of 2017 (30,000 CNY per square metre) is twenty to thirty times of that of 2000 (1,000~1,500 CNY per square metre)! Clearly, the urbanization of Hangzhou and of other major cities of China is closely linked to the promotion of mass consumption.

The capitalist market economy gains sustainable growth only when there is a correspondence between 'both the conditions of production and the conditions of [consumption]' (Harvey, 1990: 121). Such a correspondence is not easily achieved, for it involves the orchestrated efforts of all major players of the capitalist labour process—the state, big industries and labour representatives—and over an extended period of time. Harvey (1990) notices that, in the West, it took the Fordist regime of accumulation (mass production plus mass consumption) some fifty years to mature, before the regime was gradually overtaken by a more flexible post-Fordist regime of accumulation (e.g. innovative production plus quick-changing consumption) in around the mid 1970s. The Chinese case is arguably singular. For a long time the planned economy dominated, and the capitalist economy was introduced, initially only as a supplement to the planned economy, in the late 1970s. Since then, however, capitalization has been picking up speed and momentum in China, especially after 2000.[4] The global trend of flexible accumulation has clear impact on China: 'entrepreneurship' and 'innovation' were highlighted as new orientations of development in 2015 and had since become buzzwords in government reports. If, in the West, regimes of accumulation (Fordist and flexible) have experienced something of a transition from one to the other, the two are likely to be coexistent in China today. Viewed in this way, I think that China's urbanization project is part and parcel of the formational process of the Fordist regime of accumulation in the country.

## Consumers-Come-First

The laying out of the urban landscape epitomizes urban planners' customary thinking and value assumptions. Two examples below illustrate that the overall layout of Hangzhou's urban space aims to promote mass consumption.

Following Soja (2000), I first turn my eyes to the layout of Hangzhou's metro routes. Metro construction in Hangzhou was proposed as early as 1986 but was considered unfeasible due to Hangzhou's weak geological structure. Technological advances in recent years, coupled with the fast expansion of the city and its population, makes metro construction a top priority on the government's agenda. Thus, metro one (M1) started construction in 2006, M2 in 2014, M4 and M5 in 2017, and another ten metro lines (M3, M6~M14) are currently at the planning stage. The route of M1 (Figure 10.2) tells an interesting story. It starts at the northeastern part of Hangzhou (district 4), which, as of 2006, was a vast underdeveloped suburban area where huge residential projects were being planned (as they stand now), goes west until it reaches the old-town shopping centre, and then heads south, quickly leaves the central city, and finishes at a newly developed scenic attraction in district 8 (this district became a part of Hangzhou in 2001). The first metro of Hangzhou thus connects real estate projects with the shopping centre and a tourist attraction; it does not connect where most people were living and where they were working. Urban planners

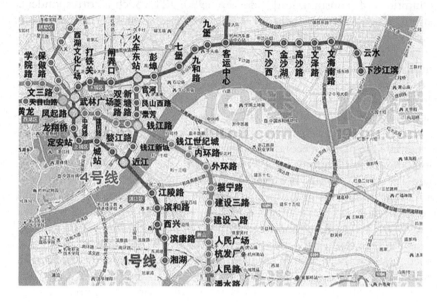

*Figure 10.2* Metro #1 (the red line).
With courtesy of www.image.baidu.com

readily 'rewarded' citizens who purchased new apartments, shopped regularly, and spent money touring.

Here is another example. In Hangzhou, road congestion became so serious recently that the government implemented, in 2014, a 'rush-hour' policy. During the morning and evening rush hours of certain workdays, some private vehicles are not allowed into central urban areas. For instance, cars licenses that end with 1 and 9 are denied accesses on Monday, those with 2 and 8 on Tuesday, and so on. This policy is a blow to salary-earners who travel significant distances between work and home relying on just one vehicle. The government, however, does not put a limit on the number of vehicles that a person, or a family, can possess.[5] In fact, if you are unlucky enough to own two cars that are banned on the same day, you are allowed to change the license number of one of them. Clearly, although the policy hits everyone, those who cannot afford a second car suffer the most. Connecting the rush-hour policy to Hangzhou's metro routes, it is not hard to see that the underlying logic of the city's urban planning is that people who have strong consuming powers are given preferential spatial treatment.

This logic—I call it 'consumers-come-first'—fits well with the Fordist regime of accumulation. A regime of accumulation is backed up and supported by its correspondent mode of regulation: a 'body of interiorised rules and social processes' (Harvey, 1990: 122). What Hangzhou's urban planners said, intentionally or not, through the laying out of urban space, is a normative message that would soon be picked by, made use of, and internalized, consciously or not, by millions of people who come to dwell in the city day in and day out. This message invites citizens to think of mass consumption (more cars, apartments, shopping and touring) as desirable and indeed normal aspects of everyday lives, in much the same way as images of driving (Ford) cars and drinking Coca Cola portrayed normal ways of consumption for Americans in the 1960s. 'Consumers-come-first' belongs to the mode of regulation that corresponds to China's urbanization project of Fordist accumulation.

Having introduced the general background of China's urbanization, and the more specific background of Hangzhou's urban planning, I will now look into three moments of Hangzhou's urban lives that correspond roughly with Lefevre's spatial triad: how urban planners redesigned roads (the conceived space), how working-class shop owners gave new meanings to space (the lived space), and how spatial practices such as square-dancing were regulated and absorbed into the city's economic lives (the perceived space). I will use Lefebvre's exchange-value/use-value logic to investigate the interrelations of these three moments.

## Redesigning Roads

The road is commonly designed to consist of several parts, each of which is reserved for the use of an identifiable group of people and usually with visible boundaries in between them: the automobile lane, the bike lane and the sidewalk. Using Lefebvre's framework, we may classify road parts as related to either use-value or exchange-value, depending on cultural contexts. In many European countries, for example, the bike lane can be considered as primarily of use-value because biking is a leisure activity in those countries. Similarly, in the UK, A/B-level roads usually do not have sidewalks, because walking from one town to another is considered economically unlikely, and inappropriate as a leisure pursuit. In China, bikes (electric scooters are classified as bikes in China) have been used mainly as a means of transport inside the city. In China, also, walking on the city sidewalk is a traditional leisure activity. The Chinese saying 'going for a walk' connotes 'going for a date': young men and women often start their relationships by window-shopping together. Thus, in major Chinese cities, the automobile lane and the bike lane are primarily of exchange-value, while the sidewalk, of use-value. In Hangzhou, the use-value of the sidewalk constantly gives way to the exchange-value of automobile space. I will illustrate with two examples.

In many parts of the city, metro construction is taking place on a large scale. Construction sites take up much of the road space, making the already congested traffic even worse. The government responds by re-designing traffic lanes. A common practice is to narrow the bike lane significantly, and to get rid of sidewalks altogether, as a temporary solution to road congestion (Figure 10.3). Changes such as these happen overnight, and they are

*Figure 10.3* The redesigned road.

Picture by author.

unpleasant for everyone. Drivers zigzag along newly routed mazes, barely able to follow freshly painted road signs. Bikers—many of them are deliverers who ride dangerously fast in order to make more money—race against each other in close combat formations, using their horns aggressively. For pedestrians it is a nightmare, for they suddenly find themselves totally and literally 'out of place'. They now tread on an undefined territory, unprotected by the kind of fences or uplifted pavements that the sidewalk once had.

Another example concerns parking. Urban planners clearly did not anticipate the dramatic increase in private cars. According to official year-book statistics (www.hangzhou.gov.cn), there were 233,000 private vehicles in Hangzhou in 2003; this number jumped to 1,849,100 in 2015. Interestingly, statistics of private vehicles before 2003 are not available, presumably because the consumption of automobiles was a relatively insignificant economic activity then. Residential apartments built around 2003 were typically six to seven storeys high with the ground-floor space reserved for garages: it was assumed that one in every six/seven families in Hangzhou owns a car. The situation today, however, is that almost every family that could afford an apartment owns at least one car. There is thus a huge gap between the number of private cars, on the one hand, and available parking space, on the other. To address this gap, the government—and this should not strike us as surprising by now—appropriates the space that previously belonged to bikers and pedestrians. One common practice is to carefully squeeze in a new 'parking lane' between the bike lane and the sidewalk. A more crude practice simply seizes the sidewalk for car parking (Figure 10.4). Local

*Figure 10.4* Using the sidewalk as car parks.
Picture by author.

authorities white-paint square boxes on the sidewalk and charge car owners for parking inside these boxes (those parking outside the boxes receive
tickets from traffic wardens). The power of the state plays a direct role in
instituting spatial changes.

'Innovation dedicated to the removal of spatial barriers in [production,
circulation and consumption] have been of immense significance in the history of capitalism' (Harvey, 1990: 232). What is significant and perhaps
unique in the disappearance of the sidewalk (temporary or permanent) in
Hangzhou is the removal of pedestrians' territorial rights. In most Western
countries, road reconstruction narrows the sidewalk, but it does not eliminate it, and pedestrians retain their exclusive use of space. This exclusiveness
is gone (in the case of road re-routing) or at least made highly ambiguous (in
the case of parking) in Hangzhou. In other words, pedestrians' space (i.e.
use-value) is made relative and drivers' space (i.e. exchange-value), absolute.
What is quite alarming is not whether people have enough sidewalks in
Hangzhou (they generally do), but the rationale that pedestrians' right to
walk *depends on* drivers' right to drive and park. This rationale, of course,
is nothing but a footnote to the 'consumers-come-first' logic that I outlined
earlier. In the conceived moment of Hangzhou's urban space, *use-value is
subjugated by exchange-value.*

*Alternative Uses of the Sidewalk*

A typical feature of many of Hangzhou's side streets is that they have residential parks on both sides of the road. Here, a scene that immediately grabs
the attention of the observer is that, on occasions, the sidewalk is used in
ways other than being walked on.

Apartment buildings with one side facing the road usually have their
ground-floor space converted to shops that conduct a number of small business: groceries, restaurants, retailers of various kinds, pet clinics, automobile maintenance, mahjong houses, laundries, and so on. These shops are,
on most occasions, run by 'new Hangzhounese'. Making a living in Hangzhou is not easy for them. Some shop owners may have worked and lived in
their shops (one sees a part of shop interiors converted to sleeping quarters)
to save apartment rents, but even if they don't, their businesses operate for
such long hours (from 9 am to 10 pm, or even later) that the shop becomes
the *de facto* place for both working and living activities. In my observations I saw people using the sidewalk—that stretch of space that their shops
open onto and which they have conveniently appropriated—for different
purposes. For instance, they dry their laundry on the sidewalk, cook and
sometimes have meals there; on several occasions I even observed people
washing their face and brushing their teeth, and one grocery owner installed
a large television *outside* his shop, so that his family and his colleagues in
adjacent shops could sit around a hot-pot stew (also placed on the sidewalk,
but hidden discreetly in the grocery when not in use) and watch television

together on summer evenings. Little children of shop owners also play on the sidewalk all the time. The shop and its surroundings are, literally, home to our Mr. and Mrs. New Hangzhounese.

It is almost impossible for people to take evening walks on sidewalks such as these. There is no place to set down steps; besides, it is awkward to walk into somebody's 'backyards'. So, would I go to local authorities to complain about the loss of my right as a pedestrian? Perhaps not. The economy behind these apparent 'misuses' of the sidewalk is more complicated than it appears. To begin with, if you observe the shops carefully, you would see that they were not initially designed for commercial activities. They were actually part of the buildings' ground-floor garage space— cubical space with no designed-in window or ventilation. If you ask shop owners about taxes and rents (I asked one or two shop owners with whom I had made acquaintance), you would see that they pay business tax to the government, *and* rents to the relevant residential committee. Each residential park is maintained by a residential committee (a kind of estate maintenance firm) that provides nearly free services to residents (cleaning, security, gardening, and so on). Every household of the residential park pays a small household fee to support the committee's functioning, but the major part of the committee's income comes from rents generated from the park's collectively owned space (e.g. parking space). Converting some garage space to shops and renting them to shop owners contributes a substantial revenue. Residential committees that make a good business out of renting can charge a relatively low household fee to residents.

A residential committee represents the major and hence collective voice of the residents. There are high-end residential parks in Hangzhou where most residents prefer paying large sums of household fees over renting out garage space. These residents have thus 'bought' surrounding sidewalks for their leisurely walks. I have no reason to complain because by purchasing my cheap apartment I have acknowledged myself as a lower-end consumer and hence, according to the consumers-come-first logic, not entitled to preferential spatial treatment (i.e. my evening walks). On the other hand, shop owners have amply demonstrated their consuming power. Through their hard labour, they are paying substantial fees for pieces of space which otherwise could be used only as garages. Thus, shop owners are rightfully entitled to preferential spatial treatments (i.e. using the sidewalk for various living activities).

The logic that justifies local authorities' appropriation of the sidewalk also justifies shop owners' unconventional uses of the sidewalk. This, I suspect, explains why the government is reluctant to check on shop owners' conduct (Figure 10.5). My suspicion was partly confirmed when I visited my regional city council one day and asked an officer in-charge whether the government has any regulation over shop owners' 'misuses' of the sidewalk. The officer explained that only under two conditions was the council allowed to take regulatory actions: when unlicensed peddlers use the sidewalk as

*Figure 10.5* Alternative uses of the sidewalk.
Picture by author.

their business sites, and when shop owners' actions endanger public safety (e.g. fire hazards). Otherwise, the officer said, all the council could do was to 'persuade' shop owners to behave more properly. A Lefebrian interpretation might suggest that since peddlers do not pay tax or rent, they demonstrate no consuming power. Likewise, public safety hazards decrease the potential consuming powers of many others and this, by a large margin, outweighs shop owners' economic contributions. Either way, the consumers-come-first logic provides a viable explanation.

As I watched these people during my evening walks, I saw only ordinary human beings trying to cope with their everyday lives. They had to keep one eye on their children while dealing with customers, watch out for the boiling kettle while unloading new deliveries, and they certainly like to lie down a bit on a bamboo sleeper (the grocery owner sometimes did this) outside their stuffy garage space when the evening was still young, thinking that it was perhaps too early to close for the day. I suspect that there is no elaborated intention to get back at urban planners, or cold calculations to squeeze planners' pressure points. People have simply *chanced upon* new ways of using the sidewalk that the planner could not say no to.

The self-positing of human beings is an ontological fact of everyday lives and the source of the latter's endless creativity (Lefebvre, 2008). Shop owners' practical engagements with the sidewalk—the 'making do' of space and life out of phenomenological necessity (de Certeau, 1988)—generate practical meanings of space with which shop owners make sense of what they do and make plans for what they are about to do; they become nodes in the Weberian web of meanings that shop owners spin for themselves. 'The idea that there is some "universal" language of space, a semiotics of space independent of practical activities and historically situated actors, has to be rejected' (Harvey, 1990: 216). In this sense, shop owners' alternative uses of the sidewalk (and local councils' silence on these acts) do more than just bringing actors extra utilities (or the government extra revenues), for they effectively redefine the sidewalk. Importantly, these action-generated definitions of space do not remain only individually relevant, for they are symbolic devices with which people gesture towards one another in the concerted efforts of conducting and concluding collective social acts (Blumer, 1969). The fact that neighbouring shop owners could dine, chat and watch television together, naturally and easily, on the sidewalk, suggests that alternative meaning frames of the sidewalk were already widely shared by the local communities of shop owners. In turn, these meaning frames would inform and sanction yet more spatial practices of similar nature. If people can cook on the sidewalk, perhaps they can also organize a dancing party on it? Before moving on, let me summarize this part by saying that in the lived moment of Hangzhou's urban space, *alternative use-values of space are created.*

## Square-dancing

Square-dancing is popular in China: popular in terms of its large number of participants but also widely incurred social critiques. The practice takes place more often on street-corner sidewalks than public squares—indeed, the public square is something of a rarity in Hangzhou. Early in the morning or late in the evening, when the weather is fine, people come out in groups and dance in unsophisticated, orchestrated motions to some rhythmic, slow-disco type of music. Dancers are often organized. Organizers provide equipment (e.g. music players, amplifiers, sometimes costumes), and being better dancers they also set the pace and lead the dance.

Participants consist mainly of elderly citizens, usually females. Square-dancing is a suitable form of physical exercise, but its primary function is social. Living in a big, fast-expanding city can be an alienating experience, particularly so for senior citizens who have newly immigrated to Hangzhou, where their children have recently found jobs, purchased apartments, and got married.[6] For these senior citizens, who initiate most dancing groups, doing the dance is almost like a social ritual. Dancing together melts down social barriers, offers useful information channels on child rearing, grocery prices, and matchmaking, and provides a welcome relief from daily household chores. Square-dancing is very popular in Hangzhou; there are dancing groups in almost every residential park, and many local citizens join them, too.

Square-dancing is a recent event. When it first appeared in major Chinese cities around 2005 (a time that coincides with the acceleration of China's urbanization), it was looked on with a mixture of curiosity and amusement. The official media (e.g. China Central Television) welcomed it, describing it as an element of the Chinese culture (it was reported that one professional dancing group gave a performance on Moscow's Red Square), as a style of a vigorous life (square-dancers prefer songs such as 'Hot Mothers'), and as a sign of urban diversity and inclusiveness. But public attitude soon turned when the practice of square-dancing proliferated in cities. Square-dancing is often noisy (dancers use powerful amplifiers), its music verges on the distasteful, and it invaded public space in such a non-negotiable manner that other less collective forms of leisure activities felt threatened.[7] Angry bickering broke out between some dancing groups and nearby residents, and for some time around 2014 and 2015, the local media was full of such conflict stories. For instance, it was reported that some residents took revenge against square-dancers by dumping garbage from higher grounds, or using even louder amplifiers to drown out dancers' music. Others littered the ground with broken glass and lubricant oil so that dancers could not set foot on it. The term 'square-dancing' was on China Central Television's list of 'ten hottest issues of 2015'. This alone speaks of the heat of the contentions.

When square-dancing was in its early, unobtrusive stage, participants bought their right of space use in much the same way as shop owners occupied the sidewalk. For one thing, by coming to stay with their families in Hangzhou, these senior dancers effectively pushed their children to purchase or rent bigger apartments in the city. But when square-dancing became a public nuisance, the interests of many other consumers were being harmed: local residents were not getting what they paid for. Responses from urban planners could thus be anticipated.

Local governments responded in a number of ways. In Hangzhou, new criteria were proposed to specify appropriate music volume and time slots for dancing practices (*People's Consultative Conference*, 30 July 2014, www.hzzx.gov.cn). Regional city councils also set up hotlines to monitor 'noise abuse' and to conciliate related disputes. In this way, small groups of square-dancers could still use street corners for the sport but were obliged not to disturb neighbouring residents. Alternatively, the government rented vacant space to be used exclusively for proper (i.e. noisy) square-dancing. For instance, an area was set aside at the city's spacious railway station, and hundreds of people came to dance every evening (Figure 10.6). A third solution was to set up government-business partnerships: 'the government makes specifications for real estate developers that a minimum amount of sport-space per household needs be designed into the public space of residential parks' (*Hangzhou Daily*, 26 May 2014).

Quite a few MBA students at my university work in the real estate industry, and I rang up some of them to find out how real estate developers responded to the government's call. It turned out that low-end and high-end

*Figure 10.6* Square-dancing at the railway station.
Picture by author.

developers both responded to the issue of square-dancing, but in different ways. For low-end residential parks, having in place some hidden-away dancing areas in parks and public green spaces is not only a government mandate, but a key to business success. 'People need a place to do square-dancing', one MBA student told me, 'and sometimes we add pavilions and roofed corridors so that they can dance on rainy days'. High-end residential parks, to the contrary, eliminate open-air dancing space. 'If we brag about having dancing areas in our (high-end) parks we'd never be able to sell any house', another MBA student said. He added that to his knowledge no high-end parks in Hangzhou ever installed open-air dancing space. If residents want some sport, they go to the park's club, which is usually a detached building with many functional areas. There people can swim, do body building exercises, and of course, square-dance, without putting other residents to inconvenience. A colleague of mine owns an apartment in a high-end water-front park. In this park, the entire public space is covered in green in order to prevent people from using it for dancing. But residential clubs charge users membership fees. What about elderly people who live in expensive parks but nevertheless hold on to their frugal consuming habits? 'Well, they usually go to a piece of water-front platform across the river and join the others (who come from nearby parks, low-end or high-end). From that distance they are unlikely to disturb anybody here.'

The regulation of square-dancing and the absorbing of it into Hangzhou's urban routines gives rise to a singular effect: people with different consuming powers are given different space to conduct the same leisure activity. High-end park residents dance in clubs, less well-off house buyers dance in open-air dancing areas, dwellers in old apartments dance on street corners, and so on. This differentiation renders square-dancing more or less enjoyable to different consumer groups in terms of both material utility (i.e. privacy, guaranteed use of space, convenience in travelling to and fro, protections against weather conditions, and the need to limit music volume) and the kind of social status that often comes together with modern consumption (Bourdieu, 2010). Thus, people who lived in expensive apartments and wanted to dance for free got pushed out to blend in with a group of nondifferentiated general consumers ('the others'). Whether people actually use the space that they are given is a matter of personal choice. The important point is that through spatial practices such as square-dancing, urban planning responds to people's lived needs, not by denying them altogether (as in the case of redesigning roads), or merely tolerating them (as in the case of shop owners), but by assimilating them into the consumers-come-first logic. In the perceived moment of Hangzhou's urban space, *alternative use-values are assimilated by exchange-value.*

## Discussion and Reflection

Above, I have looked into three examples of urban lives in Hangzhou. With the help of Lefebvre's exchange-value/use-value logic, I've outlined a process of dynamic interactions among the conceived, perceived and lived moments of Hangzhou's urban space. In the conceived moment of space, the sidewalk lost its territorial independence or simply disappeared in road redesign projects, and use-value was subjugated by exchange-value. In the lived moment of space, shop owners used the sidewalk for everyday living in such a way that their practices were at once consistent with space's conceived power rationale *and* generative of alternative use-values of space. In the perceived moment of space, through the practice of square-dancing, its emergence, development and becoming of urban routines, alternative use-values thus generated were maintained *but only to the effect* that they were assimilated by exchange-value. Thus, the urban space of Hangzhou reveals itself, in the Lefebvrian analysis, as an ongoing dynamic process that is played out among the interactions of the conceived, perceived and lived moments of social space.

Some organizational researchers believe that similar dynamic processes can be said about organizational space (Beyes and Steyaert, 2012; Zhang and Spicer, 2014). The case of Hangzhou invites us to think in this direction. I also think that further insights on organizational space as social processes could be gained from future studies that look deep into the interactions of the elements of Lefebvre's spatial triad in the organizational setting. Admittedly, studying urban space may be very different from studying organizational space. But since organizations, like cities, are essentially spatial realities (Clegg and Kornberger, 2006; Dale, 2005), and since cities are structured similar to organizations (Anthopoulos and Fitsilis, 2014), there may be lessons that studies on organizational space can learn from the case of Hangzhou. To conclude this chapter, below, I tentatively offer some observations.

My first observation concerns lived space in organizations. Some researchers invite us to see lived space as consisting of marginalized and sometimes embittered voices in organizations that seek to sidestep, disrupt, or even confront the dominant conceived space (Halford, 2004; Wasserman and Frenkel, 2011; Zhang et al., 2008). Such a view highlights the subversive aspect of lived space but in doing so unwittingly narrows the scope of the lived space to those of intentional subversions. The case of Hangzhou suggests that lived space can be subversive in non-intentional ways. Experiences of coping with basic biological desires and maximizing utilities may yet give rise to new representational forms of space which, though sporadic and incoherent, grow into poignant critiques of the existing order of spatial conceptions through daily practices. 'With daily life, lived experience is taken up and raised up to critical thinking. It is no longer disdained, regarded as an insignificant residue' (Lefebvre, 2008: 10). However, this is not to say that lived space in organizations is always subversive in its effect. Quite the opposite. Social space is incessantly dynamic, and because of this we should always expect that the conceived space is momentarily 'ready' for whatever surprises that the lived space might offer. The case of Hangzhou suggests that the conceived space is often quick to assimilate emergent lived appeals, and although the conceived space may be an empty network of abstract signifiers (Lefebvre, 1991), it is a network sophisticated enough to have 'a time and a place for and everything' (Harvey, 1990: 214). Dale and Burrell caution us against too romantic a view of lived space. They point out that what look like 'free choices of spatial practices' may be nothing but designed-in power effects (2008: 110). I think that their warning needs be taken seriously.

All this boils down to a rather subtle approach to studying lived space in organizations. One needs to observe a wide array of mundane and quotidian lived experiences that may seem little related to what is commonly known as organized work life, to look deep into their underlying tensions, and at the same time reflect whether such tensions are already accommodated by the existing order of things. I think that an approach such as this may yield further insight into the social space of contemporary organizations. Accordingly, companies like Google where the boundaries between work and life activities are wiped out may be ideal sites for study.

My second observation concerns conceived space in organizations. I suggest that we pay special attention to changes in organizations' spatial designs and treat them as revealing moments of the ongoing processes of power struggle in organizations. For instance, an organization may purposefully construct new office buildings (Wasserman and Frenkel, 2011), redecorate architectural facades and office interiors (Strati, 1996), demolish miles of internal walls (Dale and Burrell, 2008), replace the private office with hot-desking (Edenius and Yakhlef, 2007), introduce home-working schemes (Wapshott and Mallett, 2012), and so on. Daily organizational processes are often routine and repetitive, leaving the researcher little clue as to where to start her enquiry into social space. Just like the disappearance of the side-walk in Hangzhou, changes in organizations' spatial designs open up space's functionality and reveal power rationales hidden underneath.

Some scholars view major changes in architectural forms as reflective of transformations in social power paradigms (Forty, 1980; Prior, 1995). This Foucauldian approach informs studies of organizational space in important ways since organizations are necessarily embedded in their larger social contexts. However, in the organizational setting, we should not likewise assume that changes in spatial designs correspond to shifts in power relations. The case of Hangzhou tells us that the conceived space can be remarkably consistent, thanks to its ability to respond to and assimilate lived space. This links back to Lefebvre's insight that behind the physical metamorphosis of the absolute space the abstract space of capital 'nevertheless lives on' (1991: 49), adapting and remaking itself. Indeed, in Berman's (2010) analysis, the conceived space of capitalist cities achieves its consistency precisely *through* the constant demises of old physical spatial structures. All this, when translated into organizational studies, asks researchers to keep eyes open for consistent patterns of power relations underlying changes in organizational spatial designs. Organization researchers have argued that marked changes in spatial designs (e.g. the introduction of home-working schemes) often reflect management's longtime power obsessions (e.g. to colonize the sphere of living) (Fleming and Spicer, 2004). If this is so, a careful investigation into the history of conceived space and of its metamorphosis through spatial dynamics could bring out a sort of genealogy of organizational space that maps out the ups and downs of those power obsessions.

The third observation concerns perceived space in organizations. I understand perceived space as an everyday arena where multiple power relations play off against each other while space, as a whole, achieves its expected functional 'performance' (Lefebvre, 1991: 33). The spectrum of perceived space in organizations may cover a very extensive array of spatial forms, making it hard for the researcher to conduct concentrated observations. Learning from the case of Hangzhou, I would suggest that one form of perceived space merits particular attention: the space-in-between ('between' in both physical and semantic senses). The sidewalk serves as an example. It is a piece of space between the public and the private, between business and leisure, and between local residents and people who come and go, and it was on the sidewalk that some vivid forms of urban struggles were observed.

This is of course not a new discovery. Clegg and Kornberger see 'interstitial spaces'—spaces 'where things, people and knowledge overlap and interact'—as central to organizing space (2006: 154–5). Dale and Burrell point to 'liminal spaces'—spaces 'which exist at the margins of the orthodox but abut to other conventional spaces'—as one way to think about radical forms of organizing (2008: 234). Concurring with these writers, I'd like to highlight space-in-between as central to the unfolding of spatial dynamics. In the organizational setting, space-in-between can be found in communal corridors (Hurdley, 2010), 'transitory dwelling places' at work (Shortt, 2015), and perhaps in other common areas which are easily accessed by different user groups and of which there are no strictly set prescriptions for spatial uses.

My final observation is a methodological one. Lefebvre's writings on social space have inspired many organizational scholars; in contrast to this, the amount of empirical work dedicated to the unfolding of the *production* of social space in organizations looks disproportionately small. Lefebvre's spatial triad, after all, is a broad heuristic framework; it encapsulates all possible interplays of social space in one single framework but makes no attempt to elaborate these possibilities. In my opinion, such an elaboration is still much needed to further our knowledge of the social space of organizations.

But then there comes a difficulty. Being a broad framework, the triad does not lend itself as readily applicable in empirical organizational settings. If the researcher takes conceived space to mean all that is the 'representation' of space, and the lived space all that is 'representational', she may end up with data sets that look quite disconnected. There are just too many logical sets that could be subsumed into the category of 'representation' as there are into that of 'representational', so much so that a focused analysis becomes very difficult. Lefebvre's writings on urban space provide a clue to address this difficulty. It may be advisable that the researcher uses single sets of logic (derived either from theoretical deduction or initial observations), one at a time, to penetrate (so to speak) the spatial triad when investigating the dynamics of social space. The exchange-value/use-value logic that this chapter relies on is but an example of many other logic sets with which researchers could narrow focus. One example is the linear-time/biological-time logic that Lefebvre discussed in his last work *Rhythmanalysis* (2004). Lefebvre's reflections on space are closely related to his writings other than *The Production of Space*; together, they have yet much to teach us as we approach organizations and organizing as socio-spatial phenomena. It is precisely this notion that guides the effort of this chapter and the case study contained within.

## Notes

1 The Household Registration System took shape in the late 1950s in the height of China's communist movement. Citizens were classified as either 'urban' or 'rural' based on land ownership. Urban citizens do not have land ownership; they are entitled to national welfare benefits such as medicare, pension, maternity leave

and funeral benefits. By contrast, rural citizens have collective land ownership but no national welfare. Recently (around 2010), China introduced basic medical insurance and social insurance for all rural citizens. It is estimated that by 2011 50.32% of Chinese were rural citizens.

2 In practice, as rural citizens give up their collective land ownership to become rural citizens, they are entitled to whatever bonus that land yields in much the same way as shareholders draw dividends.

3 At least as late as 1997, the year I finished my undergraduate study, the barrier was still firmly in place. Only the top 15% of all undergraduates were allowed the citizenship of Shanghai.

4 And this is so despite of the country's pronounced socialist ideology. As early as 1982, 'socialism with Chinese characteristics' was proposed which allows, theoretically, the coexistence of socialism and capitalist market economy. In 1997, the Chinese Communist Party officially claimed that 'the (capitalist) market is the dominant mode of economy with other modes of economy working as supplements'. In 2016, the *Thirteenth Five-Year Plan* further specifies that the role of the government is to 'provide facilitative services to the market, and not to intervene in ways that disrupt the market's internal rationales'.

5 A new policy in 2014 limits the number of new car licenses issued everyday. Just before this policy was put in place there was a huge increase in car purchase. People (including many of my colleagues) queued overnight to buy a second or third car.

6 There are a couple of reasons why senior citizens immigrate to cities like Hangzhou. First, in China today (unlike Japan, for instance), being a housewife is not a common profession. Both the husband and the wife need to be professionally engaged in order to make ends meet. When young couples have their children, taking care of the baby becomes a full-time job that most couples could neither personally cope with nor financially afford (hiring a professional nanny is very costly). Thus, it is often the case that the retired grandparents of the baby resettle themselves in Hangzhou to take care of the baby. Second, due to the historical one-child policy (the policy was abolished in 2016), young, immigrant couples are usually the only son or daughter of their parents. The Chinese culture emphasizes family bonds, and because those parents do not have a second child with whom they could stay in their native lands, joining the new Hangzhounese couples is often their only alternative.

7 Just recently it was reported that several school boys were pushed out of their community basketball court by a group of square-dancers. The event triggered a heated debate concerning the general personality of square-dancers. Are they genial grandmas and grandpas seeking exercise and socialization, or are they the senior versions of the revolutionary terrorists forty years ago during the Cultural Revolution?

# References

Anthopoulos, L. and Fitsilis, P. (2014). Exploring architectural and organizational features in small cities. *International Conference on Advanced Communication Technology, 2014*, 190–195.

Berman, M. (2010). *All That Is Solid Melts Into Air: The Experience of Modernity*. London: Verso.

Beyes, T. and Michels, C. (2011). The production of educational space: Heterotopia and the business university. *Management Learning*, 42(5), 521–536.

Beyes, T. and Steyaert, C. (2012). Spacing organization: Non-representational theory and performing organizational. *Organization*, 19(1), 43–59.

Blumer, H. (1969). *Symbolic Interactionism*. Berkeley: University of California Press.

Bourdieu, P. (2010). *Distinction*. London: Routledge.

Boyle, M. and Parry, K. (2007). Telling the whole story: The case for organizational autoethnography. *Culture and Organization, 13*(3), 184–190.

Clegg, S. and Kornberger, M. (2006). Organising space. In S. Clegg and M. Kornberger (Eds.), *Space, Organization and Management Theory* (pp. 143–162). Koege: Liber.

Dale, K. (2005). Building a social materiality: Spatial and embodied politics in organizational control. *Organization, 12*(5), 649–678.

Dale, K. and Burrell, G. (2008). *The Spaces of Organisation and the Organisation of Space: Power, Identity and Materiality at Work*. Basingstoke: Palgrave Macmillan.

de Certeau, M. (1988). *The Practice of Everyday Life*. Berkeley: University of California Press.

Edenius, M. and Yakhlef, A. (2007). Space, vision and organizational learning: The interplay of incorporating and inscribing practices. *Management Learning, 38*(2), 193–210.

Fleming, P. and Spicer, A. (2004). 'You can checkout anytime, but you can never leave': Spatial boundaries in a high commitment organization. *Human Relations, 57*(1), 75–94.

Ford, J. and Harding, N. (2004). We went looking for an organization but could find only the metaphysics of its presence. *Sociology, 38*(4), 815–830.

Forty, A. (1980). The modern hospital in England and France: The social and medical uses of architecture. In A. King (Ed.), *Buildings and Society: Essays on the Social Development of the Built Environment* (pp. 61–93). London: Routledge and Kegan Paul.

Halford, S. (2004). Towards a sociology of organizational space. *Sociological Research Online, 9*(1). Retrieved from www.socresonline.org.uk/9/1/halford.html

Harvey, D. (1990). *The Condition of Postmodernity*. Cambridge: Blackwell.

Hernes, T. (2004). *The Spatial Construction of Organization*. Amsterdam: John Benjamins.

Hurdley, R. (2010). The power of corridors: Connecting doors, mobilising materials, plotting openness. *The Sociological Review, 58*(1), 45–64.

Jones, S. (2005). Autoethnography: Making the personal political. In N. Denzin and Y. Lincoln (Eds.), *The Sage Handbook of Qualitative Research* (pp. 763–792). Thousand Oaks: Sage.

Kornberger, M. and Clegg, S. (2004). Bringing space back in: Organizing the generative building. *Organization Studies, 25*(7), 1095–1114.

Lefebvre, H. (1991). *The Production of Space*. Oxford: Blackwell.

Lefebvre, H. (1996). *Writings on Cities*. Malden: Blackwell.

Lefebvre, H. (2004). *Rhythmanalysis*. London: Continuum.

Lefebvre, H. (2008). *Critique of Everyday Life, Vol. I, II, III*. London: Verso.

Prior, L. (1995). The architecture of the hospital: A study of spatial organization and medical knowledge. *The British Journal of Sociology, 39*(1), 86–113.

Shields, R. (1999). *Lefebvre, Love and Struggle: Spatial Dialectics*. London: Routledge.

Shortt, H. (2015). Liminality, space and the importance of 'transitory dwelling places' at work. *Human Relations, 68*(4), 633–658.

Soja, E. (2000). *Postmetropolis: Critical Studies of Cities and Regions*. Oxford: Blackwell.

Spicer, A. (2006). Beyond the convergent-divergence debate: The role of spatial scales in transforming organizational logic. *Organization Studies, 27*(10), 1467–1483.

Strati, A. (1996). Organizations viewed through the lens of aesthetics. *Organization*, 3(2), 209–218.

Taylor, S. and Spicer, A. (2007). Time for space: An interpretive review of research on organizational spaces. *International Journal of Management Reviews*, 9(4), 325–346.

Wapshott, R. and Mallett, O. (2012). The spatial implications of homeworking: A Lefebvrian approach to the rewards and challenges of home-based work. *Organization*, 19(1), 63–79.

Wasserman, V. and Frenkel, M. (2011). Organizational aesthetics: Caught between identity regulation and culture jamming. *Organization Science*, 22(2), 503–521.

Watkins, C. (2005). Representations of space, spatial practices and spaces of representations: An application of Lefebvre's spatial triad. *Culture and Organization*, 11(3), 209–220.

Zhang, Z. and Spicer, A. (2014). 'Leader, you first': The everyday production of hierarchical space. *Human Relations*, 67(6), 739–762.

Zhang, Z., Spicer, A. and Hancock, P. (2008). Hyper-organizational space in the work of J.G. Ballard. *Organization*, 15(6), 889–910.

# 11 Producing the Space of Democracy

## Spatial Practices and Representations of Urban Space in Spain's Transition to Democracy

*Inbal Ofer*

## Introduction

> Curiously, space is a stranger to customary political reflection. Political thought and the representations which it elaborates remain 'up in the air', with only an abstract relation with the soil and even the national territory. . . . Space belongs to the geographers in the academic division of labour. But then it reintroduces itself subversively through the effects of peripheries, the margins, the regions, the villages and local communities long abandoned, neglected, even abased through centralizing state-power.
>
> (Lefebvre, 1976–1978: 164)

The above citation is taken from Henri Lefebvre's work on *The State* (*De l'État*). It reflects the importance of spatial analysis to any discussion on the formation and consolidation of power relations within modern societies. At the time in which Lefebvre wrote these words they also reflected a difficulty to engage with space as a meaningful analytical category within most disciplines. As this volume well demonstrates, the ideas of Henri Lefebvre are currently experiencing a revival in the fields of urban studies, political geography, cultural and organizational studies (Brenner and Elden, 2009; Brenner, Marcuse, and Mayer, 2012; Elden, 2004; Purcell, 2002). In the field of history, space, while often referred to, is still looked upon more as a container of social relations than as an element that constitutes and is being constituted by them. This is despite the fact that Lefebvre's work offers a productive platform for integrating spatial and historical analysis, not only within the field of urban history, but also for a more general analysis of the constitution of power relations and of varied forms of social resistance.

My own work in recent years focuses on the relationship between urbanization and democratization in Spain during the period of General Francisco Franco's dictatorship (1939–1975) and Spain's transition to democracy (1975–1982). Throughout its existence, this ultranationalist dictatorship embraced urban space as a focal point of accelerated economic growth and instituted a policy that drew industry, services and capital into the city. With the same intensity, however, it also laboured to distance the Spanish working class from the centre of most Spanish cities. The regime's policies in terms of political repression and of urban planning can be understood only by paying careful attention to this simultaneous drive for industrialization and spatial segregation.

The current chapter examines the urban planning regimes, spatial practises and representations of urban space that emerged throughout the periphery of the city of Madrid during the final years of the dictatorship and the transition to democracy. Focusing on the formation and transformation of Orcasitas (one of Spain's largest squatters' settlements) I explore the interplay between spatial segregation and domination and between informality and resistance. I do so using several types of primary sources. The most important of these is a database containing information about 1,680 of the families that settled in the three *barrios* which made up Orcasitas between the years 1940–1965. I constructed the database drawing on files that were compiled by the Francoist Ministry of Housing between the years 1957–1966. The files document the legal and socio-economic status of the families who settled in Orcasitas and contain details concerning their origin; household composition; employment conditions; plans of the self-constructed homes (*chabolas*) and the legal standing of the property. The database is supplemented by a series of 34 in-depth interviews with members of the Orcasitas neighbourhood association and with individuals (7 women and 27 men) who settled in the *barrios* during the 1960s and 1970s either as children or as young adults. Further information is derived from urban plans, written texts and visual materials collected from the archives of the National Institute of Housing and from private collections and publications of architects and planners such as Pedro Bidagor, Francisco Javier Sáenz de Oiza and Fernando de Terán.

In analysing the processes which led to the formation and transformation of massive squatter settlements throughout Spain, Henri Lefebvre's prolific theory provided me with several key concepts. Of primary importance was Lefebvre's three-dimensional model for the analysis of produced space. Lefebvre pointed to three levels on which spatial change takes place: the level of spatial practises (which assign the functions of production and of reproduction to particular locations with specific spatial characteristics); the level of representations of space (that "order" and legitimize the allocation of space and the construction of spatial practises through academic and/ or professional discourses); and the level of representational or lived space (that embodies the complex symbolism of its users) (Lefebvre, 1996: 33–34). As some researchers correctly noted, this triad is not neatly drawn and much confusion exists, especially between the category of representational space and the first two categories (Shields, 1999: 161). However, the confusion, as Stuart Elden reminds us, results from Lefebvre's dialectic method (Elden, 2004: 190). If one accepts the fact that Lefebvre intentionally introduced a third term (that of lived space) which is balanced between two poles (those of conceived and perceived space) one can better understand the production of lived space as embodying new uses alongside subjective interpretations of existing representations and practises.

The above triad highlights the role of spatial practises and of spatial representations in the production of space as we know and experience it. It further encourages us to explore the struggle over space—as both a symbolic and a material resource—by looking at the ways in which competing spatial practises and discourses establish themselves. Lefebvre was less mindful, however, of the possibility that contradictions might also exist between the spatial practises and representations produced by the same stakeholder. As I show, such contradictions may surface even when the aforementioned stakeholder is a dictatorial regime looking to implement and monitor a highly structured urban planning regime.

The first period with which the chapter is concerned constitutes an example of the unfolding of what Lefebvre termed as the second critical phase in urban development. According to Lefebvre, the first critical phase in human development encompassed a period during which agricultural society was progressively subordinated by industrialization (in the European case roughly spanning the 16th century). The second critical phase, on the other hand, is characterized by the subordination of industrialized society to an all-encompassing process of urbanization. The spatial manifestation of this phase is the emergence of a critical zone in which "industrialisation, the dominant power and a limiting factor, becomes a dominant reality during a period of profound crisis" (Lefebvre, 2003b: 16).

While some view the emergence of a "critical zone" as reflecting a future reality (Elden, 2004: 137) Lefebvre himself was rather specific in describing its attributes. The critical zone is characterized by accelerated processes of implosion—explosion which lead to a process of urban concentration and extension. This process is reflected, amongst other things, in an extensive rural exodus and the subordination of the agrarian to the urban. According to Lefebvre the result of this situation is a tremendous confusion "during which the past and the possible, the best and the worst, become intertwined" (2003b: 16). My contention is that during the first period under study here the attributes of Lefebvre's "critical zone" manifested themselves most acutely in Spain. During this period grave contradictions surfaced between the regime's ideological perceptions and spatial representations (according to which the urban working classes constituted a threat to political stability and therefore had to be kept away from Spain's urban centres and channelled into well contained satellite suburbs) and its spatial practises (which strove to increase industrial output and linked the new industrial complexes to existing zones of urban concentration). Such contradictions led the dictatorship to temporarily turn a blind eye to the outpouring of working class populations into urban spaces that were not designated for their use.

The second period with which the chapter is concerned points to the circumstances under which the conditions characterizing the critical zone can nonetheless lead to a process of urban transformation: a transformation which puts the "practises of inhabitance" at the centre of the planning process. In his essay *The Right to the City* Henri Lefebvre referred to the concept of "inhabitance" as reflecting a creative use of space oriented towards its appropriation (Lefebvre in Kofman and Lebas, 1996: 158). Mark Purcell further elaborated on how the Lefebvrian concept of inhabitance might serve as a basis for a new citizenship regime: egalitarian decentralized and rooted in the experience of effectively inhabiting urban space (Purcell, 2003: 564). Following Purcell I use the term "practises of inhabitance" in order to highlight the accumulative effect of everyday engagement with lived space. However, I would like to emphasize the contingent nature of such practises: their goal might be to modify specific aspects of space in order to change specific elements in the experience of inhabiting without necessarily having a larger transformative project in mid.

Against this background, the first section of the chapter briefly explores the existing literature on urban segregation in the context of Lefebvre's analysis of spatial domination. It then goes on to examine the practises that emerged in relation to the urban during the Franco dictatorship: spatial segregation (in both political and class terms) based on functional zoning and the creation of urban peripheries. I show how these practises were legitimized through corresponding references to space as hierarchical and organic in nature, as well as produced by technical knowledge. I ask how was the concept of segregation employed during a period of maximal urban concentration and expansion and what is the nature of the relationship between spatial segregation and domination?

The second section briefly examines the existing literature on the informal production of space, while relating it to Lefebvre's scalar analysis of space and to his theory on spatial appropriation. The section then explores the production of informal space on the southern periphery of the city of Madrid between the mid 1950s and the late 1970s. Special attention is paid to the experiences of inhabiting as I reflect on the ways in which these experiences assist the users of space to apprehend and produce new knowledge regarding their lived environment. My argument in this section is that the act of squatting both complemented and challenged the regime's spatial practises. It complemented such practises by offering the most basic housing solutions to large working class populations on lands that were situated close to the capital's industrial complexes, thereby supporting the process of urbanization in the service of industrial expansion. At the same time, the reality of mass squatting during the final years of the dictatorship led the inhabitants, urban planning professionals and even the Spanish legal system to critically reconsider the rationale behind the allocation of resources and the existing system of urban development. The section analyses the experiences of informality that emerged out of the reality of the critical zone and asks under what conditions they can serve as the basis for the production of new urban knowledge?

Finally, the last section focuses on the ways in which informal knowledge can become the basis of new policies. Using examples from the Remodelling Plan of Orcasitas (the most radical and participatory of all remodelling plans in the capital) and from the Neighbourhoods' General Remodelling Plan (which affected 29 sectors in the capital) I ask how can such knowledge contribute towards the modification of existing representations and practises of spatial segregation? Pointing to the extant and limitations of change my conclusions revisit Lefebvre's notion of "right to the city" and explore the conditions under which claiming such a right is made possible.

## Social Control Through Spatial Segregation: Urban Space and the Franco Regime

What is the relationship between spatial segregation and the concept of domination? Segregation is an ambiguous term (Brun and Rhein, 1994; Grafmayer, 1994; Lehman-Frisch, 2011; Leloup, 1999). It denotes the unequal distribution of social or economic groups in urban space. As such it is generally considered a negative process by urban policy makers mostly because it impedes social integration and social cohesion processes, and does not create equal opportunities in relation to education and to people's access to the labour market. But segregation as defined by the Chicago School is also a process which refers to the tendency of "similar" people to aggregate in space (Park, 1926). In other words, segregation can be viewed as a selective process which separates different social groups, but it can also be viewed as a defensive process that provides deprived population with locally based social and symbolic resources (de Souza Briggs, 2005; Lehman-Frisch, 2011).

In the context of Henri Lefebvre's work the meaning of spatial segregation is directly tied to the understanding of urban space itself. According to Lefebvre, the urban is a product of industrial and capital accumulation. A space dominated and transformed by modern technology which introduces onto it new forms of use, closing, sterilizing and emptying it in the process (Lefebvre, 1996: 165). But space should also be viewed as a work (*oeuvre*) produced by different (and at times contradicting) processes of inhabiting. Within this context spatial segregation refers to a two-fold process: market driven processes accentuate social divisions within urban space and allocate marginalized groups into urban peripheries. This process of allocation, in its turn, has the potential of denying the same populations the right to participate in the collective creation of the urban itself (Lefebvre, 1996: 195; Hoskyns, 2014: 74–75). However, the move from spatial segregation to spatial alienation is not an automatic one. It is only when segregation is used in the service of domination that it leads to alienation, that is, to the production of space in a manner contrary to the needs of the inhabitants.

The development of the metropolitan area of Madrid under the Franco regime presents an example of acute spatial segregation at the service of domination. Throughout the late 1950s and 1960s, the metropolitan area of Madrid clearly embodied the characteristics of Lefebvre's critical zone: in 1940 (immediately following the Spanish Civil War) the capital's population stood at 1,326,647. This number doubled itself by 1960 following massive waves of internal migration from *Castilla la Mancha*, *Extremadura* and *Andalucía*. The ascendancy of metropolitan regions such Madrid, Barcelona, Valencia and Bilbao was accompanied by a corresponding "emptying out" of the Spanish countryside from both population and essential services in the fields of medicine, education, culture and commerce (Capel Sáez, 1962; Higueras Arnal, 1967; Siguán, 1959). This process was further accelerated by the annexation of "dead" rural territories into the urban. The General Plan of the City of Madrid that was published in 1941, for example, increased the capital's size by about 20%, annexing to its outer perimeter a series of half destroyed villages and small towns such as Villaverde, Orcasitas, Vallecas etc. (Sambricio, 2004).

Under the dictatorship the production of the urban was intended to maintain a strict separation between the functions of production and reproduction. The General Plan of the City of Madrid split the capital into three concentric circles and five zones, each with a distinct function. The first circle included the historical centre of the capital. This space comprised a mixture of small residential and commercial zones but was dedicated for the most part to national monuments and administrative spaces (Box Varela, 2008: 353–437). The second circle (*extrarradio*), bordering on the historical centre of the city, included residential zones built mostly during the last decades of the 19th century as well as additional commercial zones. Finally, the outer circle (that in 1941 was mostly made up of undeveloped land and half destroyed villages) was to be dedicated to residential and industrial uses (Ofer, 2017: 19–38).

The residential nuclei within the outer circle were called Satellite Suburbs, a term that pointed to their ambivalent relationship with the city. The neighbourhoods of the *extrarradio* were connected to the historical centre of Madrid via a series of roads. The Satellite Suburbs, on the other hand, were isolated both from the centre and from each other. According to the Pedro Bidagor (the initiator of the Madrid General Plan and the person in charge of its execution) Satellite Suburbs were supposed to exist as self-sufficient units. It was never made clear how this was to happen, since none of the neighbourhoods was designed so as to include commercial spaces or basic health or education services.

Following the Civil War the Spanish General Plans relied heavily on the concept of functional zoning. In accordance with the *Athens Charter* that was published in 1933, functional zoning assigned specific spaces to each of the four defined functions of the modern city: Living, working, recreation and circulation (Le Corbusier, 1973). This highly rational planning module was aimed at maximizing the use of space and reducing to a minimum the cost of urbanization. Abelardo Martínez de Lamadrid, an industrial engineer who worked alongside Pedro Bidagor on the formulation of the Madrid General Plan, reflected on the social and economic function of zoning in the Spanish case:

> The division into zones went hand in hand with the accepted planning criteria of the time: facilitating the access of primary material; enabling the distribution of products; and minimizing the inconveniences of industrial production. But zoning also facilitates the location of a mass population of workers in Satellite Suburbs—spatially independent of the city itself and with easy access to the countryside. In this way the green zones and industrial zones provided a bulwark against the invasion of the masses.
>
> (Terán, 1982: 173)

As can be understood from this citation, in Spain functional zoning had two central goals: to facilitate the needs of industry and to ensure social segregation. Workers, essential as they were to the process of production, had to be excluded from the heart of the city. Francoist cities of the 1940s and early 1950s clearly embodied what Henri Lefebvre defined as the central paradox of the spatial practises under late capitalism: an association that "includes the most extreme separation between the places it links together" (Lefebvre, 1996: 38).

The architectural form of satellite suburbs reinforced the concept of hierarchical planning and the tendency to evaluate built form through the lens of exchange value. These were dormitory suburbs that could not develop a differentiated character since they lacked spaces for socialization in which communal bonds could emerge. They met what Lefebvre defined as the lowest possible threshold of sociability, "beyond which survival would be impossible because all social life would disappear" (Lefebvre, 1996: 316). Luis Larrondo Bilbao described the sense of alienation surrounding these suburbs:

> An utter sense of failure became apparent and with it the understanding that the users themselves preferred a more traditional system of construction and felt uneasy in these homes. . . . A group of psychologists and sociologists that were contracted in order to look into the subject came to the following conclusions:
>
> > For the architect these [suburbs] symbolized the death of his creation at the hands of machinery; construction workers were weighed down by the inhuman impact of mass construction; finally, the users felt that they could not impact or reform their own home and were therefore unable to feel as if they owned it in the full sense of the word.
> >
> > (Bilbao Larrondo, 2006: 258)

Under the Franco regime, the Spanish general plans strove to design not only a segregated city, but also what sociologist Richard Sennett defined as a 'closed city'. Not only were they characterized by over determination of densities and of functions, they also aimed to create an integrated spatial system, where every part had a specific place within the overall design. Under such conditions structures that did not fit the overall design were either eliminated or acquired a diminished value and a relegated to the periphery (Sennet, 2006). The ways in which the general plans were implemented generated extraordinary imbalances during the first two decades of the dictatorship's existence. Such imbalances were noted most of all in relation to the housing market and to the construction of infrastructures.

## The Experience of Inhabiting: Producing Informal Space in the Periphery of Madrid

Despite harsh political and social repression, spatial domination in Francoist Spain was never complete. It was met with different forms of resistance: from sporadic illegal construction to more extensive alternatives which could be characterized as informal urbanism. Ananya Roy defined informal urbanism as a mode of urbanization with "an organizing logic, a system of norms that governs the process of urban transformation itself" (Roy, 2005: 148). Not all manifestations of illegal construction, therefore, can be characterized as informal urbanism. The latter term implies, in my view, a certain degree of permanence. From the researcher's point of view the analysis of different forms of informal urbanism requires an understanding that self-constructed spaces are not shaped solely by the harsh economic conditions under which they are produced. These spaces reflect the values and the material needs of their users and therefore may hold important lessons also for those engaged in formal planning.

Architect José Castillo further defined the informal in reference to three characteristics:

> First, it incorporates the notion of the casual; second, it refers to the condition of lacking precise form; and finally, it relates to the realm outside what is prescribed.
>
> I use the term urbanisms of the informal to explain the practises (social, economic, architectural and urban) and the forms (physical and spatial) that a group of stake holders (dwellers, developers, planers, landowners and the state) undertake not only to obtain access to land and housing, but also to satisfy their need to engage in urban life.
>
> (Brillembourg, 2006)

Catells and Portes focused on the contextual aspects of informality, emphasizing that "the informal economy does not result from the intrinsic characteristics of activities, but from the social definition of state intervention, the boundaries of the informal . . . will substantially vary in different contexts and historical circumstances" (Castells and Portes, 1989: 32). Research into forms of informal urban settlement in both the global south and the global north all emphasize the precarious nature of such settlements as a condition that facilitates community activism (Anders and Sedlmaier, 2017; Mayer, 2012). In this context, the concept of "appropriation," as defined by Lefebvre, proves extremely useful. Lefebvre did not view spatial proximity in itself as a guarantee for the creation of social bonds. Rather he tried to theorize the ways in which inhabiting space reinforce collective identifications and communal activism. In *L'Urbanisme aujourd'hui*, he wrote:

> For an individual, for a group, to inhabit is to appropriate something. Not in the sense of possessing it, but as making it an oeuvre, making it one's own, marking it, modelling it, shaping it. . . . To inhabit is to appropriate space, in the midst of constraints, that is to say, to be in a conflict—often acute—between the constraining powers and the forces of appropriation.
>
> (Lefebvre in Stanek, 2011: 87)

In *The Production of Space*, Lefebvre noted the appropriative potential of squatter communities but did not discuss the strategies through which squatting could in fact lead to the creation of spaces truly appropriated by their users. My contention is that under specific conditions the very nature of squatting (the context of illegality, the lack of pre-existing infrastructures, the practises of self-construction) may facilitate a more critical and purposeful engagement of people with their lived space. In order to understand under what conditions such a process may take place it is useful to consider the relationship between appropriation and spatial scales. Lefebvre proposed three scales for the analysis of space: A "private" realm, an interim level and a global level. He noted that even in the best of circumstances— when the indoor space of family life is truly appropriated by its users— the outer spaces of a community life are still mostly dominated (Lefebvre, 2003b: 86–90).

Focusing on the case of Orcasitas, I wish to point to some ways in which squatting (as an on going daily practise) can indeed lead to the appropriation of space, at both the private to the intermediate levels. This process, in its turn, can bring about the creation of communitarian "counter-spaces": spaces that are designated a specific function but through varied uses are invested with additional functions and meanings. These counter-spaces (a water fountain which functions as the community's meeting place and "billboard"; a barber's shop turned into the headquarters of a neighbourhood association etc.) are locations where new subjectivities and new forms of knowledge regarding the nature of inhabitance are produced.

What is known today as the *barrio* of Orcasitas was originally made up of three different neighbourhoods: *Meseta de Orcasitas*, *OrcaSur* and *Poblado Dirigido de Orcasitas*. The first two formed between 1955 and 1962 as a result of illegal self-construction. The patterns of squatting and of community life in Orcasitas were representative of hundreds of other squatters' settlements all over Spain. The uniqueness of Orcasitas lies in the way in which its dwellers struggled against eviction and challenged legal notions of entitlement already under the dictatorship. By forcing the local authorities to acknowledge their claim to the land they had occupied, and their status as a community of neighbours the inhabitants set a legal precedent. They also established their right to take an active part in any process of urban renovation pertaining to their *barrio*.

*Chabolismo* or *barraquismo* is a form of informal construction, which started to manifest itself around the periphery of Spanish cities in the 1920s. By the mid-1940s, however, squatting changed its face in Spain. From individual constructions that were scattered throughout the peripheries of large cities, it matured into dense areas covered by mass self-constructions. In Orcasitas alone 10,000 households lived in self-constructed homes by the late 1960s. A working paper composed in 1977 by the Commission for Planning and Coordination of the Madrid Metropolitan Area, stated:

> With the passing of time the word *chabolisimo* came to signify any type of housing that was built bypassing the official procedures of urban planning. . . . Initially, however, *chabolismo* was simply an ad hoc way in which migrants and newly formed households responded to the unsolvable housing problem.
>
> (COPLACO, 1977: 10, the author's translation)

Constructing a *chabola* was clearly more difficult than renting a shared apartment in an established working class neighbourhood. Rented apartments in the centre of Madrid enjoyed better infrastructures, transportation and educational services and shopping facilities. Why, then, did so many migrant families opt for these self-constructed *barrios*? *Barrios chabolistas* provided their inhabitants with two marked advantages in comparison to other forms of dwelling: In cities with fast growing industries the squatters' settlements were constructed in relative proximity to the new industrial complexes that provided work for many migrants. For a population deprived of any means of transportation, however, the proximity of home and work proved a marked advantage.

The *chabolas* as housing units also offered independence and flexibility. The uncertain status of the land enabled the inhabitants to use the perimeter surrounding their home in order to supplement their meagre earnings. The ability to grow vegetables and wheat and to raise farm animals was an advantage not found in established working class neighbourhoods. Furthermore, while in the countryside many young couples shared a house with their extended family, doing so in the city was often perceived as a failure of the migratory project. Having an independent home (even a *chabola*) was the hallmark of a functioning family and of adaptation to city life.

The *chabolas* also provided their dwellers with greater freedom to construct their lived space in accordance with specific needs and notions of what could be considered a "good home" (Raymond, 1974: 213–229). Most of the *chabolas* that were documented by the Spanish Ministry of Housing included a central space located at the entrance to the house, which functioned as a living room and was dedicated to socialization and eating. In some of the larger and more established *chabolas* this space also included a permanent kitchen. In most others the kitchen was made of a make-shift fireplace (which could be situated inside or outside of the *chabola* depending on the weather) and several chairs. The same space was converted at night into an additional bedroom (Ofer, 2017; 58–79). By forming make-shift bedrooms the dwellers were able to attain a certain level of coherence between the representations of "adequate" sleeping space (which dictated separation according to age and gender) and their lived (or representational) space.

The precarious structure of the *chabola* allowed for a temporary division of its internal space in accordance with the changing profile of the family that inhabited it. It also allowed its inhabitants to "expel' certain functions to the outer perimeter of the house according to weather conditions and to the structure and characteristics of communal spaces in the neighbourhood. Some of those functions were "expelled" from the *chabola* on a temporary basis (as was the case with cooking, eating and studying) and others permanently (bathing for example, which took place outside of the *chabola* in the case of young children or in public bath-houses at the centre of Madrid in the case of adults).

*Figure 11.1* Cooking outdoors in Orcasitas (Asociación de Vecinos del Barrio de Orcasitas, Archivo Fotográfico).

Between the years 2008–2012, I conducted interviews with some of Orcasitas' original dwellers. In these interviews the old *chabolas* that had been long demolished were often referred to. María (who grew up in Orcasitas) reflected on the way in which the structure of the *chabolas* influenced social life within the *barrio*:

> Here we shared everything. The houses were all open. There were no doors, only curtains. You didn't have to knock. You simply entered, and what you saw was there for the taking. It was for everyone—neighbours, friends, family members.
>
> (María, interview with the author, Orcasitas, Madrid)

Julio (who moved to Orcasitas from the centre of Madrid) recounted:

> There were many shanty homes. Some were made of wood, others of exposed brick. They looked like tiny vacation homes. Life was good then, we all knew each other. Now everything is different, we each live in a closed apartment and it's no longer the same.
>
> (Julio, interview with the author, Orcasitas, Madrid)

The "homely" feeling described above was tied by many of my interviewees to the absence of "transitional spaces." Lefebvre defined transitional spaces or objects (such as doors, windows and thresholds) that direct the movement from the inside to the outside and vice versa, defining the capacity of one space to connect or merge into another (Lefebvre, 1996: 206). In Orcasitas the open-ended structure of communal and private spaces (most notably exemplified by the lack of doors and fences) promoted a sense of intimacy and of coming together. At the same time, it is important to note that the absence of transitional spaces left the *chabolas* "naked" in a sense that could also be very dangerous. It enabled the atmosphere and the happenings on the street quite literally to penetrate the private living space of a family. Lacking in walls and doors some of these homes could not be protected from noises, smells or from the presence of outside intruders. The risk inherent in such penetration was felt most acutely when the neighbours were called to protect their homes from demolition, which in the early stages occurred due to the failure to bribe the local representatives of the forces of law and order and later on when the authorities attempted to evacuate the entire population in order to proceed with the process of reconstruction.

The most notable practises which can be identified with spatial appropriation in settlements such as Orcasitas had to do with the provision of services and the construction of communal spaces. As indicated earlier, these practises stood in stark contradiction to the spatial practises that were instituted by the regime within satellite suburbs.

*Figure 11.2* Tavern and self-constructed dancing-hall in Orcasitas.

The photos are not dated, but they were taken prior to the first wave of mass demolitions in the 1970s (Asociación de Vecinos del Barrio de Orcasitas, Archivo Fotográfico)

*Figure 11.3* Tavern and self-constructed dancing-hall in Orcasitas.

The photos are not dated, but they were taken prior to the first wave of mass demolitions in the 1970s (Asociación de Vecinos del Barrio de Orcasitas, Archivo Fotográfico)

Nearly 6% of the heads of households who lived in Orcasitas in 1958 defined themselves as independent business owners. With the nearest "established" commercial area 3 km away in the *barrio* of Usera and no public transportation at hand, the businesses that formed in Orcasitas catered for a mixed array of needs. Of the 91 businesses I know of, 12 were bars and taverns (Ofer, 2017: 70–73). They served mainly men and therefore opened on weekends and weekdays from the early afternoon and well into the night. As indicated by their names some of them functioned as hubs of socialization according to the proprietor's place of origin. Establishments such as *La Andaluza*, *Soria* and *La Asturiana* (which exist to this day) served traditional dishes and drinks and other primary products acquired during trips to the countryside. Other small businesses included a barbershop, fruit shops, bakeries, butcheries, wine shops and several shops for the sale of secondhand clothes and fabrics. To these must be added several mobile businesses for the sale of water and coal.

## The Long Road Towards Spatial Appropriation

The construction of an unauthorized school, of a communal fountain, of bars and shops all provide examples of popular production of intermediate or communal spaces. The squatters (in their capacity as consumers, housewives, and parents) identified specific needs that had to be fulfilled. They then proceeded by constructing spaces that could cater for those needs and later on invested them with additional functions and meaning according to the evolution of community life. However, the appropriation of private and intermediate spaces under such conditions should not be confused with laying claim to the urban itself. Henri Lefebvre speculated regarding the potential of spatial change to bring about political change that:

> so long as the only connection between work spaces, leisure spaces and living spaces is supplied by the agencies of political power and their mechanisms of control—so long must the project of 'changing life' remain no more than a political rallying-cry.
>
> (Lefebvre, 1996: 59)

In order for space to be fully appropriated, it would have to be produced in a way that makes its full and complete usage possible. In this respect the appropriation and creative breaking down of spatial boundaries that took place in squatter settlements across Spain during the 1960s was an essential pre-conditions for change. But a deep and long-lasting transformation of Spain's urban planning regimes awaited the emergence of a more extended structure of opportunities.

In 1964, the Franco regime sanctioned for the first time the formation of an array of new civic associations on the condition that those would be non political by nature and strictly supervised. Between the years 1968–1975 hundreds of new neighbourhood associations formed all over Spain. Sociologist Manuel Castells wrote of these associations:

> This was a large scale movement with an immense popular base. It included [associations] from squatters' settlements . . . from middle-class neighbourhoods and those arriving from neighbourhoods situated in the historical centre of Madrid. . . . It was founded by political activists of different ideological shades and by a multitude of people with no precise ideological inclination who were willing to fight for better living conditions. . . . The movement obtained the renovation of underprivileged neighbourhoods . . . and the construction of urban infrastructures not seen before. It reanimated popular cultural and street life . . . and facilitated forms of self mobilization amongst men and women. It was truly a school of democracy and leadership and made a decisive contribution to popular pressure that propelled the [Spanish] transition to democracy.
>
> (Castells, 2009: 21)

The Orcasitas Neighbourhood Association was founded in 1970, a short time before the local authorities published a *Partial Plan for the Reconstruction of Orcasitas*. The aim of the plan was to clear the area covered by *chabolas*, expropriate the land on which they stood and reconstruct a new neighbourhood while dispersing the existing squatter community throughout the Southern periphery of the capital. Aided by a team of lawyers and architects the Orcasitas Neighbourhood Association decided to oppose the implementation of the Plan. Having rejected two modified plans, in 1976 the neighbours finally accepted a third version of the reconstruction plan which was designed according to their needs and would allow them to remain on the land that they had occupied.

The 1976 plan was formulated with the active participation of the neighbours who determined both the internal structure of their apartments and the structure of the entire *barrio*. How was this done? In early 1976 the architects that worked with the neighbourhood association carried a survey that was intended to verify the priorities of Orcasitas' future dwellers. They entered the existing *chabolas*, interviewed the inhabitants and then recorded and analysed the information. One set of questions was intended to collect information on the socio-economic profile of the families (their joint income, the number of people living in the house, whether the family owned a car etc.). The second set included questions that were meant to give the architects an idea about the ways in which each family used its living space. People were asked if they wished to live in a house of a single or multiple floors and whether they preferred to live in a four-storey building without an elevator or a seven-storey building with one (Ofer, 2017: 125–129). They were also asked how far away from the house they were willing to park their cars in order to allow for the safe circulation of pedestrians. The preamble to the new reconstruction plan stated accordingly:

> We wish to reproduce the [atmosphere] experienced by the neighbours of Orcasitas, who at the moment live in a *barrio* made up of a single-storey houses, and in which the street is used and valued in its original form. . . . We wish to mix housing spaces with other spaces intended for commerce. . . . We want to reduce to a minimum the height of the buildings. This is the preference expressed by all of the neighbours, who indicated they did not want to live in high-rise apartments nor be surrounded by high buildings.
>
> (Polígono Meseta de Orcasitas, Hoja Informativa no. 3—
> La manzana, editada por el equipo de técnicos de la
> asociación de vecinos, the author's translation)

The new *barrio* was divided into six residential nuclei (which included a mix of four, eight and ten storey buildings) and structured around a Civic Centre (which to this day serves as the heart of community life in Orcasitas and houses the neighbourhood association). Each nucleus was made up of 8–10 apartment buildings that were arranged around a small courtyard and a commercial space. The ground floor of each apartment building included a nursery and a playroom for the children. The aim was to create multi-scalar spaces for socialization—from the playrooms in each building, to the courtyard that united several buildings and up to the Civic Centre and its large plaza.

In 1986, the neighbours of Orcasitas celebrated the inauguration of the new *barrio* with an exposition on 15 years of struggle (housed in the new headquarters of the neighbourhood association). In a final act which perhaps best symbolized the control they gained over their renovated living space, the neighbours named their streets. The action of naming indicated a move from the stage of an active struggle to the stage of memory conservation. *Calle de la Remodelación* (re-modeling), *calle de los Encierros* (lock-downs), *Plaza del Movimiento Ciudadano* (Citizens' Movement) are some of the more interesting names in present-day Orcasitas.

José Manuel Bringas, who was the first architect to join the technical advisory team in Orcasitas, wrote about the process of informed election that culminated in a plan for the new *barrio*:

> there are those who talk negatively of the architects [turned] activists. I did not infiltrate the association under the pretext of advising the people in order to agitate and propel them into a struggle against those in power. Anyone who knows the story of the struggle in Orcasitas personally would burst out laughing when hearing these accusations. In the *Mesta* no one had to agitate, no one! Not the president [of

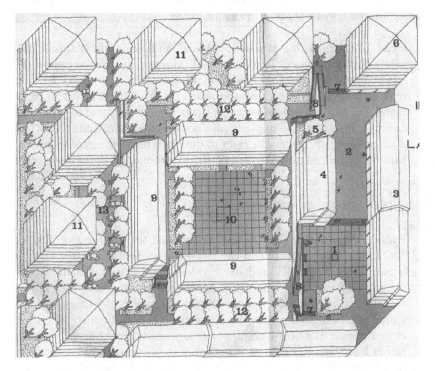

*Figure 11.4* The Structure of a Housing Nucleus, including Towers, Four-storey Apartment Buildings and Commercial and Recreational Spaces (Polígono Meseta de Orcasitas, Hoja informativa no. 3—la Vivienda, Equipo de técnicos de la asociación de vecinos de Orcasitas).

the association], not the members of the directive committee, not the technical advisors. The entire *Meseta* agitated if the people were made aware that something threatened **their** re-modeling project. . . . In this type of work the 'technical advisor', in his capacity to offer technical or academic solutions, can not be replaced by a neighbour. At the same time it is important that he or she understand that their job is to accompany the neighbours in managing [and assessing] the solutions that are being offered to them. No more and no less than that.

(Meseta de Orcasitas, 1982: 7–8, the author's translation)

Bringas' words point to developments that allowed the dwellers of Orcasitas to progress from the appropriation of their lived space and onto claiming the city in a fuller sense. Achieving the latter necessitated an understanding that controlling and shaping lived space had political implications. A right to the city was a right for spatial appropriation as well as for political participation. As Mark Purcell noted Lefebvre's right to the city was not a suggestion for reform. Rather, it was a call for:

> a radical restructuring of social, political, and economic relations, both in the city and beyond. Key to this radical nature is that the right to the city reframes the arena of decision-making in cities: it reorients decision-making away from the state and toward the production of urban space. Instead of democratic deliberation being limited to just state decisions, Lefebvre imagines it to apply to *all* decisions that contribute to the production of urban space. The right to the city stresses the need to restructure the power relations that underlie the production of urban space.
>
> (Purcell, 2002: 102)

He further elaborates:

> Because the right to the city revolves around the production of urban space, it is those who live in the city—who contribute to the body of urban lived experience and lived space—who can legitimately claim the right to the city. Whereas conventional enfranchisement empowers national *citizens*, the right to the city empowers urban *inhabitants*. Under the right to the city, membership in the community of enfranchised people is not an accident of nationality or ethnicity or birth; rather it is earned by living out the routines of everyday life in the space of the city.
>
> (Ibid.)

In the case of Orcasitas, spatial appropriation clearly generated new forms of urban knowledge. The development of a new professional and communitarian platform (in the form of a neighbourhood association) enabled such knowledge in its turn to be translated into a professional idiom and transferred into the realm of policy making. However, it is enough to look at present day Orcasitas in order to understand the limitations of change. The new *barrio* of Orcasitas was constructed as a neighbourhood onto itself. It might have been conceived as a perfectly formed *barrio* on the inside, but throughout the 1980s and 1990s it had little sustainable ties with the city around it. On a practical level this is best manifested by the fact that Orcasitas was only directly connected to the Madrid Metro line in 2008. More disquieting, however, is the fact that in the decades following the renovation the *barrio* was referred to in the Madrid press either in relation to its successful past struggle or as a current hotbed of criminal activity and of drug trafficking. While the neighbours struggled to combat drug consumption within the community, many outsiders viewed drug trafficking as one of the characteristics of the *barrio* itself. In other words, the empowering struggle and the consequent re-modelling process changed some of the existing spatial practises and the structure of representational space within the *barrio*.

But it did not bring about a lasting change in the representations of that space as a marginalized periphery in the eyes of those living outside of the *barrio*.

## Conclusion: A Democratic City versus an Open City

The current chapter analyses the ways in which micro-level research into the formal and informal practises of urban planning can benefit from Lefebvre's spatial analysis. It also raises several theoretical questions to which Lefebvre only briefly alluded in his work. Lefebvre's triad model provides us with a valuable framework for the analysis of spatial production. It highlights the ways in which space is produced through the evolution of competing practises and representation promoted by different stakeholders. However, Lefebvre did not refer explicitly in his work to the possibility that contradictions might surface between the spatial representations and the practises promoted by the same stakeholder (such as the state, city-council etc.). In reality this might happen quite often. The political and economic forces which are engaged in monitoring and shaping urban space often share common goals. But even in the rare cases where complete correlation exists between the needs and aspirations of economic and political actors, contradictions might still surface between the spatial practises which those actors promote and the representations employed in order to justify them. Under such conditions the experience of lived space (affected as it is by both) can either work in order to minimize tensions and "cover up" the contradictions, or in order to make these tensions explicit, thereby undermining the process of spatial domination. If the latter occurs we may see the beginning of a process by which urban space is claimed by its users.

In the Spanish case, the new administration which elected followed the transition to democracy clearly sought to change the exiting urban planning regimes. In Madrid, Barcelona and Bilbao the local authorities spent a large percentage of their budgets on the extension of public infrastructures. Peripheral neighbourhoods were finally brought into contact with the city through the construction of an extended system of roads, electricity and water provision facilities. Green spaces and recreational facilities were expanded all throughout the city. However, the process by which the urban was developed as a space characterized by a single gravity point (structured around a main locus of industry, services and infrastructures) and multiple peripheries was never fully reversed. The "periphery" was connected to the "centre" and gained recognition as an integral part of the city but never became a centre in itself.

The process by which the incorporation of lessons gained from the experience of informal urbanization into the new urban planning regime took place highlights, in my view, the difference between the idea of a democratic city and an "open" city. It is the latter which embodies more fully Lefebvre's notion of the "right to the city." Sociologist Richard Sennett defined the open city as a city in which constant interaction exists between physical creation and social behaviour (Sennett, 2006). Sennett suggested three design characteristics that may influence the "openness" of a city: the existence of ambiguous edges between parts of the city where different groups can interact; the creation of incomplete forms so that as the function of a building or a space changes historically so will its form; and the planning for unresolved narratives of development allowing the planner to follow rather than determine the development of urban space.

It is on the first account that the Plan for the Reconstruction of Orcasitas failed most profoundly. Urban reconstruction plans for the metropolitan area of Madrid that were approved following Spain's transition to democracy worked to diminish the hierarchical structure which the planners of the 1940s and 1950s strove to implement. The Plan for the Remodelling the Neighbourhoods of Madrid (*Programa de Barrios en Remodelación*) which was executed between the years 1979–1988, for example, created multiple commercial, cultural and educational hubs throughout the city. It also reformed the workings of the local administration, enhanced its contact with ordinary citizens, and decentralized the provision of services to the local population. However, the border between the southern periphery of the capital and its centre remains as unambiguous as the river Manzanares, which marks it. While the population of the southern *barrios* crosses the river in search of work, commerce and entertainment the periphery still has very little to offer in the minds of those living on the other bank of the Manzanares.

Finally, both Sennett's concept of the "Open City" and Lefebvre's concept of "right to the city" are based on an understanding the urban is not only the hegemonic scale at which planning is carried-out but that it should also be the level at which the political community is defined. Under the new liberal democratic state the urban continued to expand, while this particular re-scaling of the concept of citizenship was never defined as a corresponding goal. In the decade following 1986, trucks of neighbours from the southern periphery of Madrid would still occasionally pour into the capital's central Plaza. Men, women and children protested crowded classes, lack of transportation services, the administration's failure to deal with increased unemployment and drug-related problems. However, the dream of a more participatory form of government never materialized. The activists who strove to achieve higher levels of civic participation felt excluded from the beating heart of the local and the national administration. The willingness of democratic authorities to allow the "community" to take an active part in designing and regulating its living-environment was limited. Within the framework of a liberal democracy the Spanish state guaranteed an extended list of essential rights. Continued civic participation at all levels of governance, however, was never perceived as one of those rights. But it was precisely the right for active, innovative and creative participation based on the insights derived from an on-going practice of inhabiting the city, which lay at the heart of the Orcasitas success. Without it, as most neighbourhood activists understood, the ability of ordinary citizens to shape their lived space could not be sustained over time.

**Acknowledgement:** This research was supported by the Israel Science Foundation (grant no. 54/10).

# References

Anders, F. and Sedlmaier, A. (Eds). (2017). *Public Goods versus Economic Interests: Global Perspectives on the History of Squatting*. Abingdon: Routledge Studies in Modern History, Routledge.

Brenner, N. and Elden, S. (2009). Henri Lefebvre on state space and territory. *International Political Sociology*, 3(4), 353–377.

Brenner, N., Marcuse, P. and Mayer, M. (2012). *Cities for People Not for Profit: Critical Urban Theory and the Right to the City*. London: Routledge.

Brun, J. and Rhein, C. (1994). *La ségrégation dans la ville* (pp. 21–57). Paris: L'Harmattan.

Bilbao Larrondo, L. (2006). La Vivienda en Bilbao: Los años sesenta. Años de cambio. *Ondare. Cuadernos de Artes Plásticas y Monumentales*, 25, 81–86.

Box Varela, Z. (2008). *La fundación de un régimen. La construcción simbólica del franquismo* (Tesis doctoral). Madrid: Universidad Complutense de Madrid.

Brillembourg, C. (2006). José Castillo: Urbanism of the informal. *Bomb Magazine*, 94(winter), 28–35. Retrieved from http://www.bombsite.com/issues/94/articles/2798 Google Scholar

Capel Sáez, H. (1962). Las Migraciones Interiores Definitivas en España. *Estudios Geográficos*, XXIV, 600–602.

Castells, M. & Portes, A. (1989). World underneath: The origins, dynamics and the effects of the informal economy. In A. Portes, M. Castells, L. Benton (Eds.), *The Informal Economy: Studies in Advanced and Less Developed Countries* (pp. 11–37). Baltimore: Johns Hopkins Press.

Castells, M. (2009). Productores de ciudad: el movimiento ciudadano de Madrid in Pérez. In V. Quintana and P. Sánchez León (Eds.), *Memoria Ciudadana y movimiento vecinal. Madrid 1968–2008* (pp. 21–32). Madrid: Catarata.

COPLACO (1977). *Informe sobre participación pública en el planeamiento metropolitan*. Madrid: Ministerio de Obras Públicas y Urbanismo.

de Souza Briggs, X. (2005). Social capital and segregation in the United States. In Varady D. P. (Ed.), *Desegregating the City: Ghettos, Enclaves and Inequality* (pp. 79–101). New York: State University of New York.

Elden, S. (2004). *Understanding Henri Lefebvre. Theory and the Possible*. London: Continuum.

Grafmayer, Y. (1994). Regards sociologiques sure la segregation. In *La Ségrégation dans la ville* (pp. 85–117). Paris: L'Harmattan.

Higueras, Arnal, A. (1967). *La Emigración Interior en España*. Madrid: Ediciones Mundo del Trabajo.

Hoskyns, T. (2014). *The Empty Place. Democracy and Public Space*. London: Routledge.

Le Corbusier (1973). *The Athens Charter* (translated by A. Eardely). New York: Grossman Publishers.

Lehman-Frisch, S. (2011). Segregation, spatial (in)justice, and the city. *Berkeley Planning Journal*, 24(1), 70–90.

Lefebvre, H. (1976). *The Survival of Capitalism: Reproduction of the Relations of Production* (translated by F. Bryant). New York: St. Martin's Press.

Lefebvre, H. (1976–78). *De l'État*. Paris: UGE.

Lefebvre, H. (1991a). *The Production of Space* (translated by D. Nicholson-Smith). Oxford: Blackwell.

Lefebvre, H. (1996). *Writings on Cities* (translated and introduced by E. Kofman and E. Lebas). Oxford: Blackwell.

Lefebvre, H. (2003a). *Key Writings* (edited by S. Elden, E. Lebas and E. Kofman). London: Continuum.

Lefebvre, H. (2003b). *The Urban Revolution* (translated by R. Bonnano). Minneapolis, MN: University of Minnesota Press.

Leloup, X. (1999). "Distance et différence entre nationalité: La ségrégation résidentielle des populations étrangères dans un contexte urbain." *Recherches Sociologiques*, 1.

Mayer, M. (2012). The "right to the city" in urban social movements. In N. Brenner, P. Marcuse, and M. Mayer (Eds.), *Cities for People Not for Profit: Critical Urban Theory and the Right to the City* (pp. 63–85). London: Routledge.

Meseta de Orcasitas (1982). *Boletín Informativo*, no. 1 (abril).

Ofer, I. (2017). *Claiming the City and Contesting the State Squatting, Community Formation and Democratisation in Spain (1955–1986)*. London: Routledge.

Park, R. E. (1926). The urban Community as a Spatial Pattern and Moral Order. In R. H. Turner (Ed.), *Robert E Park on Social Control and Collective Behavior*. Chicago, IL: University of Chicago Press.

Purcell, M. (2002). Excavating Lefebvre: The right to the city and urban politics of the inhabitants. *GeoJournal*, 58, 99–108.

Purcell, M. (2003). Citizenship and the right to the global city: Reimagining the capitalist world order. *International Journal of Urban and Regional Research*, 27(3), 564–590.

Raymond, H. (1974). Habitat, modèles cultureless et architecture. In H. Raymond, J. M. Stébé and A. Mathieu Fritz (Eds.), *Architecture urbanistique et société* (pp. 213–229). Paris: L'Harmattan.

Roy, A. (2005). Urban informality toward an epistemology of planning. *Journal of the American Planning Association*, 71(2), 147–158.

Sambricio, C. (2004). *Madrid, vivienda y urbanismo: 1900–1960*. Madrid: AKAL.

Sennet, R. (2006). *The Open City*, LSE Cities. Retrieved from https://lsecities.net/media/objects/articles/the-open-city/en-gb/

Shields, R. (1999) *Lefebvre, Love and Struggle*. London: Routledge.

Siguán, M. (1959). *Del campo al suburbio. Un estudio sobre la inmigración interior en España*, Madrid: C. S. I. C.

Stanek, L. (2011). *Henri Lefebvre on Space. Architecture, Urban Research, and the Production of Theory*, Minneapolis, MN: University of Minnesota Press.

Terán, F. (1982). *Planeamiento urbano en la españa contemporanea (1900–1980)*. Madrid: Alianza Universidad Textos.

# 12 The 'Visible Hand' of the State

## Urbanization of Favelas as a Violent Abstraction of Space

*Daniel S. Lacerda*

## Introduction

The spatial turn observed in the field of organization studies in the past decades led to an increasing production of research on space and organization that responds to calls made by ground-breaking works in the area (Baldry, 1999; Dale and Burrell, 2008; Kornberger and Clegg, 2003, 2004). The literature on space has been particularly insightful in tackling issues of organizational control (Dale, 2005; Hancock and Spicer, 2011; Hirst and Humphreys, 2013) and organizational boundaries (Fleming and Spicer, 2008; Maréchal, Linstead, and Munro, 2013; Munro and Jordan, 2013). However, extant work has focussed on interrogating in/about the workplace or spatial theories of organization as a processual activity. There has been little work on what Dale and Burrell (2008) call the *organization of space* across organizations—in opposition to the (internal) space of organizations—that shows the lasting effects of the organizational activity in the territory and beyond.

As discussed elsewhere in this book, Lefebvre (1991) rejected the idea of space as a simple entity occupied by physical things detached from social relations. He adopted the concept of "social space" referring to a constructed space, hence a social product, and claimed that every society produces its own space. By shifting the focus of analysis from the things *in* space to space itself Lefebvre provided, thus, a critical analysis of how space is both a social product and also the means for the reproduction of history. Because *social space* incorporates social actions, it also encompasses the social relations of production, and considering that every social relation of production should be linked to the entirety—i.e. the 'totality'—of space, it follows that social space should never be detached from its totality.

That is a particularly important point if we consider that the application of Lefebvre's theory is often restricted to his spatial triad, at the expense of his wider view of the political economy of space (the production of space). This limitation is understandable, since it is not simple to extract the most important ideas from such a disruptively dense work such as Lefebvre's, but my framing of his theory will be one that attempts to do justice to the politically engaged spirit of Lefebvre's writing, as suggested by Elden (2004). I draw on Lefebvre's (1991) *The Production of Space*, which highlights the concept of abstract space in which the elements of his spatial triad are essential but subordinate concepts when considered from the perspective of the totality of the production of space. This framing reveals that the analysed social space is often linked to a particular process of abstraction operating in the development of spaces of capital accumulation.

Based on the empirical case of Brazilian favelas, which I have researched for five years, this chapter addresses this challenge of a limited application of Lefebvre's propositions. Favelas are particularly pertinent spaces for the analysis of the production of the abstract space because they have for many years been the stage of a massive and militarized presence of the state, and consequent escalation in initiatives for the development of these territories. When I conducted my fieldwork in Rio de Janeiro, the *Unidades de Policia Pacificadora* (UPP) (Pacifying Police Units) program had been in place for five years, although it was still considered a work in progress and challenged for various reasons—for a more detailed discussion of this see Lacerda (2016) where I focus on the failed construction of the state in the territory of favelas. These territories of favelas house poor communities and to a great extent have been traditionally excluded from public and market services, which had traditionally been limited to the so called 'formal city' (Davis, 2007).

The abrupt interventions carried on by the state in the UPP program transformed the everyday of many of these spaces and allowed the observation of what Lefebvre would call the abstraction of space (and the resistance to it). The characterization of abstraction as a violent process is of particular interest here (Lefebvre, 1991:289). That is certainly true because of the explanatory potential in highlighting the violence of abstraction, as pointed out by Wilson (2014: 517), "an attempt to grasp the ways in which the space of capital embodies, facilitates and conceals the complex intertwining of structural, symbolic and direct forms of violence." But even more because of the contradictory name of the program analysed in the fieldwork ('pacification'), which in practice replaces direct forms of violence emerging from historical struggles in the territory with indirect *and* concealed forms of violence imposed by the state according to the needs of the capitalist space.

Therefore, the present chapter discusses the case of urbanization of favelas in Brazil as a violent process that is inherently spatial, and examines some of the ways the violence of abstraction can be observed in practice. The main contribution offered is to analyse the process of production of the abstract space as a key argument in Lefebvre's *The Production of Space* and explain its implication for the analysis of organizations. Methodologically, it also demonstrates how the category of 'totality' can be adopted in a contextual analysis, by linking delimited organizing practices to their context of production, in the development of urban space.

Next, I describe my theoretical argument about the importance of considering the abstraction of space as the main message in Lefebvre (1991). Then, I introduce the empirical study of favelas and present the methodology of the present research, based on participatory observation performed in a favela named here as "Mucuripe."[1] Then, the data of the discussed case is presented highlighting the importance of the historical space for the description of the territory, and the violent intervention carried on by the state in an attempt to take over control of the territory, which I argue is a case of abstraction of space. Finally, I discuss the presented case pointing out that the violent actions promoted by the state favour the expansion of the space of capital accumulation through a process of negation of the previous social space, regardless of its content.

## The Production of Abstract Space

### Totality in Lefebvre

Lefebvre (1991) uses a conceptual triad to approach space as overlapping and mutually determining dimensions of the same space: spatial practices, representations of space and spaces of representation (or representational space). These three aspects are not detached but rather mutually determine each other, even though they are not coincident. This spatial triad may not constitute a coherent whole but its components are necessarily interconnected (Lefebvre, 1991: 40). To be more precise, the separation of moments for reading social space is an attempt to integrate the dimensions of space without fragmenting or superposing it *a priori*.

The separation of the social space in three dimensions is particularly useful to examine the contradictions that result in spatial transformations. Whenever the elements of each of these three dimensions clash, they are redefined through the dialectical tension that exists among them. The necessary balance that exists between the three dimensions forces the transformation of the whole. Lefebvre advanced these ideas to show the violent mechanisms of the production of space that overthrow local social spaces. That is often absent in the application of Lefebvre's theory in organization studies, but the spatial triad should be the means to analyse the production and reproduction of society as a spatial realization, and not the end in itself. It is necessary, thus, to reveal the propositions that unfold from this spatial heuristics.

In his critique of Marx's *Capital*, Lefebvre points out the reductionism in political economy in restricting its analysis only to the abstract economy, whereas the reproduction of the relations of production is found in space. Lefebvre then adds that only a "political economy of space" could save this "science" by providing it a new object of analysis—the production of space—which would reveal space as the medium of installation of capitalism (Lefebvre, 1991: 104). For Lefebvre (1991), the production of space in history leads to its abstraction in a process engendered with symbolical and material violence, which associates the commodification and the bureaucratization of everyday life with the coercive role of state. This main message unfolds from the observation of social space in the context of its historical development.

One of the main concerns in Lefebvre's work is how the relations of production are simultaneously spatial and thus how space is the means for the reproduction of social life, thus understanding space as a totality is what validates the analysis of space *from within*. It reinforces the separation from positivist views of social issues, rejects Cartesian dichotomies of real and ideal spaces, and shifts from the analysis of things "in space" to the interest in the production "of space" (Lefebvre, 1991: 37). As noted by Zhang (2006: 221), the manipulation of concepts advanced by most current literature applying Lefebvre's concepts have not been careful in preserving this idea of the totality of space.

It follows that if every society produces its own space (Lefebvre, 1991: 31) and cannot be regarded as just a collection of peoples and things in space, likewise we could say that organization is not a collection of people and resources, but must be analysed in connection with the totality in which it is included, that is, its produced space. In effect, as a consequence of organizations being forged by the social relations in space, whatever features are ascribed to the nature of space will have to be applied also to organizations. For this reason, the analysis of any organizational space should be considered within the context of its totality. Ignoring totality is precisely what often fragments the modern approach to space (including in the field of organization studies), an approach strongly criticized by Lefebvre. However, although present throughout his work, unfortunately Lefebvre provides no simple and straightforward explanation of how he understands totality, and we should turn to other authors to support this explanation.

One of the authors Lefebvre established a dialogue with was Louis Althusser, whose view on society emphasized the irreducibility of its relational structure, in contrast to sociological approaches to society as a moral community. This idea is explained by Althusser and Balibar (1970), who define social formation as a "totality of instances" (p. 207). Each instance is expressed as social relations and practices within a specific structure, in other words practices are the empirical realization of the social structure in which they are included. Each structure is in itself subordinated to the dominant structure of production. Thus, the multiplicity of practices exists always within the complex unity (p. 269) that unites the different moments of production, circulation, distribution and consumption. From this stance, the Althusserian totality unfolds from an embodied expression of the whole, distinguishing it from the Hegelian view of totality as the ideal essence derived from knowledge.

It is a whole whose unity, far from being the expressive or 'spiritual' unity of Leibniz's or Hegel's whole, is constituted by a certain type of complexity.

This structured whole contains what can be called levels or instances which are distinct and 'relatively autonomous', and co-exist within this complex structural unity, articulated with one another according to specific determinations, fixed ultimately by the level or instance of the economy. (Althusser and Balibar, 1970: 97)

Althusser and Balibar (1970) derive from these ideas the same interpretation that is present also in Lefebvre's intellectual work regarding Marx's discussion on the mode of production: "production is not the production of things, it is the production and conservation of social relations" (p. 269). Drawing on this same assumption many philosophers and geographers have written about space, since it is in space that other categories of analysis such as class or time are realized. Although the philosophical grounds may sometimes differ, the interpretation of totality is usually informed by the philosophical rule of Leibniz, for whom an object exists only as a representation, within itself, of the relationships to other objects.

In adopting the same relational thinking, Lefebvre also accepts the dialectics of spatial elements as constituent of a total space, although he conveys a more careful consideration of the philosophical content of space. As Elden (2004) puts it in relation to Lefebvre's work, before being an entity, one that can be considered an abstraction of formal logic to be attributed a feature of identity, the entity has an existence in space. Lefebvre examines this argument with a particular focus on the mediating role of the human body:

> *Before producing effects in the material realm (tools and objects), before producing itself by drawing nourishment from that realm, and before reproducing itself by generating other bodies, each living body is space and has its space: it produces itself in space and it also produces that space.*
>
> (Lefebvre, 1991: 170)

In this mediation of the body's perceived space, conceived space and lived space are not only moments to be captured by theoretical concepts, but also affect each other in the realization of social space. Each element of this triad is thus equally important in that they affect each other mutually. In other words, they are "continually and mutually informed and informing, and as such are essential in the successful negotiation of the social world" (Watkins, 2005: 220). By assuming the epistemology according to which space is manifested in totality, and that its ontological dimensions and spheres of production cannot be separated, it follows that "the physical and the theoretical and the imaginary are not separable, but are brought together through the medium of the embodied social subject who mediates both the material and the conceptual" (Dale and Burrell, 2008: 171). I will discuss next the implications of totality for the analysis of organizations, in light of their spatial (and historical) existence.

## Abstraction as a Historical Process

Lefebvre also explains that space in its totality can be engendered by theoretical understanding moving continuously from the past to the present. Every transformation becomes part of total space: "The past leaves its traces; time has its own script. Yet this space is always, now and formerly, a present space, given as an immediate whole, complete with its associations and connections in their actuality" (Lefebvre, 1991: 37). Hence, social space is a historical social product. Lefebvre compared the beginning of history to the natural world, in which things were part of nature and condemned to disappear, giving place to appropriated objects. But if social space is a constructed space, as such it is not neutral, but inherently political. Space carries a political content as the receiver and product of strategies and policies.

In effect, one of the aspects often overlooked in the literature of space and organization regarding Lefebvre's theory is his concern with the role of space as the medium and outcome for the reproduction of the relations of production of the urban space. In his analysis of the political economy of space, he attests the need of the social division of labour to be manifested in space in order to endure materiality: "The study of space offers an answer according to which the social relations of production have a social existence to the extent that they have a spatial existence" (Lefebvre, 1991: 129). As highlighted by Dale and Burrell (2008: 153) Lefebvre's approach to space has particular implications in how the enrolment of power relations in organizations transcends locality and intermingles the organizational production with the production of society. The outcome of the activity of organizations would be the production of space itself, and the analysis of space cannot be separated from the relations of production in society. In his framework for the analysis of space, Lefebvre observes in particular the production of space as a historical process, following spirals of abstraction.

The use of the term 'spiral' denotes a cycle of reproduction, which is not closed in itself but developed over time in the reinforcement of its features. The development from the absolute space of subjectivity to the abstract space of the technocrats is a continuous and advancing alienation from the *lived*. Abstract space is the dominance of the *conceived*, the mental and planned space. The supremacy of modern organizations in transforming society attests to the inexorability of this evolution. This logic of production is alienated from the concrete experience, of the *perceived* material world, in a dual sense: "as well as abstracting from it in their understanding, they then project this understanding back onto the lived level" (Elden, 2004). The concrete and abstract spaces should be linked by the lived space, and it is precisely in the alienation of this, when the conceived ideas are implemented, that space is configured as a realized abstraction. The production of abstract space of capitalism is one of the main messages in Lefebvre's work.

The observation of how the conceived space becomes fetishized in modernity over the other spatial dimensions (lived and perceived spaces) and instrumentally applied for social reproduction coincides with the change in productive activity becoming no longer directed toward the perpetuation of social life, but centred on the reproduction of its abstract space. Lefebvre (1991) highlights the prominence acquired by the dimension of representations of space in modernity with the over appreciation of mental spaces. The scientific space, supported by Cartesian logic, emerged as the only legitimate way of apprehending space, hence ignoring the socially constructed nature of space. This epistemology is intertwined with management knowledge, adopted by the capitalist production, and reproduced globally over time.

In effect, from the very beginning, Lefebvre (1991) showed how the concept of space had evolved from the Aristotelian philosophic tradition to the Cartesian realm of the absolute. Mathematicians claimed the ownership of science, detached from philosophy, and appropriated space and time making them part of their domain. From that, we can infer that as scientific management emerged with modernity (Taylor, 1911), and appropriated many mathematical tools, it is understandable that it has inherited also its particular view of space, void of social relations in an absolute realm of mental space. Critiques of this separation are provided in the literature of space and organization following various distinct approaches, and the work of Lefebvre has been applied with different purposes, ranging from social materiality in the workplace (Conrad and Richter, 2013; Dale, 2005; Wapshott and Mallett, 2012) to the embodiment of performative space of organizations (Beyes and Steyaert, 2011; Munro and Jordan, 2013; Tyler and Cohen, 2010).

The process of abstraction finds its main setting in urban space, where the reproduction of social life is highly dependent on the commodification of space. The production of abstract space is, for Lefebvre, a process unfolding from the relentless evolution of capital accumulation. This genesis is explained in the course of science and technology seeking to master nature, and in this process destroying it. Through the creation and use of tools, space becomes both the product and locus of production, resulting in the creation of urban space, as the replacement of nature: "In short, every social space has a history, one invariably grounded in nature" (Lefebvre, 1991: 110).

In the history of capital accumulation, this domination acquired different forms. That is, for Lefebvre, an inescapable mechanism of evolution in the history of the accumulation of capital, for as long as the rules of transformation are maintained. Lefebvre proposed that in capitalism abstract space was erasing distinctions of local places by reproducing social relations of the dominant space:

> *abstract space took over from historical space, which nevertheless lived on, though gradually losing its force, as substratum or underpinning of representational spaces. . . . The dominant form of space, that of the centres of wealth and power, endeavours to mould the spaces it*

dominates (i.e. peripheral spaces), and it seeks, often by violent means, to reduce the obstacles and resistance it encounters there.

(Lefebvre, 1991: 49)

In that sense, Lefebvre's abstract space should not be dismissed as simply the space that results from capitalism, for it is in how Lefebvre theorizes abstraction that concealed forms of violence become apparent (Wilson, 2014). Claiming to put forward an interpretation of Lefebvre's work "in his own terms rather than incorporating him into a pre-existing paradigm" (2014: 517), Wilson interprets abstract space as a historical and geographical reality which results from a violent process that empties the socio-spatial reality of its content, and subjects it to economic and political abstractions of money and power. Although it proceeds from abstraction, in the history of capital accumulation abstract space realized the domination of material space, which was mediated by the appearance of the urban space. Lefebvre argues that space mediated this domination in two different stages:

Urban space was thus a tool of terrifying power, yet it did not go so far as to destroy nature; it merely enveloped and commandeered it. Only later, in a second spiral of spatial abstraction, would the state take over: the towns and their burghers would then lose not only control of space but also dominion over the forces of production. . . . Surplus value would no longer have to be consumed where it was produced; rather, it would be susceptible of realisation and distribution far away from its source.

(Lefebvre, 1991: 269)

In the development of urban spaces, the urban setting becomes instrumentally organized, allowing surplus value to be consumed away from its production. The history of abstraction is thus linked to the domination of spaces of production, which are displaced to accommodate the preconceived space of technocrats. The central spaces that dominate and subjugate are often represented by organizations that mediate the production of abstract space, and which operate by denying the content of the local space that is dominated, regardless of its previous social content. In that process the symbolic and material violence of abstraction becomes apparent. This will be illustrated next with the case of a security program in the history of the so-called "pacification" of the territories of favelas in Brazil.

## Context and Methodology

Favelas (Brazilian slums) are arguably a perfectly fitting context to demonstrate the attempt to produce abstract space. Slums are a worldwide phenomenon. Various figures show the increasing presence of slums in Rio and in the world (Davis, 2007). But counting slums is not necessarily the same thing as counting favelas, and these territories need to be considered from the perspective of the construction of their space, which is revealing of particular processes of political and economic development. Likewise, 'favela' as a category cannot pretend to encapsulate the various specificities of the local cultural manifestations of hundreds of such territories in the city. Almost every favela started with temporary accommodation, which was then transformed and expanded over time, making favelas different amongst themselves. They are looked at here in terms of their common relations to the formal city, rather than as an attempt to define their essential condition.

Many authors agree that the emergence of favelas is usually related to a combination of factors, such as: the lack of housing in the city, poverty, and the proximity to job opportunities, among others. Figure 12.1 shows a picture of an urbanized favela, where the impression of chaos and confusion is conveyed by the intertwined wires and narrow alley, which almost divert the viewer from the vibrant cultural interventions painted on the walls and the ingenuity applied in the organization of this dense space to accommodate many residents. However, the classical and hegemonic definitions of favelas focus on the precariousness of these spaces, and they continue to be viewed through a prism of absence, in particular because of the lack of formal regulation in these territories.

Such an environment of loose institutional ties, where the regulation of space is unclear, opens the way for drug gangs to establish themselves as a sort of parallel state, for example by controlling access to the territory, creating an apparatus for collectively binding decisions and subjecting the population to their authority. The violent drug traffickers that benefited from the globally developing drug trade were particularly influential in privatising favelas. In a territory of residents largely excluded from consumption, drug traffickers provided for those who had given up struggling by legal and peaceful means, thus aggravating the problem of urban violence, even though these groups continued to represent a very small portion of the population in favelas.

As I have discussed elsewhere (Lacerda, 2015), the association of the identity of the inhabitants of favelas with criminality is to a great extent reinforced by discourses reproduced by the media and the government. Therefore, the definition of favelas is disputed, because the way they are categorized is also part of a political struggle. Over more than a century of existence, the strategies of the government and the elite to deal with favelas in Rio have gone through cycles of rejection/clearance and acceptance/urbanization. Across the century, not only the number of *favelados* in the city was roughly increasing but also their presence and legitimacy has been consolidated. However, the failure of the state in integrating these territories is reflected in the abiding issue of privatization of favelas by criminal organizations, which remains a key controversy. This dispute for the legitimacy of occupation and the right to the city is ultimately political, and is mediated by formal and informal (and illegal) organizations acting in the favelas.

*Figure 12.1* Alleyway in a long established favela, 2013.
Courtesy of Rodolfo Abreu.

In 2008, a rare confluence of political allies occupied the three public offices, allowing a state-level security policy to have the necessary political articulation with federal and municipal levels to launch the *Unidades de Policia Pacificadora* (UPP) (Pacifying Police Units) program. The idea was to militarily occupy the favelas where drug traffickers had existed for a long time, building police stations (the so-called "pacifying units") in these territories. The formal objective of the program was to regain control of the territories terminating the disputes between drug dealers, and in order for that to happen the first stage was the takeover by the elite squad. Therefore, the objective of the program was *not* the end of criminality or drug dealing, but to regain power and reduce the effect of armed disputes on the outside of favelas (Cano, Borges, and Ribeiro, 2012: 19). The real intentions underpinning this manoeuvre have been challenged by several authors (Fleury, 2012; Machado, 2010; Willis and Prado, 2014). This will be discussed here in light of the literature on the social production of the abstract space.

In 2014, I returned to Favela Mucuripe, where I had conducted previous work, in Rio de Janeiro, aiming to investigate the organizing space of that territory. The favela is located on the hillside, as are the vast majority of the other favelas of the city, and is roughly divided in two big communities that share the same hill. The chosen favela was a particularly rich environment because of the high number of organizations dedicated to cultural, educational and political practices. One of the main reasons for this wide range of activities was its privileged location: the favela was embedded in one of the wealthiest zones in the city. This data collection was part of a bigger project aimed at investigating what influences the organization of space of civil society organizations (CSOs) based in favelas, beyond the boundaries of their workplaces.

During fieldwork, I conducted participatory observation of the activities of civil society organizations in the territory, interviewed participants of these organizations and public representatives, and compiled documents. The twenty interviewees had a mixed background in terms of schooling, age, and type of involvement with the local organizing practices. Interviews were enriched by visual techniques: the use of timelines and drawings. The generation of data through visual methods is usually associated with interviews, which gives the opportunity for the participant to explain what is being represented. It triggers the question of how much more data is necessary to understand social relationships (Mason, 2002), and offers different entry points to the analysed data. Participants were invited to be interviewed and engage with two artistic activities: drawing and storytelling. During the first half I invited the participant to draw the favela and describe their drawing, and explain the differences between the communities, the inside and the outside, rules of living in the favela, and the main problems.

The following section presents the process of pacification in Rio focusing in the researched favela, and draws on the data collected during my research fieldwork at Mucuripe, but it includes also reference to previous research and indirect data that was compiled about the governmental programs deployed in this and other favelas.

## The Case of Mucuripe

### *The Historical Space of the Favela*

One of the first questions I asked during each interview was "If I were a Martian that had just landed on Earth, how would you describe the place where you live/work, the favela?."[2] Responses of residents often related to the past:

> *It is a place of survival of a population. A population that was . . . abandoned by the governmental institutions and did not have an option, then they had this empty space, they seized it and made their homes, and then the government came.*
> (Interview with Zico, president of ResidentsOrg)

> *In the past the morro was less dense, right. So there were more courtyards. Nowadays there aren't. Because families grew . . . then what was supposed to be a courtyard was made more and more dense . . . "my son got married," "build it over there," it's the only space we've got.*
> (Interview with Renatinha, member of CultureOrg)

> *A space of livelihood but . . . how can I say that . . . regarding the view of it, I think the favela was much more segregated in the past . . . I see, actually, in the role of some public policies that people talk so much about . . . they brought the favela to the city, to the asfalto.[3]*
> (Interview with Dani, member of EducationOrg)

> *This community [Mucuripe] is divided in three . . . erm, this morro is divided in three communities: Upper Itaperi, Itaperi and Buruti. . . . Itaperi and Buruti still today are not . . . one does not love the other [giggles], unfortunately. I thought this had got better, but it hasn't, for what I can see it hasn't.*
> (Interview with Suelen, member of MusicOrg)

Reinforcing the importance of one's history in the territory, the quotations above also support the relevance of the past for understanding the present. In most interviews, participants responded to the opening question about what the favela is at the present using direct or indirect references to the past, as illustrated above: "they seized it and made their homes," "In the past the *morro* was less dense," "the favela was much more segregated in the past," and "still today one does not love the other." They acknowledged, thus, that their present space was not arbitrary but incorporated the content of past historical systems, which subsisted in the landscape. The past is also present today in the configuration of the territory, and I will illustrate that by examining the differences between the two communities of Mucuripe, which I will call here Itaperi and Buruti.

The power and influence of drug dealers in the territory of Mucuripe has been in place for decades. Ironically, even the integration between the communities of Itaperi and Buruti that the government had recently attempted to promote with works post-UPP (pacification) apparently had a much lesser impact than the forced integration carried out by the drug dealers in the 1990s. Victor explained how the favela was first integrated then:

> *Buruti's had a chief and Itaperi's another one, then they started fighting for the control of the territory . . . until then residents that had nothing to do with the quarrel could not pass from one side to the other. So this feud lasted until 1990, when the so-called Red Command, which was a [large and well known] criminal gang, erm . . . together with a few of Itaperi's residents who had been expelled by one of these chiefs, they came back along with the Red Command and took Itaperi over. And then they also took Buruti over, which was the bordering morro. Thus, that wall had already . . . that concrete wall had been broken by a governmental intervention in nineteen eighty four, but now it was not a concrete wall anymore, that was a wall which was more in people's minds. And with the trafficking . . . only the drug trafficking managed to make these two communities unite.*
> (Interview with Victor, member of CultureOrg).

Another day, at work, Victor told me how he struggled to cross from Itaperi, where he lived, to Buruti, where he studied, before the 1990s integration: "I had to run to school without being seen because people from the two communities could not even cross each other [. . .] mate, today I work side by side with people from Buruti and Itaperi" (Field Notes, 09/04/2014). Victor referred to his colleagues from Itaperi who worked with him at the same organization in the same room, an unlikely arrangement before 1990. As contended by Victor, the separation then came no longer from the actual concrete wall, as there was "a wall which were more in people's minds," and prevented such interactions. The drug dealers who united Mucuripe have held, for at least 25 years, a territorial control of the favela, establishing new internal and external borders and boundaries. It became possible for example to work side by side with people from the other community, which was very unlikely in the past, thanks to the integration promoted by the drug dealers. The presence of drug dealers pervaded every social relation in the favela and their influence was also structured in the social relationships of the favela, which were compliant to the regulation of their own space.

Rules in favelas have fluid and uncertain origins, but they are nonetheless material. Some of these rules refer back to the period of drug dealers'

## 296   Daniel S. Lacerda

autocratic ruling, such as the dress codes. For example, wearing a swimming costume within the favela is not allowed, as a sign of respect for older people (although the beach is close by and wearing a swimming costume in public is a common habit amongst working-class people in Rio). While others emerged as a consequence of the type of territorial occupation, such as the requirement to claim a piece of land: be the first to fence it. Such norms are the result of regulatory frameworks adapting to the technical and informational content of the favela. While the historical construction of favelas made them a peculiar regulatory environment, the clash of the abstraction promoted by the recent event of 'pacification' turned Mucuripe into an even more complex organizing space.

### Intensifying the Spiral of Abstraction at Mucuripe

At the end of 2009, Mucuripe received its unit of the UPP program. This involved the previous military occupation of the territory by the elite squad—which were advertised to have expelled drug dealers and seized weapons—and the later deployment of a permanent unit with nearly 200 police officers specifically trained for the purpose of peacefully occupying favelas, a new model of action for the police in Rio. Authority over the favela would no longer be exercised by drug dealers, but should finally be given to the state.

Whereas the government made a big effort to signify the pacification as the "solution" to the "issues" of favelas, its actual presence in the territory remained very much linked to the apparatus of coercion. After decades of confrontation between the police and drug dealers, the president of the residents association (ResidentsOrg) described to me how he realized for the first time that this was a different approach being conducted by the police, changing the governance of the territory:

> if you had come here, I had to let them [drug dealers] know. I had to say when there was a journalist coming here . . . that sort of thing . . . so I would warn them, anyway, but did not accept it, I moaned over those things. Then the UPP came . . . I saw that it had come to stay with two hundred-odd men. . . . then after one week the captain went there and told me 'Zico, I came here with all this information about you, what I am going to do with you is this: I brought you my telephone number, I would like yours and I do not want any information from you, I came from the intelligence service, I know everything that happens here . . . so it's all set, if you need anything' . . . I saw that he really had come to stay.
>
> (Interview with Zico, president of ResidentsOrg)

Zico continued explaining the consequences of this change, which started a new form of governance in Mucuripe: "I had to decide whom I would obey; I told them [traffickers] that now I would only talk to the government."

This change of governance had a great impact on local organizations. However, at first this was not a negotiated process. As described above, the UPP captain addressed the president of the residents' association invested with formal authority and informed him of the new governance rather than consulting about any change: "I do not want any information from you . . . it's all set."

Zico knew that both parties exercised their domination with violence, and to him apparently it was a matter of deciding whom to obey. But as certainly known also by Zico, the actual control of the territory needed more than violence to be effective.

*Elements of Abstract Social Space*

The effect caused by the impressive initial occupation by the state resounded everywhere. Soon after the pacification of the first favelas, Rio newspapers were praising the program. The role of mass media in Rio was strong and apparently compelling in the accreditation of the success of UPPs. Among the newspaper stories I compiled regarding them, many effusively celebrated the program, as can be seen from the headlines: "Benefits way beyond the Hills";[4] "On Rocinha Occupation, the redemption of São Conrado [area];"[5] "Pacification in Rio will work as the model for national pledge."[6] This propaganda was spread over the city, and even residents reinforced this message at times.

Whereas the government made a big effort to signify the pacification as the "solution" to the "issues" of favelas, its actual presence in the territory remained very much linked to the apparatus of coercion. However, the police realized a change of representation was needed, and among this war of information they initially tried to present a new image to the residents. One of the strategies adopted by the UPP was to invite the local population for an open meeting on a regular basis to talk about the issues and build bridges with the community, who had always seen the police as hostile.

> *When the UPP got in, in 2009, they would organise a rapprochement meeting, in which we . . . every 15 days . . . we would convey to them all the difficulties we had. And we didn't want to know if UPP was a public security thing, we would throw all that shit that happened here . . . waste collection issues, neighbour quarrels, whatever problem we would get there and complain about it all [giggles]. Fuck, the state had been absent, in a way, we would report to drug dealers before. But since the state came in being 'social' and all that . . . we demanded all the shit that had not been addressed. Because before we would say to the drug dealers 'there is no water supply here', and the guy would say, "There is no water, what can I do? Would you like some money to buy medicines?"*

> (Interview with Victor, member of CultureOrg)

As Victor sharply pointed out, aside from the autocratic ruling, the drug dealers had previously to some extent played the role of the state in the territory before, providing even the means for a certain level of social wellbeing (such as medicines and financial support). However, they were not the state, and could not deliver many of the public services that citizens would expect in the city (e.g. "there is no water supply here"). Whereas the drug dealers could only do charity, the advertised presence of the state after UPP—the first stable and significant official presence until then—was perceived to mean that they would finally receive the same treatment as residents of any other part of the city, as Victor said: "we demanded all the shit that had not been addressed." Although the new meetings represented a positive channel of communication with the community leaders and representatives, the actual performance of state institutions in the territory still resembled very much that of the drug dealers.

It should be noted that, unlike other favelas in poorer areas, Mucuripe did have public services available to the population (such as a school, health unit, and street lighting), but the quality and coverage of such services were still way below what was needed, much unlike the surrounding wealthy neighbourhood. After the take over from the state, a few public representatives from various secretariats were deployed at Mucuripe. However, none of them could be compared to the presence of the police force, composed of nearly 200 officers in the territory—18 officers to 1,000 habitants, almost eight times more than the city's average, see Cano, Borges, and Ribeiro (2012: 170)—which suggested that the dominant spatial practice of the state was still violence and coercion.

In addition, after the pacification, there was a considerable increase in the number of cultural initiatives coming from the outside. During the events of the Rio+20 world summit, in June 2012, cultural presentations were organized inside Mucuripe to take the "spirit" of the conference into the favelas—as was being done at the same time in four other pacified favelas. Among the fourteen different attractions there were groups of *capoeira*, samba, *cultura nordestina*, hall dancing, poetry and even jazz and classical music, which are two very alien styles to poor communities in Brazil. No funk presentation was invited. This is surprising, since the culture of favelas is traditionally related to funk music. However, funk music has also been associated with drug cartels, and their lyrics would exalt the power of traffickers and incite violence. Funk fests were then forbidden in pacified communities, which generated many complaints by inhabitants who challenged the prohibition of their traditional funk parties.

Finally, with the improved security in the territory of favelas many market services started being offered in the 'pacified' territories. In effect, the UPPs considerably expanded the space of capital accumulation, by providing retail businesses access to the favelas' internal market, and opportunities to external contractors sponsored by the state to provide services in the new territories. The number of small businesses registered in the favelas with UPPs, for example, increased by 56% in the first year of the program, as they were accessing new credit in the financial market.[7] Even retailers' stock share prices rose thanks to the creation of new markets in the favelas, which included 280,000 new potential consumers.[8] The selective integration of these territories to the formal city also allowed energy companies to charge energy bills in many houses that had had illegal connections to the power network before.

This developed interest of businesses in favelas is unsurprising when we learn the extent of the mutual collaboration of the program: the initial funding for the UPP program, for example, was donated by a group of private companies (including Coca-Cola and Bradesco Bank),[9] jointly funding of more than USD 10 million per year for the maintenance of UPPs. The spaces of capital largely benefited from the framework of legality brought to favelas by pacification, which reduced criminality outside their territories and opened up the way for a larger market within.

## Discussion

As presented in the examples above, the struggle of the state in the favela was more than the attempt to control occupation and access to the territory; it was also an attempt to take over control from drug dealers to craft a different social space. Correspondingly, the previous control of the territory by drug dealers cannot be disassociated from the previous lack of control by the State. And for that reason the influence of the drug dealers over the territory would go, thus, beyond the drug trade. As a matter of fact, drug cartels had a well-established economic, political and ideological system. The mechanisms of institutional regulation used by the drug dealers were also vast. State services, such as social support and healthcare funding, which were considerably limited in the favela, were most of the time provided by the traffickers who would hinder even more the entrance of other market services as well. The influence of drug dealing in the enactment and dissolution of boundaries between communities, for example, demonstrate that it was embedded in the social space of the favela, as it had been over decades of influence shaping its historical space.

Disregarding the reasons that led to the emergence of drug dealers, or the particularities of the local violence founded on the absence of the state, the program of pacification was implemented not in terms of an objective proposal of services to the local population, but operated negatively by denying the content of the dominated territory. In that sense, it relates to abstract space. The state performed the direct violent action needed by the production of abstract space (Lefebvre, 1991: 280), based on the coercion of the military to support further actions of symbolic and more concealed violence enacted with the instrumental use of space. In the case of favelas, this violence can be explained in terms of the three different domains of: conceived (media reports), perceived (police occupation) and lived (cultural interventions) social space.

The propaganda illustrated in the quoted newspapers, was an important tactic for controlling the arena of representation of space. Controlling the legitimate *representations of space* (conceived space) was one of the main instruments used by the state. Instead of properly involving local civil society organizations to unify social forces, the government of Rio relied initially only on the power of propaganda and mass media, and lacked much of the necessary initiatives involving civil society, in order to assure the engagement of local residents in the construction of new representations of space. In other words, rather than territorialize the intended transformation, they reproduced inside and outside these territories their own representation of space—a favela pacified by the police—which had been conceived away from the everyday life of individuals.

In terms of perceived space, it should be noted that, because it is the site of legal and illegal trade, in favelas the control of territory is a very valuable resource. The domain of the territory enables one to decide which *spatial practices* (perceived space) can be performed, and thus means owning symbolic capital for concessions. My data suggests that the impact of the pacification on Mucuripe's residents is undisputed: most timelines had the implementation of the UPP unit as a significant event in the territory, and *UPP* was the fifth most cited term in every interview after *community*, *people*, *houses* and *favela*, occurring on average once every four minutes. However, this presence begs the question of what kind of practices were changed by the state in the territory. At Mucuripe, the implementation of pacification focused on spatial practices mainly restricted to violence and coercion, as suggested also above by the disproportionate number of police officers. Thus, with rare exceptions the involvement of civil society was to a great extent decided in offices of state representatives outside the favela (in higher 'spatial scales') and reproduced in the territory in hierarchical impositions that did not consider their local organization.

Finally, at Mucuripe the number of cultural interventions from the outside became more common after the pacification. By replacing the previous "content" of space with one that can be "grasped" by abstraction (Lefebvre, 1991: 306), the manipulation of culture plays a major role in the domination of space, as demonstrated by the pervading presence of culture in Lefebvre's articulation between the conscious and unconscious, which is depicted in the *representational space* (lived space), of symbols and images. In Mucuripe, artistic interventions of funk music were widely associated with drug dealers and the violence that would come from favelas. In effect, lived space is largely the space of resistance to planned and regulated space, where symbols marginalized by the central space are embodied (Zhang, Spicer, and Hancock, 2008). This motivated both their marginalization and the crafting of alternative cultural spaces. For that reason, the consumption of culture legitimized by the ruling class—such as the musical rhythms allowed in the Rio+20 summit—produced social signification by reproducing the kind of cultural manifestation that was adherent to the socialization of the formal city, while excluding others.

These three elements analysed above show that a new, abstract space was being crafted at Mucuripe. This is a space that overlooked local spatial practices other than military coercion; one that conveyed its spatial representation hierarchically through the media based on the 'norm' of the formal city; and that controlled which cultural events were allowed, thus censoring undesirable representational spaces. Here, it is important to recall Lefebvre's concept of abstract space as the result of processes of abstraction, and not simply the space of capitalism. The symbolic violence of abstract space is dependent on prior direct forms of violence by the state (Lefebvre, 1991: 280), such as the military occupation in Mucuripe and the resulting changes in representation and practice. The government in Rio operated then as the bearer of abstract space by ignoring any existing substance in the territory of the favela and trying to impose the norms that were necessary for the expansion of capitalist space into the favela. The new conceived relationships tried to empty the existing cultural values and replace them with the violence of a bureaucratic state, such as the reconstitution of what were deemed to be legitimate cultural expressions, forbidding funk fests. This instantiates the definition of state proposed by Lefebvre (1991) as a "realised abstraction" born of violence (p. 280).

The analysis of the data presented above reveals, thus, the connection between the violence of state and the expansion of spaces of capital accumulation. Lefebvre (1991: 281) underlines that the constitution of the state is not independent of the relations of production, and originates from the violence of homogenization that subordinates various aspects of social space—such as culture, education, and legislation. Lefebvre also adds that in the history of capital accumulation the violence of the state cannot be separated from the instrumental space of the ruling class's hegemony. The production of the abstract space is always a violent process, and in modernity this abstraction happens in the balance of the class struggle with the materiality of the state, for "it was here, in the space of accumulation, that the state's 'totalitarian vocation' took shape" (Lefebvre, 1991: 279).

Hence, following the vocation of the state to materialize in space the ruling class's hegemony, I would suggest that the major integration that the UPP program was sponsoring according to the data above was the integration of the favela to the formal market. Businesses now had free access and favela residents could now offer services to outsiders. Favela residents did not acquire the formal status of citizens, but consumers (although to an extent they have always been both); in that lies the opportunity for the production of the abstract space of capitalism (Lefebvre, 1991). Whereas the market operates through an 'invisible hand', the creation of its space depends on the 'visible hand' of the state.

The violent hand of the state was needed in the favela especially to confront a likewise violent organization that was already entwined with the space of the favela: the drug dealers. In other words, in the process of bringing the abstract space of capitalism into the favela, the state had to impose first its violent apparatus over the apparatus of violence of drug dealers.

However, the violence of drug dealers was entangled with the territoriality of the favela already. They produced space while acknowledging the previous layers of territorial formation and restricted their actions to the interests of their local trafficking activity. As a consequence, residents accommodated the pattern of violence promoted by drug dealers in their everyday life, and organized the social fabric according to—or despite—the conditioning features of trafficking (Cavalcanti, 2008). In contrast, police officers treated any resident as a potential suspect, and did not respect the existing social space. One example of this treatment was the killing of a local dancer, shot dead by the police in a frustrated operation in the favela during the period of my fieldwork.

This event, considered by most favela residents as the assassination of one of their own, triggered anger among many people, who stated that they could not differentiate the role of the police in terms of how much more or less violent than the traffickers they were, but in the different way how they imposed their norms with no respect for the local codes that characterized their social space. The police were mediators of an outsider state imposing new places in Mucuripe, by trying to enforce the legal frameworks of the formal city (such as the payment of energy bills). The signification of these new places, erasing local distinctions and reproducing social relations of the dominant space, followed the production of abstract space as described earlier through the enacted changes in social space, which entangle more concealed forms of violence that are operated through the instrumental use of space.

These spatial elements explain and contextualize the actions of various organizations operating in the territory, such NGOs that provide education and social security in the territory, which had to accommodate old and new constraints in space. In effect, many categories of analysis could have been examined here, such as the alternative structure of work, the organising practices that engender materiality, or the partnerships enacted by the cooperation between public and private organizations in the favela. However, had the totality of the produced space not been considered, the analysis of these organizations would have been considerably narrow, as it is arguably the case in many studies of non-profit and also business organizations. As I have argued in this chapter, approaching the totality of space through the analysis of the associated political economy is enlightening for it explains the conditions in which other categories operate. In effect, these categories always exist in space and should not be considered detached from its historical production.

## Concluding Remarks

As I have discussed in this chapter, the power of the drug dealers in favelas, which operated in a spatial scale that could influence the whole territory of the favela, produced an oppressive organization with strong influence in the

The 'Visible Hand' of the State 303

everyday life of individuals and organizations in Mucuripe, but this power only existed in constant dialectical tension with the formal city. The attempt to overrule this power and impose the authority of the state onto the space has created bigger tensions, because it was formed by violent actions that denied the social content of the favela space. The present analysis argued that this process is associated with the spiral of abstraction described by Lefebvre as an inescapable process in the history of capital accumulation. The production of abstract space can only happen through the dissolution of old relations of the historical space, which was attempted in Mucuripe through the program of pacification, implemented by the state to promote a hierarchical intervention in the territory of Mucuripe in order to integrate it into the space of consumption.

It should be noted that I am *not* claiming in any way that the favela had been 'absent' from market relations or state programs before, and that the program of pacification had reversed that agenda, or all the less that favelas had been detached from the urban space. Rather the contrary. Observation in favelas reveals, as it did before, market relations typical of a society organized around capitalist production, and also the presence of the state, although in different ways according to the favela. Even though there was no absolute rupture with what had gone before, there were considerable and material transformations taking place, and such transformations (as observed in Mucuripe during this fieldwork) were put in context considering two important assumptions. First, favelas had a marginal role in the organization of the urban space, mainly as the containment of cheap labour, as the agenda of the state had always reinforced. Second, the development of the urban space as a whole could not happen without the development of favelas, and the case analysed in this chapter showed attempts to promote the abstraction of these spaces oriented to the needs of its centre, i.e. in the outsider spaces of capital accumulation.

From that stance, the chapter shows that the organization of the territory is the outcome of conflicting processes of territorialization, such as the deployment of a massive police force in a favela where basic public services are still not adequately delivered. In that context, the norms that guide the production of space in favelas become disputed and contradictory, denying important features of its historical space, illustrated in this chapter through the three moments of social space: new representations of the favela by means of propaganda, the control of spatial practices with new activities in the territory, and the attempt to control cultural expressions that reflected the space of representations. As a result, I argue that this process should be considered a violent and late attempt to fully integrate favelas in the abstract space of capital accumulation, following the process described by Lefebvre. The historical space of favela subsisted entangled with the territoriality of the drug dealers at Mucuripe.

This case is ontologically attached to the concept of totality, which is often left aside in the literature of space and organization. For this reason,

304    *Daniel S. Lacerda*

this analysis contributes to organization studies in highlighting the importance of analysing the relations between organizations with their surrounding space: understanding how historical transformations affect the present organizational space; how contemporary events construct and organize space across organizations; and how organizations mediate the construction of the territory by reproducing or resisting the abstraction of their space. Scholars of organization can relate, for example, the problematic imposition of abstract managerial knowledge to marginal spaces (Cooke, 2006; Dar, 2007; Dar and Cooke, 2008; Mir, Mir, and Srinivas, 2004; Srinivas, 2008) to the inescapable violence of abstraction produced by the expansion of spaces of capital accumulation. These elements of the relation between organizations and their surroundings might be particularly important for civil society organizations, since these organizations generally do not follow abstract modes of rationality based only on efficiency and financial outcome.

## Notes

1 The names of all territories, organizations and persons were changed to preserve the informants' anonymity
2 In the data, residents refer to the favela using various names: '*comunidade*' (community), '*morro*' (hill), '*favela*' (slum).
3 The duality *morro* (hill) vs. *aslfalto* (road) is how favela residents have for a long time differentiated the favela from the formal city. This dichotomy was largely incorporated by the society of Rio, and became well known to refer to this separation across the city.
4 O Globo. Benefícios muito além dos morros: UPP agrada também a moradores do asfalto e valoriza imóveis. *O Globo*, 2010, March 13: 26.
5 Ritto, C., November 8. Na ocupação da Rocinha, a redenção de São Conrado. *Veja*, retrieved from http://veja.abril.com.br/noticia/brasil/na-ocupacao-da-rocinha-a-redencao-de-sao-conrado.
6 Dantas, P. Pacificação no RJ servirá de exemplo para pacto nacional. *Agencia Estado*, 2011, February 23, retrieved from www.estadao.com.br/noticias/geral,pacificacao-no-rj-servira-de-exemplo-para-pacto-nacional,683554,0.htm.
7 O Dia, 'Rio: abertura de empresas sobe 56% em favelas com UPPs'. O Dia, 2010, March, 20. Retrieved from http://noticias.terra.com.br/brasil/policia/rio-abertura-de-empresas-sobe-56-em-favelas-com-upps,a9291054a250b310Vgn CLD200000bbcceb0aRCRD.html
8 Biller, D., & Petroff, K., Favelas ajudam a puxar desempenho de varejistas na bolsa. Revista Exame, 2012, December 3. Retrieved from http://exame.abril.com.br/mercados/noticias/favelas-ajudam-a-puxar-desempenho-de-varejistas-na-bolsa.
9 Lobato, Elvira; Antunes, Claudia, 'Empresas ajudam a financiar pacificação'. Folha de São Paulo, 2010, November, 28. Retrieved from http://www1.folha.uol.com.br/fsp/cotidian/ff2811201040.htm

## References

Althusser, L. and Balibar, É. (1970). *Reading Capital*. Paris: New Left Books.
Baldry, C. (1999). Space—The final frontier. *Sociology*, 33(3), 535–553. Retrieved from https://doi.org/10.1177/S0038038599000346

Beyes, T. and Steyaert, C. (2011). Spacing organization: Non-representational theory and performing organizational space. *Organization*, 19(1), 45–61. Retrieved from https://doi.org/10.1177/1350508411401946

Cano, I., Borges, D. and Ribeiro, E. (2012). *"Os Donos do Morro"*: *Uma análise exploratória do impacto das Unidades de Polícia Pacificadora (UPPs) no Rio de Janeiro*. Rio de Janeiro: Fórum Brasileiro de Segurança Pública.

Cavalcanti, M. (2008). Tiroteios, legibilidade e espaço urbano: Notas etnográficas de uma favela carioca. *Dilemas*, 1, 35–59.

Conrad, L. and Richter, N. (2013). Materiality at work: A note on desks. *Ephemera: Theory & Politics in Organization*, 13(1), 117–136. Retrieved from www.ephem erajournal.org/sites/default/files/13-1conradrichter.pdf

Cooke, B. (2006). The cold war origin of action research as managerialist cooptation. *Human Relations*, 59(5), 665–693. Retrieved from https://doi.org/10. 1177/0018726706066176

Dale, K. (2005). Building a social materiality: Spatial and embodied politics in organizational control. *Organization*, 12(5), 649–678. Retrieved from https://doi. org/10.1177/1350508405055940

Dale, K. and Burrell, G. (2008). *The Spaces of Organisation and the Organisation of Space: Power, Identity and Materiality at Work*. New York: Palgrave Macmillan.

Dar, S. (2007). Negotiating autonomy: Organising identities in NGOs. *Journal of Health Management*, 9(2), 161–188. Retrieved from https://doi.org/10.1177/ 097206340700900202

Dar, S. and Cooke, B. (2008). *The New Development Management: Critiquing the Dual Modernization*. London: Zed Books.

Davis, M. (2007). *Planet of Slums*. New York: Verso.

Elden, S. (2004). *Understanding Henri Lefebvre—Theory and the Possible*. London and New York: Continuum.

Fleming, P. and Spicer, A. (2008). Beyond power and resistance: New approaches to organizational politics. *Management Communication Quarterly*, 21(3), 301–309. Retrieved from https://doi.org/10.1177/0893318907309928

Fleury, S. (2012). Militarização do social como estratégia de integração: o caso da UPP do Santa Marta. *Sociologias*, 14(30), 194–222. Retrieved from https://doi. org/10.1590/S1517-45222012000200007

Hancock, P. and Spicer, A. (2011). Academic architecture and the constitution of the new model worker. *Culture and Organization*, 17(2), 91–105. Retrieved from https://doi.org/10.1080/14759551.2011.544885

Hirst, A. and Humphreys, M. (2013). Putting power in its place: The centrality of edgelands. *Organization Studies*, 34(10), 1505–1527. Retrieved from https://doi. org/10.1177/0170840613495330

Kornberger, M. and Clegg, S. R. (2003). Reflections on space, structure and their impact on organisations. *European Spatial Research and Policy*, 10(2).

Kornberger, M. and Clegg, S. R. (2004). Bringing space back in: Organizing the generative building. *Organization Studies*, 25(7), 1095–1114. Retrieved from https:// doi.org/10.1177/0170840604046312

Lacerda, D. S. (2015). Rio de Janeiro and the divided state: Analysing the political discourse on favelas. *Discourse & Society*, 26(1), 74–94. Retrieved from https:// doi.org/10.1177/0957926514541346

Lacerda, D. S. (2016). The production of spatial hegemony as statecraft: An attempted passive revolution in the favelas of Rio. *Third World Quarterly*, 37(6), 1–19. Retrieved from https://doi.org/10.1080/01436597.2015.1109437

306    *Daniel S. Lacerda*

Lefebvre, H. (1991). *The Production of Space*. Oxford: Blackwell.

Machado, L. A. (2010). Afinal, qual é a das UPPS? *Observatório Das Metrópoles*, 1–7.

Maréchal, G., Linstead, S. and Munro, I. (2013). The territorial organization: History, divergence and possibilities. *Culture and Organization*, 19(3), 185–208. Retrieved from https://doi.org/10.1080/14759551.2013.812703

Mason, J. (2002). *Qualitative Researching* (2nd ed.). London: Sage.

Mir, R., Mir, A. and Srinivas, N. (2004). Managerial knowledge as property: The role of universities. *Organization Management Journal*, 1(October 2012), 37–41. Retrieved from https://doi.org/10.1057/omj.2004.23

Munro, I. and Jordan, S. (2013). "Living Space" at the Edinburgh festival fringe: Spatial tactics and the politics of smooth space. *Human Relations*, 66(11), 1497–1520. Retrieved from https://doi.org/10.1177/0018726713480411

Srinivas, N. (2008). Managerialism and NGO Advocacy: Handloom weavers in India. In S. Dar and B. Cooke (Eds.), *The New Development Management* (pp. 74–90). London: Zed Books.

Taylor, F. (1911). *The Principles of Scientific Management* (Vol. 7). New York: Harper.

Tyler, M. and Cohen, L. (2010). Spaces that matter: Gender performativity and organizational space. *Organization Studies*, 31(2), 175–198. Retrieved from https://doi.org/10.1177/0170840609357381

Wapshott, R. and Mallett, O. (2012). The spatial implications of homeworking : A Lefebvrian approach to the rewards and challenges of home-based work. *Organization*, 19(1), 63–79. Retrieved from https://doi.org/10.1177/1350508411405376

Watkins, C. (2005). Representations of space, spatial practices and spaces of representation: An application of Lefebvre's spatial triad. *Culture and Organization*, 11(February 2015), 209–220. Retrieved from https://doi.org/10.1080/14759550500203318

Willis, G. D. and Prado, M. M. (2014). Process and pattern in institutional reforms: A case study of the police pacifying units (UPPs) in Brazil. *World Development*, 64, 232–242. Retrieved from https://doi.org/10.1016/j.worlddev.2014.06.006

Wilson, J. (2014). The violence of abstract space: Contested regional developments in Southern Mexico. *International Journal of Urban and Regional Research*, 38(2), 516–538. Retrieved from https://doi.org/10.1111/1468-2427.12023

Zhang, Z. (2006). What is lived space? *Ephemera*, 6(2), 219–223.

Zhang, Z., Spicer, A. and Hancock, P. (2008). Hyper-organizational space in the work of J. G. Ballard. *Organization*, 15(6), 889–910. Retrieved from https://doi.org/10.1177/1350508408095819

# 13 Future Directions
## Henri Lefebvre and Spatial Organization

*Sytze F. Kingma, Karen Dale,*
*and Varda Wasserman*

## Beyond "Turn-Thinking"

This final chapter does not attempt to draw conclusions from the previous chapters but rather seeks to transcend the volume by offering some reflections on the appropriation of Lefebvre's work in organization studies and offering some suggestions for future research. Lefebvre writes "Man does not live by words alone; all 'subjects' are situated in a space in which they must either recognize themselves or lose themselves, a space which they may both enjoy and modify" (Lefebvre, 1991 [1974]: 35). In this sentence, Lefebvre makes poignantly clear both why it is important to study space and how he understands the ambiguous relationship humans, social actors and scholars alike have with space. This understanding is particularly relevant for the field of organization studies, where over the past decade spatial relations, and to some extent also the work of Lefebvre, assumed a new relevance. First, humans do indeed not 'live by words alone', but looking at the state of organization studies in the beginning of the 21st century it almost seemed as if words were all that mattered (Carlile et al., 2013). Partly related to the popularity of social constructivist approaches, organization studies were dominated by theories and methods which prioritized the role of language, cognitions, narratives, motives, discourses and legitimations. Maybe the neglect of space had to do with the false and exclusive association of space with positivist and deterministic approaches. However, space can very well be understood and studied in a constructivist way, as Lefebvre makes clear in the second part of the abovementioned quote. People cannot do without space—in Lefebvre's view, 'subjects' are part and parcel of spatial relations—but they have the capacity to change space, which is at the same time constraining and enabling their behaviour. As this volume illustrates in many ways, Lefebvre's work is concerned with how people produce a 'social space' in and through their actions, and how space can be both a product of social relations and effective in producing social relations, including organizations. As such, we believe that Lefebvre's work on space connects very well with mainstream developments in organization studies.

However, we would argue against a limited appropriation of Lefebvre by organization studies in view of his treatment of space. Some scholars talk about a 'materiality-turn' or 'spatial-turn' in organization studies, and associate Lefebvre with this. The risk here is that we both reproduce false distinctions between the spatial and the social, or, for that matter, the organizational—and thus misunderstand the significance of space itself—and miss the significance and the potential of Lefebvre's approach, which, as major interpreters of Lefebvre's work are quick to acknowledge (Shields, 1999; Elden, 2004; Merrifield, 2006), extends beyond space. As Shields puts it: 'Against the tendency of theorizing space in terms of its own codes and logic, what is necessary, argues Lefebvre, is an approach that seeks to understand the *dialectical* interaction between spatial arrangements and social organization itself' (Shields, 1999: 157). With this volume, we would like to advocate Lefebvre's work as a source of inspiration of much greater relevance for organization studies. Against the 'turn-thinking' we would argue for space as an integrated and integrating component in the full complexity of organizational dynamics and developments. This objective is not restricted to, but includes a critique of contemporary organization studies from the perspective of space, always in view of elaborating our understanding of organizations in and through space. We, the editors, believe that such an understanding of organizations is still lacking, and that Lefebvre's work can offer tools for working towards this objective, and, above all, serve as a source of inspiration which goes beyond a narrow interest in space. In analogy with Lefebvre's idea that 'every society' and indeed 'every mode of production' 'produces a space, its own space' (Lefebvre, 1991 [1974]: 31, 46), we suggest that each organization and mode of organizing produces its own space. Developing Lefebvrian organization studies, therefore, would have 'spatial organization' as the object and outcome of analyses. Spatial organization should not be confused with the spatial part of organizations (i.e. the organization of space) but addresses the full realization of organization processes as conceived from spatial perspectives. In spatial organization studies, space not only serves as an object of research but also constitutes a method for analysing organization processes.

To prevent misunderstanding, we do not suggest that this volume already offers an overview of such an innovative Lefebvrian approach to organization. We see this volume as a first attempt to bring together a number of scholars and studies who engage with Lefebvre in a comparable spirit and offer some aspects, thoughts, insights and possible directions for advancing truly spatially informed organization studies. In this sense, this volume might be considered part of the emergence of spatial organization studies rather than a result or an end product of it. In short, with this volume, one can start to envision the first outlines of a project and an image of what spatial organization studies might look like. For Lefebvre, space is a social and political product, and the production of space simultaneously (re)produces analytically distinct social structures concerning power, class, knowledge, symbols, identities, values, and legitimations. Historically, the production of space generates concrete social formations such as countrysides, households, villages, churches, cities, states and technologically advanced organizations. In this respect, urbanism was for Lefebvre—in his high days (the 1960–70s)—the culmination of history. For him, this urbanism represented an ideological structure, a 'capitalism of organization': 'Urbanism organizes a sector that appears to be free and accessible, open to rational activity: inhabited space' (Lefebvre, 2003 [1970]: 164). Although Lefebvre clearly cannot be regarded as an organization scholar, there is much of relevance about organizations and organization processes in Lefebvre's work. But then again, spatial organization studies use Lefebvre's work as a source of inspiration, rather than trying to carve specific organizational insights out of his work. For this purpose, analogies are more important than examples.

This final chapter proceeds as follows. We will not go back in detail to the chapters and assess the many significant contributions of each to the study of spatial organization. Instead, we start with an abstract ideal type, based on Lefebvre's work and the discussions about it, of what spatial organization studies are (or should) roughly (be) about. In this regard, this chapter can be regarded as a manifesto for rather than an account of Lefebvrian organization studies. We see the current volume merely as an extension and moderate next step in the appropriation of Lefebvre's work. Subsequently, we give some considerations and suggestions for future directions in the uses of Lefebvre's work and the development of spatial organization studies.

## Approaching Spatial Organization (in ten clues)

How can we recognize and analyse spatial organization? In this section we offer an ideal typical (abstract) sketch of ten basic characteristics of spatial organization and how they can be analysed.

One. Spatial organization is not about space; at least, not space as commonsensically distinguished from place, time, technology, artifacts and the body. For Lefebvre, space is all this together. Lefebvre is concerned with the substance, the materiality of human existence, including our relationship with nature. Questions of space and time and of the social/organizational always go together. Spatial organization therefore should be addressed in the broadest possible terms as referring to spatio-temporal organizational relations.

Two. Spatial organization is produced in and through time. Lefebvrian analyses are therefore dynamic, focus on processes of becoming and change, and are open ended (never teleological). Spatial organization is always a historical achievement. Time and space are conceptually connected in rhythm-analysis. These rhythms are multiple and natural (environmental and biological) as well as social. The temporal dimension includes the future. Lefebvre's method is 'regressive-progressive', meaning that analyses not only address the historical backgrounds of certain situations, moments, events, crises and revolutions, but also the future expectations, possibilities, risks, ambitions, hopes, fears and dreams of those involved. In this sense, spatial organization contains a utopian element.

Three. Spatial organization results from the interaction between three different spatial perspectives: the conceived space (representations), the perceived space (concrete practice) and the lived space (representational). These perspectives are historically produced ways of knowing space, and always exist together and constitute each other in a dialectical way. The spatial perspectives can be distinguished analytically but spatial organization can never be reduced to one of the perspectives.

Four. The three perspectives of spatial organization always operate together, but the relative importance is context-dependent and may vary over time. Ideally, the perspectives match, but in practice there often is imbalance between the three. Coherence is possible only under 'favourable circumstances, when a common language, a consensus and a code can be established' (Lefebvre, 1991 [1974]: 40). One perspective may dominate the others, dependent on the situation. This also implies that actual coherence is an empirical rather than a theoretical issue.

Five. Societies and spatial organization evolve in processes and cycles of abstraction. Capitalist relations of production and urban society are important examples, as are the clock regarding time and geographical coordinates regarding space. Abstract representations of organizations have a dominating and homogenizing effect and are often controversial and in conflict with the organization of concrete everyday life. In this respect Lefebvrian analyses are particularly sensitive to power relations, alienation, difference and resistance. Lefebvre even developed the idea of a 'right to difference' and a 'right to the city'; the latter might translate into a 'right to the organization', meaning that the production of the organization should not be restricted to the dominant views and to those in leading positions. The rights of workers are an obvious example (but there are more 'stakeholders').

Six. The economic mode of production is a crucial condition and logic of spatial organization, but not the only one. Politics and the state, and culture and everyday life are equally important. In particular, spontaneity and imagination should not be ruled out. Spatial organization is not merely produced by economic, political and cultural relations but is, in a dialectical way, also constitutive for these relations. In fact, space combines and generates these relations.

Seven. Spatial organization and its analysis is complex and plural. There are multiple times, spaces, rhythms and differentiated social formations. A Lefebvrian approach is also multi- or transdisciplinary. Of particular relevance is the combination of phenomenological (experience) and semiological (structure) analyses. These extremes are combined in Lefebvre's concept of the lived space.

Eight. The experience, and therefore also the analysis, of spatial organization starts with the body. For Lefebvre the body is a 'spatial body', which emerges from space and is constitutive of spatial relations. Social relations are always spatialized and embodied. The body is a 'bundle of rhythms' and confronts the biological in the course of everyday life with the social/organizational. The body is therefore also an important instrument for sensing spatial organization.

Nine. The proper object of analysis of spatial organization is the complete or total organization. This does not mean that every aspect and detail of organizations should be studied or discussed. It means that the analysis should address the full spectrum of the various constitutive layers; the concrete (private) level of everyday life, the (intermediary) level of social formations—'realized abstractions'—and the abstract level of (global) political, economical and cultural structures. In this sense spatial organization studies are holistic.

Ten. The analysis of spatial organization evolves in three stages, starting with detailed descriptions, followed by a regressive phase searching for historic conditions and explanations for current situations, and a progressive, future oriented, phase focusing on (unintended) consequences, contingencies, motives and decision-making. Lefebvre insists on the need for detailed empirical analyses and the recognition of the contingent and constitutive role (scientific) knowledge plays in social formations. Lefebvrian analyses are therefore also critical, in the sense that they expose contradictions and hidden interests, raise awareness, and are suspicious of rationalized knowledge (technocracy). Lefebvrian analyses do not merely want to explain and interpret but also have an emancipatory intent.

Together these clues set a standard of expectation for Lefebvrian organization studies. They can also be perceived as an ultimate goal for such studies. As all ideal-types they are of course never realized in practice, they can serve only as guidelines and may be approximated. They can also be used for the critical assessment of organization studies, in order to get an idea of the extent to which particular studies comply with the basics of spatial organization studies. In the following section, we offer some reflections on the appropriation of Lefebvre's work and suggest some future directions for research.

## Future Directions: A Critique of the Present?

Which topics and suggestions do we have for future research on spatial organization, in further developing a Lefebvrian approach? This question is difficult to answer because the options are almost infinite. On the one hand, the scope of Lefebvre's work is very extensive and only little of it has been put to use. In this respect, this volume reveals rather than fills the gaps in the appropriation of Lefebvre's work in organization studies. Lefebvre's spatial triad obviously is the major contribution which has so far been taken up in organization studies, and even in this respect we should immediately wonder whether this triad, and the dialectics behind it, are always properly understood and applied (Beyes and Steyaert, 2012; Zhang and Spicer, 2014). A first suggestion for organization studies would thus be to practice some self-critique on the current uses of Lefebvre and start further building spatial organization studies from a close(er) (re-)reading of Lefebvre's original works. This reading, in our view, can very well be combined with a systematic comparison between Lefebvre's work and current mainstream literatures, such as illustrated in the chapter by Gili Drori and Briana Preminger.

This volume clearly confirms the dominance of the spatial triad in the appropriation of Lefebvre, but at the same time, and often in combination with the triad, some interesting windows on other aspects of Lefebvre's work are opened. This is especially the case with the focus on micro aspects of Lefebvre's work concerning everyday life, the spatial body and rhythm-analysis, as illustrated in the chapters by Sarah Warnes, Tuomo Peltonen and Perttu Salovaara, Harriet Shortt, Louise Nash and Zhongyuan Zhang. Similarly, the time dimension (in combination with space) is also extremely important—as questions of space should always go together with questions of time—as particularly illustrated in the chapters by Timon Beyes, Daniel Lacerda and Inbal Ofer. The chapters by Lacerda, Ofer, Nash and Zhang further open windows for connecting Lefebvre's work with societal scale levels beyond the confines of organizational buildings, such as the city and the state. Finally, Lefebvre's work also has potential for having a fresh look at more specific organizational processes concerning for instance leadership, power, and organizational design, as illustrated in the chapters by Perttu Salovaara and Arja Ropo and by Fabio Petani and Jeanne Mengis.

On the other hand, the relevance of Lefebvre's work goes beyond particular organization processes, such as those regarding space. In this respect, we have advocated Lefebvre's work for developing a novel and systematic approach to organization studies, particularly in view of the recent interest in (socio)materiality in organization studies. In this approach—briefly addressed with the concept of 'spatial organization'—space not merely figures as an object of research, but rather figures as an analytical perspective on organization processes. For this approach we started this final chapter with an ideal-type with ten basic guidelines. It is probably because of the strength, depth and coherence of Lefebvre's overall approach that his work remains relevant today. In relation to its specific content much of Lefebvre's work may at face value perhaps be considered as outdated, but in drawing upon its approach and its application in concrete historical settings and processes, contemporary organization studies may benefit greatly. As Elden (2003: xix) remarks in his introduction to Lefebvre's *Key Writings*: 'despite the age of some of his works, he acts almost as a prehistorian of contemporary developments, with his insights into technology, globalization, popular protest and post-ideological politics open to all manner of possible uses.' In this respect, we hold Lefebvre's work extremely relevant for developing spatial organization studies.

This is also because of Lefebvre's engagement with the present—his present. Although Lefebvre's work goes in many spatial, historical and philosophical directions, this is always in view of furthering the understanding of contemporary knowledge and developments. Much of his work should be understood as contributing to a critical understanding of the present, and is often explicitly addressed as such, most prominently in *Critique of Everyday Life* (Lefebvre, 2014 [1947, 1961, 1981]); this work was designed to be 'a radical questioning of the everyday in contemporary society: industrial and technological society, and so-called "consumer" society' (Lefebvre, 2003 [1981]: 106) (cf. Elden, 2004: 115–117). Therefore, we suggest that in order to derive topics and directions from Lefebvre's work we should, paradoxically, move away from his work and start with the contemporary era, and problematize the present—our present—following Lefebvre's approach.

From a consideration of the present we see many topics and issues emerging in line with Lefebvre's interests. Many of the rapid recent changes (including the rapidity of change in Zygmunt Bauman's (2000) 'liquid modernity') would probably be beyond Lefebvre's wildest dreams (including issues of social emancipation and differentiation, virtual reality, neoliberalism, managerialism, globalization, and climate change), but also would have fascinated him. As editors we find a range of organizational issues Lefebvre's approach might be helpful in furthering the knowledge about. We recall the significance of information technology, the network enterprise and the network society, as explored by Castells (1996; 2001). Lefebvre regarded technology as the 'lord and master' of modernity. In his view the driving force of technology, and the 'related problem of controlling technology', would only continue to be of key importance in postmodernity (Lefebvre, 2014 [1947, 1961, 1981]: 724). One key issue of concern would of course be the way digital technologies are involved in reorganizing spatial relations (Thrift, 2005), including for instance the emergence of new kinds of flexible workspaces (Kingma, 2016). In an insightful discussion, Lefebvre already foresees a computerized society dominated by information networks at the global level, with 'the risk of a global monopoly of information in a transnational system'(Lefebvre, 2014 [1947, 1961, 1981]: 814). At the same time, however, he is careful to analyse and criticize the ideology of this system promoted by technocrats who sketch a technological utopia which is transparent and inevitable. Today it is not difficult to confirm this analysis: to see how many politicians, officials, managers and consultants reproduce this ideology in their technologically deterministic legitimations of ICT-projects, and to reveal the ideological nature of these accounts, given the huge problems with many of these projects, which in the end often do not produce what is promised.

Further, already mentioned as a promising direction is the significance of everyday life to organizational analysis. This direction—and the great value of Lefebvre's take on this—has recently been stressed by Courpasson (2017), who points at the importance of often neglected and apparently obvious and banal aspects of work. As examples Courpasson (2017) mentions, the 'appropriation of time and space' by employees, for instance at lunch breaks; the so-called 'useless activities' at work such as smoking and nail polishing; the 're-humanizing' friendship relations at work; and 'inhabiting' the company with subversive activities and meaningful 'dwelling places' such as analysed by Shortt (2015). As this volume illustrates, much of organization studies' interest in Lefebvre's spatial triad is actually triggered by his cultural concept of 'lived space', which immediately connects with this concern for everyday life.

Another fruitful direction may be found in juxtaposing Lefebvre's work with the abundant literature on gender in organizations. Although Lefebvre did not refer directly to the study of gender in his writings (although he does talk about 'phallic space' and analyses the role of women and men), many geographers working from a feminist perspective have adopted his spatial theory as a multilayered framework, which enables the exploring of power relations between different social groups as they are experienced, materialized and conceptualized (e.g., Simonsen, 2005). Each of the three spaces raises new and intriguing questions as to the role of the space in constructing gender within organizations. For instance, do men and women experience various organizational spaces in the same manner? How are gendered experiences constructed? How is space enacted by men and women? How are gender norms reinforced and perpetuated through spatial arrangements and everyday practices? How is the imagined space constructed and reconstructed in architectural and managerial discourses? What are the rationales as to how space should be divided, who should get more space in the organization, and how offices should be designed and with which colours and materials? Future research in (one of) these directions could expose various ways in which managerial/architectural discourses that are phallocentric (i.e., space allotment is based on hierarchy and/or achievements, disregarding gender differences and division of labour) lead to a unified conceptualization of space and male-centred planning processes that will inevitably perpetuate women's invisibility and inequality. Both Shortt and Nash mention in their chapters in this volume a few such insights that could emerge from using Lefebvre's ideas in organizational studies. Shortt, for instance, argues that eating behaviours can differ according to sexuality and gender, since these are always embodied practices that are not gender-neutral. Since the popularity of open-plan offices is still growing, eating behaviours during the working day become a public practice that is subjected to the surveilling gaze and to social gender norms. Thus, space and eating are inherently part of the construction of a gendered body at work. Expanding beyond Lefebvre's triad, Nash too mentions gendered practices, not only within the organization but also outside, in the business area of the City. Following previous studies by McDowell (1997), who examined the multiple ways in which masculinities and femininities are constructed and performed in the City, Nash too refers to business spaces in the City, but she focuses on gendered rhythmanalysis offering an innovative theoretical perspective for future studies to analyse the gendered experience of work, not only in between the organizational walls, but also outside of them.

Given Lefebvre's interest in 'organized capitalism', 'technocracy', '*autogestion*' (self-management and civil society), and 'nature', Lefebvre's approach and work surely connects with prominent organizational themes regarding New Public Management, managerialism, empowerment, and corporate social responsibility. The significance of, for instance, social movements such as Greenpeace and Anti-globalists resonate with Lefebvre's studies on the Paris Commune (1878) and the Paris student movement (1968) (Lefebvre, 1969 [1968]). Especially Lefebvre's views on the 'abstract space of capitalism', the 'conceived space', and on 'positive knowledge' and 'technocrats' may be very inspiring for analysing the management role in organizational processes. Lefebvre was particularly concerned with technocrats, especially in relation to town planning and architecture, who monopolize decision making and reduce the rest of society to passive performers (Elden, 2004: 144–145). Interestingly, the main critique Lefebvre formulates against this managerial class is not that they reduce planning to a set of technocratic considerations, but that they merely use technocratic considerations to persuade people to accept decisions and situations which in fact are hardly technocratically informed at all!

By extension, given Lefebvre's work on politics and the state, his work could be very inspiring for the study of organizational politics and the political role of organizations. The political aspects of organizations are often masked and mystified by managerial, technocratic considerations. But the political role of organizations becomes ever more prominent and apparent with the growing significance of organizations (Meyer and Bromley, 2013), with the waning power of the state—or perhaps more accurately: the mingling of state and corporate power—the complex connections between large (transnational) corporations and the state, and with the civil society in view of the current significance, and the social as well as political calls for corporate social responsibility. Lefebvre consistently argued against the tendency to neglect the spatial aspects of political processes. Brenner and Elden (2009: 360) quote Lefebvre on this: (organizational) political processes involve 'localities and regions, differences and multiple (conflictual) associations, attached to the soil, to dwelling, the circulation of people and things, in the practical functioning of space'.

Lefebvre's questioning of scale, scaling and territorialization we regard as equally significant for entering new avenues for organization studies. It should be noted that organization studies often limit themselves to what goes on within and between rather narrowly defined confines of organizations, such as the organization's buildings. This restriction may also be observed in most of the contributions to this volume. In this respect Lefebvre's approach connects well with the current interest in developing a process view on organization. This makes it possible to breach the confines and analyse processes which are equally relevant on the level of cities, nations, federations and global communities. Lefebvre was not only interested in the relevance of particular scale levels but also, and even more so, in the question of scaling, i.e. the social production of various scale levels and the territories of social formations. In this respect Lefebvre was interested in the emergence of a world scale of interaction and orientation, which he called 'mondialization'. It goes without saying that this level is now of the utmost importance for contemporary organizations, given the role of the global internet, transnational corporations, transnational institutions, the crisis of the European Union, geopolitical reconfigurations with the rise of 'Asian Tigers' and BRIC-countries, and the undermining of state power by these developments. More than ever 'the worldwide now acts as a third term in relation to the country and the city', as Elden (2004: 232) quotes Lefebvre on this. To the extent that a neglect of global processes of organizing is associated with disciplinary boundaries, we may also be inspired by Lefebvre's multi-disciplinarity, and borrow from and contribute to other disciplines such as social geography (Yeung, 1998) or international political economy (Brenner and Elden, 2009). Here we recall, as mentioned in the introduction to this volume, that the first article to introduce Lefebvre's triad in the field of organization studies was Yeung's (1998) article on 'the Social-spatial Constitution of Business Organizations'. While Yeung's problematization of the strategic, territorial and network dimension—with special reference to the global region of Hong Kong—so far has hardly been taken up in organization studies, this neglect may be re-considered and corrected especially in view of extending organization studies with a Lefebvrian approach on processes of regionalization and transnationalization. We hope that these suggestions and this volume will trigger the reader to wonder about the endless possibilities of Lefebvre's work and approach.

We would like to end with a call to organization scholars in the spirit of Lefebvre's life and work. With this, we submit to Kipfer et al.'s (2008: 300) conclusion, which refers to Merrifield's (2006) passionate remarks about this. For Lefebvre his intellectual work was inseparable from his everyday life and his critical engagement with society. However, today, scientific practice—and this certainly goes for organization studies—is more than ever commodified, 'ever more alienated, increasingly judged by performance principles, by publisher sales projections—or by their ability to *justify* the status quo' (Merrifield, 2006: 119). Possibly absorbed by our hectic everyday rat races of teaching and researching, we should perhaps pause and take a look in the mirror, held up by Merrifield (2006: 120): 'When scholars write about emancipation, about reclaiming space for others, we might start by emancipating ourselves and reclaiming our own work space, giving a nod to disruption rather than cooptation, to real difference rather than cowering conformity.' More than with any reference to space or to Lefebvre, we would be happy if his approach and this volume would in any way contribute to a liberation of the spirit of organization studies.

# References
Bauman, Z. (2000). *Liquid Modernity*. Cambridge: Polity Press.

Beyes, T. and Steyaert, C. (2012). Spacing organization: Non-representational theory and performing organizational space. *Organization*, 19, 45–61.

Brenner, N. and Elden, S. (2009). Henri Lefebvre on state, space, territory. *International Political Sociology*, 353–377.

Carlile, P. R., Nicolini, D., Langley, A., et al. (2013). *How Matter Matters: Objects, Artifacts, and Materiality in Organization Studies*. Oxford: Oxford University Press.

Castells, M. (1996). *The Information Age: Economy, Society and Culture*. Oxford: Blackwell Publishers Ltd.

Castells, M. (2001). *The Internet Galaxy. Reflexions on the Internet, Business and Society*. New York: Oxford University Press.

Courpasson, D. (2017). The politics of everyday. *Organization Studies*, 38, 843–859.

Elden, S. (2004). *Understanding Henri Lefebvre—Theory and the Possible*. London and New York: Continuum.

Elden, S., Lebas, E. and Kofman, E. (2003). *Henri Lefebvre. Key Writings*. London: Bloomsbury.

Kingma, S. F. (2016). The constitution of 'third workspaces' in between the home and the corporate office. *New Technology, Work and Employment*, 31, 176–193.

Kipfer, S., Schmid, C., Goonewardena, K., et al. (2008). Globalizing Lefebvre? In K. Goonewardena, S. Kipfer, R. Milgrom, et al. (Eds.), *Space, Difference, Everyday Life. Reading Henri Lefebvre*. New York: Routledge.

Lefebvre, H. (1969 [1968]). *The Explosion: Marxism and the French Upheaval* (translated by Alfred Ehrenfeld). New York: Modern Reader.

Lefebvre, H. (1991 [1974]). *The Production of Space*. Oxford: Blackwell.

Lefebvre, H. (2003 [1970]). *The Urban Revolution* (translated by R. Bononno. Foreword by N. Smith). Minneapolis, MN: University of Minnesota Press.

Lefebvre, H. (2003 [1981]). The end of modernity? In S. Elden, E. Lebas, and E. Kofman (Eds.), *Henri Lefebvre. Key Writings* (pp. 105–107). London: Bloomsbury.

Lefebvre, H. (2014 [1947, 1961, 1981]). *Critique of Everyday Life. One Volume Edition. Vol I, II, III* (translated by J. Moore and by G. Elliott; prefaces by M. Trebitsch). London: Verso.

McDowell, L. (1997). *Capital Culture: Money, Sex and Power at Work*. Oxford: Blackwell.

Merrifield, A. (2006). *Henri Lefebvre. A Critical Introduction*. New York: Routledge.

Meyer, J. W. and Bromley, P. (2013). The worldwide expansion of 'Organization'. *Sociological Theory*, 31, 366–389.

Shields, R. (1999). *Lefebvre, Love & Struggle. Spatial Dialectics*. London and New York: Routledge.

Shortt, H. (2015). Liminality, space and the importance of 'transitory dwelling places' at work. *Human Relations*, 68, 633–658.

Simonsen, K. (2005). Bodies, sensations, space and time: The contribution from Henri Lefebvre. *Geografiska Annaler*, 87B(1), 1–14.

Thrift, N. (2005). *Knowing Capitalism*. London: Sage.

Yeung, HW-C. (1998). The social-spatial constitution of business organizations: A geographical perspective. *Organization*, 5, 101–128.

Zhang, Z. and Spicer, A. (2014). 'Leader, you first': The everyday production of hierarchical space in a Chinese bureaucracy. *Human Relations*, 47, 739–762.

# Index

Page numbers in *italic* indicate a figure and page numbers in **bold** indicate a table on the corresponding page

Index 321

time *see* also rhythms; also temporality:
accounting of in leadership 80–81;
centrality of to the production
of space 51; "desacralisation" of
137–138; rhythmanalysis 167–169;
rhythms 137–138; walking as
rhythmanalysis *170*
'total body' 133
"totality of instances" 286–287;
abstraction as a historical process
288–290
triad *see* Lefebvre's triad
'turn-thinking' 308–309

unbuilt spaces 47; *see also* waste
'unitary theory' of space 193–194
universities, spacing leadership in
82–92, *84, 85,* **87,** *89, 90, 91*
"unresolved question of value" in
cultural center case study 59–60
UPP (*Unidades de Policia Pacificadora*)
284, 292
urban planning *see* also public cultural
center, case study: alternative uses of
the sidewalk 248–251, *250;* missed
historical possibilities 65–66; open
cities 279–280; parking 247
urban revival, city-as-oeuvre 238–239
urban segregation 264; social control
through 265–268
urban space: abstraction as a historical
process 289–290; "critical zone"
263–264; dynamics of 240; and the
Franco regime 265–268
urban studies: *autogestion* 33–34;
everyday life 34–36; industrialization
165; rhythmanalysis 167–169
urbanization: Hangzhou case study
240–243, *241;* Lefebvre's critique

of 76; second critical phase in urban
development 263
use-value 238

value creation theory 191
vertical power 73–74
"visual turn" in organizational studies
104–105, 107

walking as rhythmanalysis *170*
Warnes, Sarah 18
waste 46; in public cultural center case
study 56–57
Weber, Helmut 27
Western Wall, institutionalist analysis of
118–125, *120;* insights gained from
122; spatialized enactment 123–124;
spatialized logics 120–122, *120;*
spatialized sensemaking 122–123
workplaces: canteen 195; City of
London as performative workplace
172–177, *175, 176, 177;* and eating
207–209; and food 207–209,
209–210; 'Lunch Beat' movement
in Scandinavia 195–196; spatial
organization as means of control and
domination 191–193
workshops, in spacing leadership
process 86–87, **87**
workspace: dwelling 144–150, *145,
147, 148;* organizational dressage
150–154; sharing of food 217–219,
*218, 219;* spatial practices of eating
at work 214–217
Wright, Frank Lloyd 108
writing style of Lefebvre 3
www.91ways.org 230n1

Zhang, Zhongyuan 20, 286

Printed in the United States
by Baker & Taylor Publisher Services